The
FAITH
ONCE
DELIVERED

THE WESTMINSTER ASSEMBLY AND THE REFORMED FAITH

A Series

CARL R. TRUEMAN
Series Editor

The
FAITH
ONCE
DELIVERED

ESSAYS IN HONOR OF
DR. WAYNE R. SPEAR

Edited by
ANTHONY T. SELVAGGIO

Foreword by
W. ROBERT GODFREY

P&R
PUBLISHING
P.O. BOX 817 • PHILLIPSBURG • NEW JERSEY 08865-0817

Scripture quotations marked (NKJV) are from The Holy Bible, New King James Version. Copyright © 1979, 1980, 1982, Thomas Nelson, Inc.

Scripture quotations marked (NIV) are from the Holy Bible, New International Version®. NIV®. Copyright © 1973, 1978, 1984 by International Bible Society. Used by permission of Zondervan Publishing House. All rights reserved.

Scripture quotations marked (NASB) are from the New American Standard Bible®. Copyright © 1960, 1962, 1963, 1968, 1971, 1972, 1973, 1975, 1977, by The Lockman Foundation. Used by permission.

Scripture quotations marked (KJV) are from the King James Version.

Italics within Scripture quotations indicate emphasis added.

Printed in the United States of America

Library of Congress Cataloging-in-Publication Data

The faith once delivered : essays in honor of Dr. Wayne R. Spear / edited by Anthony T. Selvaggio ; foreword by W. Robert Godfrey.
      p. cm. — (The Westminster Assembly and the Reformed Faith)
    Includes bibliographical references and index.
    ISBN-13: 978-1-59638-020-2 (pbk.)
    1. Theology, Doctrinal. I. Spear, Wayne R. II. Selvaggio, Anthony T.
BT10.F35 2007
230'.42—dc22

                    2007012555

Contents

Series Introduction

The last two decades have seen a revolution in the way in which scholars have come to understand the nature and development of Reformed theology in the sixteenth and seventeenth centuries. It was in this context, and to further this scholarly revolution, that Westminster Theological Seminary in Philadelphia established the Craig Center for the Study of the Westminster Standards in 2002. The center provides a forum for promoting scholarly study of the history and theology of the Westminster Assembly, the various documents that it produced, and the way in which these documents have been received and used over the years.

As part of this project, the Craig Center has joined forces with P&R Publishing Company to commission a series of books, including monographs and collections of essays, that reflect this agenda. Each volume stands within the trajectories set by this new scholarship and takes seriously the theological content of Reformed orthodoxy while not naively divorcing that content from its historical or ecclesiastical context. Yet in doing this, these books do not become simply examples of antiquarianism or historicism. In fact, our desire is that this approach will free the past from the shackles and constraints of the agendas of the immediate present and thus allow voices from history to speak meaningfully to the world of today. It is thus the hope of the Craig Committee that both church and academy will benefit from this series for many years to come.

Carl R. Trueman
Chair of the Craig Committee

Foreword

W. ROBERT GODFREY

In the midst of growing political and social turmoil—leading to civil war and the execution of a king—commissioners called by the English parliament began to meet in 1643. Over a period of years they worked in the precincts of Westminster Abbey in London to compose standards that they hoped would guide a newly reformed church in Great Britain. Their work was prodigious and profound, manifesting remarkable balance and solidity in light of the chaotic conditions that often surrounded them.

The commissioners to this Westminster Assembly did not see themselves as religious revolutionaries, tearing down an old church to erect a brand-new one. They saw themselves as reformers who could at last bring the churches of England, Wales, Ireland, and Scotland into great conformity to the Word of God, to each other, and to the Reformed churches of continental Europe.

This Assembly is best remembered today for the Westminster Confession of Faith and the catechisms that it prepared. But unlike those who embrace the modern tendency to reductionism, the members of the Assembly knew that a reformed church needed more than a summary of its official doctrine. The commissioners also prepared a form of church government to structure the official organization of the church. In addition, they prepared a Directory of Public Worship to guide the churches in meeting with their God. And they arranged for the preparation of a Psalter as the praise book for public worship.

The fruit of the work of the Assembly had little effect in England. The triumph of Independency over Presbyterianism in England during the Commonwealth and the restoration of episcopacy under King Charles II prevented that. But in Scotland and in Presbyterian churches around the world, the work of the Westminster Assembly had great and blessed effect.

At the beginning of the twenty-first century, most Protestant churches in America find themselves in very serious turmoil and trouble in the very areas about which the Assembly worked and wrote with such care. In the evangelical, Pentecostal, and Reformed churches we see great confusion and error on doctrine, church government, and worship.

The depth of the current disarray in evangelical churches is well documented in a book by Mark Noll and Carolyn Nystrom, provocatively titled *Is the Reformation Over?* This book largely examines the changes in the relations between the Roman Catholic Church and evangelical churches in the last fifty years. The contention of the book is that Roman Catholics and evangelicals are much closer to each other in theology and practice than they were fifty years ago and that while the differences that remain are not trivial, many evangelicals now rightly recognize Roman Catholics as brothers and sisters in Christ.

Noll and Nystrom list a number of evangelical weaknesses ("ecclesiology, tradition, the intellectual life, sacraments, theology of culture, aesthetics, philosophical theology, or historical consciousness") and note that evangelicals in these areas "almost always" find some help in the Roman Catholic tradition.[1] Modern evangelicals seem seldom to look to the great Reformed and Lutheran traditions of the Reformation for help. In fact, Noll and Nystrom's book illustrates— largely unintentionally—how little evangelicals know or understand the concerns and work of the Reformation. Indeed, this book—again unintentionally—is further evidence that the evangelical tradition is as different from the Reformed tradition as it is from Lutheranism or Pentecostalism.

To speak just of the Reformed heritage of the Reformation, one could not charge the Reformed with a lack of concern for ecclesiology.

---

1. Mark Noll and Carolyn Nystrom, *Is the Reformation Over?* (Grand Rapids: Baker, 2005), 71.

Much study was undertaken and many books written on that subject, exploring the fullness of biblical teaching. (If the Reformed had a fault, it was not the neglect of ecclesiology, but a failure to maintain a clear witness to and practice of biblical Presbyterianism.) On tradition and historical consciousness, the Reformed studied with care the ancient fathers and medieval theologians, recognizing both value and errors in their work. The intellectual life of Reformed scholars has been second to none for over four hundred years. On sacraments the Reformed thought deeply, and they wrote widely on baptism and the Lord's Supper. They also made them an integral part of Christian worship and experience. The Reformed contributions on culture, aesthetics, and philosophical theology have been significant, especially in Dutch Reformed circles in the last hundred years.

Many evangelicals, in their pursuit of vital religion, abandoned their Reformation heritage in most of the areas of weakness highlighted by Noll and Nystrom. It is not surprising that they should find their own tradition to be shallow and impoverished. Yet it is very disappointing that they seem so driven by the pursuit of religious experience that they find more affinity with the human inventions of Rome than with the biblical, confessional commitments of the Reformed.

Dr. Wayne Spear has spent much of his ministry teaching the theology contained in the Westminster Standards. It is right that he should be honored at his retirement with a volume of essays examining the riches of the work of the Westminster Assembly. Our prayer should be that the solid Reformed teaching exemplified in his life and in this book may help reform the churches in our day according to the Word of God. Perhaps more than at any other time since the Reformation, churches today need biblical doctrine instead of human ideas of truth. They need biblical church government rather than government by offices of human contrivance. They need biblical worship rather than the vain pursuit of human rites and practices. The Reformation is not over. The Reformation is needed more today than ever, and the wisdom of the Westminster Standards is more relevant today than at any other time in recent memory.

Editor's Preface

ANTHONY T. SELVAGGIO

This volume is a celebration of Reformed systematic theology. It celebrates the theology that emerged during the years of the Reformation and reached its high-water mark at the Westminster Assembly. Celebrating systematic theology is vitally important in our current theological climate. The current trend in theological studies is to neglect traditional systematic theology. Many modern theologians have eschewed the topical and rational approach of systematic theology in favor of practical and narrative approaches. This trend is both unfortunate and dangerous. The intent of this volume is to encourage the church to once again focus on *theology*, the humble study of God through his self-revelation. Given this intent, it is therefore fitting that the volume include contributions from those engaged in systematic theology from a variety of Reformed denominations and from several different nations. It is also fitting that the volume begin with an inspiring and thoughtful essay entitled "The Vitality of Reformed Systematic Theology."

This volume is also a celebration of the teaching career of Dr. Wayne R. Spear, who taught systematic theology at the Reformed Presbyterian Theological Seminary in Pittsburgh, Pennsylvania, for over thirty years. Dr. Spear taught me the value of the traditional approach to systematic theology. The most noteworthy aspect of Dr. Spear's approach to teaching systematic theology was his insistence on using both the Bible and the Westminster Confession of Faith as the primary references. Dr. Spear recognized that systematic theology flows from the Bible itself and that there is no better summary of

Reformed systematic theology than the Westminster Confession of Faith. He unashamedly and unapologetically taught "confessional" Reformed systematic theology. Therefore, it is fitting to honor him with a collection of essays that touch on some of the great themes and theology of the Westminster Confession of Faith. In order to specially honor Dr. Spear, two of the essays in this volume were written by former students, C. J. Williams and me, and one was written by Dr. Spear's successor, Dr. Richard Gamble.

In this book the reader will be exposed to the theological topics at the core of Westminster's theology, topics such as justification, adoption, the kingship of Christ, the doctrine of Scripture, the Lord's Day, covenant theology, the atonement, and Christian liberty. These topics served as pillars of the theology that was forged in Westminster Abbey in the seventeenth century and, if the church is to adhere to the "faith which was once for all delivered to the saints" (Jude 3 NASB), must continue to serve as pillars of the Reformed church in the twenty-first century and beyond.

Introduction

JERRY O'NEILL

On more than one occasion I have heard my friend and colleague Dr. Wayne Spear lecture on the history of the Reformed Presbyterian Church of North America (RPCNA). No one is more qualified to do so. His knowledge and thoroughness in covering this subject so dear to his heart are evident to all. But when his lectures come to the latter half of the twentieth century and the early days of the twenty-first century, they omit the one man who has arguably had the most profound influence on the RPCNA for the last half-century.

In these lectures, Dr. Spear rightly discusses the continuing impact of the late J. G. Vos, and he carefully explains some of the important decisions made by our synod over these years. He mentions presidents of the Reformed Presbyterian Theological Seminary (RPTS) who have provided formal and informal leadership for the denomination because of their labors at the denominational seminary. He notes pastors such as Kenneth Smith, Roy Blackwood, and Edward Robson, who have been tremendously used by the Lord in our generation. But his humility keeps him from even considering in this context the one man who many of us think has done more than anyone else to shape pastors and ultimately congregations within our denomination in the last generation: Wayne Renwick Spear.

Dr. Spear served as professor of systematic theology at RPTS for thirty-five years. At the time of his retirement in the summer of 2005, he had spent exactly half his life serving his Lord, and his denomination, in this capacity. During many of those years he also taught church history, taught homiletics, or served as dean of faculty.

But it is not merely the fact that he served for thirty-five years in one ministry position that is so impressive. Many others in the church who have been blessed by God with good health and perseverance have labored in Christ's kingdom for an equal number of years. But few have labored more faithfully and more ably than this humble servant of the Lord.

I count it an honor to have served on the seminary faculty with Dr. Spear. He was my teacher of systematic theology when I was a student at RPTS, and I still have (and occasionally use) the notes that I took in his classes. When I returned to the seminary to serve in my current position, Dr. Spear's counsel to me in his role as dean of faculty was invaluable.

I have also had the privilege of serving with Dr. Spear in the various courts of the church—the session in the North Hills of Pittsburgh, the Presbytery of the Alleghenies, and the Synod of the RPCNA. His has always been a voice of reason in such settings. Younger men often do much of the talking in these meetings, but when Dr. Spear speaks, others listen—and learn. His service to the church has sometimes been public (chairing the Geneva College Board of Corporators, for example) and sometimes private. But he always serves humbly and without fanfare. Few who read this book will have any idea of the myriad ways in which he faithfully serves Christ and his church behind the scenes.

As intimated earlier, Dr. Spear's teaching has tremendously influenced my theological convictions, as it has those of so many others who have studied at the seminary both before and after me. He has the uncanny ability to read difficult and complicated theological works, understand what the authors are trying to communicate, critique these works from a biblical perspective, and then explain it all to others who might not even be able to wade through the original material.

Dr. Spear's knowledge of theology and church history is remarkable. Seldom is he without an answer to a student's question. Sometimes a student will ask a question on an obscure subject about which few others in the class have any knowledge whatsoever. Certain students seem to have the desire to stump the professor with these kinds of questions. But all of us who have sat in Dr. Spear's classes can recall how he will often pause (sometimes for a considerable length of time), reach back into his vast memory reservoir—almost appearing to be thumbing through his mental Rolodex—and pull out an answer that just "blows away" everyone in the class. Not only will he recall the author and the book from which he draws his answer, but he will be able to quote the author who addressed the point under consideration almost verbatim.

Dr. Spear's teaching is known to be clear, systematic, and thorough. Occasional stories, illustrations, and wise proverbs that inject both clarification and humor into his lectures also mark his teaching. Some of these were passed along from those who taught him in a previous day; some are his own. One example, given to budding preachers as they consider the preferred length of sermons, is Spear's Law: "If it is long, it had better be good!"

One story that Dr. Spear likes to tell his students in his doctrine of salvation course is passed along from one of his former professors at Geneva College about a student who was falling asleep in class just as his Bible teacher asked him whether he could explain how the sovereignty of God in election could be reconciled with the biblical teachings of human responsibility and free will. The student heard his name called, but had not heard the question. Rather than admitting this, he replied, "Yesterday I knew the answer to that question, but today I have forgotten it." To this the professor replied to the class, "This is indeed a great tragedy. Only two persons in all of history have known the answer to my question. One is God, and he has chosen not to reveal the answer to us. The other is our brother here, and he has forgotten!"

I'm reminded of one illustration that demonstrates Dr. Spear's ability to use a modern-day parable to drive a particular teaching home. When discussing the topic of redemption, he tells a story passed on to him by a former pastor of his. The story is about a young lad who, with great and loving care, built a small wooden boat. It was without any question his prized possession, and he frequently played with the boat in the small creek near his home. One night he left the boat by the creek, attempting to secure it safely to a nearby tree before he went home for the evening. During the night, a storm came up and the boat was swept away, to the boy's deep chagrin. Sometime later, though, the boy walked by a secondhand store, and he spotted his prized little boat. Quickly he ran home, gathered together all his money, and returned to the store to purchase the boat that had once been his. As he carried the boat out of the store, he looked at it fondly and said, "Little boat, you are twice mine. I made you, and now I have bought you back." How better can you teach such a profound biblical truth?

Dr. Spear was born into a preacher's family on July 24, 1935. His father, Norman, died shortly before Wayne's twelfth birthday, and he spent his teenage years on his uncle's farm in Bovina Center, New York. This agricultural background did much to shape his personality and interests, and to this day he owns, loves, and carefully tends to Haflinger horses on his small farm in Gibsonia, Pennsylvania, several miles north of Pittsburgh.

While in high school Wayne demonstrated the gifts and interests that would mark his later life when he developed an original outline of the book of Romans. At a time in life when most of us were pursuing sports or other temporal pleasures, Wayne was giving serious time to the study of God's Word. He did enjoy sports and other recreational activities, but his life was already balanced and Christ-centered.

While a student at Geneva College, Wayne distinguished himself in the classroom, ran cross-country, and fell in love with Mary Grace McCracken, whom he married after his first year at seminary. Although Wayne himself is not quick to confirm the following account, a widespread rumor has it that during his senior year of college, he not only aced the comprehensive examination in Bible, which was his major field of study, but also took the comprehensive exam in science and scored higher than all the science majors. (In those days, students were required to pass a comprehensive exam in their major field of study before graduation. Also in those days, Geneva's science department was highly esteemed, with medical schools gladly accepting most Geneva students who applied.)

After graduating from RPTS in 1960, Wayne spent six years in pastoral ministry before pursuing graduate studies at the request of Synod—at Princeton Theological Seminary, Westminster Theological Seminary (where he received a Th.M.), the University of Pittsburgh, and Pittsburgh Theological Seminary (where he received his Ph.D.).

In 1970 he began his teaching responsibilities at RPTS, where he taught until he retired.

Because RPTS has been the site of most of Dr. Spear's ministry over the years, and because the seminary is not well known to many in the Reformed and evangelical communities, it seems appropriate in these words of introduction to say just a little about the institution. An understanding of RPTS will help you, the reader, understand the context of this man's labors.

The seminary was founded in 1810, one year after the Synod of the Reformed Presbyterian Church of North America had been officially organized. The establishment of the seminary was one of the first acts of the new synod and demonstrates the priority that this fledgling church placed on preparing pastors for the gospel ministry. RPTS is the fifth oldest seminary, and the oldest evangelical or Reformed seminary, in the United States.

For many years, consistent with how other seminaries of that era operated, a professor of theology was elected by Synod and the students of theology came to study with him wherever he ministered. When the pastor-professor moved to serve a different congregation, the seminary moved with him. In its first forty-six years, RPTS operated in at least five different locations, depending on where the lead professor was serving as pastor.

In 1856 the seminary was moved to a permanent location in what is now called the North Side of Pittsburgh, Pennsylvania. In 1923 RPTS was moved to its present site in Point Breeze, in Pittsburgh's East End. This beautiful site was originally a mansion built by a retail magnate near the end of the nineteenth century, and has been extensively remodeled and enlarged to house the seminary.

For many years the seminary primarily served Reformed Presbyterian students preparing for pastoral ministry or the mission field. In the last half of the twentieth century the ministry began to expand to include students from a wide variety of evangelical and Reformed churches. In 1973 the Commonwealth of Pennsylvania granted RPTS the authority to offer the Master of Divinity degree, and in 1994 the seminary was accredited by the Association of Theological Schools.

Today the seminary is, in the judgment of those of us who are called to serve there, a very special place where the blessing of God's

Spirit seems most evident. God has, in his grace, enabled RPTS to remain firmly committed to the historic Reformed faith in its teaching while ministering to students from various cultures, nations, and denominational backgrounds. Students find the seminary to be a haven, a safe refuge, an ideal environment in which to learn the great truths of the historic faith.

The seminary also houses the Center for Urban Biblical Ministry, which works with Geneva College to provide associate's degrees for students in our city. We also provide a site for Geneva College to offer modular courses leading to a bachelor's degree in community ministry in a nontraditional evening-school format. On this one site, therefore, a student can get an associate's degree through the Center for Urban Biblical Ministry, a bachelor's degree in community ministry from Geneva College, and either a Master of Theological Studies degree or a Master of Divinity degree from RPTS.

The seminary's great desire is to be faithful to the Word of God and the mission he has given us. In God's grace, Dr. Spear has played an enormous role in enabling us to fulfill this mission for the last thirty-five years.

Because RPTS has historically been a seminary where teaching was emphasized, with little time available for professors to do research and writing, Dr. Spear has not been a prolific author and is not as widely known as some who spend much of their time writing books. Nevertheless, *The Theology of Prayer*, his first book, printed in 1974, was revised and updated in 2002 under the title *Talking to God: The Theology of Prayer*; and a new book critiquing the neoorthodox theology of Karl Barth is (at my writing of this) soon to be published. Dr. Spear has also written scholarly journal articles and contributed chapters for books edited by others. He is a respected scholar in Reformed academic circles and was asked in 1993 to present material in London, in conjunction with the celebration of the 350th anniversary of the Westminster Confession of Faith.

Dr. Spear's life and ministry were seriously threatened in 1986. While running near his home in Gibsonia, he experienced a splitting headache and realized that something was seriously wrong. He went to the emergency room of a local hospital and was diagnosed with an aneurysm in his brain. Thankfully, in response to the urgent prayers of many people and under the care of a skilled physician, the Lord spared his life, and he has had no further trouble as a result of the aneurysm.

When I first joined the RPTS faculty in 1995, Dr. Spear was already thinking of his retirement. He was quite concerned that younger men be given the opportunity to serve; and he was concerned that after his many years at the seminary, he might be growing stale in the classroom. But in the providence of God, he was asked to go with a team of men to Romania in the summer of 1997 to teach at a small seminary there. This experience seemed to recharge his batteries, reinvigorating him for his teaching responsibilities back home. He enthusiastically returned to RPTS in the fall, and taught with vigor until his recent retirement.

Personally, I look forward to seeing much of Wayne in his retirement. Not only do we serve on the same session in the North Hills of Pittsburgh, we also share certain members of our families. Wayne's youngest son, Sam, is married to my oldest daughter, Meg, and they have seven children. What a blessing for my wife, Ann, and me to share grandkids with Wayne and Mary Spear! But Wayne and Mary don't share all of their grandchildren with us. They have a total of twenty-four as of this writing, and the Lord may have others to come. Truly they have been blessed to see their children's children, and to see God's covenant promises extend from one generation to the next.

On behalf of the entire RPTS community, it is my great joy to introduce Wayne Spear (and his wife, Mary) to the readers of this volume. My prayer is that the Lord will use this work for the advancement of the kingdom of Christ, and that Wayne and Mary will be richly blessed all the days of their lives. They have given selflessly to Christ's work; may they be greatly rewarded for their labors of love.

1

The Vitality of Reformed Systematic Theology

RICHARD B. GAFFIN JR.

Toward the close of the nineteenth century, the Old School Presbyterian periodical, *The Presbyterian and Reformed Review*, published an article by the Dutch dogmatician Herman Bavinck, "The Future of Calvinism."[1] In it Bavinck's concern is with Calvinism broadly, as a worldview, not just its systematic theology. He reflects on the situation in the Netherlands and then contemplates Calvinism's future elsewhere. The article remains remarkably timely. Two points of a more general sort are particularly worth highlighting for those, more than a century later, still concerned for the future of Calvinism and the vitality of its systematic theology.

First, in surveying the period of decline in Dutch Calvinism that begins toward the close of the seventeenth century, Bavinck notes that, thankfully, "the treasure of Calvinism" continued to be preserved, but

This chapter was first delivered as a paper, entitled "The Vitality of Reformed Dogmatics," at the International Theological Congress in Noordwijkerhout, Netherlands, in June 1994 and subsequently published in the proceedings of that Congress (now out of print), J. M. Batteau, J. W. Maris, and K. Veilig, eds., *The Vitality of Reformed Theology* (Kampen: Kok, 1994), 16–50. It is offered here, with some revisions, in appreciation of the life and labors of Wayne Spear.

1. Herman Bavinck, "The Future of Calvinism," *Presbyterian and Reformed Review* 5 (January 1894): 1–24; subsequently published with a revised and shortened introduction and other slight revisions in "Het Calvinisme in Nederland en zijne toekomst," *Tijdschrift voor Gereformeerde theologie* 3 (1896): 129–63.

in a manner that can be described only as imbalanced and unhealthy. A faithful remnant, increasingly marginalized and alienated from the dominant trends in church and society, became inflexible and reactionary; they lived in the past and despised the present. Calvinism ceased to be properly radical; it lost its vitality.[2] So, Bavinck cautions, those concerned for revival "do not wish to repristinate, and have no desire for the old conditions to return," and he goes on to warn against "the deadly embrace of a dead conservatism."[3]

It would be easy enough to speculate that were Bavinck writing today,[4] with all that has transpired over the course of the twentieth century to the present, not least of all the developments within his own denomination, the Reformed Churches in the Netherlands,[5] he would adopt a different, more cautious and conservative tone. But that would be gratuitous. Bavinck was not naive. His eyes were open to "the alarming fact that unbelief is increasing on all hands."[6] He was well aware that "the tendencies prevailing at the present day in the Christian Church are not favorable to Calvinism."[7]

In a time, such as our own, of unprecedented radicalism and profligate experimentation, both theologically and ethically, the temptation

2. "In the same proportion that they felt less at home in their own time, they lived in the past, in the world of the old religious literature, in the speech and ideas of the fathers. The Reformed, who had once stood at the head of every movement and been the liberals and radicals of their time, now became conservative, reactionary, panegyrists of the old, and despisers of the new times. . . . It was no longer the old, high-minded, radical Calvinism, but a Calvinism that had become rough, harsh, unpolished, without splendor and fire, cold and dry and dead." Bavinck, "The Future of Calvinism," 10–11.

3. Ibid., 13. Similarly, Abraham Kuyper began the last of his Stone Lectures delivered at Princeton Seminary in 1898, "Calvinism and the Future," by excluding "every idea of imitative repristination." "What the descendants of the old Dutch Calvinists as well as of the Pilgrim fathers have to do," he went on to say, "is not to copy the past, as if Calvinism were a petrification, but to go back to the living root of the Calvinist plant, to clean and to water it, and so to cause it to bud and to blossom once more, now fully in accordance with our actual life in these modern times, and with the demands of the times to come." A. Kuyper, *Calvinism* (Grand Rapids: Eerdmans, 1943), 171.

4. Writing in the flush of recent developments culminating in the union of 1892 between churches of the Afscheiding and the Doleantie movements, Bavinck is keenly aware of living in a time of dawning revival and sees that union as "a prophecy perhaps also of a better and more beautiful future." "The Future of Calvinism," 12.

5. I am inclined to say, "stunning declension." Those who may find that assessment too severe, or unfair, will at least have to admit that these developments are hardly the "future of Calvinism" that Bavinck had in mind.

6. Ibid., 13.

7. Ibid., 16.

to be merely reactionary becomes all the stronger. For instance, we may believe, probably rightly, that present abuse of the Reformation's *semper reformanda* has never been more flagrant. But the prostitution of that principle, no matter how glaring, does not remove its truth. "We may not suppose that theological construction ever reaches definitive finality."[8] Today, no less than in Bavinck's time, we may be sure, to use his striking language, that "the deadly embrace of a dead conservatism" remains a live threat to the vitality of Calvinism, including its systematic theology.

Second, one of the distinctive strengths of Calvinism, according to Bavinck, is that in its theology and church life "it avoids all mechanical uniformity."[9] He has in mind especially the multiplicity of confessions in the Reformed tradition—in contrast, say, to Lutheranism. Calvinism, he says, has room for the display of individuality and for the differences that exist among various nationalities. The truth is too rich and manifold for any individual person or individual church to assimilate in all its fullness. "Only in company with all the saints can we understand the breadth and length and depth and height of the love of Christ."[10]

Again, in view of the religious and theological pluralism rampant today, it would be easy to downplay Bavinck's emphasis, not to mention his allusion to the apostle Paul (Eph. 3:8, 10, 18–19). But that would slight an important point of our Reformed heritage. Bavinck reminds us that variety and Reformed vitality are not in tension. The apostolic ideal, "together with all the saints" (Eph. 3:18),[11] and Paul's injunction that "you all say the same thing" (1 Cor. 1:10) do not mean that it has to be said in the same way or with identical formulations.

The vitality of Reformed systematic theology may no doubt be explored in a number of different ways, but these would all seem to reflect one of two basic approaches. On the one hand, we could

---

8. John Murray, "Systematic Theology," in *Collected Writings*, 4 vols. (Edinburgh: Banner of Truth, 1976–82), 4:7.

9. Bavinck, "The Future of Calvinism," 22.

10. Ibid.

11. Scripture quotations in this chapter are my translations.

accent the antithetic stance required within the broader contemporary religious and theological environment. Ours is an era dominated by postmodern pretensions, aggressively pluralistic, rife with deconstructive confusion, and celebrating doctrinal disunity and contradiction in the name of permissible, even healthy, "diversity," to note several characteristic trends. So we could concern ourselves with these and other tendencies that threaten to sap the vitality of Reformed systematic theology. Alternatively, we could concentrate on the inherent vigor of Reformed systematic theology and how best to preserve and even nurture its strengths. Neither of these approaches need exclude the other. But I have decided here to follow the latter, more positive approach, trying to stay focused always on the notion of vitality, but without entirely neglecting the antithetic stance. In doing so, I am keenly aware at a number of points of having done little more than raise issues and of the need to probe much more deeply. My hope is at least to have stimulated further discussion in a constructive fashion.

The Word of God is "living and active" (Heb. 4:12). Like God himself, it "abides forever" (Isa. 40:8; 1 Peter 1:25). That vitality, ultimately, is the source of whatever vitality, derivatively, Reformed systematic theology has and will continue to have. I assume that this truth is a commonplace for many readers of this volume, but it never becomes so obvious that we may cease reminding each other of it, particularly when it continues to be anything but obvious in the larger theological scene, where denials and enervating misconceptions about God's Word abound and persist.

If the vitality of systematic theology is the vitality of the Word and, what is equally important, of the Spirit working in the church with the Word, then systematic theology can have no more vital concern than the inscripturated Word and how it handles that Word.[12] Systematic

12. As the briefest indication of my own stance, suffice it to say here that in its heart of hearts God's Word is the incarnate Word, Jesus Christ, and, inseparable from him, the written Word, the canonical Scriptures. These Scriptures, in their entirety, both materially and formally, in diverse text forms and genre as well as varied, multifaceted content, are identified by the exalted Christ ("the self-attesting Christ of Scripture") as his very own words, and by his Spirit, he maintains them in the life of the church ("the letter written to me and to the whole Church by Christ himself"). The expressions in parentheses are from Cornelius Van Til, "My Credo,"

theology, as I take it, is a radically nonspeculative undertaking. That is, while it formulates with an eye to the confessions of the church and past doctrinal developments, as well as to the contemporary opportunities and challenges that face the church, it, like all the other theological disciplines, is essentially exegesis of Scripture.[13]

A hermeneutical dimension, then, is fundamental to the task of systematic theology. The systematic theologian is a custodial interpreter, proximately of church dogma but ultimately of Scripture. This means that at any given point in time, the basic stance that systematic theology is to adopt toward the doctrines and confessions of the church is, as Klaas Schilder has neatly captured it, "sympathetic-critical."[14] One of its most cherished ambitions is that church doctrine formulate only what is "either expressly set down in Scripture, or by good and necessary consequence may be deduced from Scripture."[15] The apostolic injunction "Do not go beyond what is written" (1 Cor. 4:6),[16] adapted to the postapostolic, completed-canon situation of the church, holds for all our theologizing, especially for systematic theology. This, the exegetical-hermeneutical facet of systematic theology in distinction

---

in *Jerusalem and Athens: Critical Discussions on the Philosophy and Apologetics of Cornelius Van Til*, ed. E. R. Geehan (Nutley, NJ: Presbyterian and Reformed, 1974), 3, 5, 8.

13. Adapting John Calvin's well-known figure for Scripture as the "spectacles" indispensable for properly understanding the revelation of the entire creation order (*Institutes of the Christian Religion*, ed. John T. McNeill, trans. Ford Lewis Battles, Library of Christian Classics [Philadelphia: Westminster, 1960], 1.6.1, 1.14.1), we may say that theology, in all its parts and whatever its encyclopedic divisions, is a kind of "optometry," concerned with the composition of lenses and frame and, more importantly, their proper use and the correct, saving "vision" they facilitate. In this sense Scripture is the *principium unicum* of theology, its sole foundational source and norm. Even church history, as Gerhard Ebeling persuasively argued (*Kirchengeschichte als Geschichte der Auslegung der heiligen Schrift* [Tübingen: Mohr, 1947]), is essentially "history of the interpretation of Scripture."

Does not such a stance eventually result in presumptuously claiming too much for theology as a special discipline? It strikes me that we can become too preoccupied with trying to circumscribe and limit theology in relation to other fields of study. The forces at work in theology are first of all centripetal, not centrifugal. When theology remains centered on Scripture, the boundary questions, though still present and important, will be less urgent, and also more likely to be resolved.

14. As quoted by J. Douma in *Oriëntatie in de theologie: Studiegids samengesteld door de hoogleraren aan de Theologische Hogeschool van De Gereformeerde Kerken in Nederland te Kampen* (Groningen, Netherlands: De Vuurbaak, n.d. but likely 1974), 20. See the afterword at the end of this chapter.

15. Westminster Confession of Faith 1.6.

16. Whatever may be the written document or material Paul had in view; see the commentaries for the problem here.

from its contemporary-contextual and doctrine-historical facets, is my larger concern in what follows.

About the same time as Bavinck's article appeared, in May of 1894 its translator, Geerhardus Vos, was installed as the first occupant of the newly created chair of biblical theology at Princeton Seminary. This proved to be a significant development because Vos, more than anyone else, deserves to be called the father of a Reformed biblical theology. He more than any other was the initiator within a Reformed context of the rich tradition of redemptive-historical exegesis we now possess.[17] But that prompts us to ask this: How, just over a century later, has Reformed systematic theology utilized this exegetical legacy? To what extent has it discharged its responsibility to redemptive-historical exegesis? Probing that area of questions will further focus the remainder of this chapter.

In his inaugural address Vos treated, appropriately, the program and encyclopedic place of biblical theology as a particular discipline.[18] In the course of articulating some advantages of this relatively young discipline, which he preferred to call "History of Special Revelation,"[19] he makes this statement: "It is certainly not without significance that God has embodied the contents of revelation, not in a dogmatic system, but in a book of history."[20] Years later, at the close of his career, he observes in a similar vein, "The Bible is not a dogmatic handbook but a historical book full of dramatic interest." And: "The circle of revelation is not a school, but a 'covenant.' "[21]

The almost identical form of these statements is noteworthy. They express what the Bible is *not* as well as what it is. It is not a "dogmatic handbook"; its structure is not that of a "dogmatic system"; its provenance is not a "school." Such pointedly contrasting formulations

17. Vos's pioneering work has been followed notably by that of Herman Ridderbos and the likes of Schilder, B. Holwerda, M. G. Kline, and (at a more popular level) S. G. De Graaf, and others too numerous to mention.
18. Geerhardus Vos, "The Idea of Biblical Theology as a Science and as a Theological Discipline," in R. B. Gaffin Jr., ed., *Redemptive History and Biblical Interpretation: The Shorter Writings of Geerhardus Vos* (Phillipsburg, NJ: Presbyterian and Reformed, 1980), 3–24.
19. Ibid., 21 n. 2; see also the preface to Geerhardus Vos, *Biblical Theology: Old and New Testaments* (Grand Rapids: Eerdmans, 1948), 23.
20. Vos, "The Idea of Biblical Theology," 23.
21. Vos, *Biblical Theology*, 26, 17.

are hardly accidental or merely rhetorical. They confront a more than purely hypothetical misunderstanding and suggest at least a degree of tension.

Whom does Vos have in mind? Clearly he is concerned about the baleful consequences of Enlightenment rationalism. But there is little question from the tenor of his comments that he is also countering an intellectualistic tendency that he finds, closer to home, in the systematic theology of Protestant orthodoxy: the tendency to view the Bible as a compendium of ahistorical first principles or static truths. That tendency can be alleviated, he believes, by biblical theology, that is, by giving greater, more adequate attention to the redemptive-historical structure and content of biblical revelation, or, in other terms, by attending to the embedding of that revelation in the dynamically unfolding history of God's covenant.

How valid is Vos's reservation? That touches on massive historical questions that I am not able to enter into here, except to warn against exaggeration. This caution is all the more necessary because of the widespread but severely distorting model abroad today for reading the history of theology since the Reformation, especially its sweepingly negative assessment of seventeenth-century Protestant orthodoxy.[22]

22. It does not seem an unfair caricature to present that model as something like this: "creation"—the Reformation; "the fall"—seventeenth-century orthodoxy (responsible more or less directly, in turn, for eighteenth-century rationalism and nineteenth-century liberalism); "redemption"—primarily Karl Barth and the trends he initiated.

On this view Reformed orthodoxy brings little other than the darkening clouds of medieval synthesis thinking with its baleful dualisms, reappearing after the temporary respite brought by the bright sunshine of the Reformation. Characteristically, this theology is branded with the pejoratives "scholastic" and "scholasticism" (though it is remarkable how seldom an effort is made to define these labels; presumably they are self-evidently bad). Under attack here, if we need reminding of what is obviously at stake, are the biblical integrity and continuing viability of major Reformed confessions such as the Canons of Dort and the Westminster Standards, which stem from a "scholastic" mind-set.

Especially worth mentioning, for a fuller evaluation of post-Reformation Reformed orthodoxy and its strengths and weaknesses, out of a growing body of literature by others, is the valuable groundbreaking work of Richard Muller in rehabilitating the Reformed "scholastics" and redressing the distortions of the currently prevailing paradigm by showing the deep and cordial continuity, despite all the differences in method, between the theology of the Reformers and that of the seventeenth century. See especially his four-volume *Post-Reformation Reformed Dogmatic Theology: The Rise and Development of Reformed Orthodoxy, ca. 1520 to ca. 1725*, 2nd ed. (Grand Rapids: Baker, 2003) and his inaugural address, *Scholasticism and Orthodoxy in the Reformed Tradition: An Attempt at Definition* (Grand Rapids: Calvin Theological Seminary, 1995).

In this regard Vos himself has made a most important balancing observation. Writing in 1916, he said of Reformed theology that it

> has from the beginning shown itself possessed of a true historic sense in the apprehension of the progressive character of the deliverance of truth. Its doctrine of the covenants on its historical side represents the first attempt at constructing a history of revelation and may be justly considered the precursor of what is at present called biblical theology.[23]

Vos reminds us here that the Reformed confessions and the theological framework they entail, particularly the doctrine of the covenant, far from being hostile, are quite hospitable toward and in fact anticipate giving greater, more methodologically self-conscious attention to the redemptive-historical substance of Scripture. Flaws there undoubtedly are in post-Reformation orthodoxy, but we must be on guard against overstating them.

With that important qualification made, however, there can be little doubt that Vos was not just "tilting at windmills." He voiced a legitimate concern—one that, over a century later, remains a live one. The primary text for producing textbooks on systematic theology is not itself a systematic-theological textbook, an elemental fact but still worth pondering. The question still needs to be asked about the tension between "covenant" and "school" that Vos noted, about those intellectualistic traces in treating doctrine that leave the life of the congregation untouched. Has that tension and have those traces entirely disappeared from Reformed systematic theology? In other words, once more, has Reformed systematic theology adequately processed the heritage of redemptive-historical exegesis and considered its fructifying and reshaping potential? These and like questions, it seems to me, are as challenging and as promising as any today for a systematic theology concerned for its continuing viability.

As already intimated, the larger issue in view here, at least in English-language discussions, concerns the relationship between

---

23. Vos, *Redemptive History and Biblical Interpretation*, 232.

biblical theology and systematic theology. Leaving to the side for now objections to either one or both of these designations, several points need to be briefly highlighted. The subsequent course of my discussion may serve to elaborate and, where necessary, to substantiate these points, at least to some degree.[24]

1. Biblical theology (= redemptive-historical exegesis) is concerned with the actual revelation process in back of the Bible. That process is in fact a history, redemptive or, more broadly, covenantal history, a history that begins at creation and, subsequent to the fall and largely incorporating the history of Israel along the way, reaches its culmination in the incarnate Christ and his work.

The clearest, most explicit biblical warrant for this fundamental theological construct is the overarching assertion with which the writer of Hebrews begins: "God, having spoken in the past to the fathers through the prophets at many times and in various ways, has spoken to us in these last days in his Son" (1:1–2a). Note how this statement captures three interrelated factors: (a) revelation as a historical process, (b) the diversity involved in that process, including, we might observe, diverse modes and various literary genres, as well as, by implication, whatever legitimate methodologies have emerged in the modern era for dealing with them, and (c) Christ as the omega point, the eschatological end point of the process.

Canonical Scripture, then, itself revelation and its own origin a part of redemptive history, is essentially a record of revelation, providing the church's sole and sufficient access to that history.

2. The history of revelation, "revelation" understood more narrowly as verbal, unfolds within the mainstream of redemptive history. Or, elementally considered, the focus of revelatory Word is redemptive deed. The Word is tethered to the deed and interprets it; without the deed there is no place for the Word.[25] In other words, God is his

24. Cf. Vos, "The Idea of Biblical Theology," 23–24, and preface to *Biblical Theology*, 12, 24–25; Murray, "Systematic Theology," 9–21; and my "Systematic Theology and Biblical Theology," *Westminster Theological Journal* 38 (1976): 281–99; in a different vein but with substantially overlapping concerns, W. D. Jonker, "Eksegese en dogmatiek," in W. D. Jonker et al. eds., *Hermeneutica: Erebundel aangebied aan Prof Dr. E. P. Groenewald . . .* (Pretoria, South Africa: N. G. Kerk-Boekhandel, 1970), 157–79.

25. "Revelation is so interwoven with redemption that, unless allowed to consider the latter, it would be suspended in the air." Vos, *Biblical Theology*, 24. When, for instance, the

own interpreter, preeminently of his activity relative to his creation and its restoration.

All biblical interpretation, then, is interpretation of interpretation—our interpretation of Scripture's God-given interpretation of (creation, fall, and) redemption. The unity of Scripture in terms of its content is, globally, a redemptive-historical unity, that is, the unity of a historically differentiated and progressively unfolding whole. In terms of the principle of context, so essential for sound biblical interpretation, the broadest controlling context is the covenant-historical context.[26] Canon and covenant are correlatives. The canonical context overall, if it is truly honored,[27] and the covenant-historical context are coterminous.

3. In its most important aspect, the relational question in view does *not* concern the placing of biblical theology and systematic theology relative to each other as distinct disciplines, although the question may be put that way. A more fundamental, functional, hermeneutical understanding of biblical theology is called for. All exegesis ought to be biblical-theological (redemptive-historical). At stake, then, in so-called biblical theology is nothing less than the exegetical lifeblood of systematic theology.[28] The focus of systematic theology, more ultimately, is not dogma but the history of redemption. The latter should

---

Westminster Shorter Catechism asserts that "the Scriptures principally teach, what man is to believe concerning God, and what duty God requires of man" (3), it is important to make it immediately clear that this teaching (*credenda*) concerns God, as the covenant God, active in creation and redemption, and that the imperatives (*agenda*) are grounded in *this* (covenant-historical) indicative. Far from denying divine aseity, this emphasis rather leaves it in the largely incomprehensible depths that Scripture does. This redemptive-historical emphasis is also an important antidote to the quasi-gnostic as well as privatized, individualistic notions of Christian truth that continue to plague the church.

26. We may say that in so-called biblical theology the principle of context, of the analogy of Scripture, that Scripture interprets Scripture, so central in the Reformation tradition of interpretation, finds its most thoroughly and pointedly biblical realization and application.

27. This, regrettably, cannot be said of the "canonical criticism," about which so much has been made in recent years (see the work, e.g., of B. Childs and J. A. Sanders). Its effort to read the Bible (the Old Testament) as canon without abandoning the historical-critical method, and its presuppositions, is ultimately self-defeating.

28. Murray incisively observes: "But systematic theology will fail of its task to the extent to which it discards its rootage in biblical theology as properly conceived and developed. It might seem that an undue limitation is placed upon systematic theology by requiring that the exegesis with which it is so intimately concerned should be regulated by the principle of biblical theology. And it might seem contrary to the canon so important for both exegesis and systematics, namely, the analogy of Scripture. These appearances do not correspond to reality.

set the agenda for the former. Doctrine, as I will try to make clearer below, is a function of redemptive history. The vitality of systematic theology is rooted in the covenant- or redemptive-historical.

A recent large-scale effort in addressing the opportunities and challenges that redemptive-historical interpretation presents for Reformed systematic theology is Gordon Spykman's *Reformational Theology: A New Paradigm for Doing Systematic Theology.*[29] As the subtitle indicates, Spykman sees himself as breaking fresh ground. He offers a "New Paradigm," and its overriding concern, in his own words, is "to give the historical-redemptive pattern of biblical revelation a firmer place in Reformed systematic theology." He wishes to highlight that "the entire biblical story line has an eschatological thrust."[30] The rest of this chapter consists largely of interactions and reflections prompted by the more prominent structural or "paradigm" elements of this proposal.[31]

1. The key biblical motifs of creation, fall, redemption, and consummation structure Spykman's presentation of the main body of systematic theology; these four categories provide the major sections of the book. This basic framework certainly succeeds in giving prominence to the overall redemptive-historical, eschatological flow of biblical revelation. Further, it has the decided advantage of highlighting the bond between creation and redemption and the characteristic Reformed emphasis that the two are not divorced or in opposition but integrally related as redemption restores and perfects creation. Also, these major divisions are sufficiently broad to allow ample room for

---

The fact is that only when systematic theology is rooted in biblical theology does it exemplify its true function and achieve its purpose." "Systematic Theology," 19–20.

29. Gordon Spykman, *Reformational Theology: A New Paradigm for Doing Systematic Theology* (Grand Rapids: Eerdmans, 1992). To my knowledge, it is the first such effort, at least in the modern era. A precursor might be sought as far back as the eighteenth century in Jonathan Edwards's *A History of the Work of Redemption*, in which he endeavored to present the "body of divinity in an entire new method, being thrown into the form of a history." Richard Lints, *The Fabric of Theology: A Prolegomenon to Evangelical Theology* (Grand Rapids: Eerdmans, 1993), 174; see generally pp. 171–81. Whether, going back even further, Johannes Cocceius and those he influenced ought to be included here is debatable.

30. Spykman, *Reformational Theology*, 135.

31. For a more thorough and balanced assessment, see my review article, "A New Paradigm in Theology?" *Westminster Theological Journal* 56 (1994): 379–90.

differences in judgment on internal development and the subtopics to be discussed under each.

We should not suppose, however, that this is the only or even the ideal format for systematic theology or that there can be only one arrangement for presenting material; nor does Spykman make that claim. In this regard, I am not as sure as is Spykman that a redemptive-historical approach necessitates abandoning the so-called *loci* method of traditional systematic theology. After all, strictly speaking, that method simply calls for a topical presentation of doctrine, and it is difficult to see why the biblical materials preclude such an approach.

For instance, we may compare the message of Scripture as a whole to a massive epic drama. This is quite an appropriate model, considering the Bible's covenant-historical main theme. Accordingly, systematic theology may be seen as large-scale, overall "plot analysis" of this metanarrative: reflection on the various actors and their actions and interaction under appropriate headings (God, man, sin, salvation, the church, etc.).

There is, to be sure, the undeniable inclination in traditional systematic theology to "dehistoricize" or decontextualize the Bible (another way of putting the concern expressed by Vos noted earlier); "the tendency to abstraction . . . ever lurks," as John Murray warns.[32] But that hardly means that an "abstract and rationalist" treatment is "inherent" in the *loci* method, as Spykman maintains.[33] A historical-redemptive awareness should go a long way toward counteracting approaches that diminish the eschatologically driven dynamic of biblical revelation as a whole or that tend toward handling topics in a way that isolates them from each other and misses important interconnections.[34]

There is also another side of the matter to consider here. If Scripture is truly *God's* Word, then its historically progressive and differentiated diversity exists not as a quagmire of doctrinal confusion and

32. Murray, "Systematic Theology," 20.
33. Spykman, *Reformational Theology*, 135.
34. Such approaches have their perhaps most substantial (and unfortunate) repercussions in conventional treatments of eschatology, where it is dealt with only in the last, often little more than appended, chapter in systematic theology, a point we will address in part below.

contradiction but as a concordant, mutually reinforcing unity, a unity in diversity. No doubt, the diversity involved will always embody a rich residue of imponderables (e.g., "the unsearchable riches of Christ," "knowing the love of Christ that surpasses knowledge," Eph. 3:8, 19). Even the most imposing systematic theology is kept from ever becoming self-confident or "system-secure," keenly aware that "for now we see in a mirror, dimly" (1 Cor. 13:12). The cohering unity of this diversity, however, not only permits but enables and authorizes the church to answer this question: What does the *Bible* (not just Isaiah, Paul, etc.) say about X (= any topic appropriate to Scripture)? Answering that question must remain a distinguishing concern of systematic theology.

2. An even better basic division of material than Spykman's fourfold motif might be the triad of creation-fall-redemption, subsuming "consummation" under "redemption" and developing it as two major subdivisions: redemption present and redemption future, the proverbial "already–not yet." This, faithful to Spykman's own intention, would highlight even more clearly the eschatological nature of Christ's work, finished as well as future, a point on which there is a virtually universal consensus across a broad front after a century or more of New Testament exegesis.[35]

Despite the rich resources resident in the Reformed confessions and theology, including the redemptive-historical sensitivity already displayed there, especially in the doctrine of the covenant, it does seem to me that the exegetical consensus just mentioned has yet to make the impact it ought. Pointedly, in both overall structure and

---

35. This consensus began forming toward the close of the nineteenth century with reassessments of Jesus' kingdom proclamation (e.g., the "consistent" eschatology of J. Weiss and A. Schweitzer), in reaction to the idealistic misreading marking the brand of theological liberalism dominant at that time (e.g., A. Ritschl and A. von Harnack). To provide the briefest sampling of New Testament teaching: the coming of Christ in "the fulness of time(s)" (Gal. 4:4; Eph. 1:10) means just that—not a particularly auspicious moment during the course of history (though that is no doubt true on other grounds), but the filling up of history, its end in an absolute sense. His sacrificial death for sin occurred "at the end of the ages" (Heb. 9:26), "in these last times" (1 Peter 1:20). As resurrected, Christ is "firstfruits" (1 Cor. 15:20); his resurrection is not an isolated event in the past but the actual, visible beginning in history of the final resurrection-harvest that will include all believers at the end of history. And so on. All told, the first and second comings of Christ are not so much two separate events as two episodes of the one eschatological *parousia* of the Lord.

internal development, systematic theology needs to make clearer that soteriology is eschatology.[36] Here I can touch, no more than suggestively, on a couple aspects of a larger complex of issues worthy of discussion.

In his monumental work on Paul's theology, Herman Ridderbos repeatedly says, echoing throughout almost like a refrain, that the apostle's interest on this or that matter is the *historia salutis*, not the *ordo salutis*.[37] In my judgment, Ridderbos somewhat overstates this point.[38] Nevertheless, if the contrast is taken as a matter of *emphasis*, not

36. By "soteriology" I have in view the total work of the incarnate Christ: the salvation he first accomplishes and then applies by his Spirit.

37. Herman Ridderbos, *Paul: An Outline of His Theology* (Grand Rapids: Eerdmans, 1975), 14, 63, 173ff., 205ff., 211; cf. 45ff., 91, 214ff., 221ff., 268ff., 365, 378, 404ff.; and *When the Time Had Fully Come* (Grand Rapids: Eerdmans, 1957), 49. This contrasting formulation, like the statements from Vos quoted earlier, is hardly accidental or simply rhetorical. It seems pointedly directed (like the Vos quotes, but three-quarters of a century later), primarily at least, at the considerable theological and pastoral use of Paul that Ridderbos still sees to be dominant in his own Reformed tradition and elsewhere. I take it, by the way, that on the one side of the contrast his concern is not just limited to the *ordo salutis* in the usual specific sense of a logically or causally concatenated sequence of acts and benefits, though it includes that idea. His *historia salutis–ordo salutis* contrast is virtually identical with the basic distinction between redemption accomplished and applied. Cf. the closely related, if not identical, orientation of Vos, especially chap. 2, "The Interaction between Eschatology and Soteriology," in *Pauline Eschatology* (1930; repr., Grand Rapids: Baker, 1979).

38. Apart from Ridderbos's valuable treatment of the role of faith (*Paul*, secs. 29, 40–41), he leaves his reader wondering what place, if any, *ordo salutis* concerns have in Paul. The question of the Philippian jailer (Acts 16:30), for instance, is a legitimate one, and Paul's answer, for one, opens up a distinct area of reflection for the church.

Spykman's treatment of redemption, under the major heading "The Way of Salvation" (pt. 4), is not only puzzling but troublesome. There the distinction between once-for-all accomplishment and ongoing application, if not entirely missing, is virtually eclipsed; it is at best implicitly in view in a section on "The Christian Life." *Reformational Theology*, 480ff.

Certainly we should agree with Spykman that traditional treatments of the *ordo salutis* have often been overextended and, at times, counterproductive (ibid., 481–83), following Anthony A. Hoekema, *Saved by Grace* (Grand Rapids: Eerdmans, 1989), 14–17; and G. C. Berkouwer, *Faith and Justification* (Grand Rapids: Eerdmans, 1954), chap. 1. Particularly in the period following the Synod of Dort, developments largely resulting from increasingly necessary resistance to Arminianism and pietism have had the enduring, though no doubt largely unforeseen, effect of blurring Calvin's sublime focus on union with the exalted Christ, by faith, through "the secret energy of the Spirit," as the Alpha and Omega of the application of redemption—union so pivotal that it both underlies and comprehends all other aspects and benefits. Calvin, *Institutes*, 3.1.1; cf. C. Graafland, "Heeft Calvijn een bepaalde orde des heils geleerd?" in J. van Oort et al., eds., *Verbi Divini Minister: Opstellen voor L. Kievit* (Amsterdam: Ton Bolland, 1983), 109–27, esp. the conclusion, p. 127.

But Spykman's notion that we become "contemporaries" with Christ (*Reformational Theology*, 481) is not helpful, particularly since the distinction between redemption accomplished and applied is not made clear. Union with Christ in his death and resurrection, with all

as mutually exclusive alternatives, then it captures an important and valuable insight, particularly in the light of his thoroughly impressive demonstration of the redemptive-historical, eschatological framework that controls Paul's teaching as a whole.[39] The ongoing application of redemption (*ordo salutis*) is a function or outworking of its once-for-all accomplishment (*historia salutis*).[40]

Among other considerations, this entails the need for systematic theology, including ethics, to be more explicit and articulate about the inalienable eschatological dimension fundamental to the Christian life and the present existence of the church. That dimension is probably illustrated most easily and graphically by the commercial and agricultural metaphors that Paul uses for the Holy Spirit presently at work in the church: "down payment" in kind on our eschatological inheritance (2 Cor. 5:5; Eph. 1:14; cf. Eph. 4:30), the actual "first-fruits" of the eschatological harvest of resurrection-adoption (Rom. 8:23). But to highlight by way of contrast, we have only to ask: how many believers think, or have been taught to think, of the Spirit's work in their lives in its entirety, including the undoubted inwardness and personal intimacy of that working, as nonetheless of one

---

the mystery involved, does not eliminate the historical distance, soteriologically, between the circumstances and conditions of my "now" and the "then" of those once-for-all events.

The present, ongoing appropriation of salvation, in both its corporate and personal dimensions, is not simply on a line or in series with the finished work of Christ. Developments that gave rise to the Reformation (e.g., Rome's soteriology and ecclesiology, focused in its doctrine of the Mass) have made perennially clear the danger in making the one essentially an extension of the other. When that happens, invariably the sufficiency and historical finality of Christ's death and resurrection become eclipsed or even denied. Ultimately the gospel itself stands or falls with the distinction between redemption accomplished and applied. See further my "Biblical Theology and the Westminster Standards," *Westminster Theological Journal* 65 (2003): 165–79, esp. 167–69.

39. See esp. Ridderbos, *Paul*, chap. 2.

40. The challenge clearly implicit in this insight is all the more compelling in view of the dominant role, especially since the Reformation, that Pauline materials, in particular, have played in formulating soteriological doctrine.

As an aside, it seems pertinent to observe that in this area the church has perennially had difficulty, in both its doctrine and its life, in maintaining proper perspective, in keeping its priorities straight. Application is a function of accomplishment, not the reverse; the latter does not exist simply to facilitate the former. Without intending to polarize among equally valid considerations, the "main point," if I may risk putting it that way, of the Christian religion, the religion of God's covenant, is not the Christian but Christ, not our experience but his work, not our needs but his glory. Only when that point is appreciated do Christian identity and experience, both individual and corporate, come to stand in a right light. Otherwise, we are on our way down the long and convoluted road toward Schleiermacher (and beyond).

RICHARD B. GAFFIN JR.

piece with the great work of God at the end of history in renovating the entire creation?

Further, there is room for systematic theology to make clearer the "already–not yet" structure that qualifies the various elements in the application of salvation. That structure is reflected in the believer's union with Christ in his death and resurrection. Between Christ's resurrection and return, according to Paul's categorical distinction between "inner" and "outer man" (2 Cor. 4:16), the believer both has already been raised and will be raised. Accordingly, the specific benefits that flow from being united to Christ as crucified and resurrected—forensic (justification, adoption) as well as renovative (regeneration, sanctification)—are both realized and still future.[41]

On the forensic side, Romans 8, for instance, shows rather plainly that adoption, our eschatological identity as God's children and co-inheritors with Christ, is both present (vv. 14–16) and still future (v. 23). But systematic-theological treatments have not usually made that clear.

For justification, it is fair to say that, in general, Reformation theology has grasped, at least intuitively, the eschatological "now" emphatically asserted, for instance, in Romans 5:1 and 8:1. It has perceived with sound instinct that the verdict pronounced on believers, declaring them righteous and entitled to eternal life, involves judgment, already realized, that is final and irrevocable.[42] But it has been much more inhibited, no doubt because of polemics with Rome, in recognizing and incorporating into its doctrinal formulations the still-future aspect of justification clearly implied if not explicitly taught in the New Testament.[43] The Westminster catechisms, for instance, confess that believers will be "openly acknowledged and acquitted in the day of judgment."[44] Such language is thoroughly forensic, and acquittal is at the heart of justification.

41. See, so far as Paul is concerned, my *Resurrection and Redemption* (Phillipsburg, NJ: Presbyterian and Reformed, 1987), 127–43; cf. the "I am" declaration of Jesus in John 11:25–26.
42. Yet it is also probably true that most often justification, like the work of the Spirit, has been viewed as a transaction in time between God and the individual sinner, without any particular reference to eschatological structure.
43. At issue is whether passages such as Rom. 2:13 and Gal. 5:5 and others on the final judgment teach that justification is in some respect future.
44. Larger Catechism 90; Shorter Catechism 38.

The integral tie between that future acquittal and present justification needs to be made clear. As a *single* justification by the sole
instrumentality of faith and based exclusively on the imputed righteousness of Christ, the one is the consummation of the other, as its
open manifestation. For now until Jesus comes, the believer's justification is most certainly settled and certain but not uncontested. Romans
8:33–34, for instance, is clear in that regard. The faith that justifies
perseveres in love (Gal. 5:6). No doubt, as so often in our theologizing, the proverbial razor's edge between the truth of the gospel and
serious error presents itself here, a narrow ledge that will have to be
negotiated with care.[45]

Alternatively, Reformed theology has certainly been clear about
the future eschatological transformation of the believer, penultimately
at death and climactically in the resurrection at Christ's return. But
it has been ambiguous at best, and certainly not decisive, that the
regeneration/renewal already experienced by believers is likewise
nothing less than eschatological in nature. At the core of their being,
believers will never be more resurrected than they already are. Their
place in the final resurrection-"harvest" (1 Cor. 15:20–23) is now as
well as still future.

For instance, in Ephesians 2:5–6, believers' having already been
"raised with Christ" is not merely "positional" or metaphorical. It is
of one piece with future, bodily resurrection. It is just as "real" and
"existential." That, an enlivening and transforming experience, is
plain in the immediate context (vv. 1–10) from the radical reversal
in "walk" it effects (vv. 2, 10): from a lifestyle of "being dead in tres-
passes and sins," with which the passage opens (vv. 1–3, 5), to the
"good works" of new-creation existence in Christ, the note on which
it closes (v. 10).

Elsewhere in the New Testament, the believer in Christ is already a
participant in the "new creation" (2 Cor. 5:17). Again, because of their
union with the crucified and resurrected Christ, believers no longer
"live" in sin as the power that dominates them (Rom. 6:1ff.). In fact,
"everyone born of God does not sin[;] . . . he is not able to sin" (1 John

45. On the relationship between justification and (final) judgment according to works
in the New Testament, especially Paul, especially helpful is the treatment of Ridderbos, *Paul*,
sec. 31.

3:9; cf. v. 6).[46] Nettlesome questions, especially anthropological, loom large here, as well as the false perfectionism that continues to plague the church. Still, Reformed systematic theology needs to process more adequately the already-realized, nonforensic eschatological "perfection" of the believer that the New Testament does teach.

At the same time, it will also be necessary to keep clear, as Reformed systematic theology has always sought to do, that the eschatologically qualified *ordo salutis* of the New Testament is not an essentially new or different *ordo* than that already present in the Old Testament. Here, too, the controlling viewpoint of the *historia salutis* is critical. The soteriological unity of the covenant of grace can never be properly appreciated or satisfactorily explained apart from recognizing that this unity is predicated on the "revealed mystery" (Rom. 16:25–26; Col. 1:26): the eschatological revelation of the righteousness of God in Christ as the fulfillment of the promise. Only on that basis may the benefits of the covenant be applied in advance, "out of season," before "the time had fully come" (Gal. 4:4), so that old-covenant believers—Abraham and David, for instance—could serve as models of justification by faith (Rom. 4; Gal. 3).

The unmistakable and substantial contrasts involved in the movement from old to new covenant are preeminently redemptive-historical, and not in terms of the *ordo salutis*. Differences in the latter there no doubt are, but these, despite the understandable tendency to be preoccupied with them, remain on the periphery of biblical revelation and resist full categorization. On the one hand, covenantal fellowship with God becomes for the New Testament believer what it was not, and could not yet be, for Abraham and David: union with the *now-exalted* Christ. But the experiential difference this makes can be only loosely captured by comparative terms such as "enlarged," "greater," "fuller" (language used by Westminster Confession 20.1 in treating Christian liberty).

The "something better," of which Hebrews speaks, does not divide new- and old-covenant believers in the personal appropriation of salvation but, as the writer says, was planned by God "so that only

---

46. See in this regard Murray's important discussion of "Definitive Sanctification," in *Collected Writings*, 2:277–84.

together with us would they be made perfect" (11:40). The sote-riological "newness" of Pentecost, for instance, is not anthropological-individual-experiential but Christological and ecclesiological. (a) The Spirit is now present, at last, on the basis of the finished work of Christ, the "life-giving Spirit" (1 Cor. 15:45); he is the *eschatological* Spirit. (b) The Spirit is now "poured out on all flesh," Gentiles as well as Jews; he is the *universal* Spirit.[47]

3. One of the remarkable features of Spykman's book is its extensive treatment of theological prolegomena. "Part One: Foundations" is nearly one-fourth of the whole, 136 out of a total of 560 pages.[48] Along with appreciating much that is useful and stimulating in this lengthy introduction, I am left with several substantial reservations.[49] For one, Spykman's theological prolegomena do not really lead into ("introduce") the redemptive-historical approach taken in the main body of his systematic theology. In fact, they tend to undermine it. There is a certain dissonance between the stance he adopts in this part and what he sets out to do in the rest of the book—a tension present, I suggest, primarily because of his conception of theology and, correlatively, of the relationship between theology and Scripture.[50]

47. For further elaboration, see my *Perspectives on Pentecost* (Phillipsburg, NJ: Presbyterian and Reformed, 1979), 13–41.

48. Spykman would probably have considered this lengthy discussion, especially the "new directions" he proposes (*Reformational Theology*, 76ff.), its most significant and valuable part. The rest of the book "is intended as a consistent following-through on [its] spirit and thrust." Ibid., 135.

49. Perhaps most valuable in this part is the exposé of synthesis thinking, especially the various outworkings of Enlightenment and post-Enlightenment thought with its controlling autonomy commitment, although beginning with Barth the critique becomes noticeably less incisive. The importance of Immanuel Kant and the noumenal-phenomenal disjunction for subsequent theology, for instance, is handled with admirable clarity. Ibid., 29–30, 41–42. Among other strengths, along with combating false and objectionable dualisms, is the emphasis on the Creator-creature distinction and on the antithesis, in a religious, directional sense, as fundamental structures in theology.

My other major reservations about this part concern (1) Spykman's virtual dismissal of post-Reformation Reformed systematic theology (everyone until Kuyper and Bavinck, apparently, and British-American Presbyterianism in its entirety) with the pejorative "scholastic" ("reformational," presumably, does not include Reformed orthodoxy); and (2) the Christological difficulties, if not confusion, attendant on his call for "three-factor" theologizing: "the Word of God as the pivotal point, the normative boundary and bridge between the revealing God and his responding creatures." Ibid., 60.

50. Again, we are into issues that call for much more extensive discussion than the comments that follow. See my *Resurrection and Redemption*, 19–30, and my "Introduction" to *Redemptive History and Biblical Interpretation*, xiv–xxiii.

(a) Is there theology in the Bible? No, says Spykman, emphatically not. The particular basis on which he reaches that conclusion is his neo-Kuyperian stress on the difference, structurally, between pretheoretical and theoretical thinking. Within that philosophical framework, the Bible, along with Christian confession, exemplifies the former, theology the latter.

This distance between theology and Scripture means that there is no single discipline, theology or any other, that has a privileged position relative to Scripture. Acknowledging this, Spykman thinks, will deliver us from the "triumphalist pretensions"[51] too long present, for instance, in the Reformed tradition, especially in its systematic theology (the proverbial "queen of the sciences" label). Put in its proper place, theology is concerned specifically with *confession* as a human activity. His preferred designation to replace "theology" is the neologism "pistology," that is, theoretical reflection on faith in its various senses.[52] The "normative movement,"[53] in which this delimited discipline has its role, runs from faith, grounded in Scripture, to a worldview, common to all believers, that in turn underlies all the special sciences, including philosophy and theology in their interaction.

I for one, however, have no hesitation about speaking of the special, even proprietary right of theology to Scripture, and so of its right to speak *about God*, in a careful, methodologically self-conscious and responsible way—speaking that at the same time can and should also be an act of worship and confession. That right the church has recognized from the beginning and proceeded accordingly, however otherwise wrongheadedly or even disastrously at times. To view theology in this way is not to enfranchise a theological guild that deprives other believers of free access to the Bible and lords it over the other special disciplines. Rather, it is to provide those disciplines and the whole church with the shepherding, ministerial services they cannot afford to be without.

At issue here is not the inevitably faith-qualified nature of all human endeavors or the notion of underlying, controlling worldview.

51. Spykman, *Reformational Theology*, 106.
52. Ibid., 104–5.
53. Ibid., 102.

20

Nor is it that for both Reformed systematic theology and Christian philosophy Scripture is "the noetic point of departure."[54] These are important insights that Spykman effectively reinforces.

Spykman is not alone in rejecting theology in the Bible. That rejection is shared by others who do not necessarily share his epistemology, or his sweeping anti-"scholastic" agenda.[55] This suggests a deeper, underlying influence, an influence that is to be found, almost certainly, in Abraham Kuyper's work on theological encyclopedia, particularly considerations that he voices most clearly in rejecting the expression "biblical theology."[56]

It is important to recognize that Kuyper's objections are not primarily in reaction to rationalistic, "critical" theology that, under the slogan "biblical theology," masqueraded its thinly veiled attacks on the authority of Scripture and orthodox Protestant systematic theology. That historical factor certainly plays a role,[57] but Kuyper's rejection has a deeper, principled basis.

His understanding of Scripture as the *principium theologiae* flatly prohibits the expression "biblical theology." Scripture is not itself theology but underlies it.[58] The biblical writers must not be called "theologians"[59] because theology is unthinkable apart from previously formed dogmas, and dogma is a product of the life of the (institutional) church.[60] The Bible itself contains no dogma but rather the "material" from which the church "constructs" dogma.[61] Biblical revelation comes in "the stylized, symbolic-aesthetic language of the East," while theology comes into being only when the "Western mind" with its penchant for "dialectical clarity" goes to work on the

---

54. Ibid., 101.

55. E.g., apparently, the authors of *Oriëntatie in de theologie*, who reject the expression "biblical theology." This rejection, apparently characteristic of Continental Reformed theology in contrast to British-American Calvinism, is probably bound up with the aversion of the former to the designation "systematic theology"; its preference is for "dogmatics."

56. Abraham Kuyper, *Encyclopaedie der heilige godgeleerdheid*, 3 vols. (Kok, 1909), 3:166–80 (where he discusses the *"historia revelationis"*).

57. Ibid., 169–70, 401–4.

58. Ibid., 167.

59. Ibid., 176.

60. Ibid., 169; cf. 395ff.

61. Ibid., 169, 404; cf. 355ff.

biblical material.[62] In short, Kuyper stresses exclusively the difference between Scripture and dogma, the discontinuity between the biblical writers and the subsequent theological activity of the church. He rejects biblical theology not only in name but in concept.[63]

Striking, and highly instructive, is the difference we find in Vos and Ridderbos on this point. In clear contrast with Kuyper, they approach the apostle Paul, say, in terms of their *continuity* with him—a continuity, moreover, that both see to be specifically *theological*. That sense of theological continuity is plain enough in Ridderbos. He subtitles his massive redemptive-historical exposition of Paul's teaching *Outline of His Theology*. But Vos is even more explicit. He speaks of "the Apostle's theological system."[64] Paul can "justly be called the father of Christian eschatology."[65] His is "the genius of the greatest constructive mind ever at work on the data of Christianity."[66] In large

<hr/>

62. Ibid., 168; cf. 2:247–48.

63. To be sure, Kuyper does approve the material interest of biblical theology—namely, its concern with the historical character of biblical revelation. He laments what he perceives to be the shortcomings of the *loca probantia* method of traditional systematic theology in this respect and looks for genuine progress in biblical understanding to result from study of the *historia revelationis*. Ibid., 170ff. Cf. Herman Bavinck, *Reformed Dogmatics* (1906; repr., Grand Rapids: Baker, 2003), 1:343–46; three of four Dutch volumes have appeared in English thus far.

64. Vos, *Pauline Eschatology*, 60.

65. Ibid., vi.

66. Ibid., 149. Such statements can be multiplied in Vos: Because the apostle's mind "had by nature a certain systematic bent, which made him pursue with great resoluteness the consequences of given premises" (ibid., 60), and because it was "highly doctrinal and synthetic" (ibid., 148), one ought to think in terms of Paul's "construction of Christian truth," his "system of truth" (ibid.), "the dogmatic coloring [of] his teaching" (ibid., 60). Paul's "energetic eschatological thinking tended toward consolidation in an orb of compact theological structure." Ibid., 61. The facile one-sidedness of many of his interpreters results in part "because Paul's mind as a theological thinker was far more exacting than theirs." Ibid., 149. "The Gospel having a precise, doctrinal structure, the doctrinally-gifted Paul was the fit organ for expressing this, because his gifts had been conferred and cultivated in advance with a view to it." Vos, *Biblical Theology*, 17.

Highly instructive is the remarkable difference between such statements, resulting from a lifetime of careful interpretation of Paul, and the following excerpt from his inaugural address. Rejecting the notion "as if in the Bible we had the beginnings of the process that later gave us the works of Origen, Augustine, Thomas Aquinas, Luther, and Calvin," he continues: "Only if we take the term Theology in its more primitive and simple meaning, as the practical, historic knowledge of God imparted by revelation and deposited in the Bible can we justify the use of the now commonly accepted name [Biblical Theology] of our science. As for the scientific elaboration of this God-given material, this must be held to lie beyond the Biblical period. It could spring only after revelation and the formation of the Scriptures had been completed. The utmost that can be conceded would be that in the Apostolic teaching of the New Testament the first signs of the beginning of this process are discernable. But even that measure, I would argue, the refreshing stimulus and fruitfulness of their work in alerting us, within a Reformed context, to the pervasively redemptive-historical subject matter of Scripture come from this approach in terms of theological continuity.

The Bible simply may not be categorized, in a single sweep, as confession but not theology, as Spykman, for one, apparently believes it should be.[67] In the case of Scripture, if the distinction between theoretical and pretheoretical thought is applicable, it describes a continuum that cuts across them as a whole. Anyone who says, categorically, that Scripture does not contain theology needs to reread much of Paul, for instance, or to reconsider large stretches of the argumentation in the book of Hebrews.[68]

I recognize, and fully share, the deep reservations about the dangers that this accent on theological continuity may occasion: abandonment of the unique authority of the New Testament writers; devaluation, say, of Paul's apostolicity; relativizing of Scripture as canon; and denial of its unity and divine authorship. These dangers are by no means imaginary, as developments, especially since the Enlightenment, show. But such disastrous consequences are not necessary or inevitable. Here, as elsewhere in our theologizing, the old maxim holds: *abusus non tollit usum* ("abuse does not invalidate legitimate use").

For there is also this to consider. The divine origin and perfections of Scripture, the canon and its closedness, apostolicity—all of these are not ahistorical abstractions but derive from and are intrinsically

---

which the Apostles teach is in no sense primarily to be viewed under the aspect of Theology. It is the inspired Word of God before all other things." Vos, "Idea," 20–21. Here, apparently, Kuyper's model still controls and is not yet questioned or qualified.

67. See, e.g., Spykman, *Reformational Theology*, 103. Confession itself, especially the corporate confession of the church, is explicitly *theological* assertion. That, at least, is how sixteenth- and seventeenth-century Protestantism understood what it was doing. Not to appreciate that understanding is inevitably to be on the way to the misuse of these creeds in the life of the church.

68. How, for instance, can Kuyper assert, as a sweeping generalization, that biblical revelation has been given in "the stylized, symbolic-aesthetic language of the East" (if that is a fair rendering of "de symbolisch-aesthetische kunsttaal," *Encyclopaedie*, 2:168)! Presumably his encyclopedic concerns have blinded him at this point to what he himself recognizes elsewhere: "What makes the letters of Paul so difficult is that there the mystical-oriental and western-dialectical streams flow into each other" (*Dictaten dogmatiek*, 10 vols. [Kampen, 1907], vol. 1, pt. 2, p. 54); "Paul is a more acute thinker than James" (*Encyclopaedie*, 2:241).

23

qualified by a covenant-historical matrix.[69] To be sure, within that matrix, at its eschatological, new-covenant end point, there is the important transition from apostolic to postapostolic to consider. The attendant distinction between inspired/canonical and noninspired/ noncanonical brings the one under the absolute authority of the other. That difference is crucial and may never be obscured.

But there is also a deeper, underlying unity. Apostolic history is *church* history, too. In "church" "apostolic" and "postapostolic" have their common (redemptive-historical) denominator.[70] In terms of that denominator a double, compounded commonness emerges: (i) a common *focus*, at least in part theologically qualified, on the subject matter of the gospel: Christ, crucified and exalted; and (ii) from a common already–not yet *context or vantage point*: now that Christ has departed and sent his Spirit, until he returns.

Far from devaluing the unique and final authority of Scripture and dragging it down to our own all-too-fallible level, such an approach, it seems to me, serves rather to ensure that the church's theological activity remains firmly within the parameters of biblical revelation. In terms of Paul's teaching about the church in Ephesians 2:11ff., this approach helps to keep that activity faithful to "the mystery of Christ, . . . as it has now [finally] been revealed by the Spirit to [God's] holy apostles and prophets." It serves to keep our theology firmly "built on the foundation of the apostles and prophets, with [the exalted] Christ Jesus himself as the cornerstone" (3:4–5; 2:20).[71]

69. See esp. Herman Ridderbos, *Redemptive History and the New Testament Scriptures*, rev. ed. (Phillipsburg, NJ: Presbyterian and Reformed, 1988).
70. "Still we know full well that we ourselves live just as much in the N.T. as did Peter and Paul and John." Vos, *Biblical Theology*, 324–25. In the same context Vos makes the perceptive and suggestive observation that the "seeming disproportion in chronological extent of the O.T. and the N.T. . . . arises from viewing the new revelation too much by itself, and not sufficiently as *introductory* and *basic* to the large period following." Ibid., 325, emphasis added.
71. In Eph. 2:20 (as well as 3:5), in view are not Old but New Testament prophets, and revelation given through them, along with the apostles, from the vantage point of the eschatological end point. The concern of the immediate context, 2:11ff., is not the unity/continuity between old and new covenants, but the newness of the new, especially the inclusion of Gentiles with Jews in the church. This view, I take it, is not subject to serious question exegetically; see, e.g., Wayne Grudem, *The Gift of Prophecy* (Westchester, IL: Crossway, 1988), 47; my *Perspectives on Pentecost*, 93; and, representative of the virtually universal consensus of recent commentators and monographs, Andrew T. Lincoln, *Ephesians*, Word Biblical Commentary (Dallas: Word, 1990), 153.

This apostolic model of the church as a building is especially suggestive for appreciating continuity. What is built on the apostolic "foundation" is not a different structure but postapostolic "super-structure." Both result from the single house-building activity of the exalted Christ (cf. esp. Eph. 4:7ff.) in the period between his resurrection and return. Scripture, we may say, then, not only is canon for the content of systematic theology but has something to say as well about its task. As *principium unicum theologiae*, Scripture not only gives us right answers but teaches us right questions to ask.

(b) Approaching Scripture in terms of a dimension of common theological activity with the New Testament writers will alert us to the models they provide for our own systematic-theological work, models in fact that hold the center of all our systematic-theological reflection where it ought to be—not simply on Christ and his incarnate person and work more generally, but on him as the embodied "fullness of the Deity" (Col. 2:10), as the consummate, eschatological revelation of the triune God.

Before noting some examples, let me again make it clear that my concern is not to force systematic theology into a single, particular format. In fact, if anything, the New Testament sponsors a variety of approaches; it is a diversity in unity.

(i) Herman Ridderbos has written, "It can be rightly said that Paul does nothing but explain the eschatological reality which in Christ's teachings is called the Kingdom."[72] This observation provides a particularly helpful unifying outlook on the New Testament, without overriding its diversity. If, appropriately, we expand Ridderbos's suggestive insight to include the other New Testament writers, and if, in turn and also properly, we take Jesus' kingdom proclamation as a grid for reading the whole Old Testament in all its parts, from the vantage point of the fulfillment Christ embodies (as Luke 24:44–47, cf. Acts 1:3, especially, suggests), then we have a kingdom model

72. Herman Ridderbos, *When the Time Had Fully Come* (Grand Rapids: Eerdmans, 1957), 48–49. This is true despite the fact that kingdom terminology recedes sharply in Paul's letters in comparison with the Synoptic accounts of Jesus' teaching. That shows how little the issue is a particular format or single vocabulary. Paul reflects on the "substance" of Jesus' kingdom proclamation primarily in his teaching on righteousness and the Holy Spirit (Rom. 14:17; cf. Matt. 6:33; 12:28).

for comprehending the history of revelation, as inscripturated, in its entirety and overall unity—a model, moreover, explicitly attuned to that history, centered on Christ, and sponsored by Scripture itself.

(ii) In English-speaking Calvinism, the expression "the whole counsel of God" has become something of a slogan, evocative of the comprehensive, God-centered concern for truth that distinguishes Reformed theology.[73] Yet in its sole biblical occurrence (Acts 20:27), a passage where Paul accounts for an entire lifetime of ministry, "the whole counsel" has a distinctly kingdom profile. There it is not in view, at least in the first place, as a topical compendium of revealed truth, but concerns, as correlative expressions in the immediate context show, the "preaching of the kingdom" (v. 25) as that preaching is "the gospel of the grace of God" (v. 24), focused in the call to repentance and faith (v. 21), and as such, then, omits "nothing profitable" for the church (v. 20). As the broader Lucan (and Pauline) context shows, the controlling preoccupation of the "counsel" is the historical-eschatological dynamic involved in the coming of the kingdom, the lordship of God in Christ exercised at the end of history for the renovation of his creation and the redemption of his people.[74]

(iii) Another notion that Paul uses to signal the redemptive-historical, eschatological orientation of his teaching in its entirety is "the revelation of the mystery" (Rom. 16:25ff.). That notion, properly exegeted, more than encompasses all that the Reformed confessions and theology have found, and must continue to find, essential for maintaining and defending what concerns the divine decree and its realization, and the promise-fulfillment structure of the covenant. But it does so without allowing that mystery-decree to become a separate topic, burdened, whenever that happens, with inevitable and counterproductive speculation. It keeps the focus where it belongs: on its *revelation*, the mystery as *revealed*.[75] It keeps the focus, in other words,

---

73. "The whole counsel of God concerning all things necessary for his own glory, man's salvation, faith and life, is either expressly set down in Scripture, or by good and necessary consequence may be deduced from Scripture . . ." (Westminster Confession of Faith 1.6). It is engraved, for instance, on the seal of Westminster Theological Seminary.

74. For fuller elaboration, see my "The Whole Counsel of God and the Bible," in John H. White, ed., *The Book of Books* (Phillipsburg, NJ: Presbyterian and Reformed, 1978), 19–28.

75. What, for instance, explains the marked de-escalation of the supra-/infralapsarian debate in recent Reformed theology if not the increasing awareness that the questions involved,

on Christ, on his death and resurrection, which, in their soteriological-eschatological significance ("for our sins") and as the fulfillment of Scripture ("according to the Scriptures"), are "of first importance," as Paul says elsewhere (1 Cor. 15:1–4), again in describing his gospel proclamation at the heart of his theology as a whole.

There can be nothing more important for Reformed systematic theology than this same *gospel* priority. To anticipate an objection without really being able to address it here, Christocentricity, at least with a proper redemptive-historical focus, and fully theocentric, Trinitarian balance are not in conflict.

These observations, I would add, should not be dismissed as a plea for some sort of biblicism in systematic-theological method. What they do reflect, again, is a concern, especially in our systematic theology, for an ever more faithful articulation of the "pattern of sound words" (2 Tim. 1:13) that Paul not only mentions as the concern of his own ministry but specifically enjoins on the postapostolic church.

(c) Approaching the New Testament in terms of common theological activity enables us to appreciate how systematic theology is a redemptive-historically qualified venture, not only because of its subject matter, as we have just seen, but also in terms of its context. That context, as already noted, it shares, despite important discontinuities, with the New Testament writers.

Systematic theology, then, like all other theological endeavors, is a "timed" enterprise. Specifically, it is for the present time of the church, that we might "know the time" (Rom. 13:11), that time "between the times," bracketed by Christ's resurrection and return. Paul neatly captures its essence in 1 Thessalonians 1:9–10: the church consists of those "turned to God from idols to serve the living and true God," just as, in that service, they "wait for his Son from heaven, whom he raised from the dead." Systematic theology is for the duration: the duration of this hiatus, this Spirit-filled and -energized interim. It, too, with the "timely" knowledge it provides and elaborates, is a part of the "waiting service" of the church. Doctrinal formulation and

---

though legitimate, cannot be resolved because the biblical writers, with their covenant-historical focus, address them only obliquely, at the "edges" of their teaching?

systematic theology are a function of redemptive history, and the formation of dogma begins in the New Testament.[76]

These observations, by the way, point us to appreciating the New Testament itself as the deepest, most far-reaching as well as "relevant" "contextualization" of the gospel. The Bible is not a composite of ahistorical truths about God, humanity, and so on, needing to be enculturated. Scripture, ultimately, is not in need of contextualization but provides its own.[77]

(d) A systematic theology intent on maintaining its vitality faces no greater danger than a situation in which Scripture can no longer correct it, and in which appeal to Scripture serves only to confirm existing formulations. Accordingly, it can have no more urgent concern than for a recourse to the Scriptures that continues to challenge and refine it.[78]

The confessional commitment, noted earlier, to the "good and necessary consequence . . . deduced from Scripture"[79] is the *commit-*

---

76. "Surely it does not become systematic theology to unravel what has been synthesized to a degree even in the Scriptures. Systematic theology ought rather to weave together the related strands yet more systematically." Meredith G. Kline, *By Oath Consigned* (Grand Rapids: Eerdmans, 1968), 29. "It is important to see the theological project as embedded in the Scriptures themselves rather than as merely an overlay on them, for this will make it easier to see how the theological project can be restructured to more nearly mirror the structure of Scripture [with reference to the author's earlier discussion of Edwards and Vos]." Lints, *The Fabric of Theology*, 261.

77. This comment is surely not meant to preempt ongoing debate on contextualization, at least not all aspects of that debate, nor to deny the legitimacy of issues raised by the distance between the biblical world and the culture of a particular time and place since.

The book of Hebrews is instructive in this regard. Originally addressed, as were the other New Testament documents, to readers in a particular time and place, under specific social, economic, and political conditions, it reveals remarkably little about these cultural factors. The date and the place and identity of the readers continue to be debated, and the perennial question of authorship remains unanswered. What the writer *is* concerned to have his readers grasp clearly is that they are "in these last days" when God has spoken his final word in his Son (1:2), when Christ "has appeared once for all at the end of the ages to do away with sin by the sacrifice of himself . . . and . . . will appear a second time . . . to bring salvation" (9:26, 28). The ultimately relevant and decisive "context" of his readers' existence, in all its undoubtedly enculturated particularity, is not that particular context but the period between the exaltation and return of Christ, in which the church has its identity as the new and final wilderness community (esp. 3:7ff.). This macro-historical and -cultural outlook is integral to the gospel. It not only transforms and redirects life in the first-century Mediterranean world, or any other particular cultural matrix, but also establishes the continuity necessary for truly meaningful transhistorical and cross-cultural contacts.

78. Jonker's comments in this regard in "Eksegese en dogmatiek," 163–66, 171–73, are particularly valuable: the concrete statements of Scripture, functioning like a "jamming station" (!), retain a disruptive element for doctrinal formulation.

79. Westminster Confession of Faith 1.6.

ment, especially, that has given rise to Reformed systematic theology. But is the particular deduction truly "good and necessary"? That *question,* especially, must continue to occupy Reformed systematic theology. Seeing ourselves as involved with the New Testament writers in a common redemptive-historical project or, even more pointedly, a common preoccupation with the *gospel* is a stance that will prove valuable in distinguishing the "good and necessary"—"everything profitable," as Paul says in Acts 20:20—from what is not.

As long as one continues, with Kuyper, to think of Scripture as providing the raw "material" from which the church "constructs" doctrines and develops its systematic theology, it is difficult to see how an illegitimate proof-texting can be effectively overcome, despite insistence to the contrary, and so the speculative, intellectualistic traces that have marred Reformed systematic theology will persist. The solution to "scholasticism" (to abuse that word), to an overly notional Christianity, to a speculative, excessively cerebral treatment of Christian doctrine, to a less than full-blooded embodiment of the gospel and its implications—the solution to all that, it turns out, is not to deny that Scripture contains theology or to slight that theology, but to recognize it and let it come to its rights.

I have lived long enough to learn that there are no easy formulas for safeguarding sound theologizing. But I submit that for the church at the beginning of the twenty-first century, the vitality of its systematic theology will be well served by our recognizing and exploring its deep theological continuity, despite the long span of intervening centuries, with the apostolic church and theology of the first century.

Afterword

Recently,[80] W. Robert Godfrey has taken decided exception to my use in the original version of this chapter (see the footnote at the outset of this chapter) of the expression "sympathetic-critical," which I borrowed from Schilder for the basic stance of systematic theology toward the church's confessions (see above at note superscript 13).

80. In David VanDrunen, ed., *The Pattern of Sound Truth: Essays in Honor of Robert B. Strimple* (Phillipsburg, NJ: P&R Publishing, 2004), 141–42.

This stance, he maintains, "misses the communal, ecclesiastical character of confessions" because it fails "to distinguish clearly between our confessions and our [systematic-theological] tradition." He even associates it with the attitude of those who "have acted as if the confessions of their churches were out-dated historical documents or pious advice that could be rejected as easily as followed or as brief systematic theologies that they were free to improve upon," or who forget that, until the church duly changes its confession, "those who have confessed their faith by subscribing a confession are under a moral obligation to uphold that confession." Instead, our attitude toward confessions as church confessions, particularly those subscribed to, ought to be one of confidence, an attitude that "in the first place is not critical, not even 'sympathetic-critical.' "

I suppose that, taken by itself, "sympathetic-critical" could be read as unsympathetically and critically as Dr. Godfrey reads it, but it hardly needs to be taken that way, and I leave it to the reader to judge whether it is not reasonably clear from the immediate context as well as the tenor of this entire chapter that my own usage, far from betraying ecclesiastical indifference (or moral insensitivity), intends, precisely, to make a *churchly* point about the proper relationship between three factors: Scripture as given to the *church*, church doctrine/confession, and systematic theology as done in the interests of the *church*. At any rate, I have retained the expression above because I remain convinced that it expresses something vital for the church in maintaining its confessions and so for systematic theology faithful to those confessions.

Helpful here is the orthodox Protestant distinction between the absolute authority of the Bible as "norming norm" (*norma normans*) and the subordinate authority of the church's confession as "normed norm" (*norma normata*). In its work, systematic theology is bound to maintain this distinction and the no-more-than-subordinate authority of the confession. In fact, all those subscribing, *ex animo*, to the Westminster Standards are bound by this very subscription to maintaining this distinction.[81] Undeniably, subscription presupposes cordial

---

81. "The supreme judge by which all controversies of religion are to be determined, . . . and in whose sentence we are to rest, can be no other but the Holy Spirit speaking in the Scripture" (Westminster Confession of Faith 1.10); cf. 20.2: "God alone is Lord of the conscience,

acceptance of the contents of the confession, and when one's views diverge, for whatever reasons, an orderly procedure ought to be in place for adjudicating whether or not such divergences are acceptable by the church or other institutional body responsible for overseeing subscription. If it needs to be said, that is not at issue for me.

But when the distinction in view above (that "critical" distinction, in fact) is lost sight of or otherwise not maintained, then the risk is great that the confession will come to function on a par with Scripture and its authority—in effect, will become absolute (an elevation that Dr. Godfrey certainly does not intend: the attitude he calls for entails "fully recognizing that our confessions are human writings and may need to be changed in light of clearer understanding of the Word of God"). May we not, then, on balance, speak of a "sympathetic-critical confidence" in our church's confession?

Dr. Godfrey connects the faulty attitude he attributes to me with the view, which he likewise rejects, that "the confession is basically a brief form of systematic theology." This latter rejection is puzzling. Certainly, the confession is more than just a systematic theology produced by one or more individuals. But if systematic theology is fairly characterized as presenting the unified teaching of the Bible as a whole on appropriate topics in an orderly fashion, then a confession or catechism is just that: a *privileged* piece of systematic theology, which the church, by adoption, has elevated to the status of a subordinate standard in its life. Is that not what is being confessed virtually, for instance, by those who subscribe to the Westminster Standards "as a summary and just exhibition of that *system of doctrine* . . . contained in Holy Scripture" or "as containing *the system of doctrine* taught in the Holy Scriptures"?[82]

As noted, the expression "sympathetic-critical" comes from Schilder. Perhaps there will be some value in quoting the passage from J. Douma where I found it.[83] Doing that will make clearer the sense that Schilder and he have in mind, and I, in turn, in taking it over.

---

and hath left it free from the doctrines and commandments of men, which are, in anything, contrary to his Word. . . ."

82. See as well the observation above in note 67.

83. See note 14 above for bibliographic details; all italics original.

The science of theology is in *the service of the church*. . . . Against those [who deny this tethering of theology to the church] we hold that God's revelation has been entrusted to the church. The one who studies this revelation can only do that in the right place: within the church. Given, too, with the office of minister of the Word (pastor and *teacher*) is training for the ministry of the Word.

This ecclesiastical bond does not mean that the theologian is shackled to an ecclesiastical tradition, as in the Roman Catholic Church. Article 7 of the Belgic Confession commands the believer to place the truth of God above everything. That is true as well for the theologians among believers. Confessional committedness is something other than confessionalistic narrowmindedness. Important in this connection is the definition that Schilder gives of dogmatics: Dogmatics is "the science, which in submission to the content and purpose of Holy Scripture, arranges and systematically treats the problems of the theological dogmas of the church [der kerkelijk-theologische dogmata] in a *sympathetic-critical reproduction* of the content of the dogmas established in the line of the ecumenical creeds" (*Dictaten compendium-dogmatiek*, 1:13).

Critical—"If, after all, the church never has exhausted nor will exhaust the truth of inscripturated revelation, and also never was nor will be free from the consequences of sin, then reflection over and reproduction of dogma, just through its tie to inscripturated revelation, will be provoked to a critical stance toward dogmas and confession" (1:12).

Sympathetic—"Naturally this critical stance may only be sympathetic, that is, the dogmatician, as believer even in his scientific thinking, has to begin with the dogmas of his church" (ibid.).

2

A Tract for the Times:
James Buchanan's *The Doctrine*
of Justification in Historical
and Theological Context

CARL R. TRUEMAN

James Buchanan (1804–70) was an outstanding member of the
generation of men who cut their theological and ecclesiastical teeth
during the struggles of the Ten Years' Conflict within the Church of
Scotland that led to the Disruption of the established church and
formation of the Free Church of Scotland in 1843. Along with the
varied contributions of contemporaries such as William Cunningham, Robert Smith Candlish, and James Bannerman, Buchanan's
lecturing and writing provided much of the intellectual muscle of the
new denomination in the middle years of the nineteenth century; yet
he also possessed a significance beyond his narrow denominational
bounds as one of the most able exponents of Reformed orthodoxy as
it came to expression in the church conflicts of Victorian Britain.

In his own day, Buchanan was better known as a philosophical
theologian and apologist than as a straightforward expounder of the
traditional Reformed faith, a reputation that rested largely on major
works he wrote on both the rationality of theism and the meaning and

use of analogy.[1] Nevertheless, his career at New College, Edinburgh, which saw his initial appointment in 1845 as professor of apologetics followed by his translation on Thomas Chalmers's death in 1847 to the chair of systematic theology, reflects the dual nature of his theological competence and interest. Indeed, as the philosophical paradigms with which he worked have dated, so as a consequence his metaphysical work has faded somewhat from view; but he is still well known among students of traditional Reformed theology for two significant systematic treatises that articulate classic orthodox positions, *The Office and Work of the Holy Spirit* (Edinburgh, 1842) and *The Doctrine of Justification* (Edinburgh, 1867), the latter of which was first delivered as the Cunningham lectures for 1866 and forms the subject of this essay.

Buchanan's Text in Context

It is, of course, a truism that the doctrine of justification was the hallmark of Protestantism. The theological confessionalization that took place in Western Christendom in the sixteenth century codified doctrinal divisions between Roman Catholicism and Protestantism and, within Protestantism, between Lutheran and Reformed. Nevertheless, on the central issue of justification, particularly with regard to the instrumentality of faith and the imputation of Christ's righteousness, there was no major dissent between the confessional documents of the Reformed churches and the Lutheran Book of Concord.

Despite the apparent consensus, however, Protestantism did not enjoy a particularly peaceful history on this matter. In the seventeenth century, the precise role of good works was the subject of some considerable debate in English Puritanism, particularly because of the fear of antinomianism at a time of considerable social and political upheaval. Richard Baxter's development of what opponents dubbed "neonomianism" is perhaps the most famous example of an attempt to recast the Reformation doctrine in a manner that avoids the pos-

1. *Faith in God and Modern Atheism Compared*, 2 vols. (Edinburgh, 1855); *Analogy, Considered as a Guide to Truth* (Edinburgh, 1864).

34

sibility of antinomian misconstruction, and his orthodoxy on this point has been subject to vigorous debate from that day to this. Debates over other related issues such as eternal justification, to what extent assurance is of the essence of faith, the conditionality of the covenant of grace, and the role of the law in the Christian life also continued to shape Protestant discussion and to lead to increased nuancing and, to an extent, fragmentation of the Reformed consensus on the issue.[2] The most famous ecclesiastical incident of this kind was the Marrow Controversy, which caused bitter dispute in the Church of Scotland in the early eighteenth century, setting Reformed orthodox theologians against each other.[3]

By the time Buchanan came to address the subject in the 1860s, further theological developments had taken place. Perhaps most significant was the advent of Tractarianism in the 1830s. A reaction to various political, cultural, and theological trends, the movement defies reduction to the simplistic categories that ecclesiastical partisans and opponents often seek to apply. Catholic Emancipation, attempts to disestablish the church, the rapid rise of industrialization, and the rise and fall of Romanticism all played their part in shaping the ethos and ideology of the movement; and in John Henry Newman, the movement found one of the most acute theological writers and elegant prose stylists of the nineteenth century, a man whose influence on modern Roman Catholicism it is hard to overestimate.[4]

At the heart of the theological campaign of the Tractarians was an attempt to reconceive historic Protestant identity in a manner that made room for what their opponents routinely decried as their "Romanizing" tendencies but that the Tractarians themselves would have seen as an attempt to locate Anglicanism within a pre-Reformation tradition of

2. See Hans Boersma, *A Hot Peppercorn: Richard Baxter's Doctrine of Justification in Its Seventeenth-Century Context of Controversy* (Zoetermeer, Netherlands: Boekencentrum, 1993); Tim Cooper, *Fear and Polemic in Seventeenth-Century England: Richard Baxter and Antinomianism* (Aldershot, Hampshire: Ashgate, 2001).

3. See David C. Lachman, *The Marrow Controversy, 1718–1723: An Historical and Theological Analysis* (Edinburgh: Rutherford House, 1988).

4. On Tractarianism, see Owen Chadwick, *The Mind of the Oxford Movement* (Stanford: Stanford University Press, 1960); also Peter Nockles, *The Oxford Movement in Context* (Cambridge: Cambridge University Press, 1994). On Newman, see Ian Ker, *John Henry Newman: A Biography* (Oxford: Oxford University Press, 1988).

catholicity.[5] The most obvious points at which this took place were those matters relating directly to church practice and aesthetics, and thus the Eucharist became a central part of the revisionist agenda. Nonetheless, given the fact that the doctrine of justification was, along with rejection of the Mass, perhaps *the* hallmark of historic Protestantism, it was inevitable that this doctrine, too, should come under some pressure. Newman himself, in his (in)famous *Tract XC*, deals with the issue relative to works before and after justification, carefully avoiding the obvious Reformation Protestant character of the Thirty-nine Articles and rather reading the relevant passages against the background of debates about congruent merit. Thus, his comments on Articles 11, 12, and 13 should be read together as one piece, moving from an emphasis on faith as justifying proleptically relative to the process of making righteous, on to a discussion of congruent merit regarding works. Thus, in dealing with justification Newman reads the Articles as consistent with an Augustinian understanding of the issues of grace, while he studiously avoids addressing the central Reformation issues of whether the righteousness of Christ is received through faith alone by imputation.[6]

Newman was not, of course, the first to attempt to bring the Thirty-nine Articles into line with Roman Catholic thinking. Indeed, the whole issue of the relationship between the Protestantism of the Anglican Church and Roman Catholicism had been a somewhat vexing issue since the first Book of Common Prayer (1549).[7] Then in the seventeenth century, at the height of the conflicts of the 1630s and 1640s, Franciscus à Sancta Clara (Christopher Davenport) wrote a Latin treatise arguing for a traditional Roman Catholic interpretation of the Articles.[8] Of course, one of the key elements of Protestant

5. See Chadwick, *The Mind of the Oxford Movement*, 16–17.
6. The text is available in William G. Hutchison, ed., *The Oxford Movement: Being a Selection from Tracts for the Times* (London: Walter Scott, 1906), 197–203.
7. E.g., Stephen Gardiner's swashbuckling use of the 1549 Book of Common Prayer to refute Thomas Cranmer's own view of the Eucharist. See Diarmaid MacCulloch, *Thomas Cranmer* (New Haven: Yale University Press, 1996), 486–87.
8. Franciscus à Sancta Clara, *On the Articles of the Anglican Church*, ed. Frederick George Lee (London, 1865). The text contains both the original Latin, *Paraphrastica Expositio Articulorum Confessionis Anglicanae*, and an English translation. The original was published in 1646. The nineteenth-century introduction to this work is interesting, demonstrating as it does the highly relativized way in which the editor understood the Articles to function. Distinguishing

understandings of justification is that it might well occupy a different constructive function in Lutheran and Reformed confessional traditions, but that in neither can it simply be taken in isolation. Rather, the teaching has implications for a number of different doctrines. Thus, Sancta Clara's attempt to read the Articles in a Roman Catholic way requires him to rework the theology underlying a number of them. On Article 11 ("Of the Justification of Man"), he elides imputation with impartation and thus blunts the force of the instrumentality of faith in Protestant theology.[9] On Article 14 ("Of Works of Supererogation"), he reads the article against the background of Roman Catholic teaching on pure nature, thus finessing the condemnation away and leaving space for merit in the context of grace.[10] Then, as one final example, on Article 22 ("Of Purgatory"), Sancta Clara argues that it is the doctrine *imputed* to Rome, not the Roman Catholic doctrine *as truly taught*, that is condemned.[11]

Two things are clear from the tradition of polemic epitomized by Sancta Clara. First, the doctrine of justification stands at the heart of the Protestant project; and Roman controversialists such as Sancta Clara knew that the success of their polemic depended not simply on addressing this issue in isolation, but on revising the body of Protestant divinity in light of such critique. Second, this type of Roman polemic depended on relativizing the controversy over justification by arguing that it was, at root, an argument over the relationship of grace, good works, and merit. This effectively sidelines the central issues of the instrumentality of faith and imputation by recasting the Reformation debate in the terms of the earlier Pelagian controversy—a recasting undoubtedly aided by the widespread belief among the Reformers that their debate with Roman Catholicism did indeed break down along lines similar to that of Augustine and Pelagius.

This attempt to relativize the differences between Tridentine Catholicism and confessional Protestantism on the issue of

---

them as articles of *religion*, not *faith*, he argues that the Articles themselves are not intended as a statement of orthodoxy, but only as statements of opinion. Some of these may indeed deal with issues of faith, but on the whole, they are not to be received as creedally authoritative.

9. Sancta Clara, *On the Articles*, 13.
10. Ibid., 17.
11. Ibid., 39–42.

justification is akin to what had become established practice by the nineteenth century whereby the focus of debate was the issue of the way in which the believer's good works could be described as meritorious. This point is made with passion and clarity by Free Church divine William Cunningham in an 1852 review of the second edition of Richard Whately's book *Essays on the Errors of Romanism Having Their Origin in Human Nature* (London, 1837).[12] In this work, Whately devotes appendix B to explaining why he has not dealt with the issue of what he calls "self-righteousness" in the main text, despite the fact that trust in the meritorious nature of human works is, for many Protestants, one of the principal errors of Tridentine Catholicism. On this, Whately comments as follows:

> The Romish Church, however, has not in reality ever set this forth as one of her tenets. If any one will consult, what is of decisive authority in that Church, the decrees of the Council of Trent, he will perceive, that though they may perhaps have made an injudicious use of the word "merit," the abstract question between them and others (not Antinomians) is chiefly verbal. For they admit, and solemnly declare, that nothing we can do can be acceptable before God except for the sake of Jesus Christ; and that we are unable to perform good works except by his Spirit working in us: so that what is called a Christian's righteousness, is, at the same time, the righteousness of Christ, although the Scriptures promise, repeatedly and plainly, that it will, through his goodness, not "lose its reward."[13]

Whately's point, combined with an assertion that the works righteousness against which Paul was writing was that of the ceremonial law, not of the law as a whole, serves to relativize the difference between Protestant and Roman Catholic positions by shifting the grounds for disagreement to that of the merit of the believer's righteousness. This, Whately correctly observes, is to be conceived of Christologically and pneumatologically, and not in any humanly autonomous or Pelagian sense. The problem, of course, is that this was not the principal point

---

12. William Cunningham, "The Errors of Romanism," in *Discussions on Church Principles: Popish, Erastian, and Presbyterian* (Edinburgh, 1863), 1–34. This is a reprint of the original that appeared in the *Northern British Review* 34 (August 1852).

13. Whately, *Essays on the Errors of Romanism*, 336. I am using the first edition of 1830.

of dispute in the Reformation: both sides agreed that justification was on the grounds of the righteousness of Christ; where they differed was over whether this was given to the believer by imputation or by impartation. Cunningham's criticism of Whately here is right on target: if Whately is correct, then the Reformation was caused by a misunderstanding of the normative Roman position, not by Protestant rejection of actual Roman error, a point the Scotsman reinforces with reference to two classic seventeenth-century works on the subject, one by John Davenant, the other by George Downame.[14]

This theological maneuvering on the doctrine of justification in the Anglican Church coincided with something of a resurgence in Scottish Episcopalianism, which put considerable pressure on the Presbyterians. This in turn merely added to the general fear of Roman Catholicism, and of Romanizing Episcopalianism, typical of many nineteenth-century British evangelicals, fueled, as noted above, by Catholic Emancipation and the growing acceptance, and influence, of Roman Catholics in British society. In the 1860s, therefore, the perennial doctrinal debates with Rome had an added ecclesiastical, social, and political urgency. While the Disruption Free Church to which Buchanan belonged was initially led by Thomas Chalmers, a man of remarkably progressive views on Catholic Emancipation, this should not be taken as any sign that she was soft on either the theology or the culture of Roman Catholicism.[15] Cunningham, who, along with Robert Smith Candlish, had been one of the more radical, younger voices to which Chalmers had paid heed, was to go on to be professor of church history and then principal of New College; and he had an exemplary track record as an anti-Roman theological polemicist.[16] In addition, the theologically less gifted but constitutionally acute and ecclesiastically influential James Begg proved to embody a fascinating

14. Cunningham, *Discussions on Church Principles*, 25, citing the second section of John Davenant, *Praelectiones de Duobus in Theologia Capitibus* (Cambridge, 1631), on habitual and actual righteousness; and George Downame, *A Treatise of Justification* (London, 1634). Cunningham cites the latter as 1633, though the Short Title Catalogue lists only editions for 1632 and 1634.

15. See Henry R. Sefton, "Chalmers and the Church," in A. C. Cheyne, ed., *The Practical and the Pious* (Edinburgh: St. Andrew Press, 1985), 166–73.

16. For example, in 1845 Cunningham edited and wrote an introduction to a new edition of Edward Stillingfleet's seventeenth-century work *The Doctrines and Practices of the Church of Rome Truly Represented* (Edinburgh, 1845).

combination of enlightened and progressive social views along with vigorously reactionary anti-Catholicism. Thus, in their attitude to Roman Catholicism, the leaders of the Free Church embodied the evangelical Protestant spirit of the age.[17]

Given this background, it is not surprising that the anti-Roman ethos of the times is reflected in the mid-century polemics on justification. This is exemplified in the treatment of justification in Cunningham's posthumously published lectures, *Historical Theology*. Here, he notes two standard Roman Catholic reactions to the Protestant understanding of justification: that which repudiates the latter outright, and that which presents it as containing *some* legitimate criticism of Rome. This second approach, Cunningham argues, is designed to prove that "there is not so great a difference between their [the Protestants'] doctrine and that of the Church of Rome."[18] It is this trajectory of discussion to which Cunningham declares he will confine his own polemics on the issue.[19] Thus, it was the relativizing tendency of contemporary discussions that perturbed Cunningham most, presumably because the social and cultural context was ripe for such views to appeal to a wider public, thus opening up the wider possibility of serious doctrinal indifferentism on an issue of central theological and pastoral concern lying at the heart of Protestant identity. He was particularly sharp in his comments on Newman in this regard, seeing the lectures on justification delivered while the latter was still an Anglican as being already driven by "Popish purposes," particularly in the radical downplaying of the declaratory nature of justification as stated in the Thirty-nine Articles.[20] Given that these lectures of Cunningham were edited for publication by Buchanan and his colleague James Bannerman, we can assume that the emphases and approach of Cunningham's arguments were very familiar to him.[21]

17. See James Lachlan MacLeod, *The Second Disruption* (East Linton, Scotland: Belknap, 2000), 22–31.
18. William Cunningham, *Historical Theology: A Review of the Principal Doctrinal Discussions in the Christian Church since the Apostolic Age*, 2 vols. (London: Banner of Truth, 1960), 2:4.
19. Ibid., 5.
20. Ibid., 33–34.
21. Cunningham comments that the doctrine of justification "was the great fundamental distinguishing doctrine of the Reformation, and was regarded by all the Reformers as of primary and paramount importance." Ibid., 1. He also notes what he sees as a worrying tendency of

Buchanan himself had exhibited interest in and concern for Trac-tarianism since his earliest days as a theological writer, publishing a small, epistolary book on the movement in 1843.[22] In this work, the issue of justification is not directly addressed at any length; instead, Buchanan focuses his criticism of Tractarian soteriology on the empha-sis that Newman and company place on the visible church, as opposed to repentance and faith, as the means by which the individual enjoys the benefits of Christ.[23] Buchanan's concern over developments in Anglican thought had also shown itself in his response in the early 1860s to the *Essays and Reviews*. Here, he had identified both Tractarianism and the later liberalizing movement as being responses to the general crisis in religious authority within Anglicanism, and as representing a softening of attitude toward Rome and a basic distrust of the principle of Scripture alone.[24]

By the mid-1860s, however, there was good reason to be focusing more on the issue of justification. Newman had, of course, converted to Roman Catholicism in 1845, and his pilgrimage to that point had been marked by his *Lectures on Justification* (1838) and *Tract XC* (1841) and by the composition of *An Essay on the Development of Christian Doctrine*, which he wrote as an Anglican, though it was not published until 1845. Whatever the full story of Newman's conversion may have been, it was publicly worked out in the context of wrestling with issues of church authority and justification.[25] Given the touch-stone nature of justification for the very existence of Protestantism as a Western theological and ecclesiastical tradition separate from Roman Catholicism, and the clear connection between this issue and

---

High Churchmen to rewrite the history of the doctrine in order to minimize the conflict with Rome. Ibid., 4.

22. James Buchanan, *On the "Tracts for the Times"* (Edinburgh, 1843).

23. "Every penitent believing soul may at once appropriate for himself, and by himself, every one of those exceeding great and precious promises, and feed on them as his daily food. But, say the Oxford divines, these promises are not made to men simply as *repenting* or *believ-ing*, but as members of THE CHURCH; and none else have a divine warrant to appropriate or apply them to themselves. What is this, again, but to interpose THE CHURCH betwixt a hungry soul and Christ, the bread of life, and to make my hope depend, not on his faithfulness, but on her fidelity?" Ibid., 99.

24. James Buchanan, *The "Essays and Reviews" Examined* (Edinburgh, 1861), 7–44.

25. On the significance of the *Lectures on Justification* for Newman, see Ker, *John Henry Newman*, 151–57.

the understanding of authority and church, it is quite understandable why Newman's pilgrimage should have addressed these issues. Indeed, even after Newman's conversion to Rome, they continued to preoccupy the minds of Anglo-Catholics. Thus, for example, in 1865, the seventeenth-century work of Sancta Clara cited above was republished, offering another attempt to read the Reformation Articles of the Church of England in as Roman Catholic a way as possible. All of this combined to place justification by faith, and its various corollary doctrines, at the center of theological debate for those determined to defend Protestant orthodoxy over against Roman Catholicism.[26]

It is worth noting at this point the difference between the theologies of confessional Lutheranism and of the Reformed churches concerning the importance of justification. For both traditions, justification by grace through faith on the basis of the imputation of the righteousness of Christ is basic. As a result, any and all attempts to drive a major wedge between the two on this point, whether as part of a nineteenth-century Tractarian agenda or as part of the tiresome contemporary campaign to find space for explicit or implicit repudiations of imputation within the Reformed confessional community, are disingenuous at best and without either historical or confessional integrity. Indeed, one might say that as far as the doctrine of justification is concerned, if you are not on the road to Wittenberg and Geneva, then the old proverb is indeed true: all roads lead to Rome.[27]

All of this is not to say, however, that the doctrine has precisely the same structural function within both traditions, Lutheran and Reformed. For Lutheranism, justification by faith operates not simply as an essential doctrine but also as a central structuring principle for the whole theological edifice, although we should beware of under-

---

26. Buchanan, quoting Robert Traill, sums up his suspicion of the contemporary maneuvering in the following pithy manner: "Such men as are for 'middle ways' in point of doctrine, have usually a greater kindness for that extreme they go half-way *to*, than for that which they go half-way *from*." *Doctrine of Justification*, 173.

27. This would certainly seem to be Buchanan's own viewpoint, as the following comment from his introduction indicates: "All these assaults on the cardinal doctrine of the Reformation, from whatever quarter they have proceeded, . . . have invariably had one and the same aim and direction—a return in substance, if not in form, to the corrupt doctrine of the Church of Rome." Ibid., 11.

standing this as a central dogma in the simplistic sense of an axiom from which all other doctrine can be deduced; rather, it provides a basic structural coherence to the system of doctrine as expressed in the Book of Concord. While Lutherans would most probably deny this vigorously, it is arguable that this structural importance is in large part the result of the personal significance of the doctrine in Martin Luther's own life.[28]

For the Reformed confessions, however, justification does not have the same structural importance as in Lutheranism. Nevertheless, it is crucial to understand that this does not mean that the doctrine's importance is somehow relativized or made negotiable. Not at all: it is still an essential truth, the denial of which would entail a fundamental revision of the overall Reformed theological system. It is one crucial part of a complex of doctrines; indeed, it stands in positive connection to a whole host of other important doctrines, such as the covenants of work and grace; the economic relations of the persons of the Trinity; the status of humanity both in original integrity and in sin after the fall; the mediatorial work of Christ; and the nature of the Christian life as it connects to God's eternal decree, good works, merit, assurance, final judgment, and glorification. Any adjustment of the doctrine of justification requires a correlative revision of all of these other doctrines, and vice versa. Thus, it may not be the central dogma of Reformed theology, but it is of vital importance to the content and stability of the system as a whole.[29]

By the time Buchanan came to lecture on the doctrine, then, the theological importance of justification, as both an integral part of Reformed confessional theology and a—perhaps *the*—key point of dispute between Protestants and Roman Catholics, had combined with the social and religious politics of the nineteenth century to

28. For the Lutheran confessional material, see Robert Kolb and Timothy J. Wengert, eds., *The Book of Concord* (Minneapolis: Fortress, 2000); on the structural significance of justification in Lutheranism, see Werner Elert, *The Structure of Lutheranism* (St. Louis: Concordia, 1962), 73–106.

29. Buchanan himself describes the Reformers as regarding the doctrine of justification by faith as that which disposed of "the whole host of scholastic errors and superstitious practices, by which, in the course of many preceding centuries, men had corrupted the simpler faith and worship of the primitive church." *Doctrine of Justification*, 9. He thus saw it as central to the whole Reformation enterprise, theological, ecclesiastical, and practical.

reinvigorate the debate surrounding the Reformation teaching and to give the whole matter an air of urgency. It was almost inevitable, therefore, that Buchanan, as a leading Free Church theologian, bound by solemn vows to uphold the theology of the Westminster Standards, should enter the lists on behalf of the Reformed orthodox position. As one committed to the Westminster Standards, he also had a rich theological heritage upon which to draw.

When we turn to the lectures themselves, we find that Buchanan approaches the topic in a manner typical of one committed to a confessional, and thus to a historically/ecclesiastically sensitive, theology. Part 1 consists of seven lectures, which move from discussion of the doctrine as it is revealed in Old and New Testaments, through the patristic and medieval periods, to the Reformation and post-Reformation eras, examining developments in both Protestantism and Roman Catholicism. He ends part 1 with a chapter devoted specifically to analyzing the history of the doctrine within the Anglican Church, a decision undoubtedly motivated by the Tractarian problem. Part 2 consists of a further eight lectures, which move from discussion of the semantics of the biblical language of justification, to a series of systematic syntheses of the biblical material, to a culminating analysis of the subjective role of the Holy Spirit. While it is not hard to find treatments of the subject that are more elaborate than that of Buchanan, these lectures nonetheless stand as one of the most significant nineteenth-century Reformed expressions of the orthodox position.

The Starting Point: The Covenant of Works

At the heart of Buchanan's argument is his belief that a correct understanding of justification is intimately connected to a correct view of divine law and righteousness: "It may be safely affirmed that almost all the errors which have prevailed on the subject of Justification, may be traced ultimately to erroneous, or defective, views of the Law and Justice of God."[30]

30. Ibid., 268.

This is crucial, as this point tracks doctrinally on the one hand to creation, to Adam, and to the fall; and on the other to the intra-Trinitarian life of God himself, to Christ as Mediator, and to salvation.

To take creation and the fall first, Buchanan clearly articulates in his lectures his belief in a pre-fall covenant between God and Adam that established Adam as representative head of all humanity and determined the nature of his obedience and reward. This issue of the pre-fall covenant is important because it will ultimately provide Buchanan with the context for understanding the nature of Christ's own sacrifice via federal headship.[31] Before we get ahead of ourselves, however, we should just note that in referring to this pre-fall administration, Buchanan uses several confessionally sanctioned terms, being comfortable with both "covenant of life" and "covenant of works."[32] The former phrase is used in Shorter Catechism 12 and Larger Catechism 20, the latter in Westminster Confession of Faith 7.2. There is nothing to suggest that Buchanan's use of one term instead of another at any point is at all theologically significant.[33]

The representative federal headship of Adam is stated by Buchanan, but no detailed argument is offered in its support. This is not surprising: Buchanan clearly assumed the importance of the confessional position on Adam to the doctrine of justification; but he did not consider it necessary to defend it at length in this specific treatise. Thus, near the start of the work he simply tells the reader that Adam was the "common father and representative of the race."[34] Later, he refers to Adam as federal head and legal representative of the whole human race and thus his sin is directly imputed to all his descendants. This precludes any notion that later generations might be able to approach

31. Ibid., 298–301.
32. E.g., ibid., 22, 270, 287.
33. E.g., ibid., 287. John Murray's preference for avoiding the language of "covenant" when applied to the arrangement between God and Adam in the garden of Eden is well known. In my opinion, this is the result of an overly critical approach to classical systematic categories, an approach rooted in a certain biblicism with regard to covenant terminology and a suspicion that the language of works carried with it implications of strict merit. It should be noted, however, that his criticism of the covenant of works is largely semantic in substance, as is indicated by his willingness to allow the catechisms' designation of "covenant of life" to stand in its place. John Murray, *Collected Writings*, 4 vols. (Edinburgh: Banner of Truth, 1976–82), 4:261–62.
34. Buchanan, *Doctrine of Justification*, 19.

God on the terms of the covenant of works: that covenant has been broken once and for all by the federal head, and no private individual can ever achieve eternal life on its basis again.[35]

This assumption of what is arguably a crucial part of the Reformed soteriological structure is ideally suited to the specific requirements of the polemics of the middle decades of the nineteenth century. Tractarian and Roman Catholic attacks on the confessional Protestant position placed the issue of merit at the center of the controversy, and it is this issue that preoccupies Buchanan in dealing with the doctrine of the covenant of works. Thus, Buchanan, standing on a long tradition of Reformed thinking, sees the covenant in the garden as being a *gracious* covenant. Care is needed here in understanding exactly what he means by this. In line with the clear teaching of Westminster Confession of Faith 7.1, he argues that the ontological distance between God and human beings is so great that even if Adam had continued in the state of integrity, God would have been under no natural obligation to reward that obedience in any way: it would simply be the due owed by a rational creature to the Creator.[36] Nevertheless, God condescended in his goodness to establish a covenant whereby a reward was annexed to obedience, and did so in such a way that the fulfilling of the stipulation consequently required that reward as a matter of justice because, as Buchanan quotes Thomas Boston, God is now a "debtor to his own faithfulness."[37] In saying this, Buchanan is doing little more than confirming the point regarding

---

35. Ibid., 278–81.

36. It is worth quoting Buchanan at length on this point: "But a Moral Law, however perfect, and although armed with the sanctions of reward and punishment, is not necessarily a covenant of life. It could only denounce punishment in the event of disobedience, and secure entire exemption from punishment, with such blessings as might be connected with obedience, while man continued in a state of holy innocence; but, considered simply as law, or an instrument of government, it could give no assurance, either that he would continue in that state, or that, by continuing in it, he would ever become a confirmed heir of eternal life." Ibid., 270–71.

37. Ibid., 21. Buchanan gives no reference, but the quotation is from Boston's *Human Nature in Its Fourfold State*, emphasizing the utter freedom of God in entering into a covenant with Adam and thereby appending a reward to obedience that was not, in the strict sense, necessary. See Thomas Boston, *Human Nature in Its Fourfold State* (Edinburgh: Banner of Truth, 1964), 49. The notion of condescension in the covenant of works is a commonplace in Reformed orthodoxy. See, for example, John Downame, *The Summe of Sacred Divinitie* (London, 1620), 1.15, 223–24; Edward Fisher, *The Marrow of Modern Divinity* (London, 1645), 10–11; John Ball, *A Treatise of the Covenant of Grace* (London, 1646), 7; David Dickson, *The Summe of Saving Knowledge, with the Practical Use Thereof* (Edinburgh, 1671), head 1.

the covenant made in Westminster Confession of Faith 7.1 concerning God's condescension in establishing a covenant with Adam, and articulating a common and established Reformed position on merit. This position was formulated in the heat of controversy with Roman Catholic opponents determined to establish the meritorious nature of the Christian's works in a redemptive context, but the basic axiom on which it rests—the infinite distance between God and creation—plays into Reformed discussions of the covenant of works.[38]

While Buchanan's use of the language of grace to describe the contingency and condescension of this covenant has a long-established pedigree in confessional Reformed theology, it is important to make sure that this is not understood either in a redemptive sense—redemptive concepts having no place in a pre-lapsarian environment—or in such a way as to relativize the difference between the so-called merit of works before the fall and those done after the fall. To slide into the latter error would be to undermine the very nature of the justice involved in rewarding good works, something that was not in the context of the established covenant an act of mere goodwill on God's part but, to develop Boston's terminology, a vital and necessary act of God's faithfulness to the stipulations of his covenant; and this would then undermine Christ's work on the cross by making the reward annexed to the atonement one of free grace and not one earned by the work of Christ. Buchanan's talk of grace refers to the condescension involved in an infinite God's first establishing a relationship with his creatures of command and promised reward annexed to obedience, a relationship by which the language of merit can then be understood. The language of grace emphatically does not refer to the subsequent dynamics of that relationship between the parties once the covenant has been established. Indeed, his thought on this point would seem to parallel that of Boston, who expands on his statement about God's being a debtor to his own faithfulness by stating that the one who fulfills the condition of work "may crave reward

---

38. See Downame, *A Treatise of Justification*, 547–660. Downame's discussion focuses on the merit of believers' works, but the general promissory structure within which language of merit can operate is clear. See, for example, his statement on page 554, citing Thomas Aquinas, *Summa Theologiae* 1a2ae.114.3, in a marginal reference: "The Lord, who is faithfull and just in performing his promises, maketh himself a debtor, not to us, but to himselfe for the gracious performance of his free and undeserved reward, which hee had freely and graciously promised."

47

on the ground of the covenant." In other words, in the context of the freely established covenant, works performed in accordance with the terms thereof are in a certain sense meritorious and can be pleaded by Adam before God as the basis of his earned reward, not because they are intrinsically valuable but because they meet the established legal criteria of the covenant, and God's faithfulness to his covenant requires that he reward them. As a clear implication of this, one might add that only works performed within the context of the covenant can be considered to be meritorious.[39]

Buchanan's approach to the covenant and to merit thus stands within the accepted bounds of the Reformed orthodox tradition. Indeed, a similar idea to that of Buchanan is found in Cunningham's *Historical Theology*, in the specific context of a refutation of the notion of meritorious works; but Cunningham's resting of his argument upon ontological considerations concerning the distance between Creator and creation makes it clear that the same argument would apply to the situation of the pre-fall covenant. The underlying religious concern is that God is in no wise and in no circumstance his creature's debtor in an absolute, strict sense. Yet, as with so many other points, the Reformed confessional tradition is not so narrow or inflexible that it is incapable of containing a variety of expression on this issue. For example, the discussion of John Owen on this matter is of some note with reference to these issues. In discussing the establishment of the covenant of works, Owen can use the language of grace when referring to the original uprightness of human nature given to Adam by God and the supernatural end that was the reward of obedience.[40]

39. "Yet while it had much grace in it, this Law is properly called a Covenant of Works; for it established a certain relation between obedience and reward, such as that which subsists between work and wages." Buchanan, *Doctrine of Justification*, 22. Likewise, Thomas Boston is careful to use the language of grace and condescension with specific reference to God's entry into and establishment of the covenant of works, not its subsequent execution. Again, we might question the wisdom of using the redemptive term "grace" in such a nonredemptive context; but against the background of the medieval and Reformed orthodox debates about God and creation, and about the nature of merit, his purpose is both clear and thoroughly orthodox, representing no attempt to relativize the difference between works and faith or humanity's pre-fall and post-fall relationship to God. See Boston, *Human Nature in Its Fourfold State*, 48–49. Cf. the similar argument of David Dickson, *Therapeutica Sacra* (Edinburgh, 1664), 1.5, 73–74.

40. John Owen, *A Dissertation on Divine Justice*, in *Works*, 24 vols. (London, 1850–53), 10:85.

He can, however, also deny that any grace was involved in the first covenant. Significantly, this kind of criticism appears in the context of underlining the radical difference between the basis of reward under the first covenant (human beings meriting reward by their own actions) and under the second (Christ meriting reward on behalf of others). In other words, the denial of the language of grace here is not linked to the way in which the covenant was unilaterally and freely established by God when he could have done otherwise; it is aimed specifically at underlining the radical difference in the ways to eternal life offered to human beings under the covenant of works and the covenant of grace.[41]

The diversity of the Reformed on this issue, within confessional parameters, is exemplified by Herman Witsius in his *Economy of the Covenants between God and Man* (1693).[42] Witsius is quite clear that God owes nothing to his creatures on the basis both of his status as their Creator and of his infinite exaltation above his creation.[43] Witsius is also clear that Adam had no claim on his Creator before, or outside, the covenant of works.[44] This position appears close to the one later articulated by Buchanan; but Witsius goes on to argue that the nature of God means that it would have been a contradiction of his own being to act in certain ways. Thus, for example, he could not have allowed a creature who had been obedient and faithful simply to sink back into a state of nonexistence because this would contradict his goodness and, quite possibly, his justice, a position clearly at odds with the view of, for example, David Dickson, Boston, and Buchanan on the same point.[45] Significantly, Witsius presents his arguments in explicit opposition to the extreme theological voluntarism of William Twisse, whose own doctrine of God was deeply indebted to Duns Scotus; thus one can read Witsius's own argument at this point as representing a more intellectualist stream within Reformed theology than that of his chosen opponent. Nevertheless, we must beware of accentuating the

41. Ibid., 5:44–46.
42. I will refer to the translation by William Crookshank, 2 vols. (London, 1822; repr., Kingsburg, CA: den Dulk Christian Foundation, 1990).
43. Witsius, *Economy of the Covenants*, 1.4.11.
44. Ibid., 1.1.14.
45. Ibid., 1.4.14–23. Contrast this, for example, with Dickson, *Therapeutica Sacra*, 1.5, 74; Boston, *Human Nature in Its Fourfold State*, 49; Buchanan, *Doctrine of Justification*, 21–22.

differences between the two approaches in a manner that might imply that this is a confessionally significant disagreement: both are represented within the bounds of the Reformed confessional community, and so this is an intraconfessional matter; it also reflects the eclectic origins of Reformed orthodoxy in both the Thomist and Scotist streams of late medieval thought; and the central point—that the reward of eternal life in the covenant of works is the result of God's goodness in establishing a covenant, not the absolute priority and intrinsic merit of human works considered in the abstract—is the common ground upon which such confessional consensus can be maintained.

This line of thinking on the nature of condescension and of merit connects Buchanan's theology not simply to the traditional formulations of Reformed orthodoxy on this issue but, as the comparison with Owen, Witsius, and Twisse shows, through that tradition, to the discussions of covenant and causality that were commonplace in late medieval theology and that scholarship has now established as providing much of the conceptual background to Protestant thinking on these matters.[46] Buchanan is, of course, self-consciously aware of the fact that his thinking is rooted in historical discussion that reaches back to the patristic era. Thus, he is prepared to argue, and to cite evidence to prove, that there are clear patristic precedents for understanding merit within the context of divine condescension and that this is sufficient to acquit classic Protestantism of any charge of novelty on this point. One major authority for this is the polemical compilation of patristic and medieval sources produced in the seventeenth century by Archbishop Ussher, which has a section specifically devoted to merit.[47]

46. See the interesting discussion in Heiko A. Oberman, *The Harvest of Medieval Theology* (Durham, NC: Labyrinth, 1983); William J. Courtenay, *Covenant and Causality in Medieval Thought* (London: Variorum, 1984). On the general question of the connections between Reformed theology and medieval thought, see Richard A. Muller, *Post-Reformation Reformed Dogmatics*, 4 vols. (Grand Rapids: Baker, 2003); also the essays in Carl R. Trueman and R. Scott Clark, eds., *Protestant Scholasticism: Essays in Reassessment* (Carlisle, Cumbria: Paternoster, 1998).

47. James Ussher, *An Answer to a Challenge Made by a Jesuite in Ireland* (London, 1686). Buchanan cites this work explicitly, *Doctrine of Justification*, 93 and n. 12, and his own list of patristic quotations indicates a probable dependence, at least in part, on the work. Ussher himself sums up his own position, and that of the patristic authors he cites, in terms similar to those of Boston: "Originally, therefore, and in it self, we hold that this reward proceedeth merely from Gods free Bounty and Mercy; but accidentally, in regard that God hath tied himself by his Word and Promise to confer such a reward, we grant that it now proveth in a sort to be an act of *Justice*; even as in *forgiving of our Sins* (which in it self all Men know to be an act of *Mercy*)

Christ and the Covenants

Buchanan sees this understanding of divine condescension and merit within the covenant of works as having clear implications for a correct understanding of justification. For a start, it shatters any notion that human beings after Adam can merit eternal life according to the terms of the covenant of works. Now, if all merit were to be understood in terms of divine condescension and covenant, it would, of course, be possible to envisage an arrangement whereby works done by fallen men and women could be regarded as meriting God's favor, not by their intrinsic value but by a covenant arranged by divine fiat. Such was the approach of the *pactum* theology of the late medieval *moderni* in which Luther was reared, and against which he rebelled, albeit selectively.[48]

Buchanan, in line with confessional Reformed orthodoxy, avoids this position by a strong emphasis on the stability of divine law, a stability coordinated with his federalism. He regards the law of God, in terms of its positive commands and its penalties for those who contravene it, as a manifestation of God's essential nature and thus as being as nonnegotiable as his divinity. God can no more abrogate the moral law than he can cease to be God.

Reformed orthodoxy held no precise consensus on this issue, as is clear from the divergence of views within the confessional tradition on the necessity of Christ's incarnation and atonement. In the seventeenth century, for example, William Twisse and Samuel Rutherford, among others, argued that Christ's incarnation and atonement were required simply because God had so willed it, and that salvation could have been granted to sinners merely by a divine decision.[49] In other words, the law of God did not reflect the divine essence but the divine will; and God could, hypothetically, act in a way contrary to it without effectively denying his own essence. John Owen, however, wrote a major attack on this position, arguing that because the law

---

he is said to be *Faithful and Just*, 1 Jn 1:9, namely, in regard of the Faithful performance of his Promise." *An Answer*, 405.

48. See Heiko A. Oberman, "Headwaters of the Reformation: *Initia Lutheri—Initia Reformationis*," in Oberman, *The Dawn of the Reformation* (Edinburgh: T&T Clark, 1992), 39–83.

49. See William Twisse, *Vindiciae Gratiae* (Amsterdam, 1632); Samuel Rutherford, *Disputatio Scholastica de Providential* (Edinburgh, 1643).

reflected the absolute and unavoidable moral claims of God over his creation, it therefore required incarnation and atonement if sin were to be forgiven.[50] Buchanan acknowledges a direct debt to Owen on this issue,[51] and clearly articulates a substantially identical position:

> Men talk lightly of His law being abrogated, modified, or relaxed, not considering that, beside being an authoritative expression of His supreme will, it is also a revelation of His essential nature, as the Holy One and the Just, and the rule of His universal empire, as the Governor and Judge of all. It is not the mere product of what Cudworth called "arbitrary will omnipotent"; His will is determined by the infinite perfection of His character, and His character is the real ultimate standard of "eternal and immutable morality."[52]

Given his convictions on this, Buchanan thus precludes the idea that God could somehow solve the problem of humanity's sin by simply lowering his standards. There is need of a second covenant head to meet the absolute terms of divine law as expressed in the covenant of works; as the law cannot be weakened, neither, by implication, can any of those embraced by Adam's breaking of the covenant hope to merit eternal life by their works. Thus, by emphasizing the absolute stability of divine law, Buchanan has put into place a crucial criterion for determining the nature of the work of Christ.[53]

When he comes to Christ's mediation, Buchanan therefore argues that Christ is placed under the same terms as the covenant of works, as federal head, not this time of the whole human race but of the elect. Again, his theology at this point is not exceptional but draws directly on the established tradition. In this context, he argues for two covenants: a covenant of grace between the members of the Trinity, which determined to overcome human sin for God's own glory and

50. See Owen, *Works*, 10:481–624; also Carl R. Trueman, "John Owen's *A Dissertation on Divine Justice*: An Exercise in Christocentric Scholasticism," *Calvin Theological Journal* 33 (1998): 87–103.
51. Buchanan, *Doctrine of Justification*, 495 n. 5.
52. Ibid., 288.
53. "The careful study of the Law as a covenant of works, is necessary at all times to the right understanding of the Gospel, as a covenant of grace: and it is peculiarly seasonable in the present age, when the eternal Law of God is supposed, by some, to have been abrogated, and by others, to have been modified or relaxed." Ibid., 24.

thus to bring about the execution of the decree of election; and a covenant of redemption between Father and Son, which established Christ as Mediator and defined the precise details of his redemptive work.[54]

It is arguable that Buchanan's commitment to the idea of an eternal covenant between Father and Son is not a doctrine explicitly required of him by his commitment to the Westminster Confession of Faith, but several comments are in order on this matter that help to underline the importance of the concept to Reformed theology.

First, it should be noted that the use of covenantal language to refer to such an eternal compact between Father and Son does not become common in Reformed theology, British and Continental, until the latter half of the 1640s.[55] Its absence from the Westminster Confession is thus partly explicable in terms of timing.[56]

Second, while the direct exegetical basis for such a doctrine is slim, it is important to realize that the concept emerges from debates surrounding the Reformed commitment to Christ as Mediator according to both natures, as opposed to the medieval idea that he was Mediator solely according to his human nature. The polemical pressure that Roman Catholic theologians exerted on the Reformed on this point forced the Reformed to refine and clarify the appointment and status of Christ as Mediator, and this process partially culminated in arguing for an eternal covenant between Father and Son.[57] As with so many

54. Ibid., 293–98.
55. I am grateful to Carol Williams, who, in her recent doctoral dissertation, demonstrates that the language of the covenant of redemption is used as early as 1638, by David Dickson in an address to the General Assembly of the Church of Scotland. See Carol A. Williams, " 'The Decree of Redemption Is in Effect a Covenant': David Dickson and the Covenant of Redemption" (Ph.D. diss., Calvin Theological Seminary, 2005), 174–75.
56. British writers in the 1640s who were instrumental in formalizing the concept and vocabulary on this issue included Edward Fisher, *The Marrow of Modern Divinity* (London, 1645); Peter Bulkeley, *The Gospel-Covenant; or The Covenant of Grace Opened* (London, 1646); and Dickson, *The Summe of Saving Knowledge*. Dickson's work was composed in the 1640s. Similar developments were taking place in Reformed theology on the Continent at the same time. See Willem J. van Asselt, *The Federal Theology of Johannes Cocceius (1603–1669)* (Leiden, Netherlands: Brill, 2001), 227–47. The most elaborate exposition of the idea in English is that by Patrick Gillespie, *The Ark of the Covenant Opened* (London, 1677). The work contains a preface by John Owen.
57. This position provoked a polemical response from Roman apologists, who pointed to the apparent logical absurdity in saying that God could be Mediator with God. It is this with which the Puritan William Ames grapples at one point in his major defense of Reformed

other formulations of doctrine, the covenant of redemption is not to be seen as comprehensible in terms of some kind of bald proof-texting; rather, it is further evidence of how complex the move from biblical text to doctrinal synthesis can be, involving, among other things, dialogue with the theological tradition, linguistic analysis, polemical concerns, and exegetical insights.

Third, one of the key dynamics in the development of Reformed theology in the late sixteenth and seventeenth centuries was the elaboration and clarification of the relationship between God as Trinity and the anti-Pelagian nature of salvation. The covenant of redemption represents, positively, an attempt to understand how the eternal Trinity thus relates to the saving actions of Christ in history.[58]

Some have raised objections to the covenant of redemption on the grounds that it seems to drive an unacceptable wedge between Father and Son, construing their relationship, and thus the eternal basis for human salvation, in commercial terms.[59] It is beyond the scope of this essay to offer a full response to such criticisms, but a few comments are in order. First, Buchanan, in line with typical Reformed orthodoxy, sees the covenant of redemption as rooted not in some kind of conflict between Father and Son, but rather in their mutual desire to see sinners saved. There is no opposition between Father and Son; the Son does not "buy" the favor of a hostile Father.[60] Second,

---

Protestantism, *Bellarminus Enervatus*. Robert Bellarmine, says Ames, lodges a series of objections to the idea of Christ as Mediator according to both natures, to which Ames responds by pointing toward the clear economic, and thus contingent, nature of incarnation and mediation; he thus implicitly invites further reflection on the grounds of incarnation within the will of the Godhead—reflection that will ultimately bear fruit in the later formalization of the covenant of redemption. William Ames, *Bellarminus Enervatus* (Oxford, 1629), 129–30.

58. On Reformed orthodoxy as, in part, an attempt to grapple with the coordination of Trinitarianism and anti-Pelagianism, see Carl R. Trueman, *The Claims of Truth: John Owen's Trinitarian Theology* (Carlisle, Cumbria: Paternoster, 1998), passim.

59. This criticism is commonplace among scholars who have accepted much of the Barthian critique of orthodoxy. See, for example, T. F. Torrance, *The School of Faith* (London: James Clarke, 1959); M. C. Bell, *Calvin and Scottish Theology* (Edinburgh: Handsel Press, 1985). Interestingly enough, Thomas Boston had similar criticism of the doctrine. See A. T. B. McGowan, *The Federal Theology of Thomas Boston* (Edinburgh: Rutherford House, 1997), 40–41.

60. Buchanan himself directly addresses the criticism that the Son somehow "purchases" the Father's love, stressing that the covenant coordinates with the spontaneous good pleasure of God in himself. *Doctrine of Justification*, 295. Cf. Witsius, *Economy of the Covenants*, bk. 2, where the covenant of redemption is explicitly set within the context of the Trinitarian God's overarching will to save fallen humanity; also Gillespie, *Ark of the Covenant*, 6–16.

that this desire to save does not extend to all sinners, in that Christ is appointed Mediator only for the elect, is clear; but to object to the particularity of the covenant is not the same as to claim that the whole idea is rooted in inappropriate commercial notions. It is also, one might add, to impose personal theological tastes upon analysis of the Reformed orthodox tradition that are simply inappropriate for historical exposition.

The covenant of redemption fulfills the crucial role in Buchanan's argument of placing Christ under the terms of the covenant of works, and thus of establishing and defining the nature of his mediatorial work, and also of respecting the stability of divine law in both creation and the economy of salvation. Given that the covenant of works provided the context for understanding both the relationship of obedience and reward and the nature and implications of the fall, then the placing of Christ under the terms of the covenant as a new federal head is clearly essential if his work is to have any salvific value whatsoever. Thus, the covenant of redemption establishes Christ's work as both meritorious and vicarious, and provides the basis for human salvation and the divine glory that accrues from this.[61] It also serves to establish his *whole* obedience as part and parcel of his mediatorial office. This is significant because Buchanan does make a formal distinction between Christ's active and passive obedience, as had been done in the seventeenth century, but does not see the two as really separable, either in terms of Christ's office or, later, in terms of the twofold imputation to the sinner.[62] The covenant of redemption established that the whole state of Christ's humiliation would serve for salvation, that his life was not merely a preparatory phase equipping him for a vicarious death, but was itself a part of his vicarious work.[63]

The history of this distinction between active and passive righteousness relative to the Westminster Confession is somewhat murky. It is well known that delegates William Twisse and Thomas Gataker both had serious reservations about seeing the active righteousness of

61. Buchanan, *Doctrine of Justification*, 300–01.
62. In tone and nuance, on this point Buchanan follows Cunningham, whom he cites in the notes: Ibid., 496 n. 7, citing William Cunningham, *The Reformers and the Theology of the Reformation* (Edinburgh: Banner of Truth, 1967), 402–6.
63. Buchanan, *Doctrine of Justification*, 301–7, 333–34.

Christ as part of his work of mediation, possibly motivated by any or all of the following: fear of antinomianism, appropriation of Anselmic notions of atonement, and exegetical concerns. For certain, Gataker was profoundly influenced by, though not entirely in agreement with, the views expressed on this matter by the Continental theologian Johannes Piscator of Herborn.[64] The question of active/passive righteousness was raised early on at the Westminster Assembly before the arrival of the Scottish delegation, at a point in the proceedings when the debate was really focused on the revision of the Thirty-nine Articles. In a series of speeches on Article 11, "Of the Justification of Man before God," Daniel Featley offered the most elaborate and significant arguments for the twofold righteousness of Christ in justification.[65] Ultimately, Featley won the day, with the majority of

64. Two significant works of Piscator on justification were published in England in the decades before the Westminster Assembly. The first, *A Learned and Profitable Treatise of Mans Justification* (London, 1599), a translation of a 1594 treatise written at the request of his friend, the soon-to-be-infamous Conrad Vorstius, was a response to the Jesuit Bellarmine on whether justification involved imparting or imputing of righteousness. Not surprisingly, Piscator argued for the latter; but, perhaps more significantly, he consistently identified justification as *remission of sins*, and focused his argument on the *death* of Christ as the basis for this remission, with the life being notable in its absence from inclusion in the work of satisfaction. E.g., *A Learned and Profitable Treatise*, 2, 5–6, 13, 105–6. The second work is a Latin treatise, presented as a three-way discussion between Piscator, Lodovicus Lucius of Basle, and Thomas Gataker: *D Ioannis Piscatoris Herbonensis et M. Lodovici Lucii Basiliensis, Scripta Quaedam Adversaria; De Causa Meritoria Nostri Coram Deo Justificationis: Una cum Thomae Gatakeri Londinatis Animadversionibus in Utraque* (London, 1641). In this work, Piscator's argument is that Christ's active obedience is that which qualifies him to act as Mediator, but is not a part of the mediatorial work itself, something reserved for the passive obedience. *Scripta Quaedam Adversaria*, pt. 1, p. 5. This argument, akin to that of Anselm, appears to lie at the heart of Gataker's own position, whereby Christ as creature is obliged to the law because of his own status as creature and is therefore no part of what one might term the work of supererogation that constitutes the vicarious work of salvation that he performs for others. Ibid., pt. 1, p. 68; pt. 3, pp. 10–11. We should be wary, however, of identifying the position of Gataker with that of Piscator, given that the former is adamant that remission of sins is not identical with, and is indeed really separable from, justification. Contrast the claims of Piscator, ibid., pt. 1, pp. 33–34, with Gataker, ibid., pt. 1, pp. 9–10, 21; cf. Thomas Gataker, *An Antidote against Errour concerning Justification* (London, 1670), 11–14, where Gataker offers linguistic and logical arguments for seeing the two as separate.

65. Daniel Featley, *The Dippers Dipt*, 5th ed. (London, 1647), 192–211. Featley represents the mainstream English Reformed view in this argument; for example, while William Perkins does not address the issue directly and precisely in the same terms as Gataker and Featley, it is clear that he regards the imputation of Christ's righteousness as involving that of both his death and his obedience to the law: see his comments in *A Golden Chaine, Works* (1603), 87, and in *A Reformed Catholike, Works* (1603), 681; cf. James Ussher, *Eighteen Sermons Preached in Oxford 1640* (London, 1660), 370–92; also Downame, *A Treatise of Justification*, 18, 24–27,

divines approving the term "whole obedience and satisfaction" in the revised article, though the adjective "whole" is pointedly absent from the later Westminster Confession 11.3.[66] Given the content of questions 70–73 of the Larger Catechism, however, it is difficult to read huge significance into this omission: it is at most a concession to the minority party of Twisse and Gataker.[67]

Buchanan's context was somewhat different from that of the Westminster Assembly. Far from facing the challenge of a Twisse or Gataker, who wished to focus atonement exclusively on Christ's death, Buchanan would have been aware of an influential stream of thinking in the nineteenth-century Scottish church that tended to identify atonement simply with incarnation. The two most obvious examples of this were John McLeod Campbell of Row (1800–72), whose views were found confessionally wanting and who was consequently removed from the Church of Scotland ministry in 1831, and influential lay theologian Thomas Erskine of Linlathen (1788–1870), who ultimately did not hesitate to make explicit the clear universalist implications of his thinking.[68] Given the significance that later theologians have ascribed to these men and their tortuously tedious writings, one might have perhaps expected Buchanan both to have heavily accented the passive righteousness of Christ in his atoning death and to have engaged somewhat with their theologies.[69] In fact, only one statement would seem to refer to them (though not by name), where Buchanan argues for active and passive righteousness as crucial, and that the life of Christ, while culminating in his death, is neither a

151–59. Downame is explicitly cited by Buchanan in his note on this section. *Doctrine of Justification*, 307 n. 7.

66. *The Westminster Standards: An Original Facsimile* (Audubon, NJ: Old Paths Publications, 1997) contains a facsimile of both the revised Articles and the final Confession.

67. It is interesting to note that when the question was put in the Assembly, Featley himself brought to the divines' attention an old letter of James I that urged the delegates to a synod in France not to divide over the issue, as being one of recent vintage and of little importance. The letter, with translation, is reprinted in Featley, *Dippers Dipt*, 212–24.

68. See John McLeod Campbell, *The Nature of the Atonement* (Cambridge, 1856); Thomas Erskine, *The Brazen Serpent* (Edinburgh, 1831); John McLeod Campbell, *The Doctrine of Election* (London, 1837); for a critique of this trajectory of Scottish theology, see N. R. Needham, *Thomas Erskine of Linlathen* (Edinburgh: Rutherford House, 1989).

69. The most significant of McLeod Campbell's modern advocates was the late J. B. Torrance; see his "The Contribution of McLeod Campbell to Scottish Theology," *Scottish Journal of Theology* 26 (1973): 295–311.

replacement for it nor merely a preparation for his mediation. Christ was federal head; and as such, he lived and died and rose again on behalf of those given to him under the terms of the covenant. It would seem, therefore, that Buchanan did not deem this incarnational school of thought as worthy of detailed refutation; and that he considered the mainstream Reformed position to require no revision, even in terms of emphasis, despite their critique.[70]

We noted at the start that it was a staple of Tractarian polemic—and, indeed, of others such as Whately—that the Reformers' dispute with the Roman Church over justification had been fundamentally misplaced because it involved a misunderstanding of Rome's teaching on merit and grace. Cunningham, among others, rightly saw this claim as incorrect, and as potentially very damaging in the ecclesiastical climate of the mid-nineteenth century: the point at issue between confessional Protestantism and Roman Catholicism was not whether justification was by grace and on the basis of Christ's righteousness; the issue was whether that righteousness was imputed or imparted to the believer, with faith alone as the instrument. Buchanan, too, sees this clearly: all of this doctrinal construction, from Adam and the covenant of works, through to the coordinate covenants of grace and redemption, serves to make the doctrine of justification by imputation unavoidable. That Adam and Christ were federal heads meant that all those they represented were bound up with their obedience; once Adam had sinned, no other could merit God's favor because merit has no meaning outside of a covenant relationship; and that covenant had been shattered by the appointed covenant representative. Only the appointment of a second covenant head, placed under the terms of the covenant of works by the covenant of redemption, could serve to gain eternal life—and then only for those given to him under the terms of the covenant of grace.

Imputation, therefore, for Buchanan means the crediting of any action done by one party to another party; and thus to make any claim that Christ's work has an effect of some kind on a third party is to make a claim about imputation. Thus, even if one argues that the law is now relaxed because of Christ's work, then some aspect

70. Buchanan, *Doctrine of Justification*, 303.

of Christ's work in fulfillment of the law has been imputed to those who now enjoy this relaxed legal dispensation; in fact, as Buchanan points out, the terms of the covenants of grace and redemption mean that the whole of Christ's obedience, active and passive, is imputed to the believer in that, for those who trust in the promises of Christ by faith and are thus united to him, this obedience is accounted theirs.[71] In this context, Buchanan accepts with reservations the language of justification as a legal fiction. No, it is not a legal fiction if what is meant is that it is something that is not really true: the federal headship of Christ means that those united to him are righteous before God, and very real blessings flow from this: pardon of sin, restoration of God's favor, renewal of God's image, assurance of his love, the privilege of adoption, and finally eternal life. In other words, the legal status granted by justification under the terms of the federal scheme is very real indeed.[72]

Conclusion

There is, of course, much more to say about Buchanan's work—particularly on the instrumentality of faith, which we have not really touched on in our analysis but which is an integral part of the whole scheme. Nevertheless, even after this incomplete analysis, two concluding points seem especially apposite.

First, Buchanan's theology is a clear example of how the Reformed orthodoxy of the seventeenth century continued to enjoy a vital, ecclesiastical existence at the highest intellectual level well into the nineteenth century. Indeed, Buchanan's lectures on justification represent a late articulation and application of the classic Reformed theology of the seventeenth century; they also demonstrate how this theology provided a nineteenth-century theologian with sufficient traditional resources to meet the challenges of his own day. Mainstream theology had moved on from strict adherence to confessional trajectories; but that did not mean that these trajectories were intellectually bankrupt, impotent in polemic, or antiquated beyond usefulness. For those who did not buy

71. Ibid., 332–34.
72. Ibid., 334–38.

into the critical moral and epistemological paradigms of post-Kantian theology, Reformed orthodoxy still provided a coherent theological structure with which to address the pressing issues of the day.

It is thus important to remember that Buchanan was not a generic evangelical who responded to the Enlightenment by privileging piety or experience over doctrinal formulation; nor was he a Bible-thumping "no book but the Bible" fundamentalist for whom the church's doctrinal tradition was just so much quasi-Roman bunkum; nor was he a reactionary obscurantist who was simply committed to mouthing the old shibboleths and talking nostalgically about a mythical golden age of doctrinal and ecclesiastical purity. Rather, he was a confessional Presbyterian, obliged by his ecclesiastical vows not only to take the historic teaching of his church seriously and to expound and defend the theology of the Westminster Standards as consistent with Scripture, but also to use these, and the tradition of theology to which they belonged, as a principal resource for combating error in his role as protector and shepherd of God's flock. Buchanan's work is marked by historical analysis, attention to confessional concerns, and a careful coordination of exegesis and doctrinal synthesis in the context of specific polemical, ecclesiastical, and pastoral concerns; and it thus provides a vintage example of the churchman-theologian in action. Analyzing the theology of the nineteenth century in Britain needs this third category—that of confessional churchman—if we are to fully understand how and why individuals such as Buchanan thought and wrote the way they did.[73]

Second, it is clear that Buchanan also provides us with a thorough exposition of the Reformed doctrine of justification. We noted at the start that justification for the Reformed confessional tradition does not have the same structural significance as for the Lutherans; yet it

73. In his article on Buchanan in the new *Dictionary of National Biography*, Michael Jinkins makes reference to his lectures on justification as being "principally remarkable for his avoidance of constructive and original thought," and then refers to his "unoriginal conservative theology," both comments seeming somewhat pejorative. A clearer grasp of what constitutes a *confessional* approach to theology might liberate us from such personal value judgments and allow us to offer an account of Buchanan that does not measure him by standards he would have considered irrelevant. After all, until a confessional position has been decisively shown to be inadequate, the church theologian who is voluntarily bound by solemn vows to upholding that position is scarcely going to prize originality in doctrine as an honorable or worthy aspiration.

is clear from our exposition of Buchanan's work in context that justification by imputation is intimately connected among other things to the doctrines of God, of creation, of the fall, of the person and work of Christ, and of the federal nature of God's dealings with men and women. This has salutary systematic significance for confessional subscription: tinkering with justification, or indeed tinkering with a host of other doctrines with which justification is connected, will serve to place one's theology outside the bounds of the Westminster Standards. Deny the covenant of works, for example, and one implicitly denies the whole structure of justification taught in the standards. Then again, if one wishes to historicize and relativize imputation by claiming that this doctrine did in the sixteenth and seventeenth centuries what some other doctrine can or must do today, one needs to revise and reconstruct a whole host of other doctrines to make the claim coherent; and in doing so, if one is being honest, one is really required to abandon anything even vaguely resembling confessional Reformed orthodoxy. One can repeat the shibboleth of, say, "union with Christ" indefinitely—and such a concept is certainly germane to Reformed theology—but unless this is clearly set within a solid, federal scheme akin to that outlined by Buchanan, the content of the phrase will not be Reformed in any meaningful, historic, confessional way. This is not to say that the Westminster Standards, or the Reformed orthodox tradition as a whole, demands precise agreement on every jot and tittle of doctrine—we noted, for example, that the covenant of redemption is not a confessional requirement—but it is to say that both the content of justification and its basic placement within the federal structure of Reformed theology are clear and nonnegotiable for those committed by church vow to upholding the theology of the Westminster Standards.

Karl Marx once commented that Georg Wilhelm Friedrich Hegel had noted that all historical facts and personages occur twice; but, he added, Hegel failed to note that the first time this was as tragedy, the second as farce.[74] His comment surely applies by way of analogy to great theological discussions as well, and only by taking history

---

74. Karl Marx, "The Eighteenth Brumaire of Louis Bonaparte," in Robert C. Tucker, ed., *The Marx-Engels Reader* (New York: Norton, 1978), 594.

seriously can such tragedy and farce be avoided. Thus, I offer in closing these final comments as a historian's passing shot across the bows of modern theologians—systematic, biblical, and all points in between—who pursue their calling with ne'er a glance at history: if they wish to avoid the tragi-farcical options either of reinventing the wheel or of privileging their own narrow interpretative horizons over those of the church throughout the centuries as reflected primarily in her creeds and confessions, they might do well to meditate on the fact that current controversies on justification are reminiscent in so many ways of the issues raised relative to this doctrine through the centuries, not least by the Tractarians of the nineteenth century. This applies, for example, to attempts to recast the Reformation as based on a misunderstanding, and to the identification by some of the Pauline "works of the law" exclusively with Jewish ceremonial distinctives. Further, they also might reflect that while Buchanan's work was in part a refutation of the theology represented by the *Tracts for the Times* of Newman, E. B. Pusey, and others, today his treatise stands as a veritable tract for our own times, an example of something to which contemporary Reformed theologians would do well to aspire: a piece of principled ecclesiastical and confessional scholarship; a demonstration of the usefulness of the resources of classic confessional orthodoxy in contemporary polemic; and an elegant and thorough example of a Reformed orthodox church theologian arguing with passion and learning for that most precious of Protestant doctrines—justification by grace alone, through faith alone, by the imputed righteousness of Christ alone.

3

Transforming Power and Comfort: The Puritans on Adoption

JOEL R. BEEKE

We have enough in us to move God to correct us, but nothing to move him to adopt us, therefore exalt free grace, begin the work of angels here; bless him with your praises who hath blessed you in making you his sons and daughters. (Thomas Watson)[1]

The Puritans have gotten a bad press for their supposed lack of teaching on adoption, that is, the biblical doctrine that every true Christian is God's adopted child. In his otherwise excellent chapter titled "Sons of God," in the classic *Knowing God*, J. I. Packer writes, "The Puritan teaching on the Christian life, so strong in other ways, was notably deficient" on adoption.[2] In his otherwise fine article on adoption, Erroll Hulse asserts that "the Puritans did little in exploring this truth apart from a few paragraphs here and there."[3] Statements such as these promote the familiar comment that adoption is *the* neglected aspect in the Puritan *ordo salutis*.

1. Thomas Watson, *A Body of Divinity in a Series of Sermons on the Shorter Catechism* (London: A. Fullarton, 1845), 160.
2. J. I. Packer, *Knowing God* (Downers Grove, IL: InterVarsity, 1973), 207.
3. Erroll Hulse, "Recovering the Doctrine of Adoption," *Reformation Today* 105 (1988): 10.

The evidence suggests that adoption, though not developed as thoroughly as several closely knit doctrines such as justification, sanctification, and assurance, was certainly not a neglected topic among the Puritans. William Ames, Thomas Watson, Samuel Willard, and Herman Witsius gave it ample treatment in their systematic theologies—Witsius devoting twenty-eight pages to it in his *The Economy of the Covenants between God and Man*.[4]

William Perkins, often denominated the father of Puritanism, addresses various aspects of adoption at some length in at least nine different places in his works.[5] William Bates, Hugh Binning, Thomas Brooks, Anthony Burgess, Stephen Charnock, George Downame, John Flavel, Thomas Goodwin, William Gouge, Ezekiel Hopkins, Edward Leigh, and John Owen all provide some treatment of the subject.[6] Other Puritans, such as Jeremiah Burroughs, Thomas Cole, Roger Drake, Thomas Hooker, Thomas Manton, Stephen Marshall, Richard Sibbes, John Tennent, and John Waite, preached one or more sermons on adoption.[7]

4. William Ames, *The Marrow of Theology*, trans. and ed. John D. Eusden (Boston: Pilgrim Press, 1968), 164–67; Watson, *A Body of Divinity*, 155–60; Samuel Willard, *A Compleat Body of Divinity* (repr., New York: Johnson Reprint Corporation, 1969), 482–91; Herman Witsius, *The Economy of the Covenants between God and Man*, 2 vols. (repr., Kingsburg, CA: den Dulk Christian Foundation, 1990), 1:441–68.

5. *The Workes of That Famovs and VVorthy Minister of Christ in the Vniuersitie of Cambridge, Mr. William Perkins*, 3 vols. (London: Iohn Legatt and Cantrell Ligge, 1612–13), 1:82–83, 104–5, 369–70, 430; 2:277–80; 3:154–55, 205; 138 and 382 of 2nd pagination.

6. William Bates, *The Whole Works of the Rev. W. Bates, D.D.*, ed. W. Farmer, 4 vols. (repr., Harrisonburg, VA: Sprinkle, 1990), 4:299–301; Hugh Binning, *The Works of the Rev. Hugh Binning, M.A.*, ed. M. Leishman (repr., Ligonier, PA: Soli Deo Gloria, 1992), 253–55; Thomas Brooks, *The Works of Thomas Brooks*, 6 vols. (repr., Edinburgh: Banner of Truth, 2001), 4:419–20; Anthony Burgess, *Spiritual Refining: or A Treatise of Grace and Assurance* (London: A. Miller for Thomas Underhill, 1652), 237–43; Stephen Charnock, *The Complete Works of Stephen Charnock*, 5 vols. (Edinburgh: James Nichol, 1865), 3:90; George Downame, *A Treatise of Ivstification* (London: Felix Kyngston for Nicolas Bourne, 1633), 239–42; John Flavel, *The Works of John Flavel*, 6 vols. (Edinburgh: Banner of Truth, 1997), 6:197–99; Thomas Goodwin, *The Works of Thomas Goodwin*, 12 vols. (repr., Eureka, CA: Tanski, 1996), 1:83–102; William Gouge, *A Gvide to Goe to God: or, An Explanation of the Perfect Patterne of Prayer, The Lords Prayer*, 2nd ed. (London: G. M. for Edward Brewster, 1636), 10–21; Ezekiel Hopkins, *The Works of Ezekiel Hopkins*, ed. Charles W. Quick, 3 vols. (repr., Morgan, PA: Soli Deo Gloria, 1997), 2:120–21, 569–76; 3:198–99; Edward Leigh, *A Treatise of Divinity* (London, 1646), 510–11; John Owen, *The Works of John Owen*, ed. William H. Goold, 16 vols. (repr., London: Banner of Truth, 1966), 2:207–22; 4:265–70; 23:255–76.

7. Jeremiah Burroughs, *The Saints' Happiness, Delivered in Divers Lectures on the Beatitudes* (repr., Beaver Falls, PA: Soli Deo Gloria, 1988), 193–202; Thomas Cole, *A Discourse of Christian*

So significant was the Puritan emphasis on adoption that the Westminster divines were the first to include a separate chapter on the subject of adoption in a confessional statement: the Westminster Confession of Faith (chap. 12). The Larger Catechism (74) and the Shorter Catechism (34) also addressed it, as have numerous commentators of the Westminster Standards ever since.[8] Most importantly, some Puritans wrote entire treatises on adoption, including:

- John Crabb, *A Testimony concerning the VVorks of the Living God: Shewing How the Mysteries of His Workings Hath Worked Many Wayes in and amongst Mankind. Or, The Knowledge of God Revealed, Which Shews the Way from the Bondage of Darkness into the Liberty of the Sons of God*;
- Simon Ford, *The Spirit of Bondage and Adoption: Largely and Practically Handled, with Reference to the Way and Manner of*

Religion, in Sundry Points . . . Christ the Foundation of Our Adoption, from Gal. 4. 5 (London: for Will. Marshall, 1698); Roger Drake, "The Believer's Dignity and Duty Laid Open, in the High Birth wherewith He Is Privileged, and the Honourable Employment to Which He Is Called," in *Puritan Sermons 1659–1689: Being the Morning Exercises at Cripplegate, St. Giles in the Fields, and in Southwark by Seventy-five Ministers of the Gospel in or Near London*, 6 vols. (repr., Wheaton, IL: Richard Owen Roberts, 1981), 5:328–44; Thomas Hooker, *The Christians Tvvo Chiefe Lessons* (repr., Ames, IA: International Outreach, 2002), 159–73; Thomas Manton, *The Complete Works of Thomas Manton, D.D.*, 22 vols. (London: James Nisbet, 1870), 1:33–57; 10:116–21; 12:111–39; Stephen Marshall, *The Works of Mr Stephen Marshall, The First Part, [Section 2:] The High Priviledge of Beleevers. They Are the Sons of God* (London: Peter and Edward Cole, 1661); Richard Sibbes, *Works of Richard Sibbes*, 7 vols. (Edinburgh: Banner of Truth, 2001), 4:129–49; John Tennent, "The Nature of Adoption," in Richard Owen Roberts, ed., *Salvation in Full Color: Twenty Sermons by Great Awakening Preachers* (Wheaton, IL: International Awakening Press, 1994), 233–50; John Waite, *Of the Creatures Liberation from the Bondage of Corruption, Wherein Is Discussed . . . [Section 5]: And Lastly Is Discussed That Glorious Libertie of the Sonnes of God into Which the Creature Is to Be Reduced* (York: Tho. Broad, 1650).

8. For example, for the Westminster Confession, see Robert Shaw, *The Reformed Faith: An Exposition of the Westminster Confession of Faith* (repr., Inverness, Scotland: Christian Focus, 1974), 137–41; for the Larger Catechism, see Thomas Ridgley, *Commentary on the Larger Catechism*, 2 vols. (repr., Edmonton: Still Waters Revival Books, 1993), 2:131–37; and for the Shorter Catechism, see John Brown (of Haddington), *An Essay towards an Easy, Plain, Practical, and Extensive Explication of the Assembly's Shorter Catechism* (New York: Robert Carter & Brothers, 1849), 162–65; James Fisher, *The Assembly's Shorter Catechism Explained, by Way of Question and Answer* (repr., Lewes, East Sussex: Berith Publications, 1998), 184–87; Thomas Vincent, *The Shorter Catechism of the Westminster Assembly Explained and Proved from Scripture* (repr., Edinburgh: Banner of Truth, 1980), 96–97. For additional confessional statements that address adoption, see Tim Trumper, "An Historical Study of the Doctrine of Adoption in the Calvinistic Tradition" (Ph.D. diss., University of Edinburgh, 2001), 5–10.

>   *Working Both Those Effects; and the Proper Cases of Conscience Belonging to Them Both;*
>
> - M. G., *The Glorious Excellencie of the Spirit of Adoption;*
> - Thomas Granger, *A Looking-Glasse for Christians. Or, The Comfortable Doctrine of Adoption;*
> - Cotton Mather, *The Sealed Servants of Our God, Appearing with Two Witnesses, to Produce a Well-Established Assurance of Their Being the Children of the Lord Almighty or, the Witness of the Holy Spirit, with the Spirit of the Beleever, to His Adoption of God; Briefly and Plainly Described;*
> - Samuel Petto, *The Voice of the Spirit. Or, An Essay towards a Discoverie of the Witnessings of the Spirit;*
> - Samuel Willard, *The Child's Portion: Or the Unseen Glory of the Children of God, Asserted, and Proved: Together with Several Other Sermons Occasionally Preached.*[9]

Sadly, none of these books has been reprinted, which, in part, serves to promote the misrepresentation that the Puritans rarely addressed this subject.

Then, too, Scottish and Dutch divines of Puritan persuasion also wrote at length on adoption; for example, John Forbes, a Church of Scotland minister who spent most of his pastoral years in the Netherlands, wrote *A Letter for Resolving This Question: How a Christian Man May Discerne the Testimonie of Gods Spirit, from the Testimonie of His Owne Spirit, in Witnessing His Adoption.*[10] Thomas Boston devoted forty pages to the subject of adoption; Wilhelmus à Brakel, twenty-five pages.[11]

The Puritan bibliographical materials recorded in this introduction amount to approximately eight hundred pages of writing on the

---

9. Crabb (London: John Gain, 1682); Ford (London: T. Maxey for Sa. Gellibrand, 1655); M. G. (London: Jane Coe for Henry Overton, 1645); Granger (London: William Iones, 1620); Mather (Boston: Daniel Henchman, 1727); Petto (London: Livewell Chapman, 1654); Willard (Boston: Samuel Green, to be sold by Samuel Phillips, 1684).

10. Middelburg, Netherlands: Richard Schilders, 1616.

11. Samuel M'Millan, ed., *The Complete Works of the Late Rev. Thomas Boston, Ettrick,* 12 vols. (repr., Wheaton, IL: Richard Owen Roberts, 1980), 1:612–53; 2:15–27; Wilhelmus à Brakel, *The Christian's Reasonable Service,* trans. Bartel Elshout, ed. Joel R. Beeke, 4 vols. (Grand Rapids: Reformation Heritage Books, 1999), 2:415–38; 3:486–87.

doctrine of spiritual adoption.[12] As far as I know, no one to date has recognized the significant amount of work done by the Puritans on this subject, nor has anyone ever done a study on it. This chapter only begins to redress this neglect by letting the Puritans speak for themselves, for the most part. Throughout, I show how Puritanism recognized adoption's far-reaching, transforming power and comfort for the sons and daughters of God.

Greatness and Comprehensiveness of Adoption, and Its Relation to Soteriology

The Puritans were fond of stressing the transforming power, superlative value, and surprising wonder of adoption. They spoke often of its greatness, excellency, dignity, and comprehensiveness.

William Perkins said that a believer should esteem his adoption as God's child to be greater than being "the childe or heire of any earthly Prince [since] the sonne of the greatest Potentate may be the childe of wrath: but the child of God by grace, hath Christ Iesus to bee his eldest *brother*, with whom he is *fellow heire* in heaven; hee hath the holy Ghost also for his *comforter*, and the kingdome of heauen for his euerlasting *inheritance*." Perkins lamented how few people realize this experientially: "At earthly preferments men will stand amazed; but seldome shall you finde a man that is rauished with ioy in this, that hee is the childe of God."[13]

Spiritual adoption is the comprehensive apex of God's salvation. The Puritans often shared the apostle John's sense of awe when he declared, "Behold, what manner of love the Father hath bestowed upon us, that we should be called the sons of God" (1 John 3:1).[14] What a stupendous wonder adoption is! Brakel put it this way:

12. This number does not include material that could be included from Puritan commentaries and additional sermons that treat the main texts on adoption, nor additional commentaries on the Westminster Standards.

13. *Workes of William Perkins*, 3:138 (2nd pagination).

14. Unless otherwise indicated, Scripture quotations in this chapter are from the King James Version.

JOEL R. BEEKE

From being a child of the devil to becoming a child of God, from being a child of wrath to becoming the object of God's favor, from a child of condemnation to becoming an heir of all the promises and a possessor of all blessings, and to be exalted from the greatest misery to the highest felicity—this is something which exceeds all comprehension and all adoration.[15]

And how comprehensive adoption is! Most Puritans place their treatment of adoption in the *ordo salutis* between justification and sanctification, following the order set forth by the Westminster divines. Logically, that makes considerable sense, given the inevitable ties between justification and adoption, and sanctification and adoption, as we will see shortly. Other Puritans, however, have pointed out that though adoption can at times be viewed as one aspect of salvation, or one part of the *ordo salutis*, at other times it can be best understood as comprehending all of soteriology. For example, Stephen Marshall writes, "Though sometimes in the holy Scriptures our Sonship is but one of our Priviledges, yet very frequently in the Scripture all the Beleevers do obtain from Christ in this world and the world to come, here and to eternity, all is comprehended in this one, *That they are made the Children of God.*" Marshall goes on to cite several examples: "I know not how often the whol Covenant of Grace is expressed in that word, *I wil be their Father, they shal be my children,*" or consider Ephesians 1:5, he says, where Paul comprehends all of salvation "in this one expression, *having predestinated us to the adoption of children.*"[16] Clearly, the Puritans ascribed a lofty and comprehensive place to adoption in their soteriology.

Adoption Compared in the Two Testaments

The Puritans believed that the metaphors of "adoption" and "sons of God" are valid for believers of both testaments, but that only in the New Testament did the transforming power of adoption come to the

15. Brakel, *The Christian's Reasonable Service*, 2:419.
16. Marshall also uses Rom. 8:23 and the beginning of Gal. 4 to buttress Scripture's frequent comprehensive use of adoption. *Works of Stephen Marshall*, 37–38.

68

fore. Herman Witsius, one of the clearest on this point, stresses that believers in the Old Testament era were also regenerated, betrothed to Christ, and adopted to become sons of God. He writes, "Believers, at all times, were the children of God. Elihu, who was not of the people of Israel, called God *his Father*." Yet the clarity on the adoption of Old Testament believers compared to New Testament believers varies as much as "the light of the stars before that of the sun."[17]

Witsius goes on to say that believers under the Old Testament were children under the "severity and discipline of tutors, who bound heavy burdens, grievous to be born, and laid them on their shoulders." Consequently, believers were "obliged to be subject to the weak and beggarly elements of the world, and like children, to be engaged all the day in the trifling ceremonies of the Mosaic institution, which were, in a manner, the play-things of the church." Compared with New Testament believers, they were taught like infants, "without being left to their own choice," and experienced little "familiarity" with their Father. They were not allowed to enter the temple, and were compelled to live under types and shadows by sacrifices and offerings in the land of Canaan, which served as a rather obscure pledge of the heavenly inheritance.[18]

New Testament believers bask in the sunlight of God's super-abounding, adopting grace and liberty merited for them by their Elder Brother. Witsius writes, "For after our elder brother, having taken upon him human nature, had visited this lower world, and freely undergone a state of various servitude for us, he brought us into true liberty, John viii. 36. removed the tutors, [and] blotted out the hand-writing of ordinances, which was contrary to us." He now brings us into the Father's "secret counsels," shows us the Father by showing us himself (John 14:9), and makes us into a royal priesthood (1 Peter 2:9). He calls us "directly to an inheritance of spiritual and heavenly good things, and appoints unto us a kingdom" (Luke 22:29). Believers are now "eminently and emphatically called *the sons of God*" (1 John 3:2), as Isaiah had prophesied (Isa. 56:4–5), and the Holy Spirit witnesses with their spirits that this is so (Rom. 8:15–16). God

17. Witsius, *Economy of the Covenants*, 1:447.
18. Ibid., 1:447–48.

consciously becomes their personal Father, and this "Father" name becomes God's new-covenant name, representing the family covenant to which he binds himself on behalf of his children, so that they now have liberty to cry, "Abba, Father" (Gal. 4:6). Galatians 4:4–7 teaches that "*when the fullness of the time was come*; namely, *that appointed time*, (till which the children were to be under tutors, ver. 2.) *God sent forth his Son to redeem that were under the law*, setting them free from the use of ceremonies, *and that we might receive the adoption*." They "receive the adoption" into Christ's kingdom provided for by the testament of Christ's blood. That kingdom consists of the whole world, so that every crumb of bread believers receive, every aspect of creation they observe, and every act of providence carried out testifies of the love of the Father and of their own good. To this spiritual kingdom entered into by adoption belong victory over sin, the bruising of Satan, inestimable riches, peace of soul, joy in the Holy Spirit, and boldness in Christ (Eph. 3:12).[19]

What Adoption Is Not

To more precisely analyze the Puritans' teachings on adoption, it is advantageous first to consider what they thought adoption is not.

Adoption Is Not Regeneration

We are prone to treat regeneration and adoption as synonymous because in regeneration the Christian is someone born from above. Adoption, at first glance, seems to be another way of describing the consequences of that new birth. The Puritans assure us, however, that this is not so. These are two distinct blessings, though all who are born again are adopted, and everyone who is adopted is born again.[20]

Regeneration and adoption deal with two different problems. Adoption deals with our status. We are by nature children of wrath and children of the devil; our status is one of alienation and condemnation. Because of the sin-removing and heaven-meriting work

19. Ibid., 1:448–54.
20. Burroughs, *The Saints' Happiness*, 192.

of Christ, our whole status changes so that we are now called the children of God.

If in adoption we would receive only the privilege and status of being God's children, something would still be missing. The adopted child retains the nature of his biological parents; he does not assume the nature of the adoptive parents. God, in his amazing grace, not only gives us the status and privileges of being his children by adoption, but also gives us the Spirit of sonship as a witness to our adoption, which abides within us by Spirit-worked regeneration. The Holy Spirit implants a new nature within us.

Regeneration, then, deals with our nature, those sinful hearts of ours that drink iniquity like water. God changes our sin-loving personalities by the new birth. In other words, after changing our status and adopting us into his family as his sons, God will not allow us to go on behaving like children of the devil. He ensures that we cannot do so; he gives us the nature and likeness to match our sonship by a birth from above. Our title as "a son of God" then becomes intimately related to our own experience. We are not what we once were (1 John 3:9). God has done what no human father and mother can do when they adopt a child—change the personality and the nature of the child they have adopted so that he or she is like theirs. But God, in regeneration, has allowed his born-again children to become partakers of his own loving, holy nature as their Father in heaven.

In short, the Puritans taught that regeneration and adoption are to be distinguished in several ways. Here is a summary of points made by Thomas Manton and Stephen Charnock:

- Regeneration brings us to close with Christ; adoption causes the Spirit to abide in our hearts.
- Regeneration is the Spirit's renewing; adoption, the Spirit's inhabiting. In regeneration, the Holy Spirit builds a house for himself; in adoption, he dwells in the house—much like bees that "first make their cells, and then dwell in them."
- Regeneration is not conditioned by faith; adoption is.
- Regeneration enables us to believe unto justification and adoption.

- Regeneration engraves upon us the lineaments of a father; adoption relates us to God as our Father.
- Regeneration makes us God's sons by conveying the principle of new life (1 Peter 1:23); adoption keeps us God's sons by conferring the power of new life (John 1:12).
- Regeneration makes us partakers of the divine nature; adoption makes us partakers of the divine affections.
- Regeneration affects our nature; adoption, our relationships.[21]

Adoption Is Not Justification

Justification is the primary, fundamental blessing of the gospel; it meets our most basic spiritual need—forgiveness and reconciliation with God. We could not be adopted without it. But adoption is a richer blessing because it brings us from the courtroom into the family. "Justification is conceived of in terms of law, adoption in terms of love. Justification sees God as a judge, adoption as a father."[22]

Justification and adoption obviously have much in common. The Puritans taught that the status of adoption, like justification, is an act rather than a process. Contrary to the ideas of Robert Bellarmine and Roman Catholicism, this act is administered by imputation, not infusion.[23] It is punctiliar, not linear. Believers are not progressively adopted, becoming more and more the children of God; adoption is no more subject to degrees than justification is. When sinners believe, they are made full children of God, and remain so. Justification declares them to be righteous—in a moment! They become his children, sons and heirs of God, joint heirs with Christ.

When an attempt is made to pinpoint more precisely the relationship of justification and adoption, three viewpoints surface among the Puritans. The first, represented by Brakel, says that since justification includes not only a negative aspect of acquittal from guilt and punishment, but also a positive aspect of the bestowal of the right of

21. *Works of Thomas Manton*, 12:113–14; *Complete Works of Stephen Charnock*, 90.
22. Gordon Cooke, "The Doctrine of Adoption and the Preaching of Jeremiah Burroughs," in *Eternal Light, Adoption, and Livingstone* (London: Congregational Studies Conference Papers, 1988), 23.
23. Downame, *A Treatise of Ivstification*, 241–42.

eternal life, in which God's children are declared heirs, adoption is best seen as being included in the positive side of justification. Hence, justification includes spiritual sonship.

The second position, represented by Thomas Ridgley, a moderate Calvinist best known for his exposition of the Westminster Larger Catechism, is that adoption is included in justification from one perspective but not from another. Ridgley maintains that adoption can be reckoned as a branch of justification in some respects and a branch of sanctification in others. He writes:

> If justification be explained as denoting an immanent act in God, whereby the elect are considered, in the covenant between the Father and the Son, as in Christ their federal head; they are then considered as the adopted children of God in Christ. Accordingly, when described as chosen in Christ unto eternal life, they are said to be "predestinated unto the adoption of children."

Both justification and adoption, Ridgley adds, are received by faith. On the other hand, if adoption is viewed from the perspective of the child of God's being made meet for his heavenly inheritance, which includes "being endowed with the temper and disposition of his children, consisting in humility, heavenly-mindedness, love to him, dependence upon him, a zeal for his glory, a likeness to Christ, a having in some measure the same mind in us which was in him, it in this respect agrees with sanctification."[24]

Third, the majority of the Puritans support the position of the Westminster Assembly, stressing that justification and adoption, though intimately related, are two distinct privileges and ought to be handled separately in theology. For example, in expounding the Shorter Catechism, Samuel Willard emphasizes that the Bible clearly distinguishes justification and adoption in Romans 8:14ff., Ephesians 1:5, and elsewhere. Scripture makes plain that it is one thing to be judged righteous and another to be placed among God's children; one thing to have God accept us as a Judge, another to do so as a Father,

---

24. Ridgley, *Commentary on the Larger Catechism*, 136–37.

with all the love and care that this involves. Justification involves a *legal* relationship; adoption, a *personal* relationship.

These three positions, practically speaking, are not far removed from one another. Theologically, however, the second and especially the third are prone to accent adoption more biblically. Though both justification and adoption are forensic concepts—the former derived from the realm of criminal law and the latter from family law—their practical outworkings differ substantially. Justification in abstraction from adoption leaves us with a rather bare, legal concept—though, of course, the privilege of having our sins forgiven and being made acceptable to God must never be underestimated. But adoption enlarges our understanding of what it means to be acceptable to God. We are acceptable not simply as moral agents but as the image-bearers of our Father who are being subjectively conformed to Christ. We are acceptable as sons of God who have the privilege of calling God our Father and bearing the responsibility of serving him as his children.

Subjectively, of course, believers grow in the knowledge of their adoption, as will be considered in more detail below.[25] Thus, the Puritans taught that adoption in its objective dimension, related to the believer's state and to justification, is instantaneous and complete; in its subjective dimension, related to the believer's condition and to sanctification, there is a growing awareness of its privileges, responsibilities, and applications.

Adoption Is Not Sanctification

Thomas Brooks asserts that sanctification is simply a living out of one's adoption and sonship (John 1:12; Rom. 8:17). He writes, "If thou art a holy person, then of a child of wrath thou art become a child of God, a child of love; and of an heir of hell thou art become an heir of heaven; and of a slave, thou art become a son."[26]

Packer's assertion about sanctification would resonate well with the Puritans: that it is "simply a consistent living out of our filial relationship with God, into which the gospel brings us. It is just a matter of

---

25. See the section on how adoption is realized experientially.
26. *Works of Thomas Brooks*, 419.

the child of God being true to type, true to his Father, to his Saviour, and to himself. It is the expressing of one's adoption in one's life. It is a matter of being a good son, as distinct from a prodigal or black sheep in the royal family."[27]

Through sanctification the believer is brought into a fuller experiential awareness of his adoption. He learns to grasp more fully what adoption is, and learns to live joyfully out of its wonders.

The Westminster Assembly's Definitions of Adoption

The Westminster Assembly, which included scores of Puritans, offers three formal definitions of adoption—a basic definition in the Shorter Catechism, an intermediate definition in the Larger Catechism, and a more comprehensive definition in the Confession of Faith:

Shorter Catechism 34: Adoption is an act of God's free grace, whereby we are received into the number, and have a right to all the privileges, of the sons of God.

Larger Catechism 74: Adoption is an act of the free grace of God, in and for His only Son Jesus Christ, whereby all those that are justified are received into the number of His children, have His name put upon them, the Spirit of His Son given to them, are under His fatherly care and dispensations, admitted to all the liberties and privileges of the sons of God, made heirs of all the promises, and fellow heirs with Christ in glory.

Confession of Faith, chapter 12: All those that are justified, God vouchsafeth, in and for His only Son Jesus Christ, to make partakers of the grace of adoption, by which they are taken into the number, and enjoy the liberties and privileges of the children of God, have His name put upon them, receive the spirit of adoption, have access to the throne of grace with boldness, are enabled to cry, Abba, Father, are pitied, protected, provided for, and chastened by Him as by a

27. Packer, *Knowing God*, 201.

Father: yet never cast off, but sealed to the day of redemption; and inherit the promises, as heirs of everlasting salvation.[28]

Several significant points may be made relative to the Westminster Assembly's work on adoption.

First, how intriguing it is that the Westminster divines, often accused of being too scholastic in their theology, provided the Christian church's first confessional chapter and formal articles on adoption—one of the least scholastic doctrines of the Christian faith! Why the Assembly decided to allot adoption a separate *locus* is not clear. Both the published and unpublished minutes of the Westminster Assembly tell us no more than the basic dates and facts that it happened.[29] Perhaps the divines were motivated by a growing awareness of the scripturalness and importance of adoption both doctrinally and experientially as it relates to justification, sanctification, assurance of faith, perseverance, and other ancillary doctrines.

Second, there are good reasons for the Westminster divines' brevity in treating adoption, including the lack of treatment in former confessions, the lack of dissent or heresy that needed to be addressed, and the overlap of material with the chapters on assurance and perseverance. All of these factors assist the divines to expound a large doctrine with remarkably succinct brevity.[30]

Third, the Westminster divines were concerned to apply predestination soteriologically. That is already evident in Westminster Confession of Faith 3.6, where the first reference to adoption is made in conjunction with predestination: "They who are elected being fallen in Adam, are redeemed by Christ; are effectually called unto faith in Christ by His Spirit working in due season; are justified, *adopted*, sanctified, and kept by His power through faith unto salvation. Neither are there any other redeemed by Christ, effectually called, justified, *adopted*, sanctified, and saved, but the elect only" (emphasis added). Later, the Assembly stressed that adoption originates as "an act of

28. Joel R. Beeke and Sinclair B. Ferguson, eds., *Reformed Confessions Harmonized* (Grand Rapids: Baker, 1999), 107.

29. See Trumper, "An Historical Study of the Doctrine of Adoption in the Calvinistic Tradition," 227–29, for a detailed study of Westminster's minutes relative to adoption.

30. Chad Van Dixhoorn, "The *Sonship* Program, for Revival: A Summary and Critique," *Westminster Theological Journal* 61 (1999): 235–36.

the free grace of God,"[31] and involves being "taken"[32] or "received into the number" of the elect.[33] Tim Trumper rightly concludes that "as the Westminster commissioners were as concerned as Calvin to apply predestination soteriologically, there is little purpose in driving a wedge between Calvin and the later Calvinists" on this issue, as is often done.[34]

Fourth, union with Christ is inseparable from adoption. The sonship we receive is Christ's in the first place. Adoption transpires "in and for His only Son Jesus Christ," so that the adopted "have His name put upon them, the Spirit of His Son given to them."[35] Justification, adoption, and sanctification all flow from union with Christ.[36] Contrary to what some scholars have suggested, the Westminster divines were as concerned as Calvin to maintain that "to be adopted is to be united with Christ in his Sonship."[37]

Fifth, the Westminster divines harmonized the forensic and familial elements of adoption. They spoke of both the judicial pronouncement of adoption[38] and the adoptive experience of sonship, referred to as the "liberties and privileges" of adoption.[39] This is evident in the chapter on justification also, where forensic and familial aspects are united in stating that though the justified "can never fall from the state of justification, yet they may, by their sins, fall under God's *fatherly* displeasure."[40] Adoption, therefore, is not exhausted by its forensic aspects; rather, the forensic aspects imply an ensuing familial life of sonship that manifests itself in the visible church, which is described as "the house and family of God."[41]

31. Larger Catechism 74; cf. Shorter Catechism 34 and Westminster Confession of Faith 3.5.
32. Westminster Confession of Faith, chap. 12.
33. Shorter Catechism 34; Larger Catechism 74.
34. Trumper, "An Historical Study of the Doctrine of Adoption in the Calvinistic Tradition," 231.
35. Larger Catechism 74; Westminster Confession of Faith, chap. 12.
36. Larger Catechism 69.
37. Trumper, "An Historical Study of the Doctrine of Adoption in the Calvinistic Tradition," 232.
38. Larger Catechism 74; Westminster Confession of Faith 8.5, chap. 12.
39. Larger Catechism 74; Westminster Confession of Faith, chap. 12.
40. Westminster Confession of Faith 11.5, emphasis added.
41. Westminster Confession of Faith 25.2; Trumper, "An Historical Study of the Doctrine of Adoption in the Calvinistic Tradition," 234–36.

Finally, the Westminster divines emphasize that adoption is an act of free grace.[42] In adoption, the unlovable sinner is freely loved by God and taken into the divine family. Watson puts it this way: "Adoption is a mercy spun out of the bowels of free grace; all by nature are strangers, therefore have no right to sonship, only God is pleased to adopt one, and not another, to make one a vessel of glory, another a vessel of wrath. The adopted heir may cry out, 'Lord, how is it, that thou wilt show thyself to me, and not unto the world?' "[43]

The Transforming Power of Adoption

When we are born again, God delivers us from Satan's enslaving family and, by his astounding grace, transfers us to the Father's sonship. He calls us sons; we are adopted into his family, transferred "from a state of sin and misery" to "a state of excellency [and] dignity," writes Watson. "It were much for God to take a clod of dust and make it a star; it is more for God to take a piece of clay and sin and adopt it for his heir."[44]

Adoption in the time of the apostle John usually took place in adolescence or adulthood, not infancy. Under Roman law, adoption was a legal act by which a man chose someone outside of the family to be an heir to his inheritance. Likewise, believers become children of God through the gracious act of God the Father, who chooses them to be his heirs and joint heirs with Christ.

Ames identifies four differences between human and divine adoption:

- Human adoption relates to a person, who, as a stranger, has no right to the inheritance except through adoption. But believers, though by natural birth they have no right to the inheritance of life, are given it because of rebirth, faith, and justification.

42. Shorter Catechism 34; Larger Catechism 74; Westminster Confession of Faith, chap. 12.
43. Watson, *A Body of Divinity*, 155.
44. Ibid., 156.

- Human adoption is only an outward designation and bestowal of external things. But divine adoption is so real a relationship that it is based on an inward action and the communications of a new inner life.
- Human adoption was introduced when there were no, or too few, natural sons. But divine adoption is not from any want but from abundant goodness, whereby a likeness of a natural son and mystical union is given to the adopted sons.
- The human adoption is ordained so that the son may succeed the father in the inheritance. But divine adoption is not ordained for succession, but for participation in the inheritance assigned. Both the Father and his first-begotten Son live forever and this admits no succession.[45]

How astonishing it is that, unlike people's heirs, who don't share their estates with their friends, we as God's adopted children share the same privileges that belong to God's only-begotten Son! The Puritans reveled in what Christ prays in John 17:23: ". . . and hast loved them, as thou hast loved me."[46] This love is the essence of God's fatherhood. It shows us how far God is willing to go to reconcile us to himself.

How great is the love the Father has lavished on us that we should be called children of God (1 John 3:1)—we who have deserved his judgment, dethroned him from our lives, spurned his love, and defied his laws. Here, surely, is the great assurance of the child of God, that God the Father loved him when he was bound for hell. How wonderful is the assurance of the Father's words: "I have loved thee with an everlasting love" (Jer. 31:3).

Love and communion with God lie at the heart of adoption, according to John Owen. Owen listed five elements of adoption, which Sinclair Ferguson summarizes as follows:

(1) that the person first belongs to another family; (2) that there is a family to which he has no right to belong; (3) that there is an authoritative legal translation from one family to another; (4) that

---

45. Ames, *The Marrow of Theology*, 165–67.
46. Anthony Burgess, *CXLV Expository Sermons upon the Whole 17th Chapter of the Gospel According to John* (London: Abraham Miller for Thomas Underhill, 1656), 641–48.

the adopted person is freed from all the legal obligations of the family from which he came; and (5) that by virtue of his translation he is invested with all the rights, privileges, and advantages of the new family.[47]

The Puritans emphasize that all the members of the Trinity are involved in our adoption. Marshall summarizes it this way: Adoption is the gracious act of God the Father whereby he chooses us, calls us to himself, and gives us the privileges and blessings of being his children. God the Son earned those blessings for us through his propitiatory death and sacrifice, by which we become children of God (1 John 4:10), and applies them to us as Elder Brother. And the Holy Spirit changes us from children of wrath, which we are by nature, into children of God by means of regeneration; unites us to Christ; works in us a "suitable disposition" toward God and Christ; and seals our sonship as the Spirit of adoption, witnessing with our spirits that we are the sons of God. In that witnessing, the Spirit shows us God's work of grace in our hearts and lives, and also "carries our hearts to God, and testifies to the Soul that God is [our] Father."[48]

Pastoral Advice in Promoting Adoption

As pastors, the Puritans distinguished people in four ways with regard to adoption.

First, some are visibly adopted into God's church family but lack adoption's experiential power. Their adoption, says Thomas Shepard, is

> external, whereby the Lord takes a people by outward covenant and dispensation to be his sons, and thus all the Jews were God's "first born," (Ex. iv. 22,) and unto them did "belong the adoption," (Rom. ix. 4, 5;) and hence their children were accounted "sons" as well as

---

47. Sinclair B. Ferguson, *John Owen on the Christian Life* (Edinburgh: Banner of Truth, 1987), 90–91; cf. *Works of John Owen*, 2:207ff.
48. *Works of Stephen Marshall*, 43–48.

saints, and "holy," (1 Cor. vii. 14; Ezek. xvi. 20, 21;) but many fall from this adoption, as the Jews did.[49]

Today, this visible adoption applies to the New Testament church. Many have professed the gospel as members of the church, but do not know the gospel's power. Not being born again, they do not possess the Spirit of adoption. That is not the gospel's fault, but their own. Manton writes, "They are strangers to the grace of the covenant under which they live, by their own negligence and folly." Manna is around their tents, Manton continues, but they would rather starve than gather it. "The Spirit is ready, but they are lazy," he concludes.[50]

Such people are "under a visible administration of the covenant of grace." Christ often gives them "common gifts which he giveth not to the heathen world: knowledge of the mysteries of godliness; abilities of utterance and speech about spiritual and heavenly things; some affection also to them, called 'tasting of the good word, the heavenly gift, and the powers of the world to come,' Heb. vi." Despite having these common gifts of superficial Christianity, they lack "the real Christianity with special graces."[51]

Ministers must warn such people of the danger of remaining members of Satan's family inwardly while they appear to be members of God's family. They must plead with sinners to repent and believe in Christ and trust God's mercy for adoption. Roger Drake says, "Art thou an alien? O never rest till thou get into a [saving] state of sonship."[52]

Second, some professing members of the church are under "the Spirit of bondage," that is, those who are under the Holy Spirit's power to convict of sin but do not as yet have liberty in Christ. Some Puritans—though by no means all—understand this to mean what is at times called "a preparatory work of grace." Ezekiel Hopkins lays out the essence of this approach more succinctly; his key thoughts form an apt summary:

---

49. Thomas Shepard, *The Sincere Convert and the Sound Believer* (repr., Morgan, PA: Soli Deo Gloria, 1999), 251. Cf. Burgess, *Spiritual Refining*, 238–39; Drake, "The Believer's Dignity," 329–30; Watson, *A Body of Divinity*, 155.

50. *Works of Thomas Manton*, 12:116.

51. Ibid.

52. Drake, "The Believer's Dignity," 340.

1. The preparatory work of conversion is usually carried on in the soul by legal fears and terrors.
2. This legal fear is slavish, and engenders bondage.
3. This slavish fear is wrought in the soul by the Spirit of God, though it be slavish.
4. When the soul is prepared for the work of grace by the work of conviction, when it is prepared for comfort by the work of humiliation, the same Spirit, that was before a Spirit of bondage, becomes now a Spirit of adoption.
5. To whom the Spirit hath once been a Spirit of adoption, it never more becomes to them a Spirit of bondage and fear.
6. A reverential, filial fear of God, may and ought to possess our souls, while the Spirit of God, who is a spirit of adoption, is, by the clearest evidences, actually witnessing our sonship to us.[53]

Pastorally, the Puritans advised those who were under the Spirit of bondage of their danger, their invitation, and their encouragement. Their danger is that they will perish if they do not take refuge in Christ with penitent faith and come to know the Spirit of adoption. Their invitation is to come to Christ immediately, confessing their sins—including the sin of lacking childlike fear. They must ask the Spirit to drive them out of their self-confidence and cause them to storm the mercy seat. And their encouragement is, according to Simon Ford, that God will not keep his elect indefinitely in bondage for several reasons: religion would become uncomfortable and unappealing, people would faint under their burden of sin, and they would develop hard thoughts of God. God will lead those under bondage into liberty to show that serving him is not in vain; he wants to wean his own from this world, and he wants to commune with them often.[54]

Third, some sincere children of God have, at best, a weak sense of their own sonship. Objectively, all of God's children are equally sons of God, as we have seen. But as Manton says, "All God's children have the spirit of adoption in the effects, though not in the sense and

53. *Works of Ezekiel Hopkins*, 2:569–74.
54. Ford, *The Spirit of Bondage and Adoption*, 212–16.

feeling of it. They have the spirit of comfort, though not the comfort of it. . . . There is a child-like inclination and impression left upon them, though they know it not, [and] own it not." Christ had the Spirit without measure, but Christians, though having the whole Spirit, enjoy him and his work in different degrees. Christians are not all of the same size and growth. Moreover, Manton concludes, "Some do more improve their privileges than others do; now they cannot rationally expect the best and richest fruits of this gift, and to be enabled and enlarged by the Spirit, who do not give such ready entertainment and obedience to his motions, as the more serious and fruitful Christian doth."[55]

Manton then explains the difference between these people who have a weak sense of sonship and those who are still under the Spirit of bondage. The weak ones have a childlike inclination to God, though they lack childlike familiarity and boldness. They have a childlike reverence for God as Father (1 Peter 1:17), though they lack a childlike confidence in him as their Father. They have a childlike dependence on God's general offers of grace, but are not persuaded of the sincerity of their particular claim. They have a childlike love for God, though they lack assurance of his paternal love for them. They possess the childlike adherence of faith without the mature full assurance of faith. Unlike those under the Spirit of bondage who seek God out of a mercenary spirit, these seek him from a childlike spirit.[56]

Manton gives four counsels to assist the weak in faith in being able to call God their Father: First, "disclaim when you cannot apply." If you cannot say, "Father," plead on your "fatherless" condition, using such texts as Hosea 14:3, "In thee the fatherless findeth mercy." Second, "own God in the humbling way." Come to the Father like the Prodigal Son, confessing your unworthiness, or like Paul, as the chief of sinners. Come to him as your Father-Creator if you cannot come to him as your Father-Savior. Third, "call him Father in wish." If you cannot call him "Father" with directness, do it with desire. "Let us pray ourselves into this relation, and groan after it, that we may have a clearer sense that God is our Father in Christ," Manton counsels.

55. *Works of Thomas Manton*, 12:116–17.
56. Ibid., 1:34–36; 12:117–18.

Fourth, make "use of Christ Jesus." Since Christ's name means so much in heaven, "if you cannot come to God as your Father, come to him as the God and Father of our Lord Jesus Christ (Eph. 3:14). Let Christ bring you into God's presence. He is willing to change relations with us. Take him along with you in your arms. Go to God in Christ's name: 'Whatsoever you ask in my name, shall be given to you.' "[57]

Finally, many believers experience the joy of knowing that they are sons and daughters of God. That knowledge is grounded in objective truth—ultimately, in God's election. God's will is the foundation in this building: "Having predestinated us unto the adoption of children . . . , according to the good pleasure of his will" (Eph. 1:5). Election is executed via Christ's bloody atonement: Christ was "made of a woman, made under the law, . . . that we might receive the adoption of sons" (Gal. 4:4–5). Christ purchased the adoption of his brothers and sisters by his obedience and satisfaction. He also sends out his ministers, as Boston says, "to proclaim the offer of adoption unto them, that whosoever of them will leave their father's house and people [i.e., Satan and the unsaved] shall be adopted into the family of heaven." Satan rages against this message, but "unto the elect among them God sends his Spirit, which opens their ears, awakens their conscience, and rouses them so, that they can no longer" live without a Savior.[58] The Spirit then applies Christ's satisfying atonement in regeneration, which immediately enters the believer, by faith, into the status of adoption: "[To] as many as received him, to them gave he power to become the sons of God, even to them that believe on his name: which were born, not of blood, nor of the will of the flesh, nor of the will of man, but of God" (John 1:12–13).[59] From the moment of regeneration and faith, the believer is spiritually united with Christ as part of the Son of God's body and is thus judged by the Father to be one of his adopted children (Eph. 1:23).[60] Willard

57. Ibid., 1:36, 50–51; cf. Ford, *The Spirit of Bondage and Adoption*, 200, and Petto, *The Voice of the Spirit*, 56–62.
58. *Works of Thomas Boston*, 1:619, 621.
59. *Works of Thomas Manton*, 12:123.
60. Brakel, *The Christian's Reasonable Service*, 2:420.

summarizes, "*Though we were appointed to it [adoption] from Eternity, yet it is conferred upon us in Believing.*"[61]

The believer may also subjectively realize adoption. "There must in order of nature be the *certitude objecti*, before *certitude subjecti*, for I can never be sure of a thing before it is," writes Ford. Years may transpire, he goes on to say, before the believer who is adopted by God may *know* he is adopted. In fact, since the subjective consciousness of adoption is not essential to eternal life, Ford concludes that it is *possible*—though not normative—for a believer to "go to heaven without that particular actual assurance, or a particular confidence to address himself to God as his Father."[62]

The Puritans believed that all God did outside of the Christian for his salvation has its counterpart within him. The Christ who merited salvation for his elect also applies it to them. This he does by means of what Forbes called his "experienced word": God "speakes the word of trueth to the heart," causes the heart "to believe that which it hath heard and received," and adds "his spirit: and by the testimonie thereof . . . makes Adoption and eternall life, most certain and sure to the soule."[63]

Most Puritans were fond of calling this certainty the witnessing testimony of the Holy Spirit, which they usually identified with the consciousness of the sealing of the Spirit and assurance of faith. Westminster Confession of Faith 18.2 refers to "the testimony of the Spirit of adoption witnessing with our spirit that we are the children of God." Samuel Petto defines the Spirit's witnessing ministry as "a worke whereby the Spirit doth that towards the clearing up unto a soule of its Adoption, that a witnes doth amongst men for the decision and determination of a matter dubious and uncertaine."[64]

The Puritans varied in their interpretation of how the Spirit's witnessing testimony was experienced by the child of God.[65] Some, such as Jeremiah Burroughs, Anthony Burgess, and George Gillespie,

---

61. Willard, *A Compleat Body of Divinity*, 487.
62. Ford, *The Spirit of Bondage and Adoption*, 201–2.
63. Forbes, *How a Christian Man May Discerne the Testimonie of Gods Spirit*, 37.
64. Petto, *The Voice of the Spirit*, 7.
65. Cf. my *Quest for Full Assurance: The Legacy of Calvin and His Successors* (Edinburgh: Banner of Truth, 1999), 142–47.

emphasize that the witnessing testimony of the Holy Spirit coincides with assurance gleaned from inward evidences of grace, which the Puritans also called the marks or fruits of grace.[66] They believe that the Spirit's witness refers exclusively to his activity of uniting the adopted child's conscience with the Spirit's witness that the Christian is a child of God. According to that view, the witness of the Holy Spirit conjoins *with* the witness of the believer's spirit. Romans 8:15 (receiving the Spirit of adoption) and 8:16 (the Spirit's bearing witness together with the believer's conscience) are thus synonymous.[67] Therefore, when the Spirit's witness and the witness of the believer's conscience unitedly confirm that the believer possesses the marks and fruits of grace to some degree, the believer, assured that he is a child, may then cry out, "Abba, Father" (Gal. 4:6).[68]

Manton describes the Spirit's witness with our spirit in six thoughts:

1. The Spirit lays down marks [of grace] in scripture.
2. He worketh such graces as are peculiar to God's children, and are evidences of our interest in the favour of God.
3. He helpeth us to feel and discover those acts in ourselves.
4. The Spirit helps us to compare them with the rule [of Scripture], and accordingly to judge of their sincerity.
5. The Spirit helps us to conclude rightly of our estate.
6. He enlivens and heightens our apprehensions in all these particulars, and so fills us with comfort, and raiseth our joy upon the feeling of the sense of the favour of God; for all this is the fruit of his operation.[69]

Other Puritans, such as Petto, Witsius, Samuel Rutherford, William Twisse, Henry Scudder, Thomas Cole, and Cotton Mather, concur with much of what has been said thus far, but feel that all of this is

66. Burroughs, *The Saints' Happiness*, 196; Burgess, *Spiritual Refining*, 44; George Gillespie, *A Treatise of Miscellany Questions* (Edinburgh: Gedeon Lithgovv for George Svvintuun, 1649), 105–9.
67. Cf. Perkins's exegesis of Rom. 8:16 in *Workes of William Perkins*, 2:18–19; Burgess's exegesis of Rom. 8:15–16, Eph. 1:13, and 1 John 5:8 in *Spiritual Refining*, 49–50.
68. Cf. *Workes of William Perkins*, 2:277–80; *Works of John Owen*, 4:265–70.
69. *Works of Thomas Manton*, 1:51–53.

included in the previous expression in Westminster Confession of Faith 18.2, which refers to assurance obtained through the inward evidences of grace. They believe that the witnessing testimony of the Spirit involves something more, that the witness of the Spirit described in Romans 8:15 contains something distinct from that of verse 16.[70] They distinguish the Spirit's witness *with* the believer's spirit from his witnessing *to* the believer's spirit by direct applications of the Word. As Heinrich Meyer pointed out, the former works the self-conscious conviction, "*I* am a child of God," and thus finds freedom to approach God as Father. The latter involves the Spirit's pronouncement on behalf of the Father, "*You* are a child of God," and the believer thus approaches the Father with the familiarity of a child, crying out, "Abba, Father," on the basis of hearing one's own sonship pronounced from God's Word.[71] Witsius says that this comes with such power, "immediately assuring God's beloved people of their adoption, no less than if they were carried up to the third heavens, and had heard it audibly from God's own mouth."[72] Mather distinguishes these two grounds of assurance this way:

> There is a *Testimony* of the Holy SPIRIT unto our *Adoption*, which comes as a *Mighty Light*, more *Directly* breaking in upon our Minds, to assure us, that we are indeed the *Adopted* of GOD. There is a *Discursive Assurance* of our Blessedness; which is drawn from the *Marks* and *Signs* of a Soul become an *Habitation of God thro' the Spirit*. And then there is a more *Intuitive Assurance* of it; In which the Holy SPIRIT, more Immediately, and most Irresistibly, and with a *Mighty Light*, bears in upon the Mind of the Beleever a powerful perswasion of it, That he is a *Child* of GOD, and his GOD and *Father* will one day bring him to *Inherit all things*. The Soul of the Beleever

70. Petto, *The Voice of the Spirit*, 67–97; Samuel Rutherford, *The Covenant of Life Opened, or A Treatise of the Covenant of Grace* (Edinburgh: Andro Anderson for Robert Broun, 1655), 65ff.; William Twisse, *The Doctrine of the Synod of Dort and Arles, Reduced to the Practice* (Amsterdam: G. Thorp, 1631), 147ff.; Henry Scudder, *The Christian's Daily Walk, in Holy Security and Peace* (repr., Harrisburg, VA: Sprinkle, 1984), 338–42; Witsius, *Economy of the Covenants*, 1:465ff.; Cole, *Christ the Foundation of Our Adoption*, 357–62; Mather, *The Sealed Servants of Our God*, 16–22.

71. Heinrich Meyer, *Critical and Exegetical Hand-book to the Epistle of the Romans* (New York: Funk & Wagnalls, 1889), 316.

72. Witsius, *Economy of the Covenants*, 1:466–67.

is now wonderfully moved and melted and overpowered with such Thoughts as these; *GOD is my Father, CHRIST is my Saviour, and I have an Inheritance in the Heavens reserved for me.*[73]

However the Puritans may have varied here, they all agreed that the Spirit is essential in every aspect of adoption and assurance, and that the Spirit's testimony is always tied to, and may never contradict, the Word of God.[74] They knew that without Word and Spirit at work, all spiritual experience is counterfeit and can easily degenerate into a host of errors, such as unbiblical mysticism, excessive emotionalism, introspective bondage, or barren antinomianism.

The mature child of God, therefore, grows in the consciousness of his adoption and assurance through Word and Spirit. That growth has some ups and downs, however. Ford says:

> Of those that have this assurance and enlargement thereupon, very few or none keep it *at all times alike,* and can alike improve it on every occasion. Great sinnes, and great troubles &c. may many times cloud, and sometimes as to the act, blot out the evidence of their Adoption. Thus *David* wanted this Spirit, *Psal.* 51.11,12. A child having offended, may scarce dare call Father, whiles that guilt remains uncovered.[75]

Manton puts it succinctly: "The workman that made a thing can best warrant it to the buyer. First he [the Spirit] sanctifieth, and then he certifieth; sometimes we overlook our evidences through the darkness and confusion that is in our hearts." He goes on to say that the Spirit "helpeth us not only to see grace, but to judge of the sincerity of grace." The Spirit helps us conclude with boldness, comfort, and joy from the evidences of our lives that we are adopted sons or daughters of God. This comfort enables us to pray and embrace God's promises with freedom.[76] Those divine promises always remain the

---

73. Mather, *The Sealed Servants of Our God,* 16.
74. *Works of Thomas Manton,* 12:127; Witsius, *Economy of the Covenants,* 1:463; Petto, *The Voice of the Spirit,* 23–41.
75. Ford, *The Spirit of Bondage and Adoption,* 201.
76. *Works of Thomas Manton,* 12:128–29.

primary ground of the assurance of our adoption. The Spirit comforts us with God's promises of our adoption, and grants us grace to apply them to ourselves.[77]

Such believers are advised by the Puritans to hold fast to their profession, to grow in the grace and knowledge of Jesus Christ, to witness of the Father's goodness to others, and to lead lives of service to God and man. In short, as adopted children they should daily engage in the responsibilities and duties expounded below.

The Marks of Adoption

The Puritans gave clear marks for us to determine which family we belong to—God's or Satan's. They believed that when self-examination is undertaken biblically, the Holy Spirit often uses it as a positive transforming power in the lives of God's children.

Perkins provides six marks that may help certify one's adoption:

- An earnest and heartie desire in all things to further the glorie of God.
- A care and readiness to resigne our selues in subjection to God, to bee ruled by his word and spirit, in thought, word, and deede.
- A sincere endeauor to do his will in all things with cheerfulnesse, making conscience of euerything we know to be euill.
- Vpright walking in a mans lawfull calling, and yet still by faith to relie vpon Gods prouidence, being well pleased with Gods sending whatsoeuer it is.
- Euery day to humble a mans selfe before God for his offences, seeking his fauour in Christ vnfainedly, and so daily renuing his faith & repentance.
- A continual combate between the flesh and the spirt, corruption haling and drawing one way, and grace resisting the same & drawing another way.[78]

---

77. Ford, *The Spirit of Bondage and Adoption*, 204–5.
78. *Workes of William Perkins*, 3:154.

Roger Drake offers these marks: a spirit of faith and dependency (2 Cor. 4:13), a spirit of prayer (Acts 9:11), a spirit of evidence (Rom. 8:16), a spirit of liberty (2 Cor. 3:17), a spirit of waiting (Rom. 8:23), and a spirit of love (1 John 5:2).[79]

Mather says that we belong to God's family when we can positively answer that our only trust for salvation lies in Jesus Christ and his atoning blood, that we are effectually called by the Spirit, and that we exercise vital piety, which consists of fearing God, giving glory to him, and loving our neighbor.[80] Marshall said that we must answer such questions as these: "Is the Holy Ghost come to dwel in you to unite you to Christ? Doth the Holy Ghost work a Childs heart in you? Can you honor God, and reverence him, and turn to him? And can you walk before God as obedient Children, at least in the constant bent and tenure of your Souls?"[81]

Transformed Relationships in Adoption

The consciousness of personal adoption into God's family affects the believer's entire life. The Puritans would agree with Packer: "Sonship must be the controlling thought—the normative category, if you like—at every point."[82] Every relationship in the believer's life is transformed by it.

Christ himself is the best proof of this truth. Jesus' consciousness of his unique filial relationship with the Father controlled all of Christ's living and thinking: "I seek not mine own will, but the will of the Father which hath sent me" (John 5:30); "If I do not the works of my Father, believe me not," Jesus says in John 10:37, and "As my Father hath sent me, even so send I you" (John 20:21). Jesus likewise urges his disciples to let their thoughts and lives be controlled by the conviction that God is now their Father and they are his children, and that he knows all their needs (Matt. 6:32). The child of God is to

---

79. Drake, "The Believer's Dignity," 344.
80. Mather, *The Sealed Servants of Our God*, 9ff.
81. *Works of Stephen Marshall*, 54–55.
82. Packer, *Knowing God*, 190.

pray and to live his whole life in relation to his Father, remembering that the Father has promised each child his kingdom.

John Cotton makes plain in expounding 1 John 3 that the significance of adoption affects the following relationships:

1. *Our relationship to God* (1 John 3:1a). God's adopted children learn that the only place in the universe where true security can be found is in the household of the heavenly Father. Jesus taught his disciples this truth in many ways. He urged them to think about God's fatherly love by comparing it to the love of a human father: "If ye then, being evil, know how to give good gifts unto your children, how much more shall your Father which is in heaven give good things to them that ask him?" (Matt. 7:11).

The comparison is between the imperfect fatherhood of earthly fathers, who are evil (i.e., they have fallen natures and show flaws, failures, and sins), and the perfect fatherhood of God. God's fatherhood is flawless, despite our shortcomings that incline us to confess what Cotton says: "Surely I am not a child of God, because I find much pride in my heart, and much rebellion and corruption in my spirit. Surely if I were born of Christ, I should be like him. But what says St. John here? We are the sons of God even now, though there is much unbelief in our hearts, and much weakness and many corruptions within us."[83] Despite all this, Jesus will show us that our heavenly Father's love is expansive and glorious beyond imagination.

2. *Our relationship to the world.* The believer's adoption by God the Father also affects his relationship to the world. First John 3:1b tells us that this relationship is a troubled one: "Therefore the world knoweth us not, because it knew him not." On the one hand, the believer shares with Jesus the unspeakable love of the Father, but on the other hand, he shares with Jesus the hostility, estrangement, and even hatred of the world.

This reaction of the world is one evidence of the believer's adoption into God's family, for the world did not know Jesus either: "He

83. John Cotton, *An Exposition of First John* (repr., Evansville, IN: Sovereign Grace Publishers, 1962), 319.

came unto his own, and his own received him not" (John 1:11). He was in the world he created, but the world knew him not. The world did not recognize him as the Son of God; ultimately, it crucified him. "If God saw it meet that his Son should be thus afflicted in the world and drink of such a bitter portion of God's wrath," writes Cotton, "let us not think we shall go to heaven and partake of those heavenly mansions which Christ has prepared for us, without also drinking of the same cup that he drank of. Let us account ourselves happy that God will so esteem us as to make us his sons."[84]

3. *Our relationship to the future.* We cherish a great hope. John goes on to say, "It doth not yet appear what we shall be: but we know that, when he shall appear, we shall be like him; for we shall see him as he is" (1 John 3:2). The prospects for God's adopted family are great, for his children will receive a glorious inheritance. They cannot even imagine the extent of that inheritance. God keeps that hidden, says Cotton, so that they may (a) be like their suffering Head, (b) have their faith kept in exercise and be watchful, and (c) be tolerated to some degree in this world, for "if God should allow them to be perfectly holy in this world, the men of the world would not allow them to live among them long (Deut. 7:22)."[85]

If our present privileges as God's adopted children are so great that the world cannot grasp them, our future prospects are so glorious that even we cannot fully grasp them. As 1 Corinthians 2:9 says, "Eye hath not seen, nor ear heard, neither have entered into the heart of man, the things which God hath prepared for them that love him." Because God is our Father and we are his adopted children, we have a full inheritance awaiting us. The best is yet to be. Today we experience great blessings, despite our infirmities and sins; but one day we will be in glory, free from sin and living in perfect communion with God. Our heavenly Father keeps the best surprises for his children until the end, when he will turn all their sorrow into joy.

84. Ibid., 318.
85. Ibid., 320–21.

4. *Our relationship to ourselves.* The children of the heavenly Father embrace his will and purpose for them. Every adopted child of God also knows that holiness is an important part of God's purpose for his happiness in God's family. First John 3:3 says, "Every man that hath this hope in him purifieth himself, even as he is pure." Cotton draws this doctrine from that text: "Every child of God has hope in Christ, to be made like him at his appearing." That hope is "a patient, certain, and grounded expectation of all those promises in Christ which by faith we believe to belong to us." God gives this hope through the means of grace so that we "might not be tossed and hurried up and down the world."[86]

So we are to purify ourselves daily, using Christ as our pattern. Holiness means putting off everything that is dishonoring to our Father, who has loved us, and to the Savior, who has died to save us. It means putting on "mercies, kindness, humbleness of mind, meekness, [and] longsuffering" (Col. 3:12). Purifying ourselves involves "the whole man," says Cotton, including what we do with our minds, affections, will, thoughts, tongue, eyes, hands, disappointments, injuries, and enemies.[87] Purifying ourselves involves loving all that the Father loves and hating all that the Father hates. From the moment of conversion to the time we take our final breath, we have one pursuit: to purify ourselves before our Father in order to be more like Christ.

5. *Our relationship to the church as the family of God.* As God's adopted sons and daughters, we have been placed in a great family. If we rightly understand this, our attitude toward our brothers and sisters in the family of God will be profoundly affected (1 John 3:14–18). We have not been adopted to live apart from that family, but to live within its network of relationships. God's purpose in adopting children is to create a family in which Christ will be glorified as the firstborn among many brethren. He wants the love that exists between the Father and the Son and the Holy Spirit to be extended through the love between brothers and sisters in Christ. As Cotton

86. Ibid., 327–29.
87. Ibid., 331.

says, "The sons of God ought to be the men of our love and delight (3 John 1, 2, 5; 1 Pet. 2:11; Phil. 4:1)."[88]

The way we behave toward other Christians proves whether or not we are adopted children of God (1 John 3:14–15). We are to love fellow adoptees of God, Cotton says, because of (a) "God's singular love to them," (b) "their love to God," and (c) "the truth that is in every Christian believer (2 John 1, 2)."[89]

Those who have experienced much love from him cannot help but love others. As Cotton concludes, "The lack of love to any of our brethren is a sign of abiding in the state of damnation, or in an unregenerate and carnal state."[90]

Privileges and Benefits of Adoption

The Puritans spend more time expounding what are variously called the privileges, liberties, benefits, blessings, or rights of adoption than any other aspect of adoption. This is also evident in the Westminster Confession of Faith, chapter 12, and the Larger Catechism, question 74, where more than half the material on adoption is devoted to a listing of these "liberties and privileges," each of which the Spirit uses to exercise his transforming power and comfort in the lives of God's children.

The overarching privilege can best be summarized as *heirship*. God's adopted children are all royal heirs apparent and coheirs with Christ (Rom. 8:16–17). "Men may have many children yet but one is an heir," writes Burroughs. "But all the children of God are heirs."[91] Hebrews 12:23 calls them "firstborn" heirs.

The Puritans make much of joint heirship with Christ. As coheirs with Christ, believers share in Christ's kingship, and therefore partake of the kingdom of heaven as their inheritance. Believers are made kings of the Father in his spiritual kingdom in three respects, writes Thomas Granger. "1. Because they are Lords and Conquerors

88. Ibid., 316.
89. Ibid., 317.
90. Ibid., 372.
91. Burroughs, *The Saints' Happiness*, 192.

94

of their enemies, Sinne, Satan, the World, Death, Hell. 2. They are partakers of the kingdome of Christ and of saluation; for wee haue receiued of Christ grace for grace, and glorie for glorie. 3. They haue interest, dominion, and soueraigntie of all things by Christ."[92] Witsius stresses that this "all things" includes the right of "possession of the whole world," which was given to but lost by Adam (Gen. 1:28; 3:24), promised to Abraham (Rom. 4:13), and repurchased by Christ "for himself and his brethren" (Ps. 8:6), so that now all things, both present and to come, are his people's.[93] Ultimately, believers are lords and possessors of all things because they belong to Christ, who belongs to God (1 Cor. 3:21–23).[94]

Nothing in this world can match the inheritance of believers. It knows no *corruption* (1 Peter 1:4)—not "by outward principles, as fire, violence, &c.; nor by inward principles, as sin and other taints which defile" (1 Peter 1:18). It has no *succession.* The heavenly Father and his children always live out of the same inheritance, so believers' inheritance is as unchangeable as Christ's priesthood is (Heb. 7:24). It faces no *division.* Every heir enjoys the whole inheritance, since God is both "infinite and indivisible." "God gives his all, not half, but his whole kingdom" (Gen. 25:5; Rev. 21:7).[95]

Specific blessings that accrue for us as believers from his divine inheritance and spiritual adoption include the most wonderful privileges one could ever imagine, both in this world and in the world to come. Here is a summary of them, drawn from the Puritans:

1. Our Father cuts us off from the family to which we naturally belong in Adam as children of wrath and of the devil, and engrafts us into his own family to make us members of the covenant family of God. "Adoption translates us out of a Miserable estate, into a Happy estate," writes Cole. "God is in covenant with us, and we in him."[96] By nature, Marshall says, we are "Children of wrath, Children of *Belial*, Children of old *Adam*, Children of Sin and Death, we are

---

92. Granger, *A Looking-Glasse for Christians*, 26.
93. Witsius, *Economy of the Covenants*, 1:452–53.
94. *Workes of William Perkins*, 1:82, 369.
95. Drake, "The Believer's Dignity," 334; cf. *Works of John Owen*, 2:218–21, and Burroughs, *The Saints' Happiness*, 196.
96. Cole, *Christ the Foundation of Our Adoption*, 351.

cut off from that Family, no longer to be reckoned of it, [or of its] Bondage, Baseness, Obligations, Curses," and are "taken into Gods Family as his Sons and Daughters, that is, . . . he hath ingaged himself perpetually forever" to us, so that this family relationship will last forever (John 8:35).[97]

2. Our Father gives us freedom to call on him by his "Father" name and gives us a new name, which serves as our guarantee of admission to the house of God as sons and daughters of God (Rev. 2:17; 3:12). We are a peculiar people—his people, called by his name (2 Chron. 7:14). That means, says Boston, that our "old name is for ever laid aside. [We] are no more called children of the devil, but the sons and daughters of God" (Heb. 12:5).[98] Cotton goes a step further, expressly saying that this name is "Adoption": "[We] have this white Stone, that is Absolicall for sin, and in that a new name written, that is, Adoption: and if we be of a meek, humble, innocent, frame of mind, we have this comfort."[99] By the Spirit of adoption, we have access to God as a reconciled Father through Christ. We have liberty to call God "Father," which "is more worth than a thousand worlds" (Jer. 3:4).[100]

3. Our Father gifts us with the Spirit of adoption. Believers are, by grace, partakers of the Holy Spirit. This Spirit, Burroughs tells us, enlightens our minds, sanctifies our hearts, makes God's wisdom and will known to us, guides us to eternal life—yes, works the entire work of salvation in us and seals it to us unto the day of redemption (Eph. 4:30).[101]

Willard writes that the Spirit "ratifies our Sonship to be immutable, and confirms our title to all the Promises irreversible. As such a Spirit, he gives his testimony in us, to ratify all our evidences, and fully assure us of our Sonship and Heirship."[102]

97. *Works of Stephen Marshall*, 50–51.
98. *Works of Thomas Boston*, 1:624.
99. Quoted in Jesper Rosenmeir, " 'Clearing the Medium': A Reevaluation of the Puritan Plain Style in Light of John Cotton's *A Practicall Commentary upon the First Epistle Generall of John*," *William and Mary Quarterly* 37, no. 4 (1980): 582.
100. *Works of Thomas Boston*, 1:623.
101. Burroughs, *The Saints' Happiness*, 196.
102. Willard, *A Compleat Body of Divinity*, 489.

4. Our Father grants us likeness to himself and his Son. The Father imparts to his children a filial heart and disposition resembling his own. Drake writes, "All God's adopted children bear their Father's image, as Gideon's brethren did his (Judg. 8:18). They are like God, in holiness [and] in dignity" (Matt. 5:44–45; Rom. 8:29; Heb. 2:7; 1 John 3:2–3).[103]

Cole writes similarly from a Christological perspective: "Christ is formed in them all, *Gal.* 4.19. As Christ is, so are they, each one resembles the children of a King, *Judg.* 8.18. They will be exactly like Christ at the Resurrection, *Psal.* 17.15. *They were from Eternity predestinated unto this, Rom.* 8.29."[104] Burgess reminds us that this includes the privilege of being "made conformable unto Christ in his sufferings" (Phil. 1:29).[105]

5. Our Father especially strengthens our faith through his gifts of promises and prayer. "If we are adopted," writes Watson, "then we have an interest in all the promises: the promises are children's bread." They are like a garden, Watson goes on to say, in which some herb is found to cure every ailment.[106] Or, as William Spurstowe put it, God's promises are like a bag full of coins that God unties and pours out at the feet of his adopted children, saying, "Take what you will."[107]

Concerning prayer, we are given limitless access to our heavenly Father. Children have the right of access to their father, no matter how busy or important he is—even if he is president of the nation. So in the New Testament, adopted sons are encouraged to come boldly to the throne of grace through the God-man Savior at any time to find grace and mercy to help in time of need (Heb. 4:14–16), notwithstanding the exaltedness of their God.

The Spirit teaches us that the Father in heaven is more pleased to see his adopted children come through the door of prayer into his throne room than we are pleased to see our children come through the

---

103. Drake, "The Believer's Dignity," 333.

104. Cole, *Christ the Foundation of Our Adoption*, 350; cf. Burroughs, *The Saints' Happiness*, 195–96.

105. Burgess, *Spiritual Refining*, 242.

106. Watson, *A Body of Divinity*, 160.

107. William Spurstowe, *The Wells of Salvation Opened: or A Treatise Discovering the Nature, Preciousness, and Usefulness, of the Gospel Promises, and Rules for the Right Application of Them* (London: T. R. & E. M. for Ralph Smith, 1655), 34ff.

door into our living room. Willard writes that the Spirit "enlivens" the faith of believers, enabling them "to go to God as a Father, and claim this relation, and upon the claim, believingly to plead with him for the acceptance of their persons, the audience of their Prayers, the granting of their requests, and supplying of all their wants" (Rom. 8:15).[108]

6. Our Father corrects and chastens us for our sanctification. "He chasteneth, and scourgeth every son whom he receiveth" (Heb. 12:6). All chastisements involve discipline that comes from our Father's hand and works together for our best welfare (2 Sam. 7:14; Ps. 89:32–33; Rom. 8:28, 36–37; 2 Cor. 12:7). Our sufferings are "for our education and instruction in his family," writes Owen;[109] or, as Willard puts it, "All our afflictions are helps toward heaven." They contribute to the "increase of their eternal glory: every reproach and injury doth but add weight to their Crown."[110] We foolishly think that God chastens us to destroy us, but 1 Corinthians 11:32 teaches us, "We are chastened of the Lord, that we should not be condemned with the world."[111]

God's chastenings are badges of our sonship and of the Father's love (Heb. 12:3–11). They are meant only for believers in this life. Owen says, "There is no chastisement in heaven, nor in hell. Not in heaven, because there is no sin; not in hell, because there is no amendment."[112]

7. Our Father comforts us with his love and pity, and moves us to rejoice in intimate communion with him and his Son (Rom. 5:5). He does that in several ways, as Willard notes: "He applies the precious promises to their souls, he gives them cordials of comfort, communicates unto them the sips and foretasts of glory, [and] fills them with inward joyes and refreshings."[113] The Father commends and encourages us even for the smallest act of obedience.[114] He comforts us in accord with the afflictions he has measured out for us.[115]

---

108. Willard, *The Child's Portion*, 21.
109. *Works of John Owen*, 24:257.
110. Willard, *The Child's Portion*, 28.
111. *Workes of William Perkins*, 1:82; see also Willard, *The Child's Portion*, 18–19; Granger, *A Looking-Glasse for Christians*, [31–32].
112. *Works of John Owen*, 24:260.
113. Willard, *The Child's Portion*, 22.
114. Ibid., 19.
115. *Workes of William Perkins*, 1:369.

How precious, then, is the love of the heavenly Father toward his children! Burroughs writes, "God, who is the infinite glorious first-being, embraces them with an entire fatherly love. All the love that ever was in any parents towards children, is but as one drop of the infinite ocean of fatherly love that there is in God unto his people."[116]

8. Our Father offers us spiritual, Christian liberty as his sons and daughters (John 8:36). This liberty releases us from bondage (Gal. 4:7). It delivers us from the slavish subjection, the servile pedagogy, the condemning power, the intolerable yoke, and the thundering curses of the law as a covenant of works (Gal. 3:13), though not from the law's regulating power.[117] We are not dependent on our obedience to the law for our justification and happiness (Rom. 3:28), but as sons of God—not mercenaries—we obey the law as "a service of love."[118]

Christian liberty delivers us from the impugning, condemning, and reigning power of sin (Rom. 6:12; 8:1; 2 Cor. 5:21), making possible the enjoyment of peace with God as his children. But that liberty must not be abused. As Cole writes, "'Tis a dangerous thing to speak too freely of Christian Liberty, because many under that pretence, allow themselves in very unwarrantable courses, running into excess, laying aside all Moderation."[119]

Spiritual liberty delivers us from the world and all its powerful temptations, persecutions, and threatenings (1 John 5:4). It delivers us from the bondage of Satan, from hypocrisy and anxiety, and from the traditions of men, so that we may freely bind ourselves to the teaching of God. It grants us liberty to live transparently before God, to serve and love God and his ways with heart, mind, and strength (Ps. 18:1), so that we gladly take his yoke upon us and serve him with filial obedience each day (1 Peter 1:14), confessing, "This is my Father's world."[120]

9. Our Father preserves us and keeps us from falling (Ps. 91:11–12; 1 Peter 1:5). He restores us from every backsliding way, recovering

---

116. Burroughs, *The Saints' Happiness*, 194.
117. *Works of Thomas Boston*, 1:625; Cole, *Christ the Foundation of Our Adoption*, 352–53.
118. Burroughs, *The Saints' Happiness*, 194.
119. Cole, *Christ the Foundation of Our Adoption*, 355.
120. Willard, *The Child's Portion*, 23–27.

and humbling us, always preventing our hypocrisy.[121] Willard says, "Gods Sons in this life are like little Children, always tripping, and stumbling, and falling, and so weak that they could never get up again but for him: but by reasons of his hand that is upon them, his everlasting Arm that is under them."[122]

10. Our Father provides everything that we need as his children, both physically and spiritually (Ps. 34:10; Matt. 6:31–33), and will protect us from all harm. He will defend us from our enemies—Satan, the world, and our own flesh—and right our wronged cause. He will assist and strengthen us, always lending us a helping hand to carry us through every difficulty and temptation (2 Tim. 4:17). We may safely leave everything in his fatherly hands, knowing that he will never leave us nor forsake us (Heb. 13:5–6). We are children under our Father's special inspection and care (1 Peter 5:7) for the entirety of our earthly pilgrimage, "sealed to the day of redemption"[123] in glory, where we will be beyond all danger (Rev. 21:25).[124]

11. Our Father gives his angels, as ministering spirits, to serve us for good (Ps. 34:7; Heb. 1:14).[125] They guard us and watch for us. Willard calls them "tutelary Angels" who guard and defend us from evil and watch for our good (Ps. 91:11).[126] "They pitch their tents round about [believers], *Psal.* 34.1, they bring down messages of peace from heaven, even answers of their Prayers, *Dan.* 9.23, strengthen and confirm them in their secret conflicts, *Luk.* 22.43, and when they come to die, they are a convoy to carry their Souls home to eternal rest, *Luk.* 16.22."[127]

Responsibilities or Duties of Adoption

The Puritans taught that every privilege of adoption had a corresponding responsibility or duty, each of which transforms the way believers think and live. These may be summarized as follows:

121. Ridgley, *Commentary on the Larger Catechism*, 136.
122. Willard, *The Child's Portion*, 17.
123. Westminster Confession of Faith, chap. 12.
124. Willard, *The Child's Portion*, 16–18; *Works of Thomas Boston*, 625.
125. *Workes of William Perkins*, 1:83, 369.
126. Willard, *The Child's Portion*, 27–28.
127. Granger, *A Looking-Glasse for Christians*, [30–31].

1. Show childlike reverence and love for your Father in everything. Reflect habitually upon your Father's great glory and majesty. Stand in awe of him; render him praise and thanksgiving in all things. Remember, your holy Father sees everything. Children sometimes commit dreadful acts in the absence of their parents, but your Father is never absent. Burgess explains:

> *There is nothing done in secret, but thy Father seeth it.* There is no heart-pride, no heart-earthlynesse, but thy Father seeth it. There is never a time thou prayest, hearest the word, but thy Father seeth with what form of Spirit it is. Oh therefore if thou art a Son of God, thou wilt discover it in thy whole carriage: a Son feareth the frowns of his Father; I dare not do this; my father will be offended; and I, Whither shall I go? Thus the Apostle Peter, *If ye call him Father, passe your sojourning here with fear,* 1 Pet. 1.17.[128]

Let childlike reverence overflow in love to your Father—a love that constrains you to employ all the means of grace, to obey his commands, and to work for him. Burroughs writes, "Do all you do out of love, be not mercenary. A servant doth not care to do anything any further than he may be paid for it, but a child doth not so; he doth what he doth out of love."[129]

2. Submit to your Father in every providence. When he visits you with the rod, don't resist or murmur. Don't immediately respond by saying, " 'I am not a child of God, God is not my Father, God deals harshly with me; if He were my Father, He would have compassion on me; He would then deliver me from this grievous and especially this sinful cross'—to speak thus does not befit the nature of an upright child," writes Brakel. Rather, "it is fitting for a child to be quiet, to humbly submit, and to say, 'I will bear the indignation of the LORD, because I have sinned against him' " (Mic. 7:9).[130]

---

128. Burgess, *Spiritual Refining*, 239.
129. Burroughs, *The Saints' Happiness*, 199.
130. Brakel, *The Christian's Reasonable Service*, 2:437.

Burgess says, "If thou hadst a Child-like disposition, thou wouldst say, although all I feel be bitter, yet he is a Father still. I have been an ill Child, and this makes him a Good Father in chastising."[131]

3. *Obey and imitate your Father, and love his image-bearers.* Strive to be like him, to be holy as he is holy, to be loving as he is loving. We are to be "imitators of God" (Eph. 5:1 ESV) to show that we bear the family likeness.

We are, then, to love the Father's image wherever we see it. Willard writes, "The Saints are living Images of the Lord, we may see in them, not only the likeness to, but the shining reflection of his communicated perfections: Hence we should love the Saints."[132] We are to live as God's children in mutual love and patience with each other, having the same Father, Elder Brother, and indwelling Spirit. "It is enough that the children of the world wrangle one with another and fight; let not those that profess God to be their Father, oh let them not in the presence of their Father wrangle and fight one with another, for certainly the Spirit of God cannot bear it," Burroughs concludes.[133]

4. *Resist every hindrance that keeps you from relishing your Father's adopting grace.* Ford lists these hindrances:

- A secret *murmuring* frame of spirit against Gods present dispensations towards thee.
- A kind of *delight in complaining* against thy self, and taking Satans part many times in bearing false witness against thy own soul.
- An *unthankful denyal* of the works of Gods sanctifying spirit in the heart.
- An unwarrantable *thrusting off* those promises and comfortable truths which God in the Ministry of the Word or otherwise brings home to our condition.

131. Burgess, *Spiritual Refining*, 239.
132. Willard, *The Child's Portion*, 43.
133. Burroughs, *The Saints' Happiness*, 200.

- A groundlesse *surmising* of an irrecoverablenesse in our condition from such and such *threatenings of Scripture* as con-
  cerne us not.
- *Keeping Satans counsel.*
- Secret *tempting of God*, and *dependence* upon such means and
  such men for *peace*, and *limiting* God to such and such a
  time, and *resolving* not to wait on God beyond that time, or
  not to expect it from any other meanes.
- A sinfull *ambition of self-preparations* for comfort and peace:
  were I so much humbled, saith the poor soul, so kindly and
  ingenuously affected with my sins; could I recover of this
  deadnesse, and flatness of spirit into any measure of liveli-
  nesse and spiritualnesse in my performances; then I would
  believe comfort, and assurance of Gods love belonged to
  me.
- Giving too much way to *prejudices against God*, and his love,
  from *present sense and feeling*.
- *Slacknesse* and *remissnesse in* (occasioned by successelesse-
  nesse of) Ordinances and Duties.
- *Over-scrupulousnesse, and scepticall-question-fulnesse.*[134]

5. *Rejoice in being in your Father's presence.* Delight in communing
with him. Burgess writes, "A Son delights to have letters from
his Father, to have discourse about him, especially to enjoy his
presence."[135]

In heaven, this joy will be full; our adoption will then be perfected
(Rom. 8:23). Then we will enter into the Father's "presence and
palace," where we will be "everlastingly enjoying, delighting, and
praising God."[136] Let us wait and long for that time, as children who
eagerly anticipate our full inheritance, when the triune God will be
our all in all.[137]

---

134. Ford, *The Spirit of Bondage and Adoption*, 258–87.
135. Burgess, *Spiritual Refining*, 240.
136. *Works of Thomas Manton*, 12:125.
137. Drake, "The Believer's Dignity," 342; cf. Willard, *The Child's Portion*, 71.

Concluding Applications

The classic Puritan statement on adoption in the Westminster Standards leaves much unsaid. Trumper makes a case for its being insufficiently Pauline, insufficiently pervasive, and insufficiently redemptive-historical.[138] Though the first two of these concerns are adequately addressed in Puritan literature, the Puritans are by no means exhaustive in their doctrine of spiritual adoption. For example, they have not adequately addressed the centrality of sonship in biblical doctrine or as an organizing principle for understanding salvation along the lines that Ferguson suggests.[139]

Nevertheless, the Puritans teach us a great deal more about spiritual adoption and its transforming power than has been acknowledged. They teach us the importance of fleeing from sin and pursuing a conscious sense of our adoption.[140] They show us, as Packer helpfully summarizes, that our adoption helps us better grasp the ministry of the Holy Spirit, the power of gospel holiness, our own assurance of faith, the solidity of the Christian family, and the glory of the Christian hope.[141]

The Puritans also warn us of the danger of remaining a member of Satan's family—especially while under the means of grace. "Many a gospel-call has sounded in your ears, sinner," writes Boston; "hast thou not come away on the call? Then thou art yet a child of the devil, Acts xiii. 10. and therefore an heir of hell and of wrath." When the unbeliever objects, Boston responds: "Whose image dost thou bear? Holiness is God's image, unholiness the devil's. Thy dark heart and unholy life plainly tell the family thou art of."[142]

As strongly as the Puritans admonish, so strongly they invite. Willard writes, "What do you think of it, who have been often invited in the Gospel to embrace [Christ]? Will not [adoption] present him before

138. Trumper, "An Historical Study of the Doctrine of Adoption in the Calvinistic Tradition," 238–48.

139. Cf. Ferguson, "The Reformed Doctrine of Sonship," in *Pulpit and People: Essays in Honour of William Still on His 75th Birthday*, ed. Nigel M. de S. Cameron and Sinclair B. Ferguson (Edinburgh: Rutherford House, 1986), 84–87.

140. *Workes of William Perkins*, 3:205.

141. Packer, *Knowing God*, 198–207.

142. *Works of Thomas Boston*, 1:627; cf. Mather, *The Sealed Servants of Our God*, 23–28.

you as one worth the entertaining? Receive him by a true Faith, and he will make you, not only Friends, but Children unto God."[143]

Above all, the Puritans use the truth of adoption as a sower to transform God's needy children through powerful comforts. Thomas Hooker shows how adoption comforts them in the face of the sight and sense of the contempt of the world and their own unworthiness, outward poverty, infirmities, afflictions, persecutions, and dangers.[144] When oppressed with sin, buffeted by Satan, enticed by the world, or alarmed by fears of death, believers are encouraged by the Puritans to take refuge in their precious heavenly Father, saying with Willard, "Am I not still a Child? And if so, then I am sure, that though he correct me (and I deserve it, nor will I refuse to submit my self patiently unto it) yet he cannot take away his loving kindness from me."[145]

Willard concludes: "Be always comforting of your selves with the thoughts of your Adoption: Draw your comforts at this tap, fetch your consolations from this relation; be therefore often chewing upon the precious priviledges of it, and make them your rejoicing. Let this joy out-strip the verdure of every other joy. Let this joy dispel the mists of every sorrow, and clear up your souls in the midst of all troubles and difficulties" as you await heavenly glory, where you will live out your perfect adoption by forever communing with the triune God. There you will "dwel at the fountain, and swim for ever in those bankless, and bottomless Oceans of Glory."[146]

---

143. Willard, *The Child's Portion*, 34–42; cf. Mather, *The Sealed Servants of Our God*, 28–36.
    144. Hooker, *The Christians Tvvo Chiefe Lessons*, 170–74.
    145. Willard, *The Child's Portion*, 51–52.
    146. Ibid., 54, 66–70.

4

The Benefits of Christ: Double Justification in Protestant Theology before the Westminster Assembly

R. Scott Clark

Question 57 of the Westminster Larger Catechism asks, "What benefits hath Christ procured by his mediation?" The answer is that "Christ, by his mediation, hath procured redemption, with all other benefits of the covenant of grace."[1] This essay pursues what the West-minster divines meant by the phrase "benefits of the covenant of grace." What is the background for this phrase, and how should it be interpreted? Did it signal a turn away from the earlier Protestant doctrine of justification?

This essay interprets the language of the Larger Catechism by placing it in the broader context of the development of the Protestant doctrine of justification in the sixteenth century. It argues that when the divines spoke of the "benefits of the covenant of grace," they were giving expression to the Protestant doctrine of double justification as it had been taught by the magisterial Protestant theologians (e.g., Martin Luther, Philipp Melanchthon, Martin Bucer, and John Calvin) and the Reformed orthodox following them.

1. *The Humble Advice of the Assembly of Divines . . . concerning a Larger Catechisme* (London, 1648), 8.

R. Scott Clark

Introduction

It is clear from the Book of Concord (1580) and the *Harmony of the Reformed Confessions* (1581) that by the late sixteenth century, there was virtual unanimity among confessional Protestants on the basics of the doctrine of justification.[2] Whereas, since the Second Council of Orange (A.D. 529) it had been a given that one is justified only to the extent that one is sanctified, the magisterial Protestants rejected the doctrine of progressive justification in favor of a punctiliar, definitive doctrine of justification on the grounds of the imputed righteousness of Christ received through trust in Christ alone. Some older scholarship at least, represented by R. Seeburg, B. B. Warfield, and the more recent scholarship of T. H. L. Parker, Berndt Hamm, François Wendel, W. Stanford Reid, David Steinmetz, and Brian Gerrish, held that this pan-Protestant doctrine of justification by imputation had its roots in Luther.[3]

According to some recent scholarship, however, the Protestant consensus on the forensic doctrine of justification should not be traced to Luther or Calvin. Further, some writers do not find a pan-Protestant doctrine of justification; and some who find agreement, for example,

2. E.g., Augsburg Confession art. 4, Apology art. 4, Epitome art. 3, and Solid Declaration art. 3, in Robert Kolb and Timothy J. Wengert, eds., *The Book of Concord*, trans. Charles Arand et al. (Minneapolis: Fortress Press, 2000); Jean François Salvard, ed., *Harmonia Confessionum Fidei* . . . (Geneva, 1581), sec. 9; Jean François Salvard, ed., *An Harmony of the Confessions of the Faith* . . . , trans. Peter Hall (Cambridge, 1586).
3. R. Seeburg, *Textbook of the History of Doctrines*, trans. Charles E. Hay, 2 vols. (Philadelphia: Lutheran Publication Society), 2:392–93, 402–5; B. B. Warfield, *Calvin and Augustine*, ed. S. G. Craig (Philadelphia: Presbyterian and Reformed, 1956), 489–90; T. H. L. Parker, "Calvin's Doctrine of Justification," *The Evangelical Quarterly* 25 (1952): 101–7; Berndt Hamm, "What Was the Reformation Doctrine of Justification?" in C. Scott Dixon, ed., *The German Reformation: The Essential Readings* (Oxford: Blackwell, 1999); François Wendel, *Calvin: The Origins and Development of His Religious Thought*, trans. Philip Mairet (London: Collins, 1963), 255–63; W. Stanford Reid, "Justification by Faith According to John Calvin," *Westminster Theological Journal* 42 (1980): 290–307; David Steinmetz, *Calvin in Context* (New York and Oxford: Oxford University Press, 1995), 117–18; B. A. Gerrish, "John Calvin on Martin Luther," in J. Pelikan, ed., *Interpreters of Luther: Essays in Honor of Wilhelm Pauck* (Philadelphia: Fortress Press, 1968), 69. See also Joseph Wawrykow, "John Calvin and Condign Merit," *Archiv für Reformationsgeschichte* 83 (1992): 74–75, who argues that Calvin and Luther fundamentally agreed on forensic justification. These views are in contrast to that of Adolph von Harnack, who argued that Melanchthon and other "*epigones*" of Luther "abandoned the '*sola fides*' doctrine" in favor of "synergism." See Adolph von Harnack, *History of Dogma*, trans. Neil Buchanan, 7 vols. (New York: Dover Publications, 1961), 7:256.

between Luther and Calvin argue that they taught justification by union with Christ, not by imputation.

The revisionist account comes from several quarters. The new Finnish interpretation of Luther advocated by Tuomo Mannermaa and others claims that Luther did not teach a forensic soteriology, but rather *theosis* or divinization.[4] Mannermaa argues that, for Luther, there was no real distinction between justification and sanctification.[5] Stephen Strehle has argued that the concept of forensic justification came not from Luther but from Melanchthon's adaptation of nominalism beginning in his 1532 commentary on Romans. In this view, for Luther and Calvin, the ground of justification was not imputation of an alien righteousness, but union with Christ.[6]

Craig B. Carpenter argues that Calvin's reply to session 6 of Trent turned to union with Christ rather than to imputation. Carl Mosser claims that because of ignorance of Patristic theology and the undue influence of Adolph von Harnack, scholars have overlooked Calvin's doctrine of *theosis* through union with Christ. Following on, Julie Canlis writes that Calvin's reaction to Andreas Osiander has blinded interpreters to his own interest in deification through union with Christ.[7]

Certainly this chapter cannot address all the issues raised by the literature, but the revisionists raise two major questions: whether there

4. Tuomo Mannermaa, "Why Is Luther So Fascinating? Modern Finnish Luther Research," in Carl E. Braaten and Robert W. Jenson, eds., *Union with Christ: The New Finnish Interpretation of Luther* (Grand Rapids: Eerdmans, 1998), 6.

5. Tuomo Mannermaa, "Justification and Theosis in Lutheran-Orthodox Perspective," in *Union with Christ*, 38. For a response to the Finnish School, see Carl R. Trueman, "Is the Finnish Line a New Beginning? A Critical Assessment of the Reading of Luther Offered by the Helsinki Circle," *Westminster Theological Journal* 65 (2003): 231–44; R. Scott Clark, "*Iustitia Imputata Christi*: Alien or Proper to Luther's Doctrine of Justification?" *Concordia Theological Quarterly* (forthcoming, 2007).

6. Stephen Strehle, "*Imputatio iustitiae*: Its Origin in Melanchthon, Its Opposition in Osiander," *Theologische Zeitschrift* 50 (1994): 201–19; see also Mark Seifrid, "Paul, Luther, and Justification in Galatians 2:15–21," *Westminster Theological Journal* 65 (2003): 215–30.

7. Craig B. Carpenter, "A Question of Union with Christ: Calvin and Trent on Justification," *Westminster Theological Journal* 64 (2002): 363–86; Carl Mosser, "The Greatest Possible Blessing: Calvin and Deification," *Scottish Journal of Theology* 55 (2002): 36–57; Julie Canlis, "Calvin, Osiander and Participation in God," *International Journal of Systematic Theology* 6 (2004): 169–84. As a provisional response, one might ask whether Mosser and Canlis are reading Calvin's doctrine of union in isolation from his doctrines of God and man, which, for Calvin, were logically prior and which conditioned his soteriology.

was a pan-Protestant doctrine of justification, that is, whether it is correct to think of Luther, Melanchthon, Bucer, and Calvin as teaching essentially the same doctrine of justification; and, if so, whether that doctrine was justification by imputation or by sanctification (e.g., union with Christ) or both. This essay argues against the revisionist approach and in favor of that reading of the Reformation holding that Luther, Melanchthon, Bucer, Calvin, and the Reformed orthodox (including the Westminster Assembly) taught essentially the same doctrine of justification grounded on Christ's righteousness imputed and that each of them related their doctrine of justification closely to their doctrine of sanctification through the use of the doctrine of double justice (*duplex iustitia*).

This is a particularly interesting test case, since some (e.g., Jonathan Rainbow and Peter A. Lillback) have seen Calvin's doctrine of double justification as a point of departure from Luther, others have seen Bucer's doctrine of justification as a departure from Luther (David F. Wright and Wilhelm Pauck), some (von Harnack) have found Melanchthon abandoning Luther, and still others have found in Luther's doctrine of double justice evidence that he did not really teach justification *coram Deo* by imputation (the new Finnish school).[8] If we find them teaching substantially the same doctrine of justification by imputation there, then we may conclude that the case is not yet made that there was no pan-Protestant consensus on justification or that the magisterial Protestants were more committed to justification by sanctification than by imputation.

Duplex Iustitia at Regensburg

Despite formal similarities with various Roman formulations of double justice and despite the agreement at Regensburg (April 27–May 22, 1541), Luther, Bucer, and Calvin all used the doctrine

---

8. Jonathan Rainbow, "Double Grace: John Calvin's View of the Relationship between Justification and Sanctification," *Ex Auditu* 5 (1989): 101–2; Peter A. Lillback, *The Binding of God* (Grand Rapids: Baker, 2001), 190–93; D. F. Wright, "Martin Bucer 1491–1551: Ecumenical Theologian," in D. F. Wright, ed., *Common Places of Martin Bucer* (Abingdon, Berkshire: Sutton Courtenay Press, 1971), 21, 43.

duplex iustitia, duplex iustificatio, or *duplex beneficium* to express the Protestant dogma concerning justification.[9]

By 1518, having rejected the medieval consensus of progressive justification, Luther still faced the question of how to relate justification and sanctification. Having denied progressive justification, the Protestants had to provide a coherent explanation for the positive role of sanctification in Christian theology and living. The theological function of *duplex iustitia* for Luther, *duplex iustificatio* for Bucer, and *duplex beneficium* for Calvin was to unite justification and sanctification without confusing them.

In the sixteenth century, a number of Roman and Protestant theologians taught versions of double justice. Johannes Gropper (1503–59), Gasparo Contarini (1483–1542), and Albert Pighius (ca. 1490–1542) were among its leading Roman proponents.[10] Indeed, the doctrine of double justice figured prominently in the Tridentine deliberations on the doctrine of justification (1546).[11] Among the Protestants, Luther

9. On the continuing relevance of *duplex iustitia*, see Walter von Loewenich, *Duplex Iustitia: Luthers Stellung zu einer Unionsformel des 16. Jahrhunderts* (Wiesbaden: Franz Steiner Verlag, 1972); James McCue, "Double Justification at the Council of Trent: Piety and Theology in Sixteenth Century Roman Catholicism," in *Piety, Politics, and Ethics*, vol. 3 of Carter Lindberg, ed., *Sixteenth Century Essays and Studies* (Kirksville, MO: Sixteenth Century Studies, 1984), 39; E. Yarnold, "*Duplex Iustitia*: The Sixteenth Century and the Twentieth," in G. R. Evans, ed., *Christian Authority: Essays in Honour of Henry Chadwick* (Oxford: Oxford University Press, 1988), 222–23; Mark Noll, "The History of an Encounter: Roman Catholics and Evangelicals," in Charles Colson and R. J. Neuhaus, eds., *Evangelicals and Catholics Together: Toward a Common Mission* (Dallas: Word, 1995), 85, 101; *Union with Christ*.

10. In his *Enchiridion* (1538), Gropper had taught that one is justified by an infusion of divine justice (*iustitia inhaerens*), which would lead to the addition of further justice through sanctification (*iustitia acquisita*). Yet he was prepared to accept Melanchthon's definition of imputation as an addition to his own doctrine of justification. Gropper's doctrine of *duplex iustitia* developed from circa 1538 to 1544 to include imputation and infusion of justice. See Yarnold, "*Duplex Iustitia*," 208–9. In his *Epistola de Iustificatione* (1541), Contarini propounded a scheme that attempted to synthesize Gropper's and Bucer's view. He defined "*iustificari*" to mean "to be made just and therefore also to be considered just." See Yarnold, "*Duplex Iustitia*," 211; G. *Contareni Cardinalis Opera* (Paris, 1571), 588.

11. On the question of the development of the doctrine of double justice generally, see also Basil Hall, "The Colloquies between Catholics and Protestants, 1539–41," in G. J. Cuming and D. Baker, eds., *Councils and Assemblies* (Cambridge: Cambridge University Press, 1971); A. E. McGrath, *Iustitia Dei: A History of the Christian Doctrine of Justification*, 2 vols. (Cambridge: Cambridge University Press, 1986), 2:54–86; Carl E. Maxcey, "Double Justice, Diego Laynez, and the Council of Trent," *Church History* 48 (1979): 269–78; Peter Matheson, *Cardinal Contarini at Regensburg* (Oxford: Oxford University Press, 1972); Anthony N. S. Lane, *Justification by Faith in Catholic-Protestant Dialogue: An Evangelical Assessment* (London and New York: T&T Clark, 2002), 46–60. On the discussion of *duplex iustitia* at Trent, see Hubert

(1483–1546), Melanchthon (1497–1560), Bucer (1491–1551), and Calvin (1509–64) all made use of the language of double justice. The Roman and Protestant doctrines of double justice met most famously at Regensburg in 1541.

When Charles V convened the Imperial Reichstag and a theological conference at Regensburg, he was threatened by France to his west and Muslim armies to his east. He needed a unified empire, and to get that he needed at least a formal resolution of the chief issue of the Reformation, the question of justification.[12]

In attendance at Regensburg were some of the greatest and most interesting theologians of the sixteenth century. Among the Protestants were Melanchthon and Bucer, with Calvin watching from the side. Among the Roman delegates were Pighius (later one of Calvin's staunchest critics), Contarini the papal legate, and Johann Eck (1486–1543).[13]

The compromise reached at Regensburg was possible only after two earlier conferences at Hagenau (June 1540) and Worms (January 1541). At Worms, Melanchthon and Eck worked out a formal agreement on original sin. The question outstanding, however, was not whether we are sinners but rather concerning the effects of sin: are the effects of original sin such that humans are utterly passive in justification? The Protestants affirmed the strong Augustinian view, and the Roman theologians denied it. Worms had not resolved this difference. The fundamental reason for the failure of these conferences was that there was no way to merge the prevailing Roman doctrine of justification on the basis of cooperation with infused grace with the Protestant (*Confessio Augustana* art. 4) doctrine of justification on the basis of imputed justice received through faith alone.

Jedin, *A History of the Council of Trent*, trans. E. Graf, 2 vols. (St. Louis: Herder Book Company, 1957), 2:166–96, 239–316.

12. This line of interpretation is suggested in Wilhelm Möller, *History of the Christian Church*, trans. J. H. Freese, 3 vols. (New York: Macmillan, 1900), 3:139. See also Martin Greschat, *Martin Bucer: A Reformer and His Times*, trans. Stephen E. Buckwalter (Louisville: Westminster John Knox Press, 2004), 176; Heinz Mackensen, "The Diplomatic Role of Gasparo Cardinal Contarini at the Colloquy of Ratisbon of 1541," *Church History* 27 (1958): 319–320.

13. Albert Pighius, *De Libero Arbitrio et Divina Gratia Libri Decem* (Cologne, 1542). Calvin responded in 1543 with *Defensio Sanae et Orthodoxae Doctrinae de Servitute de Liberatione Humani Arbitrii Adversus Calumnias Alberti Pighii Campensis* (Geneva, 1543).

To serve the interests of Charles V, the theologians needed to find language on which both sides could agree that would preserve their quite different doctrines of justification. The formula on which they settled was *duplex iustitia*. To this end, before Regensburg, Bucer and Gropper had developed an alternative document, which became known as the *Regensburg Book*.[14] This book formed the basis for the discussions at Regensburg.[15] With the groundwork laid, the participants quickly agreed on the first four articles regarding original sin and Pelagianism. After only five days, they reached agreement on Article 5, *"De iustificatione hominis."*[16]

From the outset it was clear that the Roman delegates wanted a clear statement that it is the morally transformed who are reconciled to God because they are morally transformed, so that they could continue to hold and teach that sanctification is logically and temporally prior to and causally and instrumentally necessary for reconciliation with God. They did not accept the Protestant position that sanctity is the logically and morally necessary result of justification but not causally or instrumentally necessary to justification. Thus, Article 5 says that no one can claim to be reconciled to God and remain a slave to sin. Moreover, it says that justifying faith is such that through it (*hic motus est per fidem*) "the mind of man is moved by the Holy Spirit toward God through Christ."[17]

For their part, the Protestant representatives insisted on language teaching imputation as the ground of justice, and faith as the instrument of justification. So Article 5 declared that faith (*fiducia*) includes assent to all that God has handed down to us and believing the divine promises "most certainly and without doubt" (*certissime et sine dubio*). From God's promises one obtains confidence that "for the sake of the promise of God" (*propter promissionem Dei*),

---

14. See Yarnold, *"Duplex Iustitia"*; McGrath, *Iustitia Dei*, 2:57.

15. On the authorship of the *Regensburg Book*, see Hastings Eells, *Martin Bucer* (1931; repr., New York: Russell and Russell, 1971), 288–301; Hastings Eells, "The Origin of the Regensburg Book," *Princeton Theological Review* 26 (1928): 355–72; Greschat, *Martin Bucer*, 178–80.

16. C. G. Bretschneider, ed., *Corpus Reformatorum*, 101 vols. (Halle, 1834–1959), 4:198–201 (hereafter *CR*). A portion of Article 5 is also published in B. J. Kidd, ed., *Documents Illustrative of the Continental Reformation* (Oxford: Oxford University Press, 1911), 343–44. The translations in this essay are mine unless otherwise noted.

17. *CR*, 4:198. "A Spiritu sancto movetur hominis mens in Deum per Christum, et hic motus est per fidem." Ibid., 4:199.

"the forgiveness of sins, the imputation of justice and innumerable other goods" are freely offered.[18] This was the heart of the Protestant doctrine of justification. The sinner's liability to the divine justice is removed, Christ's obedience is imputed, and the sinner is graciously accounted (*imputatio iustitiae*) as righteous. This benefit is conditioned not on moral renewal (or cooperation with grace) but on trust in Christ. In the Protestant view, these sorts of expressions gave justification a definitive rather than a progressive character and allowed that one could have assurance of justification in this life. That the Roman delegates agreed to the use of "*fiducia*" is significant, if only because just a few years later, the Council of Trent would use it as a synonym for "presumption" and reject it as a definition of "faith" and as an instrument of justification.[19] Because of this language, Anthony Lane has concluded that Regensburg "does not teach double justification."[20]

Nevertheless, the definition of "faith" included other important qualifications. Only those have "*fiducia*" who have "repented of their former life and by this faith are lifted up to God by the Holy Spirit."[21] These gifts are received through a "living faith" (*fidem vivam*), which they further defined as that "which apprehends mercy in Christ, and believes that justice which is in Christ is imputed to him by grace and at the same time receives the promise of the Holy Spirit and love. Therefore, justifying faith is that faith which is efficacious through love."[22] On the basis of this language, Irwin Iserloh, Joseph Glazik, and Hubert Jedin have also concluded that at Regensburg, there "is no question of a 'twofold righteousness,' but of the one righteousness

---

18. Ibid.

19. Canon 12 of Trent, session 6, condemns anyone who says, "Fidem justificantem nihil aliud esse quam fiduciam divinae misericordiae peccata remittentis propter Christum, vel eam fiduciam solam esse, qua iustificamur." H. Denzinger, ed., *Enchiridion Symbolorum*, 32nd ed. (Barcinone: Herder, 1963), 1562.

20. Lane, *Justification by Faith*, 58.

21. *CR*, 4:199. "Quos prioris vitae poenituerit, et hac fide erigitur in Deum a Spiritu sancto, ideoque accipit Spiritum sanctum, remissionem peccatorum, imputationem iustitiae, et innumera alia dona."

22. Ibid., 4:199–200. "Fides ergo viva ea est, quae apprehendit misericordiam in Christo, ac credit iustitiam, quae est in Christo, sibi gratia imputari, et quae simul pollicitationem Spiritus sancti et charitatem accipit. Ita quod fides quidem iustificans est illa fides, quae est efficax per charitatem."

of Christ the Mediator, which produces full grace, favor, and reconciliation with the Father and renews and sanctifies man but has not yet come here fully into effect."[23]

In favor of the Protestants, however, "*fides*" was defined not as a theological virtue or intrinsic disposition created by grace, but as a trust or confidence, as an apprehensive instrument (*apprehendit misericordiam*) the object of which was Christ's imputed justice (*credit iustitiam . . . imputari*).[24] This Protestant language notwithstanding, a living faith was also said to receive sanctification. The conferees carefully avoided the traditional medieval language "*fides formata caritate*," but their phrase, "*efficax per charitatem*," was close enough to satisfy the Roman delegates and at the same time different enough to suit the Protestants. The former could say that faith exists only to the degree that it is formed by love, and the latter could say that they were only following Galatians 5:6 ("*fides quae per caritatem operatur*") in teaching that a justifying faith works through love.[25] Is faith efficacious because it apprehends Christ or because it transforms? Regensburg allowed theologians with quite different answers to this question to have it both ways simultaneously.

With this brilliantly and deliberately equivocal language, the Protestants were able to interpret sanctification as the fruit and evidence of justification and the Roman delegates were able to interpret sanctification as the primary basis for justification with imputation serving as a reserve.[26]

23. Irwin Iserloh, Joseph Glazik, and Hubert Jedin, *Reformation and Counter-Reformation*, trans. Anselm Biggs and Peter W. Becker, vol. 5 of *History of the Church*, ed. Hubert Jedin and John Dolan (New York: Seabury, 1980–1982), 278.

24. Trent (6.7) would make it clear that being reputed just is not sufficient, but one must actually be just before God, "et non modo reputamur, sed vere iusti nominamur et sumus. . . ." *Enchiridion Symbolorum*, 1529.

25. *Biblia sacra iuxta vulgata versionem*, 3rd ed. (Stuttgart: Deutsche Bibelgesellschaft, 1983). Theodore Beza's Latin New Testament, *Iesu Christi D. N. Novum Testamentum Sive Novum Foedus* (Geneva, 1565; repr., London, 1834), attempted to strengthen the Protestant reading of this clause by translating it "fides per charitatem agens." This is clearer than "efficax" and avoids the implications of "formata," but it does not seem very distinct from "operatur."

26. Lane, borrowing from John Henry Newman, says that the article is "ambitious of a Protestant interpretation, though patient of a Catholic one." *Justification by Faith*, 59. Iserloh, Glazik, and Jedin also understand Regensburg to have achieved substantive unity between the two positions, but interpret the article to teach justification on the grounds of inherent righteousness. See Iserloh, Glazik, and Jedin, *Reformation and Counter-Reformation*, 277–78.

With this background established, we are prepared to assess how three Protestants made use of or developed the doctrine of double justice to serve Protestant theological purposes.

Luther's Doctrine of *De Duplici Iustitia*

Despite the impression created by some accounts, double justice was a Protestant doctrine well before Regensburg.[27] In the years 1513 through 1521, Luther gradually rejected the medieval scheme of progressive justification by the infusion of grace and the creation of proper (intrinsic) justice in favor of the doctrine of definitive justification by the imputation of Christ's alien (extrinsic) justice.

As part of his development of the forensic doctrine of justification, Luther set the pattern for the way in which Bucer and Calvin would later relate justification to sanctification, in which definitive justification and progressive sanctification are considered as twin benefits or graces of Christ. Between them, however, justification is logically necessary for and prior to sanctification. This *ordo salutis* established a trajectory on which Bucer and later Calvin elaborated.[28]

In his *Sermo de Duplici Iustitia*, probably given in late 1518 or early 1519, Luther preached that since the "sin of man is *duplex*" (i.e., since it is both original and actual), the "justice of Christians is twofold" (i.e., it is both forensic and progressive).[29] For Luther, however, there was a distinction between the first justice and the second. In contrast to the views of Gropper and Contarini, he assigned a definite priority to the extrinsic, definitive first justice over the progressive, distributive second justice. The first justice comes "without our works through

27. In his account of Luther's criticism of the Regensburg formula, James M. Kittleson, *Luther the Reformer: The Story of the Man and His Career* (Minneapolis: Augsburg, 1986), 278, leaves the impression that Luther never taught double justification and that it was a creature of the Regensburg Colloquy.

28. I am grateful to David Bagchi for suggesting this useful phrase.

29. "Duplex est iusticia Christianorum, sicut et duplex peccatum est hominum." Martin Luther, *Sermo de Duplici Iustitia*, in Luther, *Luthers Werke Kritische Gesamtausgabe*, ed. J. K. F. Knaake et al. (Weimar, 1883), 2:145–52 (hereafter *WA*). The English translation is in Martin Luther, *Luther's Works*, trans. and ed. J. Pelikan et al., 55 vols. (Philadelphia and St. Louis: Concordia Publishing House, 1955), 31:295–306 (hereafter *LW*).

grace alone." It is received "*per fidem.*"[30] This "primary" justice is the "ground," the "cause," and the "origin" of all our "proper or actual justice."[31]

This is the sort of language one expects to find in Luther. This sermon was relatively early in the development of the forensic view. Thus, it is not completely surprising that he also said that the first justice is also that which is simultaneously "alien" and "infused."[32] This sentence presents a minor challenge to the contention of this essay, that Luther, Bucer, and Calvin had fundamentally the same doctrine of justification despite verbal differences. How should one interpret this sentence? Luther's combination of the two categories "*aliena*" and "*infusa*" has caused some to conclude that in this sermon he was not teaching what would become the doctrine of the *Confessio Augustana* (art. 4). Because, in this passage in the sermon, Luther was still speaking of infusion as part of the first justice, Mannermaa has concluded that he was teaching *theosis* rather than imputation.[33]

A less revolutionary explanation of this sentence is that Luther's theological vocabulary had not yet caught up to his developing theological categories, but that the substance of his later doctrine was already present. The same "already–not yet" phenomenon is also evident in his language about the Holy Supper. At this point, however, he was formally teaching transubstantiation, but his later view was not far below the surface.[34] In the same way, on justification, even though he made the first justice both "*aliena*" and "*infusa*," it appears that he was making a qualitative distinction between the first and second justice so that the latter was understood realistically whereas the former was understood forensically. This distinction explains why he concluded the first section of the sermon, describing the second

30. *WA* 2:145–46. "Arbitramur hominem iustificari per fidem."

31. Ibid., 2:146. "Et haec iusticia est prima, fundamentum, causa, origo omnis iusticiae propriae seu actualis . . . ." This interpretation substantially agrees with that offered by Robert Kolb, "Luther on the Two Kinds of Righteousness," in Timothy J. Wengert, ed., *Harvesting Martin Luther's Reflections on Theology, Ethics, and the Church* (Grand Rapids: Eerdmans, 2004), 47–54.

32. *WA* 2:145. "Prima est aliena et ab extra infusa." On the next page he said, "Haec igitur iusticia aliena et sine actibus nostris per solam gratiam infusa nobis . . . ." Ibid., 2:146.

33. Mannermaa, *Union with Christ*, 38.

34. See *Ein Sermon von dem Hochwürdigen Sakrament des Heiligen Wahren Leichnams Christi und von den Brüderschaften*, in *WA* 2:742–758; *LW* 35:49–73.

justice by saying, "For all justice is not immediately infused, but begins, progresses and is finally perfected through death."[35] He treated the first justice as definitive and the second as progressive.[36]

Whereas the first justice is "*aliena*," the second justice (sanctification) was said to be "ours" and "proper" "because we cooperate" with that first and alien justice.[37] Note that he did not say that we receive the first justice because we cooperate with grace, but rather, cooperation with grace is the result of justification. It is the second justice that requires cooperation with grace; but even sanctity, to the degree it exists, is a result of divine grace. That this is the correct interpretation is also confirmed by the language that appeared in Luther's much less well known sermon, *De triplici iustitia* (1518), which was not fundamentally different from the sermon on double justice—the chief difference between them being that *De triplici* included consideration of predestination in addition to imputation and sanctification.[38]

Though Luther did not continue to use the language of double justice, in the *Sermon against Latomus* (1521) he did continue to distinguish in the *ordo salutis* between imputed extrinsic righteousness and imparted intrinsic righteousness.[39] To the elector Frederick (1519) his chief consolation was the imputation of "Christ's merits," in which the Christian may boast "as if he had won them all himself."[40] In 1521, he wrote to monks tempted to trust in condign or congruent merit, pointing them to Christ's "merits and works" received through

35. *WA* 2:146. "Non enim tota simul infunditur, sed incipit, proficit et perficitur tandem in fine per mortem." The translation of the *LW*, "For alien righteousness is not instilled all at once . . . ," suggests that Luther has confused the forensic and the distributive, but this is not clearly the case in the Latin text. One might also question the judgment of Walter von Loewenich that Luther's doctrine of double justice "sounds strongly pre-Reformed" ("stark vorreformatisch klingt," *Duplex Iustitia*, 8).

36. In an unpublished response to this essay, David Bagchi notes that, regarding the first justice, in other writings from this time, Luther did not regard the language of infusion ("*infundere*") as connoting distribution as opposed to imputation. See his 1520 *Disputatio de Fide Infusa et Acquisita*, where he treated "[*fides*] *infusa*" as a synonym for "*divina*." Faith is a divine gift, not a human quality. *WA* 6:89. Thus, it is not surprising that he treated extrinsic righteousness in this way.

37. Ibid., 2:146. "Secunda iusticia est nostra et propria, non quod nos soli operemur eam, sed quod cooperemur illi primae et alienae."

38. Luther, *De Triplici Iustitia*, *WA* 2:43–47.

39. See *WA* 8:43–128.

40. Martin Luther, "The Fourteen of Consolation," in *Works of Martin Luther: The Philadelphia Edition*, 6 vols. (Philadelphia: Muhlenberg Press, 1915), 1:169.

trusting in Christ alone.[41] This was his mature teaching as well. In his 1535 lectures on Galatians, he contrasted *"meritum de congruo et condigno"* with Christ's meritorious obedience.[42] Faith believes that Christ has performed "a superabundance of works merits of congruity and condignity" and that the same have been imputed to us.[43] In the 1536 *Disputation concerning Justification*, Luther's reliance on Christ's obedience for us was even more pronounced.[44] Christ's righteousness is "outside us" and cannot be obtained "by our works." Christ's righteousness is like an umbrella protecting us from the heat of God's wrath.[45]

Melanchthon, Bucer, and Calvin followed Luther by distinguishing without separating justification and sanctification as two logically discrete but closely related benefits of Christ that believers receive *sola gratia, sola fide*.

Melanchthon's Doctrine of Justification

The history of Melanchthon's doctrine of justification quite rightly has been the focus of considerable attention. On the basis of his doctrine of double justification, von Harnack regarded him as a synergist,[46] and other scholars now argue that it was Melanchthon, not Luther, who gave us the doctrine of imputation.[47] The scope of this chapter requires us, however, to focus narrowly on how Melanchthon expressed himself on double justification. Given his central role at Regensburg, it is clear that Melanchthon supported the Protestant use of the language of double justification, but what did he mean by it? Did he make fatal concessions to the Roman doctrine of progressive justification? Despite

41. *LW* 44:286–87.
42. Ibid., 26:122–33.
43. Ibid., 2:132.
44. *WA* 39¹, 82–126.
45. *LW* 34:153.
46. Von Harnack, *History of Dogma*, 7:256.
47. See Strehle, *"Imputatio iustitiae,"* 201–19; Seifrid, "Paul, Luther, and Justification in Galatians 2:15–21," 215–30; Mark Seifrid, *Christ Our Righteousness: Paul's Theology of Justification* (Leicester and Downers Grove: Apollos and Inter-Varsity Press, 2000), 175; Mark Seifrid, "Luther, Melanchthon and Paul on the Question of Imputation: Recommendations on a Current Debate," in Mark A. Husbands and Daniel J. Trier, eds., *Justification: What's at Stake in the Current Debates* (Downers Grove and Leicester: InterVarsity, 2004), 137–76.

his pragmatic moves during the Leipzig Interim (1548) and his admittedly ambiguous language during the Majorist Controversy (1551 et seq.), his doctrine of justification as found in the *Loci Communes* did not fundamentally change from the 1521 to the 1543 editions.

By 1519 Melanchthon was expressing the rudiments of the doctrine of imputation. For his B.A. he proposed and defended this thesis: "All our righteousness is the gracious imputation of God."[48] Two years later, in the first *formal*, systematic summary of Protestant theology, the *Loci Communes*, Melanchthon wrote directly against the medieval doctrine of progressive justification by inherent righteousness. Christ's *"iustitia"* is ours, his *"satisfactio"* is ours, his *"expiatio"* and *"resurrectio"* are ours.[49] "Nothing of our good works, however good . . . are righteousness . . . but faith alone is righteousness" because it apprehends Christ's righteousness.[50] Faith is not mere assent; neither does it justify because it is "formed by love" (*fides formata caritate*).[51] In the act of justification, faith is nothing less than "a hearty trust [*fiducia*] in the divine mercy promised in Christ."[52] The *iustitia* that faith apprehends is not intrinsic to the sinner.[53] It is Christ's. "Furthermore, Christ, the intercessor for us, whom God gave as a victim and satisfaction, merited good will for us."[54] In his summary on justification, Melanchthon declared that since faith alone justifies, the basis for that declaration is the merits of Christ.[55]

Even before he finished laying out the Protestant view, however, Melanchthon addressed the question of sanctification. Immediately

48. "Omnis iustitia nostra est gratuita dei imputatio." Philipp Melanchthon, *Melanchthons Werke in Auswahl [Studienausgabe]*, ed. Robert Stupperich, 7 vols. (Gütersloh: Gütersloher Verlagshaus Mohn, 1955–1983), 1:24. See also Lowell Green, "Faith, Righteousness, and Justification: New Light on Their Development under Luther and Melanchthon," *Sixteenth Century Journal* 4 (1973): 81.

49. Philipp Melanchthon, *Loci Communes von 1521*, in *Melanchthons Werke*, 2.88.12–14.

50. Ibid., 2.88.16–19. "Nihil igitur operum nostrorum, quantumvis bona . . . iustitia sunt, sed sola fides . . . iustitia est."

51. Ibid., 2.88.35–89.1–13.

52. Ibid., 2.92.25–27. "Est itaque fides non aliud nisi fiducia misericordiae divinae promissae in Christo adeoque quocunque signo."

53. Melanchthon used the verb *"prehendo"* in accounting for the role of faith. The power of faith is in its object, not its own virtue. See ibid., 2.107.25–26.

54. Ibid., 2.106.12–14. "Porro bonam voluntatem meruit Christus, quem pro nobis intercessorem, quem pro nobis victimam et satisfactionem dedit."

55. Ibid., 2.123.1–3.

after he characterized faith as *fiducia*, which first "pacifies" (*pacificat*) our hearts, he continued: "next it enkindles us in order that we shall have given thanks to God for his mercy, so that we perform the law spontaneously and joyously."[56] The "works which follow justification" come from the "Spirit of God, who has captured the heart of the justified. Nevertheless, because they are done in the flesh, those works are in themselves unclean. For justification has commenced, but has not been consummated."[57]

Melanchthon's 1543 edition of the *Loci* is of interest to us not least because it was the first revision to appear after the discussions at Regensburg. If that colloquy marked a fundamental change in Melanchthon's doctrine of justification, it should have appeared here, but the text contains no evidence of any fundamental change in his doctrine of justification. At every point where he might have revised his doctrine to make it more congenial to progressive justification, he resisted. Indeed, the 1543 edition was considerably more sophisticated in its handling of the central points of contention with Rome.

The word "justification" does not signify God's recognition of our Spirit-infused, intrinsic righteousness. Rather, it signifies "the forgiveness of sins and *reconciliation* or acceptance of a person to eternal life."[58] By definition it is a forensic act, a declaration by God. Nevertheless, at the same time (*simul*) God remits sins, he gives (*donat*) the Holy Spirit, "beginning new virtues" (*inchoantem novas virtutes*) in us.[59] We are justified "*propter filium Dei*," not "*propter nostram dignitatem*."[60] This "*beneficium*" is to be "apprehended by faith or trust and the merit of Christ is to be opposed to our sin and damnation."[61]

The Roman critics misunderstood the Protestant definition of "faith." The faith by which sinners receive justification is not mere

56. Ibid., 2.92.28–30. "Deinde et accendit velut gratiam acturos deo pro misericordia, ut legem sponte et hilariter faciamus."
57. Ibid., 2.108.18–22. "Quae vero opera iustificationem consequuntur, ea tametsi a spiritu dei, qui occupavit corda iustificatorum, proficiscuntur, tamen quia fiunt in carne adhuc impura, sunt et ipsa immunda. Coepta enim iustificatio est, non consummata."
58. *CR* 21:742. "JUSTIFICATIO significat remissionem peccatorum et reconciliationem seu acceptationem personae ad vitam aeternam."
59. Ibid., 21:742.
60. Ibid., 21:750.
61. Ibid. "Et quod hoc credendum sit, seu quod hac fide vel fiducia apprehendendum sit beneficium et opponendum meritum Christi peccato nostro et damnationi nostrae. . . ."

"*notitia.*" Faith includes knowledge, but it also includes *fiducia* in Christ the Mediator and his merits.[62] As in 1521, Melanchthon categorically rejected the medieval doctrine of *fides formata caritate.* Faith is not a work, but an "instrument . . . by which we apprehend the Mediator interceding for us."[63] "Grace" is not the infusion of medicine, but the "remission of sins, or mercy promised for the sake of Christ or gracious acceptance."[64]

In the *Locus de bonis operibus,* Melanchthon included a subsection responding to eighteen syllogisms proposed by his Roman opponents (*de argumentis adversarium*). The "monks" do not understand the Protestant doctrine of justification because they do not "distinguish" law and gospel.[65] They think of faith as an infused virtue and not the instrument of justification because they think more like Plato and Aristotle than Paul. They "command us to doubt."[66] Melanchthon appealed to the distinction between law and gospel as the fundamental source of the disagreement between Protestants and Rome. They are right to say that we are justified by works—yet not by *our* works, but rather by those of the Mediator, Christ.[67] "Faith is imputed to us for righteousness" only because it apprehends Christ.

Two things stand out about Melanchthon's discussions of justification in 1521 and 1543. First, in neither edition of the *Loci Communes* did he explicitly speak of a *duplex iustitia.*[68] The substance of the doctrine is evident in the architecture of his treatment. Justification is always definitive, grounded in Christ's merits imputed to the sinner and apprehended *sola fide.* This forensic, definitive justification, however, always produces sanctity. Second, it is evident throughout

62. Ibid., 21:785.
63. Ibid., 21:786. "Instrumentum . . . quo apprehendimus Mediatorem pro nobis interpellantem. . . ."
64. Ibid., 21:752. "Gratia est remissio peccatorum, seu misericordia propter Christum promissa, seu acceptatio gratuita. . . ."
65. Ibid., 21:783. "Sed quod aliter Monachii scripserunt, et fit, quia non discernebant Legem et Evangelium. . . ."
66. Ibid., 21:784.
67. Ibid.
68. He did use the expression in his 1536 *Disputatio* with Luther. See Philipp Melanchthon, *Epistolae, Iudicia, Consilia, Testimonia Aliorumque ad Eum Epistolae Quae in Corpore Reformatorum Desiderantur,* ed. H. E. Bindseil and R. Stupperich (1874; repr., Hildesheim and New York: Georg Olms Verlag, 1975), 345.

this section of the *Loci* that Melanchthon was concerned to correlate justification and sanctification without confusing them. The sentence quoted above, that justification has been "commenced" but not "consummated," is especially striking. Taken in abstraction, one could put this sentence in the mouth of any medieval or Roman theologian, who all denied a present definitive justification and who anticipated a future justification. It seems clear, however, that Melanchthon did not intend to contradict his entire doctrine of justification. Rather, he was giving expression to the fact that though believers are already legally righteous, they are not yet experientially righteous or fully sanctified. Though justification produces good works, those works are never perfect in this life.[69] From 1521, Melanchthon attempted to correlate justification and sanctification without confusing them. This move was nothing other than the Protestant doctrine of *duplex iustitia*.

Bucer's Doctrine of *Duplex Iustificatio*

According to Martin Greschat, though personally conflicted and not wanting to betray the Protestant cause, Bucer substantially agreed with Gropper on justification in the discussions leading up to Regensburg.[70] It has seemed to others that because of Bucer's doctrine of double justice and his politics and rhetoric, his doctrine of justification should be considered dissimilar to Luther's and Calvin's or even sub-Protestant.[71] One might see Bucer's view differently, however, if one interprets his soteriology in the light of Luther's doctrine of double justice before him and Calvin's doctrine of double grace after him. Bucer's doctrine of justification was substantially the same as Luther's, and as for Luther, Bucer's doctrine of double justification united justification and sanctification without confusing them.[72]

69. See *Melanchthons Werke*, 2.112–14 and 2.114–25.
70. Greschat, *Martin Bucer*, 175–81.
71. E.g., Peter Stephens mentions Eduard von Ellwein, *Vom neuen Leben. De novitate vitae* (Munich: Chr. Kaiser, 1932). See W. P. Stephens, *The Holy Spirit in the Theology of Martin Bucer* (Cambridge: Cambridge University Press, 1970), 48 n. 2. See also Wilhelm Pauck, *The Heritage of the Reformation* (Oxford: Oxford University Press, 1961), 75; Joel Edward Kok, "The Influence of Martin Bucer on John Calvin's Interpretation of Romans: A Comparative Case Study" (Ph.D. diss., Duke University, 1993).
72. See Stephens, *Holy Spirit*, 52–54.

This was partly because Luther's influence on Bucer was direct, strong, and lasting.[73] It is significant that Bucer heard Luther at the Heidelberg Disputation (1518) because the seed of Luther's doctrine of double justice was already present in the theses Luther propounded there.[74] Double justice was a well-established feature of Bucer's soteriology well before Regensburg. In his 1523 tract *Basic Instruction in Christian Love*, Bucer was working with categories very much like those established by Luther in 1518–19.[75] There, faith was "trust" that "Christ by his blood has placed" believers again in the sonship and grace of the Father.[76] As Luther had preached in the 1522 *Invocavit* sermons, Bucer taught that faith "brings self-denial, dedication of self to the service of other men, forgetfulness of self and living wholly for others to the glory of God."[77] Even in this popular tract, it is evident that Bucer's chief interests were to stimulate assurance and confidence that those who trust Christ really are just before God and thence to stimulate them to good works in gratitude.

The same basic structure is also evident in his more mature work, for example, his *Brief Summary of the Christian Faith* (1548) and his massive (507-page) 1536 commentary on Romans.[78] About this commentary, T. H. L. Parker says that it "crushed into insignificance all but two or three of our others and its influence for a few years was immense."[79]

In his most direct expositions of justification, Bucer did not always appeal to *duplex iustitia* explicitly, but it was implicit throughout. In his exposition of Romans 3, Bucer wrote that it was Paul's chief concern

73. Martin Brecht, "Bucer und Luther," in C. Krieger, ed., *Martin Bucer and Sixteenth Century Europe* (Leiden, Netherlands: Brill, 1993).

74. *WA* 1:364. "XXV. Non ille iustus est, qui multum operatur, sed qui sine opere multum credit in Christum." By way of explanation he said, "Sine enim opere nostro gratia et fides infunditur, qua infusa iam sequuntur opera."

75. *Das ym Selbs Niemant Sonder Anderen Leben* . . . (Strasbourg, 1523); Martin Bucer, *Basic Instruction in Christian Love*, trans. P. T. Fuhrmann (Richmond: John Knox Press, 1952).

76. Bucer, *Basic Instruction*, 42.

77. Ibid., 48.

78. Martin Bucer, *Common Places of the Christian Religion*, trans. and ed. D. F. Wright (Appleford, Berkshire: Sutton Courtenay Press, 1971), 76–94; Bucer, *Metaphrases et Enarrationes Perpetuae . . . in Epistolam ad Romanos* (Strasbourg, 1536).

79. T. H. L. Parker, *Commentaries on the Epistle to the Romans* (Edinburgh: T&T Clark, 1986), 35. See also Bernard Roussel, "Martin Bucer: Lecteur de l'Epitre Aux Romains" (Ph. D. thesis, University of Strasbourg, 1970); Kok, "The Influence of Martin Bucer."

to show that the only justification with God that actually exists and should be expected is that which is "by Christ alone through faith."[80] Considering what Luther called the "first justice," Bucer says that law and gospel are "antithetical."[81] To Bucer, it was manifestly clear that no one is justified with God "by the works of the law." At the same time it was also clear that justification *sola gratia, sola fide* was not to become a license for immorality, since "God does not justify, i.e., give eternal life to either the unjust or the wicked." According to Bucer, it is not that God justifies sinners because they become good, but rather that those who are justified will not continue to live impenitently. The foundational justice before God is forensic. The secondary justice is progressive such that those whom God justifies do not remain in their former state.[82]

In his exposition of Romans 4, Bucer was even more explicit about the forensic basis of our justice before God. Abraham was not justified "*ex operibus*," that is, by sanctification, since that is an impossibility in this world.[83] Scripture testifies to this impossibility because faith was imputed to Abraham for justice (*fidem imputatam ad iustitiam*). Therefore, justice and salvation are given freely without merit.[84]

It was well for Bucer to follow Luther in teaching imputed justice as the ground of justification, but he might have smuggled sanctification into justification in his definition of "faith." That he did this in his Romans commentary, however, is not obvious. In his preface to the commentary, in which he gave a summary of Paul's argument, he

80. Bucer, *Metaphrases in Romanos*, 170–71. "Iam dictum aliquoties est, Paulum hoc ubique praecipue aut in hac epistola, et prima ista epistolae huius parti agere, ut ostendat a solo Christo per fidem omnem salutem, hoc est iustificationem apud Deum expectandam, eoque nulla re alia, quaecunque illa sit."

81. Ibid., 180. "Antitheton est Evangelii et legis namque dixit sine lege manifestatam iustitiam Dei."

82. Ibid., 176. "Hinc iam manifesto id sequebatur, ex operibus legis iustificari neminem. Obtinente enim tanta apud omnes impietate et iniustitia, idque apud ipsos quoque Iudaeos operiubus legis nitentes, quis non videat, ex hisce operibus iustificari apud Deum neminem posset neque enim iustificat Deus, hoc est, vita aeterna donat, tam iniustos et sceleratos."

83. Ibid., 214. "Probatio est huius, Abraham non est iustificatum ex operibus, idque ratione ducente ad impossibile in hunc mundum."

84. Ibid. "Huius vero impossibilitatem ex eo probat cumque Scriptura testat illi fidem imputatam ad iustitiam. Quod ut dictum, idem est, atque gratis, absque ullo merito, iustitiam et salutem ei divinitus donatam esse." See also his comments to the same effect, on Rom. 4:3, "et imputatum est ei ad iustitiam." Ibid., 415.

defined "faith" as "the same persuasion through the Holy Spirit of God's love and fatherly kindness, in reliance upon our Lord Jesus Christ, who by his death has expiated our sins, and by his life now reigns, makes us partakers of his righteousness."[85] He taught the same thing in his Cambridge lectures on Ephesians 2 (1550–51), during which he defined "true faith" as "a gift of God and a certain persuasion" that God has willed to save men and make them participants of eternal life and blessedness.[86] True, justifying faith necessarily produces good works. Indeed, says Bucer, "we glorify God and this benefit," that is, the gift of justifying faith, with "most holy works" that are commanded by God's Word and wrought within us by the Holy Spirit, but he did not identify faith with works.[87] He argued that James 2 neither contradicts Paul nor teaches justification by works, but rather teaches "double justification." The word "justification," he said, can be used to describe not only justification by faith, but also "justification of works," which depends on "justification of faith." In this scheme, good works "flow" (*manant*) from a "true and living faith."[88] It is not that works perfect faith or make faith justifying, but rather that the existence of justifying faith is declared (*declaraverit*), is made clear (*perspicuam*), and is "shown" (*ostensum*) by works.[89] Good works are not faith, but they are evidence and fruit of justifying faith. Clearly, this is substantially Luther's doctrine of faith and works.

Some who have suggested that Bucer had a different doctrine of justification from Luther and Calvin seem to rely on circumstantial evidence more than on Bucer's words. For example, Wilhelm Pauck concluded that Luther and Bucer had different doctrines of justification not on the basis of Bucer's definition of "justification" or "faith,"

---

85. Ibid., 6. See also Bucer, *Common Places*, 172.

86. Martin Bucer, *Praelectiones doctiss. in Epistolam d. P. ad Ephesios* (Basel: Petrus Perna, 1562), 60. "Est enim vera fides donum Dei et certa persuasio, quòd Deus velit hominem servatum et participem vitae, et aeternae felicitatis, cohaeredemque Christi propter meram bonitatem suam in Christo."

87. Ibid., 60–61. "Deum, et hoc beneficium Christi celebremus sanctissimis operibus, quae illo verbo nobis à Deo mandantur, quatenus vis illius spiritus nos regit, et cohercet in nobis rebellem carnem."

88. Ibid., 63–64. "Duplex est iustificatio, non una, fidei et operum. Sed haec, id est, iustificatio operum à iustificatione fidei pendet, & constat illis bonis operibus, quae ex vera & viva fide manant."

89. Ibid., 63.

but on the basis of Bucer's *De Regno Christi* (1550). He seems to have reasoned that since Bucer proposed a different vision of the civil order from Luther, he must have held a different doctrine of justification. It does not follow, however, that because Bucer related the two kingdoms differently from Luther, he therefore had a different doctrine of justification.[90] More recently, Joel Kok has suggested that Bucer disagreed with Calvin's doctrine of justification, noting that Bucer used a different rhetorical strategy in dealing with Jacopo Sadoleto and that he interpreted Romans 2:6 and 2:13 somewhat differently from Calvin.[91] Neither of these facts, however, means that Calvin and Bucer disagreed on justification, and Kok concedes that despite these minor differences, Bucer "denies that believers can be justified by moral law or by anything else except for faith."[92]

Thus, we should agree with Peter Stephens, who says that Bucer was attempting to account for the variety of biblical expressions regarding justice and that "his way is not to choose between them, but to reconcile them."[93] Bucer was teaching imputation as the *justification* of the impious and the second justice as the *vindication* of the pious because, for Bucer, as for Calvin and much of the tradition following him, "justification is not an end in itself."[94]

Calvin's Doctrine of *Duplex Beneficium*

Before it ever began, Luther expected Regensburg to fail, and when he read the agreement reached there, he repudiated it as a patchwork of irreconcilable views.[95] In contrast, Calvin, in the midst of the colloquy, recorded a rather different reaction. In his letters of

90. See the chapter "Bucer and Luther," in *The Heritage of the Reformation*; Wilhelm Pauck, ed., *Melanchthon and Bucer* (London: SCM Press, 1959), 156.

91. Kok, "The Influence of Martin Bucer," 63–74.

92. Ibid., 63.

93. Stephens, *Holy Spirit*, 52.

94. Ibid., 53.

95. *WAB* 9:459, no. 3627; F. Lau and E. Bizer, *A History of the Reformation in Germany to 1555*, trans. B. A. Hardy (London: Adam and Charles Black, 1969), 169. See also Möller, *History of the Christian Church*, 3:139–43; M. Brecht, *Martin Luther: The Preservation of the Church 1532–1546*, trans. J. L. Schaaf (Minneapolis: Fortress, 1993), 215–28; McGrath, *Iustitia Dei*, 2:61. Simo Peura, "Christ as Favor and Gift: The Challenge of Luther's Understanding of Justification," in *Union with Christ*, 64–66, argues that Luther did not reject Article 5 because it

May 11 and 12, 1541, Calvin wrote to William Farel, describing the
proceedings of the Regensburg Colloquy:[96]

> The debate in controversy was more bitter [*acriores*] over the doc-
> trine of justification. At length a formula was drawn up, which
> on receiving certain corrections, was accepted on both sides. You
> will be astonished [*miraberis*], I am sure, that our opponents have
> conceded [*concessisse*] so much, when you read the extracted copy,
> as it stood when the last correction was made upon it, which you
> will find enclosed in the letter. Our side [*nostri*] have thus retained
> also the substance [*summam*] of the true doctrine, so that nothing
> can be comprehended within it which is not to be found in our
> writings. You will desire, I know, a more distinct explication and
> statement of the doctrine, and in that respect, you will find me
> in complete agreement with yourself. If, however, you consider
> with what kind of men we have to agree upon this doctrine, you
> will acknowledge that much has been accomplished [*multum esse
> effectum*].[97]

Calvin's more positive appraisal of Regensburg Article 5 has been
seen by some as evidence that he held a different doctrine of justification from Luther.[98] This conclusion, however, does not follow
from the evidence available from Regensburg.

In its own time, the Regensburg settlement was interpreted in
a variety of ways and rejected for a variety of reasons. For example,
Luther was not alone in rejecting Regensburg. The Roman consis-
tory (May 27, 1541) also rejected Article 5 for the same reasons the
"duplex iustitia" formula was later rejected at Trent: because it was

---

represented a threat to his forensic doctrine of justification, but because he did not understand
that it was really advocating *theosis*.

96. Calvin's relations to Bucer have received a fair amount of attention in the secondary
literature. Pauck called Bucer the "father of Calvinism." *The Heritage of the Reformation*, 99. See
also W. van't Spijker, "Bucer's Influence on Calvin: Church and Community," in D. F. Wright,
ed., *Martin Bucer: Reforming Church and Community* (Cambridge: Cambridge University Press,
1994); Kok, "The Influence of Martin Bucer," 1–19.

97. *CR*, 38:215. Translation revised from John Calvin, *Selected Works of John Calvin*, trans.
Henry Beveridge, 7 vols. (1844–1858; repr., Grand Rapids: Baker, 1983), 4:260.

98. See Lillback, *The Binding of God*, 190–93; Armand J. Boehme, "Justification by Grace
through Faith: Do Wittenberg and Geneva See Eye to Eye?" *Logia: A Journal of Lutheran
Theology* 11 (2002): 17–27.

seen as an unstable arrangement that might tend to give a foothold to the Protestant doctrine of justification by imputed righteousness.

It is clear from his letters to Farel that, on the one hand, Calvin considered Article 5 to be a victory for the Protestant side because Roman delegates had conceded the definition of "faith" as "*fiducia*" and the doctrine of imputation, not because he had managed to wedge sanctification as a ground or instrument of justification into the Protestant doctrine. Nevertheless, his support of Article 5 was not unqualified. He was not naive about the game afoot at the conference, that both sides were constructing a statement that could and would later be interpreted by both sides in a way that allowed them to retain their distinctive views. Therefore, he knew that Article 5 was not an unambiguous victory for the Protestant side. The "sum" of true doctrine is present, that is, Christ's righteousness graciously imputed to sinners and received by a passive faith alone; but the article could have been clearer.

Like Bucer and Melanchthon, Calvin was willing and able to interpret it in a way that agreed with what he had published in the *Institutes* and in his 1539 commentary on Romans 2:13.[99] If Regensburg signaled a shift in Calvin's doctrine of justification away from Luther's, it was not evident in Calvin's 1548 commentary on Galatians 5:6, where he said, "Therefore when you move to the subject of justification, be careful about making any mention of charity or works, but hold on tenaciously to the exclusive particle."[100] Calvin did want, as Lane has argued, to hold justification and sanctification "in balance," but in so doing, he was quite unprepared to concede the central Roman contention regarding justification.[101]

The most likely interpretation of the difference between Calvin's reaction to Regensburg and Luther's is that Calvin and Luther did not differ regarding justification as much as they did in their politics. In the heat of battle, Calvin believed that the Protestant side had won

99. Ioannis Calvini, *Commentarius in Epistolam Pauli ad Romanos*, ed. T. H. L. Parker, in *Opera Omnia*, series 2, *Opera Exegetica* (Geneva: Droz, 1999), 44–46.

100. "Ergo quum versaris in causa iustificationis, cave ullam charitatis vel operum mentionem admittas, sed mordicus retine particulam exclusivam." Ioannis Calvini, *Commentarii in Pauli Epistolas*, ed. H. Feld, in *Opera Omnia*, series 2, vol. 16, *Opera Exegetica* (Geneva: Droz, 1992), 120.

101. Lane, *Justification by Faith*, 57.

concessions on which they could capitalize toward the advancement of the Protestant cause.

Calvin's interest in relating justification and sanctification as twin graces or benefits of Christ did not begin or end at Regensburg. He had taught *"duplex beneficium"* in the 1536 edition of the *Institutio*, and it was a major theme in the final Latin edition of 1559.[102] The earlier doctrine of *duplex iustitia* evolved to the doctrine of *duplex beneficium* or *duplex gratia*. The difference between 1536 and 1559 was not in the substance of his doctrine of justification. On that, he agreed with Luther and Bucer: We are definitively justified by the imputation of Christ's alien justice. From justification flows the Christian life of progressive sanctification.[103] Like Luther and Bucer, Calvin rejected the medieval *duplex* scheme, and because of his concern for a genuinely Protestant doctrine of *duplex beneficium*, he singled out for criticism Peter Lombard's *"duplex spei fundamentum,"* that is, *"Dei gratiam et operum meritum (3.2.43)."*[104]

Thus, Jonathan Rainbow is quite right to say that, on this point, Calvin was as "'Lutheran, as emphatic, and as polemical as Luther." Rainbow provides no evidence, however, for his claim that for Calvin, "sanctification does not come, as it were, from justification" but comes directly from the cross in strict parallel to justification.[105] In fact, Calvin learned his doctrine of justification from Luther and ordered the relations between justification and sanctification as Luther did.

After Regensburg, the change Calvin made to the *"duplex iustitia"* scheme was accidental, not substantial. In place of *duplex iustitia* and *duplex iustificatio*, he taught a *duplex beneficium* or sometimes *duplex gratia*. Thus, in book 2 of the *Institutes*, he taught that Christ's death and burial propounds a *"duplex beneficium,"* first that we have

102. Calvin used a quite different version of the double-justice idea in his commentary on Job. See Susan E. Schreiner, *Where Shall Wisdom Be Found? Calvin's Exegesis of Job from Medieval and Modern Perspectives* (Chicago: University of Chicago Press, 1994), 105–20.

103. For an excellent account of Calvin's doctrine of *duplex gratia*, see Cornelis P. Venema, "The Twofold Nature of the Gospel in Calvin's Theology: The *Duplex Gratia Dei* and the Interpretation of Calvin's Theology" (Ph.D. diss., Princeton Theological Seminary, 1985).

104. P. Barth and W. Niesel, eds., *Joannis Calvini Opera Selecta* (Munich: Chr. Kaiser, 1926–1954), 4.54.15–17 (hereafter *OS*). Calvin was referring to *Sententiae* III, dist. 26.1. See Peter Lombard, *Sententiae in IV Libris Distinctae*, 2 vols. (Rome, 1971).

105. Rainbow, "Double Grace," 101–2.

been liberated from death, and second that because of that liberation we are able to pursue the mortification of the flesh (2.16.7).[106]
Of course, the *"duplex"* theme is most pronounced in book 3, the
very title of which suggests this idea: "On the Means of Learning
the Grace of Christ and Thence What Fruit Comes to Us and What
Effect Follows."[107]

But perhaps the clearest discussion of the *duplex beneficium* was
in *Institutes* 3.11.1, where Calvin argued that Christ has been given
to us "by the kindness of God" and is "apprehended and possessed
by faith," whereby we obtain a *"duplex gratia,"* the first of which is
reconciliation to God by Christ's justice and the second of which,
having been sanctified by the Spirit of Christ, "we may consider
innocence and purity of life."[108]

It is in this light that one should read Calvin's argument against
Osiander's doctrine of double justice.[109] His argument with Osiander
was not against all *"duplex"* schemes per se, but against Osiander's version, because under it he hid the "monster" of "essential righteousness"
(3.11.5).[110] For Osiander, the verb "to justify" not only meant "to be
reconciled to God" by which Christ's justice is graciously imputed
to sinners, but also included "sanctity and integrity" inspired by the
essence of God dwelling in us (3.11.6).[111] In his version of double

---

106. *OS* 3.491.38–492.2. "Proinde duplex in morte sepulturaque Christi beneficium nobis
fruendum proponitur, liberatio a morte cui mancipati eramus, et carnis nostrae mortificatio."
This was Luther's message in *Tractatus de libertate Christiana* (1520). See *WA* 7:49–73 and the
Disputatio de iustificatione thesis 31, "Sed sic dicendum: Ego credo in Christum; Et post facio
opera bona in Christo vere." *WA* 39¹.83.

107. *OS* 4.1. "De modo percipiendae Christi gratiae et qui inde fructus nobis proveniant,
et qui effectus consequantur."

108. Ibid., 4.182.3–10. "Summa autem haec fuit, Christum nobis Dei benignitate datum,
fide a nobis apprehendi ac possideri, cuius participatione duplicem potissimum gratiam recipi-
amus: nempe ut eius innocentia Deo reconciliati, pro iudice iam propitium habeamus in caelis
Patrem: Deinde ut eius Spiritus sanctificati, innocentiam puritamemque, vitae meditemur."

109. See W. Niesel, *The Theology of Calvin* (Philadelphia: Westminster, 1956), 133–39;
James Weis, "Calvin Versus Osiander on Justification," *The Springfielder* 30 (1965): 31–47.

110. *OS* 4.185.19–22. "Verum quia Osiander monstrum nescio quod essentialis iustitiae
invexit, quo etsi noluit abolere gratuitam iustitiam, ea tamen caligine involvit quae pias mentes
obtenebratas serio gratiae Christi sensu privet."

111. Ibid., 4.187.9–14. "Nam in hac tota disputatione nomen iustitiae et verbum iustificandi ad duas partes extendit, ut iustificari sit non solum reconciliari Deo gratuita venia, sed
etiam iustos effici: ut iustitia sit non gratuita imputatio, sed sanctitas et integritas quam Dei
essentia in nobis residens inspirat."

justice, Osiander "confounds" the distinction between justification and moral renewal.[112]

Thus, in *Institutes* 3.11.11, Calvin rejected what he regarded as a perversion of the "*duplex*" scheme, not the scheme itself.[113] It was the "intolerable impiety" of teaching justification by sanctification under the "pretext" of double justice to which Calvin objected, not the "*duplex*" scheme he had inherited from Luther.[114]

Conclusions

The Protestant doctrine of double justice was not, as has some-times been suggested, a deviation from or substantial modification of the Protestant doctrine of justification. It was rather a development of that doctrine in the service of a pan-Protestant doctrine. Luther, Melanchthon, Bucer, and Calvin used *duplex iustitia* or its offspring, *duplex beneficium* and *duplex gratia*, to advance their agenda of uniting, without confusing, definitive justification and progressive sanctification, and it was this doctrine that came to expression in the Protestant confessions and orthodox Reformed theology.

Thus, the life of the doctrine of *duplex iustitia* or *duplex beneficium* did not end with Calvin. The German Calvinist theologian Caspar Olevianus (1536–87) appropriated it and used it as one of the organizing principles of his federal theology. For Olevianus, "Christ has been made not only our righteousness, but also our sanctification." Christ died not only to justify, but also to inwardly renew his people.[115] Under his exposition of the article *credo sanctam Ecclesiam catholicam*, Olevianus asked, "Why is the Church called 'holy'?" He answered,

112. Ibid., 4.194.11–13. "Hoc discrimen iustificandi et regenerandi (quae duo confundens Osiander, duplicem iustitiam nominat) . . . ."
113. Ibid., 4.192.33–193.2. "Verum haec minime tolerabilis est impietas, praetextu duplicis iustitiae labefactare salutis fiduciam, et nos raptare supra nubes, ne gratiam expiationis fide amplexi, Deum quietis animis invocemus."
114. See also Calvin's comments on Rom. 3:21, in which he considered and rejected a double basis for justification. Calvini, *Commentarius in Epistolam Pauli ad Romanos*, 68–69.
115. "Christus non solum factus est nobis iustitia, sed etiam sanctification." Caspar Olevianus, *In Epistolam d. Pauli Apostoli ad Romanos Notae*, ed. Theodore Beza (Geneva, 1579), 207. See also R. Scott Clark, *The Substance of the Covenant: Caspar Olevian on the Double Benefit of Christ* (Edinburgh: Rutherford House, 2005).

"The Church is holy on two accounts, by renewal and imputation (John 13). That same holiness is only begun in renewal itself (Romans 7) . . . but by imputation her holiness is most perfect in Christ."[116]

One also finds the *duplex beneficium* in William Perkins (1558–1608), certainly the greatest of the sixteenth-century English Calvinists. In 1590 he asked, "What benefits doth a man receive by faith in Christ? Hereby he is justified by faith in God and sanctified."[117]

Speaking for Dort-era Reformed theology, Johannes Wollebius (1586–1629) wrote repeatedly of Christ's *beneficia*. Preaching is "partly the offer of the benefit of redemption."[118] The substance of the covenant of grace or the *"interna materia"* (as distinct from the external and accidental) is "heavenly." The *"res significata"* of the sacraments "is certainly Christ with all his benefits."[119] Under "Justification," Wollebius defended the imputation of the active obedience of Christ as a benefit of Christ.[120] According to Reformed theology, definitive justification produces sanctification. As a transition to sanctification, the last article under "Justification" says, "Justification before God is distinct from justification before men; the former is by faith, the latter is by works."[121] Under "The Sacraments," he argued that "the effects of the sacraments are not justification and sanctification," as if they occurred *"ex opere operato,* but the confirmation and sealing of both benefits."[122] So early seventeenth-century Reformed orthodoxy continued to express substantially the same *duplex iustitia* doctrine as Luther and *duplex beneficium* doctrine as Calvin.

116. "Dupliciter autem Ecclesia sancta est: Renovatione & imputatione, Iohan. 13. Renovatione in semet ipsa sanctitas illa tantum est inchoata, ad Rom. 7 . . . Imputatione vero sanctitas eius est perfectissma in Christo." Caspar Olevian, *Expositio symboli apostolici, sive articulorum fidei, desumpta ex concionibus catecheticis G. Oleviani* (Frankfurt, 1576), 178.

117. See William Perkins, *The Foundation of the Christian Religion Gathered into Six Principles* (1558), repr., Perkins, *The Works of William Perkins* (Appleford, Berkshire: Sutton Courtenay Press, 1970), 159.

118. Johannes Wollebius, *Compendium christianae theologiae*, ed. Ernst Bizer (Munich: Kreis Moers, 1935), 1.20.4.

119. Ibid., 1.22.12. "Materia interna et coelestis est res significata, Christus nimirum cum omnibus beneficiis."

120. Ibid., 1.30.14, 17.

121. Ibid., 1.30.23. "Justificatio coram Deo alia est quam justificatio coram hominibus; illa ex fide est, haec ex operibus."

122. Ibid., 1.22.21. "Effecta sacramentorum non sunt iustificatio aut sanctificatio tanquam ex opere operato, sed utriusque beneficii confirmatio et obsignatio."

When the Westminster divines articulated their doctrine of justification, they were the heirs of over a century of Protestant theological reflection on the doctrine. In that time the same doctrine had sustained a variety of formulations that, despite that variety, were essentially identical. When the divines spoke of Christ's "benefits" in the Westminster Confession of Faith (7.6; 19.3; 27.1, 3; 29.1, 7) and in the Westminster Larger Catechism (57, 58, 65, 153, 154, 162, 167, 170, 175, 176), they were using established Protestant shorthand. In the Westminster Standards, as in Reformed orthodoxy and in sixteenth-century Protestantism, "benefits" was merely a synecdoche for the two distinct but closely related doctrines of definitive justification and progressive sanctification.

5

From Popery to Principle: Covenanters and the Kingship of Christ

David McKay

Covenanters, the Scottish Presbyterians who bound them-selves in national covenants during the seventeenth century, along with their spiritual descendants, have no monopoly of belief in the kingship of Christ. They share this belief with a multitude of other Bible-believing Christians throughout the history of the church. Nevertheless, in the providence of God, Covenanters have put particular emphasis on the fact that Christ reigns. When the Covenanter army under General Alexander Leslie faced the forces of Charles I at Dunse Law in 1639, in what became known as the First Bishops' War, blue banners were unfurled by the Covenanters. On them were the national arms of Scotland and the words "For Christ's Crown and Covenant." In the struggle with the House of Stuart, ecclesiastical and political, the Covenanters fervently believed that they were asserting and defending the "crown rights of King Jesus."

It must be recognized that Covenanters' understanding of the doctrine of Christ's kingship has developed in the course of their history. In this they demonstrate the truth of the old maxim that "a Reformed Church is always reforming." This is the case with the doctrine of Christ's mediatorial kingship over the nations. In the 1990 *Testimony of the Reformed Presbyterian Church of Ireland*, we read: "Nations, as such, by the immutable decree of God the Father, have been given to Jesus Christ that He may rule over them as their supreme Lord. They are, therefore, required to acknowledge and serve Him in all their ways, and submit to His mediatorial authority insofar as it has been revealed to them."[1]

Rather different sentiments were expressed by Samuel Rutherford, writing in 1646. In considering the relationship between church and state, Rutherford does maintain that Christian magistrates have a duty to promote the well-being of the church. He also insists, however, that "the Magistrate as a Magistrate is not the Deputie of Jesus Christ as Mediator," a view that he goes on to describe as "the heart and soule of Popery."[2] The intervening centuries clearly witnessed a major shift in Covenanter thinking.

In the course of this chapter we will trace the views of Covenanters on the kingship of Christ from the seventeenth century up to the present day. At many points there will be a striking consistency in those views across time, but on occasion, particularly with regard to the mediatorial kingship of Christ over the nations, substantial changes will be noted. Thus, what was once derided as "Popery" has become a defining and distinctive principle of contemporary Covenanters.

The Westminster Assembly Commissioners

Several Scottish ministers were among the commissioners sent to consult with the English members of the Westminster Assembly under the terms of the Solemn League and Covenant (1643). Among them were the outstanding theologians George Gillespie and Samuel Rutherford, both of whom played outstanding roles in the Assembly debates.

The Scots, in their National Covenant of 1638, had already taken a firm stand against the absolutist claims of Charles I to sovereignty over the church. The Covenanters asserted that Christ alone is head of the church, with the implication that no man could usurp that

1. *Testimony of the Reformed Presbyterian Church of Ireland* (1990), 24.
2. Samuel Rutherford, *The Divine Right of Church-Government and Excommunication* (London, 1646), 601.

position. In doing so, they were simply repeating the view of Andrew Melville, expressed in his famous speech to James VI in 1596, when he reminded the king: "There are two Kings and two kingdoms in Scotland. There is Christ Jesus the King and, His kingdom the Kirk."[3] At the Westminster Assembly, in debates and pamphlet exchanges with various opponents, the Scots commissioners defended the same view.

George Gillespie (1613–48)[4]

Although less well known than Rutherford, his older and more prolific associate, Gillespie proved himself to be an able controversialist and defender of a high view of the kingship of Christ.

It comes as no surprise that Gillespie wholeheartedly endorsed the view that Christ alone is head of the church. He does so, for example, in his *One Hundred and Eleven Propositions*, printed by order of the General Assembly of the Church of Scotland in 1647. In Proposition 100 Gillespie speaks of "the King of kings and Lord of lords, Jesus Christ, the only monarch of the Church."[5]

In a number of terse statements scattered through the work, Gillespie indicates something of what Christ's royal office means for his church. He states in Proposition 1, for example, that the Lord Jesus Christ "doth invisibly teach and govern his church by the Holy Spirit."[6] Not only that, but he also gathers, preserves, builds, instructs, and saves the church, so that in every way the church owes its existence to Christ, its King and head. All valid authority exercised within the church is also derived from Christ, a most important principle to assert in opposition to King Charles's claims to ecclesiastical authority. Gillespie goes on to say that Christ uses ministers as his instruments

3. Quoted in J. D. Douglas, *Light in the North* (Exeter: Paternoster Press, 1964), 19.
4. For a fuller examination of Gillespie's views on the kingship of Christ, see W. D. J. McKay, *An Ecclesiastical Republic: Church Government in the Writings of George Gillespie* (Carlisle/Edinburgh: Paternoster, 1997), chap. 2.
5. George Gillespie, *One Hundred and Eleven Propositions concerning the Ministry and Government of the Church* (Edinburgh, 1647). The work can be found in *The Presbyterian's Armoury*, vol. 1 (Edinburgh, 1846). The quotation is on page 21.
6. Gillespie, *Propositions*, prop. 1, p. 5.

and that he has instituted a particular order in his church, such that there are pastors to teach and a flock to learn.

Authority is the most prominent element in Gillespie's understanding of Christ's reign over the church. In Proposition 5 he refers to Christ as "our only lawgiver and interpreter of his Father's will,"[7] who has prescribed the rule for the worship and government of his own house, a rule revealed in Scripture. It is this belief that Christ the King has expressed in Scripture—his law book—a pattern to which the church must conform that explains the Scots' adherence to Presbyterianism as *jure divino* (by divine right). They tenaciously defended this view of church government in the Assembly debates. For a man such as Gillespie, Christ's royal law was as binding with regard to church government as it was with regard to doctrine.

Gillespie also argues in Proposition 5 that it is high impiety to wrest this rule of Christ from him and give it to the counsels, wills, or laws of men. Rather, "the law of faith commandeth the counsel and purposes of men to be framed and conformed to this rule."[8] Christ's law must always prevail in his church, and no human law is to supplant it.

Gillespie's view of Christ's kingship in relation to the nations is extensively set out in the pamphlets he wrote in answer to the publications of the Rev. Thomas Coleman, an Assembly commissioner and rector of St. Peter's Church, Cornhill, in London. Coleman held Erastian views, believing that the church should be subject to the authority of the state—a view anathema to Scots Presbyterians. In three pamphlets, entitled *A Brotherly Examination, Nihil Respondes*, and *Male Audis*,[9] Gillespie set out his very different position.

At the heart of the debate is Coleman's view that Christian magistrates are to manage their office "under Christ and for Christ," a principle that might be expected to receive hearty assent from Gillespie. Coleman, however, bases his position on the view that all government has been given by Christ *as Mediator*, support for this claim being drawn from Ephesians 1:21–23. Gillespie responds that such a view robs pagan or infidel magistrates of their title to rule, since

7. Ibid., prop. 5, p. 5.
8. Ibid.
9. All three are to be found in volume 1 of *The Presbyterian's Armoury*.

there is no way by which a pagan magistrate can derive authority from Christ as Mediator. This serves to expose the fundamental difference between Gillespie and Coleman. While both believe that Christ as Mediator is head of the church and that he is also supreme over the nations, they disagree as to whether the latter is as the eternal Son or as the incarnate Mediator. As Gillespie asserts, "God and nature hath made magistrates, and given them great authority; but from Christ as Mediator they have it not."[10]

It is in his debate with Coleman that Gillespie draws on the crucial distinction that informs everything he says about the reign of Christ, particularly in relation to nations and governments. He agrees with his opponent that the Son of God has absolute authority over all things. Thus he says, "I know that Christ, as he is the eternal Son of God, . . . doth, with the Father and the Holy Ghost, reign and rule over all the kingdoms of the sons of men."[11] As God, Christ has all power in heaven and on earth, an allusion to Matthew 28:18; it has been given to him, says Gillespie, "by the eternal generation, and by the declaration of him to be the Son of God with power, when he was raised from the dead, Rom 1:4."[12] Gillespie agrees that the Mediator has, as God, power to subdue the enemies of his church, but "as Mediator he is only the church's King, Head and Governor, and hath no other kingdom."[13]

As far as Gillespie is concerned, the basic weakness in Coleman's case is that it makes Christ to be head over those who are not members of his spiritual body, the church, specifically in this case unbelieving magistrates. In understanding Christ's mediatorial work, we are not to think of him as King over those for whom he is not also Prophet and Priest. This principle colors Gillespie's interpretation of biblical texts relating to Christ's kingship. In dealing with Ephesians 1:22, for example, Gillespie contends that the verse should be translated "him who is over all, [God] gave to be head over the church." This allows

---

10. George Gillespie, *A Brotherly Examination of Some Passages of Mr Coleman's Late Sermon upon Job xi.20 as It Is Now Printed* (London, 1645), in *The Presbyterian's Armoury*, 1:10.

11. Ibid., 11.

12. Ibid.

13. Ibid.

him to argue that Christ, who is over all *as God*, has been given to be head over the church *as Mediator*.

In no way is Gillespie seeking to deny Christ's supremacy over all things. Rather, his concern is to distinguish, he believes on biblical grounds, the ways in which Christ reigns over the church and over those outside the church. His position may be summed up in the title given to chapter 5 of book 2 of his famous treatise *Aaron's Rod Blossoming*: "Of a twofold kingdom of Jesus Christ: a general kingdom, as he is the eternal Son of God, the head of all principalities and powers, reigning over all creatures; and a particular kingdom, as he is Mediator reigning over the church only."[14]

Samuel Rutherford (1600–61)

Gillespie's view of the reign of Christ is shared by his more famous compatriot and fellow commissioner, Samuel Rutherford. Much of his polemical writing deals with issues of church government, in particular the defense of divine-right Presbyterianism, and the fundamental principle that Rutherford asserts is the sole and absolute headship of Christ over his church. To take but one example, in his introduction to *The Divine Right of Church-Government and Excommunication* (1646), Rutherford states:

> Christ is the head and only head of the Church, for by what title Christ is before all things, he in whom all things consist, and is the beginning, the first borne from the dead, and hath the preheminence in all things; and he is onely, solely and absolutely all these, by the same title he is the Head, and so the onely Head of the Body the Church, Col 1:17,18.[15]

This headship relates to both the visible and invisible aspects of the church: "He is the head of his Politick body, and so a head in all externals, as well as of mysticall and invisible body."[16]

---

14. George Gillespie, *Aaron's Rod Blossoming; or the Divine Ordinance of Church Government Vindicated* (London, 1646), repr., in *The Presbyterian's Armoury*, vol. 1, and by Sprinkle Publications (1985).

15. Rutherford, *Divine Right of Church-Government*, 13–14.

16. Ibid., 14.

Inevitably in his historical context, Rutherford had to wrestle with the vexing question of the relationship between church and state, as had Gillespie. Rutherford is adamant that Christian magistrates have a duty to promote the well-being of Christ's church, yet he also insists, "The Magistrate as a Magistrate is not the Vicar nor Deputie of Jesus Christ as Mediator."[17] This doctrine, as we noted in our introductory comments, is described by Rutherford as "the heart and soule of Popery."[18] It is clear that Rutherford, like Gillespie in his debate with Coleman, is reacting against the Erastian conclusions drawn by others from the view that Christ is mediatorial King over the nations, and he is also concerned to show that heathen magistrates who do not acknowledge Christ are nevertheless truly magistrates.

Rutherford shares Gillespie's belief that Christ cannot be mediatorial King over those who have not exercised faith in him. Thus, he says, "Christ is not King as Mediator in any sort or title of such as are Heathen Magistrates."[19] He bases such statements on the conviction that the subjects of Christ as mediatorial King have been given to him by God's eternal decree of election and by its outworking in Christ's work of redemption. There is here the same concern that we have noted in Gillespie to hold together the three elements that have traditionally been viewed as making up the "office" of Christ as Mediator. Thus, Christ is not to be described as King over those for whom he is not Prophet and Priest. As Rutherford puts it, "Christ is as Mediator King and Head, or mediatory King and Head of those that are the subjects, and redeemed conquest of this King, and of those who are members of the body of which he is Head, now this body is his Church only."[20] In Rutherford's thinking, if Christ were mediatorial King over all men (or nations), then nature and grace would be coextensive.

Gillespie's distinction between the two kingdoms governed by Christ is thus repeated exactly in Rutherford's writings. Rutherford finds a reference to Christ's mediatorial power in Matthew 28:18 and

17. Ibid., 601.
18. Ibid.
19. Ibid., 610.
20. Ibid., 612–13.

claims that it "is all spirituall, all Ecclesiasticall power."[21] This is not to deny that there is a sense in which Christ has power over the nations: "Now as God and Creator of the world, Christ could not deny but he had a kingdom worldly, and that he hath a regnum potentiae, a universall Kingdom of power as Lord of Hosts."[22] On this account Christ is able to dispose of all earthly realms as he wills. The same idea is to be found in a sermon on Revelation 19:11–14 preached by Rutherford at a Communion Thanksgiving in Kirkcudbright in the 1630s, in which he says, "All the Kingdoms of the earth are His; all the crowns in the world; (of Britain, France, Spain, Israel and Judah, and tell it until the morn), they are all Christ's as God Creator."[23]

In holding to such a position, Gillespie and Rutherford are giving expression to the view common among Reformed theologians of the time, not only in Scotland, but throughout Europe.[24] It is significant, for example, that the statement of how Christ as Redeemer executes the office of King given in Larger Catechism 45 is cast entirely in terms of the church. The Scots commissioners stood in the mainstream of contemporary Reformed thinking.

Days of Struggle and Persecution

The years following the end of the First Civil War in 1647 sadly witnessed increasing divisions among the Covenanters as some continued to put their hope in a restoration of the Stuart dynasty while others sought strict adherence to the spirit and the letter of the 1643 Solemn League and Covenant. The instability that characterized the government of England after the execution (to Scots outrage) of Charles I and the institution of the Commonwealth led to the restoration of the monarchy in the person of Charles II in 1660. Those who had remained steadfast in their commitment to the covenants

21. Ibid., 611.
22. Ibid.
23. Samuel Rutherford, *Fourteen Communion Sermons* (1877; repr., Edinburgh: Blue Banner Productions, 1986), 15–16.
24. A representative sample can be found in Heinrich Heppe's *Reformed Dogmatics Set Out and Illustrated from the Sources*, rev. and ed. Ernst Bizer, trans. G. T. Thompson (1950; repr., Grand Rapids: Baker, 1978).

now felt the wrath of the king as he sought to reassert royal authority over the church. In the ensuing persecutions many Covenanters paid for their convictions with their lives, while many others fled to the Continent.

Inevitably in such circumstances, the Covenanters' attention concentrated on Christ's kingly authority over the church, which was directly challenged by Charles II. The nature of Christ's kingship over the nation(s) did not vanish from Covenanter writings, but at times the clarity evident in Gillespie and Rutherford became somewhat blurred.

An Apologetical Relation (1665)

While in exile in Holland on account of his Covenanter convictions, John Brown "of Wamphray" (1610–79) penned a thorough defense of the stand taken by the Covenanters in opposition to the claims of Charles II. Under the title *An Apologetical Relation*, published in 1665, Brown provided copious biblical and historical evidence demonstrating that the actions of the Covenanters were just and necessary when they stood aside from the Church of Scotland as it had been shaped by royal decree. Godly men such as James Guthrie (1616–61) had already laid down their lives for their convictions.

Brown's attention is centered on the fact that the king's claims to exercise supreme authority in the church robbed the rightful King of the church of his just prerogatives. The mediatorial kingship of Christ over his church requires that Charles lay down his false claims.

One issue considered by Brown is the swearing of the oath of allegiance, an act refused by consistent Covenanters. They refused not because they would deny proper, biblically warranted loyalty to the king, but because the statement that "the king is the only supreme governor, over all persons and in all causes," was ambiguous if not further explained. The danger that Covenanters rightly perceived in this phrase was, in Brown's words, that of "wronging the Lord Jesus Christ, who is king and head of his church."[25] The words and

25. John Brown, *An Apologetical Relation of the Particular Sufferings of the Faithful Ministers and Professors of the Church of Scotland since August 1660* (Edinburgh, 1845), 69.

actions of the king on many occasions showed that he required of the church that which, in the eyes of Covenanters, belongs only to King Jesus.

Another issue considered by Brown is the authority of the ministers of the church, in particular the Church of Scotland. In a lengthy historical argument, Brown seeks to demonstrate that ministers who receive their commission to carry out their ministerial functions from the civil ruler are not to be acknowledged by the Lord's people. In this context Brown cites several statements drafted by the General Assembly and presented to the king of the time for approval. The 1582 Assembly, for example, complained, with reference to James VI, that "his Majesty, by advice of some counsellors, was about to take the spiritual power and authority upon himself, properly belonging unto Christ, as the king and head of his church."[26] As Brown notes, the Assembly was rightly afraid that in this way the two jurisdictions that God had separated would be confused, "to the wreck of all true religion."[27] An article drafted by the next Assembly refers to the fact that "the jurisdiction of the church was granted by God the Father, through our Mediator Jesus Christ,"[28] only to those church officers whom he had chosen and called. The Covenanters saw clearly that the claims of the Stuarts could not coexist with the claims of King Jesus.

At a later point Brown engages with the views of Bishop Edward Stillingfleet (1635–99), who advocated a union between Anglicans and Presbyterians that treated forms of church government as inessential. Brown accused the bishop of "pleading against the privilege and prerogative of the Crown of Christ, whom God hath made king in Zion, and who will reign until all his enemies be made his footstool."[29]

It is natural that in a context of defending Covenanters' rejection of the Restoration Church of Scotland, Brown should concentrate on Christ's position as "king, and sole king, in his church and kingdom."[30]

26. Ibid., 97.
27. Ibid.
28. Ibid.
29. Ibid., 108.
30. Ibid.

Richard Cameron (d. 1680)

Cameron, who died fighting at Airsmoss on July 20, 1680, was one of the leading preachers among the Covenanters during the "Killing Times." Although he did not write anything for publication, a number of his sermons were recorded and published.[31]

On May 20, 1680, Cameron preached from Hosea 13:9–10, giving particular attention to the Lord's word to Israel, "I will be thy king."[32] As the Covenanter preachers often did, Cameron applies the text to Scotland: to the Church of Scotland, to its ministers, and to the people of Scotland. Church and nation become blurred, perhaps partly because there was only one church, to which almost all the people were in some sense connected. Cameron laments the low spiritual state of Scotland and also the attempts of the civil authorities to usurp the rule of Christ in his church.

In considering the phrase "in me is thine help," Cameron challenges his hearers with great evangelistic fervor. He imagines Christ telling the people on what terms they may have his help: "if you would have help from Me you must take Me to be your King; you must take Me to be the Head of the Church."[33] Cameron continues:

> Our Lord Jesus is and must be King upon His holy hill of Zion. There is no king in the Church besides Him. The Lord has given Him to be King to rule in you and over you. What say ye to this? Our Lord is now dethroned, and that tyrant is entered into His place. . . . Now, are ye content to let the King of Glory—the Lord of Hosts—enter into your hearts and souls? . . . Will you take Christ to be your King, and to be the anointed King of the Church? Will ye acknowledge no lord over God's heritage but the Lord Jesus Christ Himself?[34]

Cameron then turns to the words "I will be thy king" and asserts that, though many in Scotland want only Charles as their king, "we must cry we will have no other king but Christ."[35] This does not mean,

---

31. See *Sermons Delivered in Times of Persecution in Scotland, by Sufferers for the Royal Prerogatives of Jesus Christ* (1779; repr., Edinburgh, 1880).
32. Scripture quotations in this chapter are from the King James Version.
33. *Sermons Delivered*, 413.
34. Ibid.
35. Ibid.

Cameron says, that Covenanters seek the abolition of civil authority but rather that they require rulers who "employ their power for the cause and interest of God."[36] Scotland, he argues, will never see good days until the present ungodly rulers are replaced, and such a radical change God may yet bring about. Quoting Jeremiah 30:21 ("And their nobles shall be of themselves, and their governor shall proceed from the midst of them"), Cameron says: "Indeed by governor we principally understand our Lord Jesus Christ. But when He turns back the captivity of His Church and people, none shall be governors but such as be for Him, at least by profession."[37] Cameron goes on to express his hopes for his native land:

> I know not if this generation will be honoured to cast off these rulers, but those that the Lord makes instruments to bring back Christ, and to recover our liberties civil and ecclesiastic, shall be such as shall disown this king and these inferiors under him, and against whom our Lord is denouncing war.[38]

Political and religious issues seem to merge in Cameron's thinking, much as they did in the National Covenant of 1638. The distinctions drawn by Gillespie and Rutherford tend to fall into the background in Cameron's rhetoric: Christ is to be King over Scotland, over all its people, whether viewed from the civil or the ecclesiastical point of view.

Like his Covenanter brothers, Cameron held to a postmillennial eschatology. This emerges in a most interesting way in a sermon preached just two days before his death. His text is Psalm 46:10 ("Be still, and know that I am God: I will be exalted among the heathen, I will be exalted in the earth"). At one point Cameron recalls better times in Scotland: "Yea, the Church of Scotland has been very high. . . . The day has been when Zion was stately in Scotland."[39] His eschatological vision then comes to the fore: "We are of the opinion that the Church shall yet be more high and glorious, as appears from

36. Ibid., 414.
37. Ibid.
38. Ibid., 415.
39. Ibid., 457.

the book of Revelation, and the Church shall have more power than even she had before. . . . Our Lord shall be exalted on earth; and we do not question much but that He shall be yet exalted in Scotland."[40] Christ's standard, Cameron asserts, will be carried to the very gates of Rome, which will be burned with fire. The Scots must embrace King Jesus if blessing is not to be lost. In the eschaton, it seems, the citizens of the nations will be the church, under Christ's royal authority.

A Hind Let Loose (1687)

The most extensive defense of the principles of the Covenanters produced during the days of persecution was entitled *A Hind Let Loose*, first published in 1687 by Alexander Shields (1660–1700), a former amanuensis to the great theologian John Owen. Shields sought to provide a survey of the spiritual history of Scotland from primitive times that would serve to vindicate the position of the strict Covenanters in relation to the contemporary Church of Scotland.

Of particular significance for our purposes are statements made by Shields at the beginning of part 3 of his work, where he begins a statement and vindication of the present testimony of the Covenanters. He summarizes the heart of the Covenanters' witness as being

> for the glory and crown prerogatives and imperial regalia of the King of kings, with reference to his visible kingdom, of which the government is laid upon his shoulders, against the heaven daring usurpations and encroachments made thereupon, both as he is Mediator, and King, and Head of the church, and as he is God and universal King of the world.[41]

Shields's language here contains clear echoes of the views of Gillespie and Rutherford on the kingship of Christ noted above. This impression is confirmed as Shields continues his exposition.

40. Ibid., 457–58.
41. Alexander Shields, *A Hind Let Loose; or, An Historical Representation of the Testimonies of the Church of Scotland, for the Interest of Christ. With the True State thereof in All Its Periods* (1687; repr., Glasgow, 1797), 248.

He defines first of all the dominion exercised by Christ as Mediator:

> As he is Mediator, it is his peculiar prerogative to have a supremacy and sole sovereignty over his own kingdom, to institute his own government, to constitute his own laws, to ordain his own officers, to appoint his own ordinances, which he will have observed without alteration, addition, or diminution, until his second coming: this his prerogative hath been, and is invaded by erastian prelacy, sacrilegious supremacy, and now by antichristian popery, which have overturned his government, inverted his laws, subverted his officers, and perverted his ordinances.[42]

Shields clearly believes Christ to be mediatorial King over the church, where he exercises absolute authority. As we have previously seen, these prerogatives of Christ were challenged by the claims of the Stuarts, the reference here to "antichristian popery" being a reminder that in 1687 the monarch was the overtly Roman Catholic James II, who would be replaced two years later by the Protestants William III and Mary in the "Glorious Revolution." (Mary, we may note, was also a Stuart.)

Shields next considers the reign of Christ in relation to civil government. A different kind of reign is exercised in this regard:

> As he is God and universal King, it is his incommunicable property and glory, not only to have absolute and illimited power, but to invest his deputed ministers of justice with his authority and ordinance of magistracy, to be administered in subordination to him, to be regulated by his laws, and to be improved for his glory, and the good of mankind.[43]

Civil government and national affairs, according to Shields, belong to the kingdom over which Christ reigns—as God, not as Mediator. Once again these prerogatives of Christ have been usurped by James II and his subordinates.

42. Ibid.
43. Ibid.

This way of understanding civil government is reinforced later by Shields when he writes of magistracy as the ordinance *of God*, deriving its authority *from God*. Shields writes, "It is that great ordinance of God, most signally impressed by a very sacred and illustrious character of the glorious majesty of the Most High, who hath appointed magistracy."[44] He alludes to Romans 13 regarding the ordaining of the powers that be by God and reaffirms that civil rule exists by divine institution. It is not merely the result of a law of nature, but rather "the special investiture of it, in institution and constitution, is from God."[45] This being the case, rulers' lofty task can be described in these terms: "Being God's ministers, they sit in the throne of God, anointed of the Lord; judging not for man, but for the Lord, as the scripture speaks."[46]

Shields also argues that civil rulers have an even higher duty: "the main thing for which government is given, to wit, the gospel and the coming of Christ's Kingdom."[47] The civil ruler is to facilitate the work of Christ's mediatorial kingdom, the church, without himself, in his capacity as ruler, coming under that mediatorial authority. In this connection Shields quotes a text used very often by the Covenanters, Isaiah 49:23, which is regarded as instructing kings to be "nursing fathers" to the church. Rulers relate to the Mediator in this way: "Out of reverence and respect to his absolute sovereignty, they shall take the law from him, without daring to contract, far less to take upon them to prescribe in the house of God, as they in their wisdom think fit."[48]

It is significant that this is written in the context of a covenantal understanding of government in which two covenants are envisaged, a view previously expounded by Rutherford in his 1644 treatise *Lex Rex*. As Shields puts it, with reference to Jehoiada in 2 Kings 11:17, "Here are two distinct covenants; the one made with God, about things eternally obligatory, wherein the king and people engage themselves upon level ground to serve the Lord. . . . The other covenant

44. Ibid., 316.
45. Ibid.
46. Ibid., 317.
47. Ibid., 355.
48. Ibid.

149

was civil, about things alterable, relating to points of government and subjection."[49] The language used throughout is of a commitment made in covenant *with God*, not with Christ the Mediator.

The position of Gillespie and Rutherford is still to be found among the Covenanters of the Killing Times, yet a certain lack of clarity among some may suggest that greater changes are in prospect.

The Eighteenth Century: Covenant Renewal and Controversy

Covenant Renewal at Auchensaugh (1712)

One of the distinctive practices that developed among the spiritual descendants of the first Covenanters was that of covenant renewal—or "renovation," as it was often termed. Fundamentally this involved a renewal of the National Covenant of 1638 and of the Solemn League and Covenant of 1643, often with additional statements applying Covenanter principles to the pressing issues of the day, where necessary taking account of changed historical circumstances. Beginning in Scotland, the practice of covenant renewal spread as Covenanters put down roots in, for example, Ireland and North America.

One particularly significant "renovation" took place in 1712 at Auchensaugh, near Douglas, in Scotland. The event is described as a renewal "with accommodation to the [then] present times."[50] The document signed at Auchensaugh begins with a lengthy historical introduction that seeks to justify from Scripture and from history the action the Covenanters are about to take. There is reference to God's gracious initiative in salvation and to believers' "striking hands with Him through a Mediator (which covenant is commonly called the Covenant of Grace)."[51] The national acts of covenanting are then described in these terms:

49. Ibid., 354.
50. *The Auchensaugh Renovation of the National Covenant and Solemn League and Covenant; with the Acknowledgment of Sins and Engagement to Duties, as They Were Renewed at Auchensaugh, Near Douglas, July 24, 1712* (Philadelphia, 1880), 9.
51. Ibid., 10.

So these three kingdoms of Scotland, England and Ireland con-
junctly, and Scotland by itself, as an independent nation, had in an
eminent way and manner the honour, above most nations of the
world, to dedicate and surrender themselves to the Lord, by a most
voluntary, free and deliberate choice, and to come under the bond
of a most solemn oath, in a most religious manner, devoting their
all to Christ, his interest and honour, the flourishing and thriving
of his kingdom, the success of his gospel, and reformation of his
churches; and openly avouching him for their Lord and Master, to
the honour of his name, and confusion of his enemies.[52]

The framers of the document emphasize that the historic covenants
are not to be regarded as the same as the covenant of grace, but are
thought of as "a solemn superadded and new obligation, tying us to
all the duties, as well of a particular Christian conversation, as those
which tend to the public and national advancement of reformation
in religion."[53]

Significant for our study is the document's description of the three
kingdoms' commitment to Christ, quoted above, and also this statement of the result of such covenanting: "Then the Lord delighted to
dwell in the nations."[54] The evidences of such dwelling by the Lord
are not confined to the church but embrace the whole life of the
nations. The Lord, for example, poured out the gracious influences
of the Holy Spirit, "as our land can afford many instances."[55] Not
only were the churches freed from the familiar oppressors, prelacy
and Erastianism, but the people as a whole were stirred up to act for
the cause of Christ. Indeed,

Numberless were the advantages and privileges which did redound
to these nations by, and were the lovely attendants and sweet con-
sequents of, these covenants; whereby God did set to his seal of
approbation, and gave clear evidence and demonstration of his

52. Ibid.
53. Ibid.
54. Ibid., 11.
55. Ibid.

acceptance of his people's cheerful and willing adventures in this
duty of covenanting with him.[56]

Equally well, when the nations abandoned their covenant obligations
to the Lord, the consequences were also comprehensive. The document refers to "the many sad and fearful plagues, distractions, con-
fusions and miseries"[57] that have resulted from national covenant-
breaking, and continues,

> Which courses of declension and grievous apostatizing from God
> and his covenant, all the three kingdoms and in special this nation,
> and every individual therein capable of such a work are . . . called to
> bewail and confess before God, and by speedy judgments, and turn
> away justly impendent wrath and long threatened strokes.[58]

Although the attention of those who engaged in covenant renewal
at Auchensaugh is chiefly on the church, and therefore on Christ's
reign over the church, prominence is also given to the authority of
Christ that was nationally recognized in the 1638 and 1643 covenants.
While it is not always clear whether the title "Lord" refers to God or
specifically to Christ, it is evident that by this period there is a more
pronounced articulation of Christ's supremacy over the nation, as
well as over the church, without reference to different ways in which
he exercises that supremacy (as God or as Mediator). The distinctions formulated by Gillespie and Rutherford are falling further into
the background, although there is no evidence that the Covenanters
were consciously rejecting their view.

Controversy with the Seceders

The "Glorious Revolution" of 1688–90, which saw the replacement of the Roman Catholic James II by the Protestants William and
Mary, at first seemed to promise better days for the Covenanters. They
soon realized, however, that the new sovereigns had no sympathy

56. Ibid.
57. Ibid.
58. Ibid., 12.

for their views regarding the historic covenants. The Act Rescissory of 1661, which had swept aside the covenants at the Restoration of Charles II, was not repealed, and the covenants continued to be disregarded. The loyal Covenanters, now known as "Cameronians" and meeting as the United Societies, felt compelled to remain separate from the Revolution Church of Scotland.

The first secession from the Church of Scotland took place in 1733, under the leadership of Ebenezer and Ralph Erskine, after a prolonged struggle over a variety of issues, including the influence of the civil power in church affairs. These "Seceders," who organized themselves as the Associate Presbytery, had much in common with the Covenanters in most aspects of their theology. Nevertheless, rather than working together, the two bodies engaged in vitriolic polemical exchanges over the issues dividing them, in particular the nature and role of civil government. Involved in these disputes were differing conceptions of the kingship of Christ. The exchanges became all the more bitter when in 1743 Thomas Nairn left the Associate Presbytery, embraced Covenanter views, and joined what shortly thereafter became known as the Reformed Presbyterian Church.

The differing views of Christ's relationship to the nation held by Seceders and Covenanters appeared in their debates about the civil application of the historic covenants and the necessity for political dissent from the government of Great Britain after 1688.

The position of the Covenanters is expounded at length in the "Judicial Testimony" drawn up in connection with the covenant renewal at Ploughlandhead in 1761. Entitled *Act, Declaration and Testimony*, this document seeks to defend Covenanter dissent from the Revolution Settlement by means of a historical review covering the period from 1638 (the National Covenant) onward, along with a doctrinal summary in eighteen articles. Its purpose is stated thus: "The intent therefore of this work is of very great importance; no less being proposed, than the right stating of the testimony for the covenanter interest of Christ in these lands, and judicial vindication of all the heads thereof, after such a long and universal apostasy therefrom."[59]

59. *Act, Declaration and Testimony, for the Whole of Our Covenanted Reformation, as Attained to, and Established in, Britain and Ireland; Particularly betwixt the Years 1638 and 1649, Inclusive* (Philadelphia, 1876), introduction.

Central to the Covenanters' dissent is their conviction that the Revolution Settlement, particularly in relation to ecclesiastical matters, is in essence institutionalized covenant-breaking. Their first objection, and indeed the fundamental objection, to the Settlement is

> because that in the civil constitution, these nations once united together in a scriptural and covenanted uniformity, unmindful of their former establishment upon a divine footing, wherein king and people were to be one perfect religion, and the supreme magistrate obliged by solemn oath to maintain and preserve the same inviolable, did call and invite William and Mary, prince and princess of Orange, unto the possession of the royal power in these lands, in a way contrary to the word of God.[60]

The Covenanters then turn their attention to differences with the Seceders. While acknowledging the stand for truth taken by the latter in a number of issues, the Covenanters launch a stinging attack on the Seceders "for their error in doctrine, treachery in covenant, partiality and tyranny in discipline and government."[61] It is especially with regard to the legitimacy of the civil government established by the Revolution Settlement that Covenanters and Seceders, united on so much else, stood deeply divided.

The view of the Seceders, set out in detail some years later by one of their leading spokesmen, Adam Gib, in his *Display of Secession-Testimony*, was that while moral qualifications for rulers are highly desirable for the *well-being* of a nation, they are nevertheless not essential for the *being* of civil government as such. The desirable situation, as stated by Gib, is that civil government,

> in all the appurtenances of its constitution and administration, run in agreeableness to the word of God; be subservient unto the spiritual Kingdom of Jesus Christ, and to the interests of the true religion and reformation of the Church: as otherwise they cannot truly prosper in their civil concerns, nor be enriched by the blessings of the gospel.[62]

---

60. Ibid., pt. 2.
61. Ibid., pt. 3.
62. Adam Gib, *Display of Secession-Testimony*, 2 vols. (Edinburgh, 1774), 1:280.

In the absence of such an outlook on the part of rulers, the people could still choose rulers, who were to be acknowledged as legitimate authorities in the nation. According to the Seceder perspective, all governments that exist by God's providence, with the consent of the governed, are of God and are to be obeyed as the ordinance of God (as Rom. 13:1–7 indicates). Thus, the Seceders held that the legitimacy of the rule of William and Mary could be acknowledged by Christians.

In the Ploughlandhead Testimony, the Covenanters set out in detail their utter rejection of such a view. Since government is God's ordinance and since God has provided unchanging laws in his Word to guide rulers, the legitimacy of government, in Covenanter eyes, depends on conformity to these divine requirements, especially in a nation bound in covenant to God. As they put it, "When therefore a nation acts according to divine rule, in the molding of government, and advancing persons to the exercise of it; there the government and governors may be said to be ordained of God."[63] When this was not the case, the government could not be acknowledged as being ordained of God. On this basis the Covenanters rejected the legitimacy of William and Mary and their successors, and sought to distance themselves from national covenant-breaking that robbed Christ of his prerogatives. Claims that a government exists "by God's providence" could not, according to the Covenanters, establish its legitimacy.

Out of the debate between Covenanters and Seceders, in ways that are not entirely clear from this distance, comes a more definite commitment on the part of Covenanters to the mediatorial kingship of Christ over the nation. They were at one with the Seceders in asserting Christ's sole headship over the church, but the Seceders' view of Christ's relationship to the nation is much closer to that of Gillespie and Rutherford. Gib, for example, was concerned that the Covenanter position blurred the necessary distinction between nature and grace because, it seemed to him, Christ as Mediator was, in the Covenanter view, said to have purchased by his death a reign over all things. As Gib puts it, "From whence it would natively follow, that the common enjoyment of all outward things, by all unbelievers through the world

63. *Act, Declaration and Testimony*, pt. 3.

155

as well as by believers, yea by beasts as well as man,—were properly from Christ as Mediator, and through the channel of his blood."[64]

The Covenanters, of course, would not accept such a charge, and the statement regarding Christ as Mediator in *Act, Declaration and Testimony* is free from any confusion of nature and grace.[65] Nevertheless, it does not appear that the doctrine of the kingship of Christ over the nations was thought out with any great theological or exegetical precision in this period—perhaps ironically, in view of the Covenanters' thoroughness on so many other issues. By the following century, however, the doctrine is taken as an essential element of the Reformed Presbyterian Testimony, complete with exegesis of a number of texts, yet with little apparent awareness that it is not the doctrine of the early Covenanters.

The Nineteenth Century: A New Orthodoxy

By the early years of the nineteenth century, we find Covenanter writers in North America, Scotland, and Ireland expounding and defending the doctrine of the mediatorial kingship of Christ over the nations in considerable detail. It appears that by this time the doctrine has become universally accepted in the various branches of the Reformed Presbyterian Church and is regarded as one of its distinguishing marks. That this is what Covenanters should believe appears unchallenged.

North America

Alexander McLeod (1774–1833). One concise and influential defense of the Covenanter view of Christ's kingship was penned by Alexander McLeod, a Scotsman who was ordained to serve the New York Reformed Presbyterian congregation in 1801. In his day he was widely read and respected as a defender of biblical orthodoxy. The focus of our attention is McLeod's short work *Messiah, Governor of the Nations of the Earth*, published in 1803.

---

64. Gib, *Display of Secession-Testimony*, 2:299.
65. *Act, Declaration and Testimony*, pt. 4, art. 7.

McLeod takes as his starting point Revelation 1:5, where Christ is referred to as "the prince of the kings of the earth." As McLeod indicates, the Greek term *"archōn"* used in this verse is a general word for "ruler," and so, he argues, Christ is a ruler and his subjects are the kings of the earth "in their official characters."[66] This assertion is fundamental to McLeod's view of Christ's relationship to the nations: it is over kings *as kings*, not merely in their private capacity, that Christ reigns.

Two issues then occupy McLeod's attention: first a defense of his view that Christ as Mediator rules over the nations of the earth, and second an exposition of some of the acts of Christ's government.

1. *Christ as Mediator ruling over all the nations of the earth.* McLeod asserts that the great truths regarding Christ's gracious mediatorial work are known only through divine revelation. To establish the fact of Christ's mediatorial rule over the nations, appeal can be made both to the explicit teaching of the Bible and to inferences legitimately drawn from explicit statements. On this basis McLeod offers six lines of argument.

First, there is *the character of Jesus Christ.* By this McLeod means what he terms "a moral fitness in the mediatorial person to be the Governor among the nations."[67] It is particularly the moral character Christ possesses that fits him for the exercise of ruling over the nations. As God, he is characterized by supreme moral excellence.

Second, there is *the necessity of Christ's rule.* As McLeod puts it, "It is necessary that Messiah should rule the nations because otherwise the mediatorial office would be inadequate and imperfect."[68] Here a link is made between the atonement offered by Christ at the cross and the application of that atonement in the salvation of sinners. The fulfillment of the Great Commission entails Christ's supremacy over the nations: "Unless his authority were paramount to that of the existing governments, it would have been a usurpation inconsistent with divine perfection to have sent his ambassadors to negotiate with the

66. Alexander McLeod, *Messiah, Governor of the Nations of the Earth* (1803; repr., Elmwood Park, NJ: Reformed Presbyterian Press, 1992), 3.
67. Ibid., 5.
68. Ibid., 7.

inhabitants of the earth."[69] It is this supreme authority of Christ that ensures the effective preaching of the gospel in spite of the opposition of rulers and peoples, and that preserves his church in the midst of its enemies.

Third, there is *the promise of the Father to the Son*. McLeod begins with Old Testament passages such as Psalm 2:8 and Psalm 89:19, 23, 25, 27, which he sees as being fulfilled in Christ's royal reign. McLeod is here drawing on the concept of a covenant of redemption, which, in some varieties of federal theology, is the pretemporal covenant established within the Trinity in order to provide redemption for God's elect. In McLeod's words, "The Scriptures uniformly teach that the Father has engaged to place the Mediator on the throne of the nations upon condition that he should become a substitute for sinners and make atonement for them."[70] The repeated quotation of Psalm 2 in such New Testament books as Acts, Hebrews, and Revelation is regarded as particularly significant for understanding Christ's mediatorial reign.

Fourth, there is *Christ's authorization to rule the kingdoms of the earth*. Two passages are cited as proof of the giving to Christ of a commission that authorizes him to rule over all the nations. The first is Daniel 7:13–14, the vision in which "one like the Son of man" comes to "the Ancient of days" and receives from him "dominion, and glory, and a kingdom, that all people, nations, and languages, should serve him." The one like the Son of Man is, according to McLeod, the Mediator, and to him is given authority over the nations. The second passage is Revelation 5:1–2, 5–7, where only "the Lion of the tribe of Juda, the Root of David," is found worthy to open the sealed book of God's purposes. In the taking of the book and the opening of the seals, says McLeod, the reign of the Messiah over all things, including the kings of the earth, is depicted.

Fifth, there is *the testimony of Christ himself*. McLeod cites texts such as John 17:2, where Jesus says to the Father, "Thou hast given him power over all flesh," and Luke 10:22, where he says to his people, "All things are delivered to me of my Father." The incarnation did

69. Ibid., 8.
70. Ibid., 11.

not entail the giving up of any of the essential perfections possessed by the eternal Son. He always possessed the *ability* to govern the nations, McLeod argues, but in his official capacity as Mediator he required the *authority* to rule, and this the Father has conferred on him. Christ on this basis can lay claim to universal authority, as he does in Matthew 28:18.

Finally, there is *the confirmation of other witnesses.* McLeod appeals, for example, to the witness of the Holy Spirit in various Scriptures that he has inspired, in particular Psalm 8:6, as expounded in Hebrews 2:8 and applied to Christ. A second set of witnesses are the four living creatures who testify to Christ's headship over the nations in Revelation 5:8–9, along with the twenty-four elders who join in their song. McLeod interprets the living creatures as faithful ministers of Christ, and the elders as the saints of both Old and New Testaments.

2. *The acts of Christ's government.* Rather more briefly, we may note several aspects of Christ's royal work listed by McLeod. He recognizes that it would be impossible to list all the acts of Christ in his capacity as ruler of the nations, but the selection he provides in fact covers a wide range of activity.

First, *Christ executes God's purposes for the nations.* McLeod applies to Christ Paul's reference in Ephesians 1:11 to "him who worketh all things after the counsel of his own will." The rise, development, and fall of all nations are in his hands.

Second, *Christ opens doors for the gospel.* Christ directs the actions of rulers and nations in such a way that the gospel spreads through them and the elect are saved.

Third, *Christ calls their subjects into his kingdom.* He has authority to take citizens of all the nations of the earth into his kingdom as his Holy Spirit accompanies the preaching of the gospel and secures a positive response.

Fourth, *Christ instructs earthly rulers how they are to conduct themselves with respect to the church.* Unsurprisingly, McLeod holds that rulers are to promote true religion and protect the true church. As Psalm 2:12 puts it, they are to "kiss the Son." This they do by removing impediments to the progress of the church and also by supporting the church in ways appropriate to their particular circumstances.

Fifth, *Christ overrules the disobedience of rulers and renders all national acts subservient to his own glory and the church's good.* Whether or not rulers wish to serve Christ, they in fact do so. This is but one example of man's wrath praising God. No weapon formed against Zion will prosper.

Sixth, *Christ punishes the powers of the earth for the neglect of their duty.* Although Christ overrules the actions of rulers to serve his cause, that does not reduce the sinfulness of their rebellion, and now, or at the last day, he will punish them.

Other North American Voices. We have spent some time considering McLeod's exposition of Christ's mediatorial kingship because it in many ways set the agenda for those who followed him. In numerous Reformed Presbyterian publications produced in the course of the nineteenth century, the same themes are considered, and the same positions expounded, developed, and defended. We may note here several other significant Covenanter writers who addressed the subject.

In 1832 James R. Willson, pastor of the Reformed Presbyterian congregation of Albany, published *Prince Messiah's Claims to Dominion over All Governments.* One of the chief points of this concise treatise is that "the ordinance of magistracy is subjected to Prince Messiah."[71] Among texts cited in support of this assertion we find Psalm 89:27, Daniel 7:14, and Revelation 1:5, all of which were used by McLeod. Willson goes on to state, "He exercises authority over Kings, as their Lord,"[72] drawing support from a number of Old Testament passages and claiming, for example, that Christ was the angel in the pillar of cloud and the pillar of fire in Exodus who "troubled" the hosts of Pharaoh. Furthermore, since Christ will judge all men, Willson argues, they must now be subject to him.

Willson also asserts, "Nations are bound in the constitutions of their governments to recognise formally the authority of the Mediator as their King."[73] The obedience that Christ requires of all people

71. James R. Willson, *Prince Messiah's Claims to Dominion over All Governments* (Albany, 1832), 13.
72. Ibid.
73. Ibid., 14.

includes that of the rulers of the nations, who to a significant degree set an example (good or bad) to their people. This obedience on the part of rulers, says Willson, will manifest itself in legislating according to the Lord's law, in excluding his open enemies from office, in being "nursing fathers" to the church (quoting Isa. 49:23, a favorite text for Covenanter authors), and in pledging them to do all this "by solemn oath, vow and covenant."[74] The major part of Willson's work then subjects the United States Constitution to rigorous examination in the light of these principles.

The two aspects of Christ's mediatorial kingship—ecclesiastical and civil—are examined in some detail by Samuel B. Wylie of Philadelphia in his 1850 publication *The Two Sons of Oil*, subtitled "The Faithful Witness for Magistracy and Ministry upon a Scriptural Basis." The title draws on the vision of the two olive trees in Revelation 11:3–4, which Wylie interprets as symbolizing the two sources of nourishment for Christ's church, namely, ministers and (godly) magistrates. While most of the book is devoted to explaining the respective responsibilities of ministers and magistrates and answering objections to his position, Wylie does also lay down as a fundamental presupposition the supremacy of Christ over both: "They agree in this, that both are subjected to the Mediator, though under different considerations. Matt xxvii.18, John v.22 and 27, Eph i.21,23 with many other portions of Scripture, leave no room for the candid mind to doubt of the universality of the donation."[75] Interestingly, Wylie states that rulers receive their commission directly from God but that under "the new covenant economy" they owe allegiance to the Mediator.[76]

The final North American voice is that of William L. Roberts, pastor of the Reformed Presbyterian congregation in Sterling, New York. His 1853 work *The Reformed Presbyterian Catechism* is devoted entirely to issues of ecclesiastical and civil government, political dissent, and covenanting. Although expounded in greater detail here, the same themes are dealt with as in the other writers quoted. His foundational principle is stated thus:

74. Ibid.
75. Samuel B. Wylie, *The Two Sons of Oil* (Philadelphia, 1850), 19.
76. Ibid.

Q. Are we to believe that the Lord Jesus Christ exercises a moral supremacy over the civil or political associations of men, simply as such?

A. Yes. Directly in their secular or political character, he claims dominion over them, and demands their public recognition of his authority.[77]

By this time such principles are considered to be, as Roberts puts it in his preface, among "the peculiar principles of the Reformed Presbyterian Church."

Scotland

William Symington (1795–1862). The most thorough examination of the doctrine of the mediatorial kingship of Christ in all its aspects is undoubtedly *Messiah the Prince,* written by the Scottish Reformed Presbyterian pastor William Symington and published in 1839 (second edition, 1840) at the beginning of his long pastorate in the Glasgow congregation.[78]

Before dealing with Christ's relationship to the church and to the nations, Symington first considers the necessary presupposition: the universality of Christ's mediatorial dominion. He asserts, "No doctrine in Scripture is supported by clearer or more abundant evidence than the universality of Christ's mediatorial supremacy."[79] He distinguishes the essential authority that Christ possesses by nature from the mediatorial authority that has been given to him, but stresses that the sphere of the latter need not be different from the former. The difference is that "the kingdom over which he, as the Son of God, rules by inherent and original right, he, as Mediator, is authorised to manage and direct for a new end, namely, the salvation of men, and the best interests of the church."[80]

77. William L. Roberts, *The Reformed Presbyterian Catechism* (New York, 1853), 63.
78. A full-length study of Symington's life and writings is provided by Roy Blackwood in "William Symington: Churchman and Theologian" (Ph.D. thesis, University of Edinburgh, 1963).
79. William Symington, *Messiah the Prince* (1884; repr., Edmonton: Still Waters Revival Books, 1990), 73.
80. Ibid., 73–74.

162

Symington then provides a number of proof texts for his position, each of which is considered briefly. He begins with Matthew 11:27, where Jesus' words to his disciples, "All things are delivered unto me of my Father," indicate a dominion that he did not possess by nature. Even clearer, in Symington's view, is Matthew 28:18, "All power is given unto me in heaven and in earth." Several other texts are quoted to the same effect: Acts 10:26; 1 Corinthians 15:27; Ephesians 1:22; Colossians 2:10. Symington concludes by making reference to the quotation of Psalm 8:6 ("thou hast put all things under his feet") in Hebrews 2:6–8, where the words are applied to the Messiah.

In a later chapter, Symington turns specifically to Christ's mediatorial dominion over the nations. He begins by indicating that this is in fact a logical consequence of what has already been proved regarding the universality of Christ's reign: "For if all things are delivered to him of his Father, if all power is given to him in heaven and in earth, if all things are put under his feet, it is not easy to see on what principle any thing so vast and important as the civil associations of mankind could be excepted."[81] Indeed, asserts Symington, Christ could not carry out his work as head of the church without such dominion.

Proof that Christ exercises dominion over the nations as Mediator is then drawn from several sources. Symington begins with the injunction to civil rulers in Psalm 2:10–12 to submit to the Mediator. As the rulers have rebelled against God's Anointed in their official capacity, so they must submit to him in that same official capacity. Symington next draws on a number of texts that, he claims, predict such a dominion to be exercised by the Messiah. The texts in question are Psalms 47:2–9; 72:10–11, 17; Isaiah 49:22–23; 60:10, 12, 16; Ezekiel 45:17; Daniel 7:13–14; and Revelation 11:15; 21:24, 26. Although others might well disagree with Symington's exegesis of these passages, his conclusion is not lacking in confidence: "No-one, therefore, who has any respect for the word of God, can hesitate to admit that Christ possesses mediatorial dominion over

81. Ibid., 193.

the nations of the earth."[82] He follows up this assertion with a third line of proof, namely, some of the designations given to the Messiah in Scripture. These include "governor among the nations" (Ps. 22:28), "higher than the kings of the earth" (Ps. 89:27), "King of nations" (Jer. 10:6–7), "prince of the kings of the earth" (Rev. 1:5), and "King of kings" (Rev. 17:14; 19:16).

Symington next turns to consider the nature of Christ's administration over the nations. His list shows several similarities to that of McLeod considered earlier. Thus, Christ is said to give the nations their existence, watch over them, demand obedience from them, overrule their rebellion for the advancement of his purposes, execute judgments upon them, open a way for the gospel, and protect his church from injury. As we have noted in other Covenanter writers, Christ's dominion over the nations secures the bringing in of the elect through the spread of the gospel. Reflecting his postmillennial eschatology, Symington finally asserts that "the Mediator will ultimately bring about an entire change in the character and constitution of the nations of the world."[83] By the Lord's power and grace, the nations, he believes, will be Christianized.

The nations in turn have duties toward the Mediator. Symington lists the following: to respect his glory, to take his law as their rule, to have respect to the qualifications of their rulers, to have regard to him in their subjection to rulers, and to swear allegiance to him. The issues treated are the same as those to be found in North American Covenanter writers, as is Symington's belief that rulers have a duty to protect and promote true religion.

Other Scottish Voices. While *Messiah the Prince* was one of the most comprehensive examinations of Christ's mediatorial dominion over the nations, William Symington was expounding a position well established among Scottish Reformed Presbyterians.

A most interesting example is a lecture by William Symington's brother Andrew, Reformed Presbyterian minister in Paisley, on the subject of "The Headship of Christ over the Nations," published in 1841.

82. Ibid., 205.
83. Ibid., 228.

It is one of a series of lectures by Reformed Presbyterian ministers and sets out essentially the same position that William would later defend. There is a certain irony in Andrew Symington's lecture in that he presents this principle as coming from the Second Reformation in Scotland, when in fact the leading theologians of the period, such as Rutherford and Gillespie, as we have seen, held a different view. Symington makes an admiring reference to Gillespie, but it is in relation to his polemics against Erastianism.[84] His own position is that "the distinction between the essential and mediatorial kingdom is only theoretical."[85]

Confessional status was given to this doctrine by the Reformed Presbyterian Church of Scotland in her *Testimony* of 1842. Thus we read:

> Nations are placed in a state of moral subjection to the Lord Jesus Christ, the Prince of the kings of the earth; and they are under obligation to acknowledge his mediatorial authority, and submit to his sceptre; framing their laws, appointing their rulers, and regulating their obedience, in agreeableness to the moral principles of the gospel, and in subserviency to the interests of the kingdom of Christ.[86]

Proof texts cited are Psalms 2:10, 12; 72:11; Isaiah 49:23; Daniel 7:14, 27; Hebrews 2:8; and Revelation 1:5; 21:24.

Ireland

Covenant Renewal in 1853. The commitment of the Reformed Presbyterian Church of Ireland to the same position regarding the mediatorial dominion of Christ that we have found in North America and Scotland is evident in the covenant renewal that took place at Dervock, County Antrim, in 1853.[87]

After the "Confession of Sins," a standard element in such covenant documents, there is then an "Act of Covenant-Renovation," which is described as a renewal of the 1638 and 1645 covenants "in

84. Andrew Symington, *The Headship of Christ over the Nations* (Glasgow, 1841), 29 n.
85. Ibid., 16.
86. *Testimony of the Reformed Presbyterian Church of Scotland* (Glasgow, 1842), 331.
87. The text of the 1853 Covenant is included in Thomas Houston, *A Memorial of Covenanting*, repr., in *Works Doctrinal and Practical of the Rev Thomas Houston, DD* (Edinburgh, 1876), 3:357–89.

accommodation to the present time."[88] The sole headship of Christ over his church is reasserted in response to the challenges of the day. The Covenanters then go on to state their belief that the welfare of both nation and Reformed religion depends to a great extent on the establishment of a biblical pattern of civil government, together with biblical character on the part of civil rulers. In view of this belief, "We engage, with all sincerity and constancy, to maintain, in our several vocations, with our prayers, efforts and lives, the doctrine of Messiah's Headship, not only over the Church, but also over the civil commonwealth."[89]

The practical implications of this engagement include a promise "that our allegiance to Christ shall regulate all our civil relations, attachments, profession and deportment,"[90] along with efforts by teaching, prayer, and example to bring others to confess Jesus Christ as Lord. It is significant that the Covenanters regard Christ's kingship over the earth as an evangelistic imperative, such that they can say, "[We] desire to dedicate ourselves, in our respective places, to the great work of making known his light and salvation throughout the nations."[91]

With particular reference to Christ's authority over the nations, the Covenanters express their aspirations in these terms:

> And we shall constantly endeavour, by all scriptural means, as far as in our power, to bring these nations to own the Mediator as the Head of all principality and rule, to subject the national polity to his authority, and to set up those only as rulers who submit to Christ the Lord, and are possessed of a due measure of scriptural qualifications.[92]

Thomas Houston (1803–82). The outstanding theologian of the Reformed Presbyterian Church of Ireland in the nineteenth century was Thomas Houston of Knockbracken, County Down, the author of *A Memorial of Covenanting*, quoted above. He deals in detail with

88. Ibid., 3:366.
89. Ibid., 3:370.
90. Ibid.
91. Ibid., 3:371–72.
92. Ibid., 3:370.

Christ's mediatorial kingship in a paper entitled "The Redeemer's Crown Flourishing," published in *The Dominion and Glory of the Redeemer* (1880).

Basing his study on Psalm 132:18 ("but upon himself shall his crown flourish"), Houston examines several aspects of Christ's reign. After noting the universal dominion exercised by Christ as the eternal Son, he goes on to speak of a dominion given to Christ as Mediator, "for mediatorial purposes."[93] This of course includes the Mediator's exclusive headship over the church, which owes its very existence to him. All that Christ does serves the welfare and growth of the church. In addition, says Houston, "He wears the crown of the nations of the earth, and has supreme dominion over the universe,"[94] citing a number of texts, including such now-familiar ones as Psalm 22:28 and Revelation 19:6.

The implications of this assertion are much as we have found in other Covenanter writings. Fundamental to Christ's reign over nations is the fact that "he claims, by proper right, the submission of civil rulers of whatever rank, and that national homage should be rendered to Him."[95] Christ's role in relation to the nations is, according to Houston, comprehensive: "He organises nations, and gives them a national existence; He fixes the times and bounds of their dominion; He claims that their constitution and law should be accordant with His revealed will."[96] Nations are rewarded or punished for their responses to Christ's law, and rulers are to possess biblical qualifications and are to promote the welfare of the church.

Houston's eschatology is clearly postmillennial. "The end of all national changes and revolutions will be the universal visible establishment of the dominion of Christ."[97] This, he says toward the conclusion of his paper, "is fitted to inspire all confidence respecting the future destinies of the church and the world."[98] He ends on a high note, as far as believers are concerned: "Brought to sit down with the Redeemer

93. Thomas Houston, *The Dominion and Glory of the Redeemer, the Support and Confidence of the Church and the Joy of the Saints* (Edinburgh, 1880), 281.
94. Ibid., 283.
95. Ibid.
96. Ibid., 284.
97. Ibid.
98. Ibid., 293.

DAVID McKAY

on His throne, they shall behold with ecstatic wonder and delight His crown flourishing upon Himself; and they themselves reflecting, as sparkling jewels, the brightness and beauty of His glory for ever."[99]

The Twentieth Century: An Established Principle

By the twentieth century the doctrine of the mediatorial kingship of Christ over the nations was an established and undisputed principle in the testimony of the various branches of the Reformed Presbyterian Church that regarded themselves as heirs of the Second Reformation in Scotland. While in the nineteenth century many books and pamphlets on the subject had been published, especially in North America, in the twentieth century publications devoted to this issue alone were rare. In the wider evangelical and Reformed community, knowledge of the Reformed Presbyterian position was, at best, limited. The principle, however, was regularly restated in the "testimonies" published by the North American and Irish branches of the denomination. The small Scottish Reformed Presbyterian Church did not produce a testimony in the twentieth century.

We may note the following official statements:

Sovereignty belongs to Almighty God alone, who has committed all authority to his Son, our Saviour, the Lord Jesus Christ. It is the duty, therefore, of every nation, in setting up its government, to acknowledge the authority of Christ, and to enter into covenant with Him as its King and Saviour. (RPCNA, 1928)[100]

God has given the exercise of all authority to the Lord Jesus Christ. Christ is the Divine Lawgiver, Governor and Judge. . . . Every nation ought to recognize the Divine institution of civil government, the sovereignty of God exercised by Jesus Christ, and its duty to rule the

99. Ibid., 294.
100. *The Declaration and Testimony of the Reformed Presbyterian Church of North America*, adopted 1806, amended 1823–1928, in *The Constitution of the Reformed Presbyterian Church of North America* (Pittsburgh, 1949), 205.

168

civil affairs of men in accordance with the will of God. (RPCNA, 1980)[101]

Nations, as such, have been, by the immutable decree of God the Father, given to Jesus Christ that He may rule over them as their supreme Lord. They are therefore required to recognise Him as their Head; to submit to His mediatorial authority; and to appoint their rulers, frame their laws, and regulate their whole administration, according to His revealed will and in subservience to the interests of His kingdom. (RPCI, 1901)[102]

Nations, as such, by the immutable decree of God the Father, have been given to Jesus Christ that He may rule over them as their supreme Lord. They are, therefore, required to acknowledge and serve Him in all their ways, and submit to His mediatorial authority in so far as it has been revealed to them. (RPCI, 1966)[103]

The transition was complete. If anyone noticed the journey that had been undertaken from the position of Rutherford and Gillespie, no mention was made of it. It does not appear that, at least in recent centuries, an extensive theological analysis and comparison of the differing views was made. By the twentieth century, Rutherford's "heart and soule of Popery" had become one of the foundational principles of the churches tracing an unbroken line of descent from him and his fellow Covenanters.

101. *The Testimony of the Reformed Presbyterian Church of North America*, adopted August 1980, in *The Constitution of the Reformed Presbyterian Church of North America* (Pittsburgh, 1989), A-70.

102. *Reformed Presbyterian Testimony, Part 1, Doctrinal and Practical* (Belfast, 1901), 107.

103. *Testimony of the Reformed Presbyterian Church of Ireland, Doctrinal and Practical* (Belfast, 1966), 18–19. The identical statement is used in *Testimony of the Reformed Presbyterian Church of Ireland*, 24.

6

Good and Necessary Consequence in the Westminster Confession

C. J. WILLIAMS

The whole counsel of God concerning all things necessary for His own glory, man's salvation, faith and life, is either expressly set down in Scripture, or by good and necessary consequence may be deduced from Scripture: unto which nothing at any time is to be added, whether by new revelations of the Spirit, or traditions of men. Nevertheless, we acknowledge the inward illumination of the Spirit of God to be necessary for the saving understanding of such things as are revealed in the Word: and that there are some circumstances concerning the worship of God, and government of the church, common to human actions and societies, which are to be ordered by the light of nature, and Christian prudence, according to the general rules of the Word, which are always to be obeyed. (Westminster Confession of Faith 1.6)

The first chapter of the Westminster Confession has left the Reformed church with a definitive statement of the perfection and completeness of the Holy Scriptures that is unrivaled in confessional literature. B. B. Warfield said of this chapter, "There is certainly in the whole mass of confessional literature no more nobly conceived or ably wrought-out statement of doctrine than the chapter 'Of the Holy Scripture,' which the Westminster Divines placed at the head of their

171

confession and laid at the foundation of their system of doctrine."[1] Although that is a bold claim, it is hard to disagree with Warfield. The doctrine of Scripture propounded by the Westminster Confession has withstood the test of time as a remarkably sound and precise confessional statement of the biblical doctrine of the Holy Scriptures.

The comprehensiveness of Scripture is the initial emphasis of paragraph 6 ("The *whole* counsel of God concerning *all things* necessary . . ."). This emphasis leads into a statement of the principal scope of Scripture: the glory of God and the salvation, faith, and life of man. The whole counsel of God on these exalted matters is not limited by the confession to "what is expressly set down in Scripture." An important distinction at this point identifies another mechanism by which biblical truth is comprehended. The confession states that the whole counsel of God includes what "by good and necessary consequence may be deduced from Scripture." This essay will explore the background, formulation, and application of this important provision.

At the time of the Westminster Assembly, the belief that one could deduce scriptural verity and arrive at certain aspects of biblical truth that were not expressly stated was the subject of spirited debate. A major criticism of this method came from the Anglican Church, as represented in the writings of Richard Hooker. Hooker was a staunch defender of the established church and fierce critic of the Puritans. His major work, *The Laws of Ecclesiastical Polity*, was first published in 1593. Hooker's main purpose in this work was to defend Episcopal polity and worship against the reforms proposed by the Puritans. He asserted that the Scriptures give little detail in all but the greatest matters of doctrine, and that much of the life and practice of the church is comprehended in general principles or left to man's judgment. In a chapter entitled "How Laws for the Polity of the Church May Be Made by the Advice of Men," he wrote:

> A number of things there are for which the Scripture hath not provided by any law, but left them unto the careful discretion of the church; we are to search how the church in these cases may be well

---

1. B. B. Warfield, *The Westminster Assembly and Its Work* (Cherry Hill, NJ: Mack Publishing, 1972), 155.

directed to make that provision by laws which is most convenient and fit. And what is so in these cases, partly Scripture and partly reason must teach to discern.[2]

With this limited view of the sufficiency of Scripture, Hooker was wary of the idea that a distinct form of church government could be deduced from Scripture. He chided the Puritan writers for their deductive hermeneutics and laid down this challenge:

> And we may boldly deny, that of all those things which at this day are with so great necessity urged upon this church under the name of reformed church-discipline, there is any one which their books hitherto have made manifest to be contained in Scripture. Let them if they can allege but one properly belonging to their cause, and not common to them and us, and shew the deduction thereof out of Scripture to be necessary.[3]

Besides Hooker and the Anglican Church, the Socinians also held the belief that biblical authority must be limited to its literal statements, leaving no room for authoritative scriptural deductions. The Anabaptists pointed to the lack of any explicit biblical statement on pedobaptism. Roman Catholicism, particularly within the context of the Council of Trent (1545–63), also left the Reformed church with a greater need to fortify and elucidate certain points of its theology and its methods for arriving at them.

It was within this atmosphere that the assembly of divines met. It would be wrong to assume, however, that in light of its historical context the affirmation of "good and necessary consequence" was merely polemical in nature. The Westminster Assembly was committed to the principle that everything necessary for faith and life can be derived from the comprehensive teaching of Scripture and stated in a concise confession. The divines were unwilling to concede that God had simply left the church adrift and undirected in certain matters, or that human judgment was to make up the balance of what

2. Richard Hooker, *The Laws of Ecclesiastical Polity*, 2 vols. (London: J. M. Dent and Sons, Ltd., 1958), 1:325.
3. Ibid., 1:216.

was lacking in Scripture. The Westminster Confession's doctrine of Scripture therefore takes into account the *implications* of Scripture, comprehended by deduction, as being part of the whole counsel of God. The confession affirms that true doctrine is comprehended in the whole sense of Scripture and in the full scope of its implicated meaning. This important provision was given systematic expression by one of the Assembly's most notable members, George Gillespie.

Gillespie, a Scottish commissioner to the Assembly, articulated this point in chapter 20 of his work *Treatise of Miscellany Questions*. The title of the chapter contains the argument itself: "That necessary consequences from the written Word of God, do sufficiently and strongly prove the consequent or conclusion, if theoretical, to be a certain Divine truth which ought to be believed, and, if practical, to be a necessary duty which we are obliged unto, *jure divino*." In this treatise Gillespie directly responded to Hooker:

> Although Hooker in his *Ecclesiastical Polity*, and other prelatical writings, did hold this difference between the Old and New Testament, that Christ and His apostles hath not descended into all particularities with us as Moses did with the Jews, yet, upon examination, it will be found that all the ordinances and holy things of the Christian church are no less determined and contained in the New Testament, than the ordinances of the Jewish church were determined in the Old, and that there were some necessary things left to be collected by necessary consequences from the law of Moses as well as now from the New Testament.[4]

Gillespie demonstrated how the deduction of good and necessary consequences is a valid method of interpretation that is used by Scripture itself, and how essential this method is in our understanding of divine truth. He demonstrated how deductions were employed in biblical argumentation to affirm great truths, such as the doctrine of the resurrection and the divinity of Christ. For example, Christ proved the resurrection to the Sadducees, who did not believe in the resurrection, by quoting Exodus 3:6, "I am the God of Abraham, the

4. George Gillespie, *Treatise of Miscellany Questions* (Edinburgh: Robert Ogle, and Oliver & Boyd, 1844), 102.

God of Isaac, and the God of Jacob."[5] Speaking to Moses long after the patriarchs were dead, God in this self-identification implies the continuing and future existence of the patriarchs because "God is not the God of the dead, but of the living" (Matt. 22:32). Gillespie also showed how the divinity of Christ is proved by a necessary consequence in Hebrews 1:6. Based on such biblical examples, he cautiously formulated his thesis on the use of good and necessary consequences, which is worth reproducing at some length:

> This assertion must neither be so far enlarged as to comprehend the erroneous reasonings and consequences from Scripture which this or that man, or this or that church, apprehend and believe to be strong and necessary consequences (I speak of what *is*, not of what is *thought to be* a necessary consequence): neither yet must it be so far contracted and straitened as the Arminians would have it, who admit of no proofs from Scripture, but either plain explicit texts, or such consequences as are *nulli non obvice*, as neither are, nor can be, controverted by any man who is *rationis compos*; by which principle, if embraced, we must renounce many necessary truths which the reformed churches hold against the Arians, Antitrinitarians, Socinians, Papists, because the consequences and arguments from Scripture brought to prove them are not admitted as good by the adversaries.
>
> This also I must, in the second place, premise, that the meaning of the assertion is not that human reason, drawing a consequence from Scripture, can be the ground of our belief or conscience; for although the consequence or argumentation be drawn forth by men's reasons, yet the consequent itself, or conclusion, is not believed or embraced by the strength of reason, but because it is the truth and will of God. . . .
>
> Thirdly, let us observe with Gerhard, a distinction between corrupt reason and renewed or rectified reason; or between natural reason arguing in divine things from natural and carnal principles, sense, experience and the like, and reason captivated and subdued to the obedience of Christ, judging of divine things not by human, but by divine rules, and standing to scriptural principles, how opposite

5. Unless otherwise indicated, Scripture quotations in this chapter are from the New King James Version.

soever they may be to the wisdom of the flesh. It is the latter, not the former reason, which will be convinced and satisfied with the consequences and conclusions drawn from Scripture, in things which concern the glory of God, and matters spiritual or divine.[6]

Gillespie provides valuable insight into the confession's doctrine of good and necessary consequence, which obviously bears his influence. First of all, the practice of deducing truth from the Scriptures is to be moderate and judicious; no deduction can be affirmed as doctrine if it is only possible or even probable. Only an objectively necessary deduction can be promulgated as biblical truth. Second, such necessary deductions are not always marked by unanimous agreement or universal acceptance. Many orthodox truths are held by good and necessary consequence, yet are not recognized by the Arians, Antitrinitarians, and others. Third, Gillespie affirms that the locus of authority always remains with the Scriptures rather than with the reason of man. Though he asserts confidence in the deductive ability of sanctified reason, his intention is to place assurance not in man's reason, but in the Bible itself in its whole scope of intended meaning. Reason and deduction are simply the means by which the truth may be comprehended. Finally, Gillespie affirms that spiritual truths are spiritually discerned; only regenerate reason is able to deduce and embrace the good and necessary consequences of Scripture concerning spiritual and divine matters.

Gillespie makes another point that is worth notice: that God is entirely consistent with himself and that proper deductions from his Word will therefore be in harmony with his will. Whereas consequences can be drawn from a man's word that the man himself did not intend, God perfectly understands and designs the consequences that will be drawn from his Word. Thus, Gillespie contends, "if we say that necessary consequences from Scripture prove not a *jus divinum*, we say that which is inconsistent with the infinite wisdom of God."[7]

Gillespie's argument is concluded by pointing out how often we depend on the good and necessary consequences of Scripture:

6. Gillespie, *Treatise of Miscellany Questions*, 100–101.
7. Ibid., 102–3.

Divers other great absurdities must follow if this truth be not admitted. How can it be proved that women may partake of the sacrament of the Lord's Supper, unless we prove it by necessary consequence from Scripture? How can it be proved that this or that church is a true church, and the ministry thereof a true ministry, and the baptism ministered therein true baptism? Sure no express Scripture will prove it, but necessary consequence will. How shall this or that individual believer collect from Scripture, that to him, even to him, the covenant of grace and the promises thereof belong?[8]

Robert Baillie, another Scottish commissioner, also typified the Assembly's doctrine of good and necessary consequence. His insistence on the authority of scriptural deductions arose out of the controversy with the Anabaptists. He made the following remark on the Anabaptists' rejection of good and necessary consequences:

When in their debate against the baptism of infants they are straited with consequences from the circumcision of infants, and the promises of the Covenant made with Abraham, and his children; refusing with the Jesuit Veron in their reasonings all deductions though never so necessary and clear, requiring for everything they will admit, expresse and syllabicall Scriptures.[9]

In his work *Jus Divinum* or *The Divine Right of Church Government*, Baillie used biblical deductions extensively and judiciously, for example, to prove that the office of ruling elder was biblical.[10]

Samuel Rutherford, another notable member of the Scottish Commission, also explicated Scripture by necessary deductions, and sought to demonstrate the use of this method in Scripture itself. To cite but one example, in his work *Christ Dying and Drawing Sinners to Himself*, he showed how Christ confirmed the resurrection by necessary consequence in Matthew 22:31–32 and Luke 20:37–38.[11]

8. Ibid., 103.
9. Robert Baillie, *Anabaptism, the True Fountain of Independency* (London: Samuel Gellibrand, 1646), 37.
10. Scott Thomas Murphy, "The Doctrine of Scripture in the Westminster Assembly" (Ph.D. diss., Drew University, 1984), 155.
11. Ibid.

Many agree that Gillespie and Baillie, and the Scottish commissioners in general, bore a great influence on the Westminster documents, so much so that *The Cambridge Modern History* speculates that "it is uncertain whether they [the Westminster documents] owe their origin to the divines of the assembly or to the Scottish Commissioners."[12] No doubt, this "uncertainty" is a bit of an exaggeration, but the point remains that the Scottish Commission was very influential. That influence is unmistakable in the Assembly's formulation of the principle of good and necessary consequence, to which we now turn.

The Assembly formulated this doctrine with obvious care and caution, for such a point lays itself open to misunderstanding and abuse. In paragraph 6 of chapter 1 of the confession, it is first of all to be noticed that the good and necessary consequences of Scripture are held on equal footing with the express statements of Scripture; together they constitute the whole counsel of God. There is no varying level of authority that depends on the method by which we comprehend a certain truth of Scripture; good and necessary deductions have the same authority as the "thou shalts" of the law. Because God is the Author of Scripture, he is also the Author of the *implications* of Scripture. As B. B. Warfield put it, "It is the Reformed contention, reflected here by the Confession, that the sense of Scripture is Scripture, and that men are bound by its whole sense in all its implications."[13]

Most important are the two qualifications that biblical deductions must meet: *good* and *necessary*. The qualification "good" surely means that any biblical deduction must be in harmony with other Scripture. In paragraph 9, chapter 1, the confession establishes this equitable principle: "The infallible rule of interpretation of Scripture is the Scripture itself." This, of course, would apply to scriptural deductions, and this would be the measure by which any deduction was deemed "good." It must be in agreement with the known corpus of truth that Scripture teaches, and it must be in harmony with "other places that speak more clearly."

The second qualification is that such deductions must be "necessary." They must be demonstrably certain and not reasonably

12. A. W. Ward, G. W. Prothro, and Stanley Leaths, eds., *The Cambridge Modern History*, 13 vols. (New York: Macmillan, 1906), 4:363.
13. Warfield, *Westminster Assembly*, 226.

deniable—or, to borrow a familiar courtroom phrase, they must be "beyond a reasonable doubt." This qualification is a much-needed safeguard against creative theological inferences based on meager biblical evidence. Biblical inferences that are merely possible or conceivable are not the stuff on which to build the doctrine and practice of the church. For a scriptural deduction to be necessary, it must occupy its own needful place within the structure of biblical truth and be in harmony with the other truths that it touches.

"Good" and "necessary" may also be seen as the terminological equivalents of the two standard criteria for sound, logical deductions. For any argument to be sound, it must meet two specific criteria, namely, (1) the premises must be true and (2) the conclusion must follow necessarily from the premises ("deductive validity"). True premises make an argument "good," while deductive validity makes its conclusion "necessary." Therefore, a "good and necessary consequence" requires verifiably true premises and deductive validity.

Paragraph 6 is careful to discriminate between the occasional need to deduce biblical truth and the view that Scripture is in need of supplementation, "whether by new revelations of the Spirit, or traditions of men." The occasional need to deduce biblical doctrine does in no way imply that Scripture is inadequate or unclear. It may be observed that traditions in which "good and necessary consequence" is not acknowledged or practiced as a method for arriving at biblical truth are also those most likely to have some form of extrabiblical authority. This was true at the time of the Westminster Assembly in regard to the Roman and Anglican churches, which depended on the authority of tradition, and the Sectarians, who often claimed new revelation. There are several other modern examples—to say no more—of this denial of good and necessary consequence with a corresponding dependence on extrabiblical authority.

The confession is just as careful on this point to avoid the impression that human reason is the ground of authority when it comes to doctrines or duties inferred from the Scriptures. "Nevertheless we acknowledge the inward illumination of the Holy Spirit of God to be necessary for the saving understanding of such things as are revealed in the Word." The mind of man must be enlightened by the Spirit and subjected to the Scriptures if any saving truth is to be comprehended and embraced, whether that truth comes in the form of a plain statement or in the form of a good and necessary consequence. The confession in no way implies that reason is its own authority, nor does it unduly exalt human reason as anything more than an instrument for understanding the Word of God under the good guidance of the Spirit. While a necessary consequence may be deduced from Scripture by the use of reason, the ground of authority is still Scripture.

In question 105 of the Larger Catechism, among the sins forbidden in the first commandment, the divines listed "bold and curious searching into His secrets," with Deuteronomy 29:29 as a proof text: "The secret things belong unto the LORD our God: but those things which are revealed belong unto us and to our children for ever, that we may do all the words of this law" (KJV). The Assembly's doctrine on this point is careful to avoid the exaltation of human reason, the indiscreet handling of Scripture, presumptuous theological creativity, and bold philosophical curiosity. Scriptural deductions must be good and necessary, not "bold and curious."

In spite of these cautions, the confession acknowledges the sanctified use of reason as an indispensable method of discovering scriptural truth. The right use of reason and the ability to deduce were so important to the Westminster divines that "skill in logick and philosophy" was among the ordination requirements that they listed in The Form of Presbyterial Church Government. On this point the divines stood within the heritage of Augustine, who wrote:

> The science of reasoning is of very great service in searching into and unraveling all sorts of questions that come up in Scripture. . . . The validity of logical sequences is not a thing devised by men, but it is observed and noted by them that they may be able to learn and teach it; for it exists eternally in the reason of things, and has its origin with God.[14]

In this same spirit, the confession affirms that Scripture is meant to engage our minds and challenge us to reason, think, and deduce.

14. Quoted in Elihu Carranza, *Logic Workbook for Logic by Gordon H. Clark* (Jefferson, MD: The Trinity Foundation, 1992), 97, 99.

The principle of good and necessary consequence reveals this quality of Scripture.

The confession has been criticized on this point for not seeming to take into account the problem of human subjectivity in the process of deduction.[15] While the Westminster divines placed an obvious degree of trust in sanctified reason, they were not blind to the potential errors and abuses in the deduction of consequences. John Delivuk observes, "Like any method of biblical interpretation, the drawing of implications can be abused. One method used by the authors of the confession to prevent this abuse was comparing their conclusions with other theologians."[16] For example, Cornelius Burges took the caution of comparing his use of biblical deductions concerning infant baptism with the work of other theologians, saying, "Nor have I been my own judge, or expounded them out of my head, but take such expositions as the most learned, judicious, reverend, and eminent Divines of this last age, as well as others of less note . . . ."[17] The Westminster divines never gave the impression that deduction is a foolproof process, or that human reason is immune to error. As a safeguard against human error, they placed a high value on counsel and consensus in matters of doctrine, as is evident by their proceedings as an assembly. As Jack Rogers summarizes, "They did not . . . discount the opinions of theologians, either individually or in council. But they claimed that all opinions of men were valid only insofar as they agreed with Scripture."[18]

It should be observed that the problems of fallibility and subjectivity are not unique to the process of deduction. There is necessarily an element of human judgment at the level both of interpreting the letter of the text and of drawing good and necessary inferences. Both demand the exegete to use his mind under the guidance of the Holy Spirit and the rest of Scripture. There is no way of raising doubts about deduction as a hermeneutical method without also raising

15. Jack Bartlett Rogers, *Scripture in the Westminster Confession* (Grand Rapids: Eerdmans, 1967), 336, 346–47.
16. John Allen Delivuk, "Biblical Authority in the Westminster Confession and Its Twentieth Century Contextualization in the Reformed Presbyterian Testimony of 1980" (Th.D. diss., Concordia Seminary, 1987), 151.
17. Quoted in ibid.
18. Rogers, *Scripture in the Westminster Confession*, 430.

doubts about the process of interpreting the more explicit statements of Scripture. Either way, the exegete must subject his mind to the guidance of the Spirit and the Word, but he must *use* his mind. We cannot escape the need to interpret the text, and deduction is one element of interpretation.

The Assembly placed other prudent limitations on the principle of good and necessary consequence. For instance, paragraph 6 asserts that "there are some circumstances concerning the worship of God, and the government of the church, common to human actions and societies, which are to be ordered by the light of nature and Christian prudence. . . ." In other words, not *everything* may be deduced, and we need not force any deduction if it does not present itself. The light of nature, Christian prudence, and "the general rules of the Word" are enough to illumine our path in certain subsidiary matters. The method of deduction by good and necessary consequence does not hold the potential to answer every question that we may think to ask, nor should it be pressed beyond its capacity.

Earlier we saw how Richard Hooker argued for the more extensive use of human judgment in the worship and polity of the church. The Westminster Confession of Faith does not deny the need to use Christian prudence or sanctified judgment in certain circumstances of the life of the church. It simply emphasizes the need to follow the inferences of Scripture when such inferences may be properly made. In doing so, we may find more authoritative direction than the light of nature or Christian prudence. We must not look for inferences where there are none, but we must not deny them when they may be rightly drawn.

We may discern another caveat in paragraph 7 of chapter 1, which reads:

> All things in Scripture are not alike plain in themselves, nor alike clear unto all; yet those things which are necessary to be known, believed, and observed for salvation, are so clearly propounded and opened in some place of Scripture or other, that not only the learned, but the unlearned, in a due use of the ordinary means, may attain unto a sufficient understanding of them.

The point of this paragraph has clear application to the doctrine of good and necessary consequence. The great gospel truths of Scripture do not require the power of deduction in order to be understood. The saving truth of the gospel, in all its power and simplicity, is accessible to all. The occasional need to employ logical deductions does not make the Bible too complicated for all but the most learned. The doctrine of good and necessary consequence is by no means a barrier to the purpose of Scripture, which includes man's salvation, faith, and life. Paragraph 8 of chapter 1 of the confession affirms that all of God's people "have a right unto, and interest in the Scriptures." The occasional need to deduce biblical truths is not a complication that impedes the right and interest of God's people, who "through the patience and comfort of the Scriptures may have hope." The Bible may contain its intellectual challenges, but its gospel of salvation in Christ is clear and radiant.

Furthermore, it is not the rules of logic that ultimately commend biblical truth to us. While biblical deduction must be sound, it is not the precise logical structure of the argument that commends it to us as believable. Paragraph 5 of chapter 1 lists the several things that may move us to "a high and reverent esteem of the Holy Scripture." The sound logic of rightly deduced doctrine may be one of those things that garner esteem for the Scriptures, but it is not what persuades fallen men to embrace the truth. That is the work of the Holy Spirit alone. Paragraph 5 goes on to say that "our full persuasion and assurance of the infallible truth and divine authority thereof, is from the inward work of the Holy Spirit bearing witness by and with the Word in our hearts." Sound logic, important as it is, is no substitute for saving grace. As the Reformed Presbyterian Testimony puts it, "The truthfulness of God, and not the reasonableness of any doctrine, is the ground of our faith."[19] Sound biblical deductions are not believable because they are logical; they are believable because they are from God.

A good and necessary consequence drawn from Scripture may, therefore, lead us to an article of truth that must be accepted entirely

---

19. *The Constitution of the Reformed Presbyterian Church of North America* (Pittsburgh: Crown and Covenant Publications, 2004), A-8.

on faith. A good and necessary consequence may, in the end, be counterintuitive to the reason and experience of man. A proper biblical deduction must have a sound logical structure, with true premises and deductive validity, but the conclusion might be beyond the bounds of human reasoning. The doctrine of the Trinity is a prime example; good biblical reasoning can lead us to a knowledge of this truth, but this truth itself must be embraced by faith. It is thus seen how reason can be rightly used without being the final criterion of judgment.

The Westminster divines were aware of this fact—that although biblical deductions must be sound, biblical truths are not judged by the reason of man. For example, Anthony Tuckney, who was by some accounts the most influential writer of the Shorter Catechism,[20] said, "Logic rules do not circumscribe God, nor should our reason."[21]

George Gillespie, who formulated the doctrine of good and necessary consequence with great care and conviction in his *Treatise of Miscellany Questions*, also clearly expressed the believer's need to submit to biblical truth even when it is beyond the bounds of reason, using the Trinity as an example. In the same work he remarked:

> Let reason be brought into captivity to the obedience of Christ. That which made the Antitrinitarians and Socinians fall away from the belief of the trinity of persons in the godhead, and the union of the two natures of God and man in the person of Christ, was, because their reason could not comprehend these articles, which is the ground of their opinion professed by themselves. When I speak of captivating reason, I do not mean implicit faith. The eyes of my understanding must be so far opened by the Holy Ghost, that I may know such an article is held forth in Scripture to be believed, and therefore I do believe that it is, though my reason cannot comprehend how it is.[22]

Finally, we may observe that, to the Westminster divines, the use of good and necessary consequence as a method of interpretation does not lay the text open to a confusing array of various meanings.

---

20. Samuel William Carruthers, *Three Centuries of the Westminster Shorter Catechism* (Fredericton, NB: University of New Brunswick, 1957), 5.

21. Quoted in John H. Leith, *Assembly at Westminster: Reformed Theology in the Making* (Richmond: John Knox Press, 1973), 47.

22. Gillespie, *Miscellany Questions*, 59.

Paragraph 9 of chapter 1 affirms that the sense of any Scripture "is not manifold, but one." While the confession is clearly refuting the allegorical method with this phrase, it also has application to the point at hand. Scriptural inferences do not open up an uncharted world of interpretive possibilities. Biblical inferences are not another layer of meaning in the text. We do not need to demand implications from every passage, or look for a deeper, latent meaning behind every biblical phrase. Good and necessary consequences will propound specific truths, not unveil mysterious layers of meaning in Scripture.

We can conclude that the Westminster Confession formulates its doctrine of good and necessary consequence within a context of many prudent cautions. The method of biblical deduction is always to be controlled and tested by the criteria "good and necessary," and it is always to be subject to the authority of the Word and the good guidance of its Author. Human reason is not exalted, nor is Scripture overcomplicated, by the occasional need to deduce biblical truth; but for biblical truth to be rightly deduced, it must be followed as the Word of God. While some truths require sanctified deduction, Scripture itself remains clear, sufficient, and complete. In the historical context of the Assembly, the Roman and Anglican churches staked their doctrine on the authority of councils and ancient writers, while the Sectarians claimed to have new revelations of the Spirit that went beyond the Scriptures. The Westminster Confession returned a balanced, biblical answer to both of these extreme positions.

It now remains to examine how the Westminster Assembly applied this principle in its proceedings. Concerning the question whether a divine warrant can be found for a specific rule of church government, the minutes of the Assembly reflect the resolution that necessary consequence can be used as a valid method to reach this conclusion, based on Scripture's own use of this method. From session 640 on May 15, 1646:

> *Proofs that a necessary consequence is a sufficient argument of Christ's will.*
> Resolved upon the Q., First proof; "Christ proves the resurrection in Matt xxii. 31, 32: 'As touching the resurrection of the dead, have you not read that which was spoken unto you by God, saying, I am the God of Abraham, the God of Isaac, and the God of Jacob? God

185

is not the God of the dead, but of the living;' which is proof of the resurrection of the dead by a consequence only."

This proof; "Christ, John x., refutes the Jews reproaching Him with blaspheming for saying that He and the Father were one, by a consequence drawn from Scriptures," calling princes gods.

Resolved upon the Q., Acts xiii. 34, "And as concerning that He raised Him up from the dead, now no more to return to corruption, He said on this wise, I will give you the sure mercies of David," which proves the resurrection of Christ by consequence only.

Resolved upon the Q., Heb. i. 6, "And again, when He bringeth in the first Begotten into the world, He saith, And let all the angels of God worship Him," where it is proved that Christ is the Son of God by a consequence.[23]

In session 641 on May 18, 1646, it was ordered that the use of good and necessary consequence "may be cleared by sundry other instances, many more of the articles of faith being proved by Christ and His apostles out of the Old Testament only by consequence."[24]

Based on Scripture's use of good and necessary consequences, the Assembly debated the question whether biblical examples can be used to deduce abiding commandments.

Resolved upon the Q., "Some examples show a *jus divinum* and the will and appointment of God; as in the Old Testament the building of altars to the Lord and offering sacrifices by the fathers from Adam to Abraham, which was done in faith and acceptance, for which there is no foregoing precept recorded in Scripture."

Resolved upon the Q., "The same may be said of the duty of the surviving brother's marrying the wife of his brother deceased without issue, of which we have no evidence that it was the will and appointment of God before the law given by Moses, but the example of Judah's sons, Gen. xxxviii."

Resolved upon the Q., "In the New Testament we have like instances of the observation of the first day of the week for the Christian Sabbath."[25]

23. Alexander Mitchell and John Struthers, eds., *Minutes of the Sessions of the Westminster Assembly of Divines* (Edinburgh and London: William Blackwood and Sons, 1874), 231–32.
24. Ibid., 232.
25. Ibid., 237–38.

The foregoing examples resulted in the following conclusions:

> *Resolved* upon the Q., "In all which examples, as we have cause
> to believe that the fathers at the first had a command from God of
> those things whereof we now find only their example for the ground
> of their posterity's like practice for many generations, so likewise,
> though we believe that Christ, in the time that He conversed with
> His disciples before and after His resurrection, did instruct them
> in all things concerning the kingdom of God, yet nothing is left
> recorded to show His will and appointment of the things instanced
> in, but the example and the practice of the Apostles and churches
> in their time."
>
> *Resolved* upon the Q., "Those examples, either of the Apostles,
> evangelists, or of the church planted and ordered by them, which are
> recorded in the New Testament, and are no where therein disallowed,
> and the particular reason whereof still abides, do show a *jus divinum*,
> and the will and appointment of Jesus Christ so as to remain."[26]

These conclusions were reached in the context of the Assembly's
debate over church polity, which was perhaps the greatest point of
contention at Westminster. Several men who believed in Episcopa-
lian government were invited, but only one, Daniel Featley, actually attended the Assembly. There was a contingent of independents,
including Thomas Goodwin, Jeremiah Burroughs, and Philip Nye, but
Presbyterians were in the clear majority. Among them it was debated
whether Presbyterian polity was *jus humanum* or *jus divinum*, that is,
by human right or divine right. Some thought that Presbyterianism
was amenable to Scripture yet not clearly commanded, but the principled use of good and necessary consequences enabled the Assembly
to finally conclude upon *jus divino* Presbyterianism in its document
The Form of Presbyterial Church Government. This is but one example
of how the scrupulous use of good and necessary consequences was
part of the Assembly's proceedings.

The deduction of good and necessary consequences from Scripture is much more than a historical curiosity of Westminster. It is
a significant aspect of the faith and life of God's people in all ages.

26. Ibid., 238–39.

The use of consistent deductions and logical thought in order to arrive at distinct statements of biblical truth is absolutely essential for an orderly and consistent approach to theology, preaching, and the application of Scripture to the various situations of the Christian life. B. B. Warfield went so far as to say that the denial of good and necessary consequences from Scripture would involve the denial of all doctrine whatsoever, "since no single doctrine of whatever simplicity can be ascertained from Scripture except by the use of the process of the understanding."[27] Not only simple doctrines, but *central* doctrines depend on good and necessary consequences, such as the doctrine of the Trinity. That doctrine is not the product of a single proof text; rather, it is an authoritative inference based on the premises of many passages, and obviously, it is a central truth of the Christian faith. It is truly amazing how intertwined the principle of good and necessary consequence is with so many doctrines of the Christian faith. The Westminster divines simply gave confessional acknowledgment to this principle, and did so with admirable care and caution.

It is also rather amazing how often the Bible itself, and Christ in particular, uses the method of good and necessary consequence. Several notable instances have already been cited from the writings of the divines and the work of the Assembly, but many more examples exist, such as Matthew 12:9–14:

> And when he was departed thence, he went into their synagogue:
> And, behold, there was a man which had his hand withered. And they asked him, saying, Is it lawful to heal on the sabbath days? that they might accuse him. And he said unto them, What man shall there be among you, that shall have one sheep, and if it fall into a pit on the sabbath day, will he not lay hold on it, and lift it out? How much then is a man better than a sheep? Wherefore it is lawful to do well on the sabbath days. Then saith he to the man, Stretch forth thine hand. And he stretched it forth; and it was restored whole, like as the other.
> Then the Pharisees went out, and held a council against him, how they might destroy him. (KJV)

27. Warfield, *Westminster Assembly*, 227.

In this passage, Christ uses a good and necessary consequence to teach that works of charity are lawful on the Sabbath. His argument takes the form of a categorical syllogism. Based on the first premise that it is lawful to do good to an animal on the Sabbath, and the second premise that men are more valuable than animals, he concludes that it is lawful to perform acts of charity toward men on the Sabbath. It is of interest to note that it was the Pharisees who denied the use of good and necessary consequences in this instance. They insisted on the "letter of the law" (or their own tradition) when it came to the question of how to observe the Sabbath, and they probably expected a proof text from Christ. Good and necessary biblical inferences, such as Christ presented, were not a part of their thinking. They were only incensed at Christ's doctrine and his deductive method of presenting it.

Good and necessary consequences drawn from the Bible also continue to aid the church in its witness to the world in current times. The relevance of biblical truth to the shifting sands of modern culture is often discerned through the deduction of good and necessary consequences. For instance, what is the church to say about abortion? No passage of Scripture says, in so many words, that "abortion is wrong." It simply was not a pressing issue in the days of Moses or Paul. But by applying the principle of good and necessary consequence, we can arrive at the will of God on this matter:

PREMISE 1: It is a sin to murder another human being (e.g., Ex. 20:13).

PREMISE 2: Children in the womb are human beings (e.g., Ps. 139:13–16).

CONCLUSION: It is a sin to murder children in the womb.

In this and other ways, the deduction of good and necessary consequences from Scripture remains an important aspect of the life, faith, and witness of the church.

This principle, as articulated in the Westminster Confession, is built on a desire to be true to the whole counsel of God as it applies in every age, whether plainly expressed in Scripture or rightly deduced from Scripture. This must still be the priority of the church today.

George Gillespie pointed out a very practical implication of this doctrine when he asked, "How," without the use of good and necessary consequence, "shall this or that individual believer collect from Scripture, that to him, even to him, the covenant of grace and the promises thereof belong?"[28] By good and necessary consequence, the gospel promises of Christ that are given in general to all his people may be appropriated in personal terms, and the individual believer may find particular comfort and assurance. "Good and necessary consequence" is more than a little-noticed phrase in a centuries-old confession. It is a principle of great importance to the faith and life of each believer. By it you may know that the promises of the gospel belong to *you*.

---

28. Gillespie, *Miscellany Questions*, 103.

7

The Lord's Day and the Westminster Confession

ROWLAND S. WARD

In the creedal history of the Reformed church, relatively few explicit statements have been made about the Lord's Day. In fact, there are really only two prior to the Westminster Assembly. In the Heidelberg Catechism of 1563, question 103, we read:

> Q. What does God require in the fourth commandment?
> A. First, that the ministry of the gospels and the schools be maintained; and that I, especially on [the Sabbath, that is] the day of rest, diligently attend the church of God, to learn God's word, use the sacraments, to call publicly upon the Lord, and to give Christian alms. Second, that all days of my life I rest from my evil works, let the Lord work in me by his Holy Spirit, and thus begin in this life the eternal Sabbath.

The words in brackets were added in the Dutch translation of 1566 but are not in the original German.

In the Irish Articles of 1615, a basic source for the Westminster Confession of Faith, Article 56 reads,

> The first day of the week, which is the Lord's Day, is wholly to be dedicated unto the service of God; and therefore we are bound

therein to rest from our common and daily business, and to bestow
that leisure upon holy exercises, both public and private.

This statement may be regarded as embryonic of the much fuller
statement in paragraphs 7 and 8 of Westminster Confession of Faith
chapter 21, which read as follows:

> As it is the law of nature, that, in general, a due proportion of time
> be set apart for the worship of God; so, in his Word, by a positive,
> moral, and perpetual commandment binding all men in all ages, he
> hath particularly appointed one day in seven, for a Sabbath, to be
> kept holy unto him: which, from the beginning of the world to the
> resurrection of Christ, was the last day of the week; and, from the
> resurrection of Christ, was changed into the first day of the week,
> which, in Scripture, is called the Lord's Day, and is to be continued
> to the end of the world, as the Christian Sabbath.
>
> This Sabbath is then kept holy unto the Lord, when men, after a
> due preparing of their hearts, and ordering of their common affairs
> before-hand, do not only observe an holy rest, all the day, from their
> own works, words, and thoughts about their worldly employments
> and recreations, but also are taken up, the whole time, in the public
> and private exercises of his worship, and in the duties of necessity
> and mercy.

Each of these statements can be shown to reflect the consensus at
the time of its publication. While each marks out a day of rest involving public worship, only Westminster asserts that the command is of
a moral character and so binds all, only Westminster is explicit that
the Lord's Day has a sabbatic character in line with the fourth commandment, and only Westminster is explicit on a transfer of the day
of rest from the last to the first day of the week.

The teaching of the confession on the subject has not escaped
criticism. In particular, the distinction the confession draws between
the moral, ceremonial, and civil laws in the law of Moses (19.2–4) is
regarded as without justification. The law is a seamless robe that cannot
be divided into parts. Given that the Mosaic covenant is superseded
by the new covenant, the argument runs that we receive the law of love
from the hands of the greater than Moses, and he gives no command

for observing special days but calls us to live all our days as in his presence. A more valid criticism relates to the lack of an eschatological emphasis. The Heidelberg Catechism has such a reference, but it cries out for development, which Westminster has not given.

In the light of this background, it is fitting in a volume dedicated to a man who has sought to uphold the teaching of the Westminster Confession that a defense of the confession's teaching be offered from Scripture, emphasizing the connection of the Lord's Day with God's creation rest and the goal of creation. Some brief comments on historical developments will form an appendix following the conclusion of our study.

The Creation Rest

God instituted the Sabbath or rest day at creation (Gen. 2:2–3). It was thus part of the order established for man from the first. As Jesus said, "The Sabbath was made for man" (Mark 2:27).[1] It follows that

1. the Sabbath is of universal relevance quite apart from the later entrance of sin into the human race;
2. significance that might become attached to the Sabbath day because of the entry of sin and the subsequent provision of redemption cannot alter its basic character; and
3. lack of references to the Sabbath prior to Moses is no argument against its institution at creation, since (a) an argument from silence is risky: for example, there is no mention of the Sabbath between Moses, circa 1400 B.C., and the time of Elijah, circa 840 B.C. (2 Kings 4:23), yet its existence cannot be doubted, and (b) corruption or neglect of Sabbath observance is amply explained by human sinfulness.

Genesis 2 does not use the noun "Sabbath," but only a related verbal form, "*shabat*," "to cease from labor." Nevertheless, later passages

1. Unless otherwise indicated, Scripture quotations in this chapter are from the New International Version.

link man's weekly rest day with the creation pattern as its foundation (e.g., Ex. 20:8).

God "had finished" his work, he "rested," he "blessed," he "made holy" the seventh day.

Meaning

The simple affirmation that the Sabbath originates at creation does not explain its character. To that question more than one answer has been given. Yet even if one does not understand the creation days to be of the same length as our solar days, it is agreed by all that the narrative of God's creation week aims to provide a pattern for human activity. So humanity's life is not to be one of ceaseless activity. It is to have a rhythm of work and rest based on a seven-day cycle, the day of rest also providing opportunity for worship of the Creator.

Yet while the Sabbath undoubtedly points to the Creator and his work, and emphasizes man's dependence on God, it seems a somewhat imprecise way of speaking to call the Sabbath a "memorial of creation" in the manner of some writers. Note that the climax of the creation narrative is *not* man's creation, but God's rest. Genesis 2:1–3 forms part of a single literary unit with Genesis 1. In other words, the Sabbath is not a mere weekly memorial day for a past work, nor is it a kind of afterthought tacked on to something more important, but it points forward to creation's purpose and goal. Days 1 to 6 record God's creative acts, but for what purpose were things created? That is what the seventh day tells us. God relates to man, his covenant partner. God rests, and humanity is to share in this rest on the recurring seventh day. The weekly rest will be climaxed by a participation in God's rest when humanity's work is complete.

What follows from this? Those who think of the Sabbath as first and foremost a memorial of creation tend to think that the original creation was beyond improvement, and so they expect a restoration of the original Edenic state at the end of the world. They also tend to insist on a seventh-day Sabbath and reject the legitimacy of a change of day. But those who think of the Sabbath as pointing to the goal of creation think that a higher destiny was in prospect for the creation, so that although "very good" at the first (i.e., precisely as God intended), it was not at the highest and most perfect level possible.

Now, the "goal of creation" view best fits the biblical data:

1. The rest of God to which creation is called is *unending* blessedness with God; hence the seventh day of the creation week is not closed by reference to evening and morning—no mere oversight in such a carefully crafted narrative. David Pareus (1548–1622), the irenic Reformed theologian of the Palatinate, had already noted this in his Latin *Commentary on Genesis* (1609).

2. The Tree of Life in the middle of the garden bears witness to a higher and eternal life in prospect for man but not yet his possession (Gen. 3:22).

3. The blessings of Genesis 1 are covenant blessings for God's son (Luke 3:37), and a son may expect an inheritance.[2] There is an eschatology before sin enters the world: the prospect of greater blessings.

4. The history of the chosen people in the Old Testament shows the pattern of redemption from bondage and a bringing in to the place of God's rest—the Promised Land; ultimately the expectation is the New Jerusalem as the city of God.

5. The fulfillment of the Scriptures in Christ shows the same pattern realized. Scripture affirms that Christ does not simply restore the Edenic state of creation, but brings creation to a higher and abiding form in blissful, unlosable harmony with God (e.g., Rom. 8:18ff.; 1 Cor. 15:42ff.).

The correctness of this "goal of creation" position will be borne out in the following paragraphs. Meanwhile, we should keep in mind that man's recurring weekly Sabbath on earth was a pledge and a

---

2. When the original blessing of our first parents is repeated to Noah (Gen. 9), it is called a covenant. Therefore, the original relationship to Adam was covenantal. Gen. 6:18 refers to continuing an existing relationship, not commencing a new one. Those blessings in Gen. 1 are covenantal blessings. To the same effect is Jeremiah's reference to God's covenant for day and night (33:20ff.). This passage refers back beyond Gen. 9:8ff. to Gen. 1 and God's blessing of his good creation, as Jer. 31:35 makes clear. Thus, we see God's covenant commitment at the very beginning of creation.

foretaste of his higher destiny. It is important to note that the Sabbath rest should deliver us from the notion that man's worth or value is to be defined simply in terms of his economic output. A day without productive work may seem a waste, but it is not. Rather, man is made for more than work—he is made for God; it is that purpose and destiny that gives his work its true meaning.

The Sabbath for Sinners

The entry of sin into human life could not fail to affect the observance of the weekly rest day, as of the other laws written on man's heart. The Sabbath as a sign of a higher destiny with God is somewhat meaningless for sinners who can never achieve that destiny. No doubt it was soon neglected as men invented their own holy days to suit their religious inclinations. There is no clear historical evidence of the weekly Sabbath outside Israel, although we do not have adequate data from early times.

The Sabbath for Israel

Whatever happened in other nations, it is admitted by all that the Sabbath became a special feature in the life of Israel. Before the giving of the Ten Commandments at Mount Sinai, we find evidence of a weekly Sabbath at the time God gave the manna (Ex. 16:26). There is a good deal to be said for the view that the Sabbath had been disregarded and is here restored to Israel preparatory to the giving of the law at Sinai (ca. 1450 B.C. on the traditional reckoning), but if so, this does not deny its origin at creation.

When the fourth commandment (Ex. 20:8–11) is given, its introductory word is "remember": "Remember the Sabbath day by keeping it holy." This word looks back to the experience of Exodus 16 and to the Genesis 1–2 narrative, and also involves a commitment for the future, as if to say, "From this time forward, keep the Sabbath in mind." But the reason given for Sabbath observance, just as for work, is one that applied before the entrance of sin into human life, namely, the pattern of God in creation. Man's rest is related to God's rest, and points to the destiny in rest with God that belongs to man when his work is done.

When the Ten Commandments are given again a generation later, the reason given to enforce observance does not refer to creation at all but to the redemption of the people from Egyptian bondage (Deut. 5:12–15). That deliverance had no special connection with the six days of creation but everything to do with the goal of creation. And so the redemptive reason is not an additional but a secondary emphasis, yet is closely allied to the basic meaning of the Sabbath. How can fallen man reach the goal of eternal fellowship with God apart from redemption? And yet God redeemed the people of Israel, their destiny is with him, and they are therefore to keep the Sabbath.

Duration

The ancient Egyptian time system was based on a ten-day week with days reckoned from morning to morning. In Mesopotamia the day was reckoned from evening to evening, and this system was followed by Israel (Lev. 23:32), with a seven-day cycle based on the creation account. In Israel the days were identified by ordinal numbers (first, second, etc.).

Sequence

One may suggest that the emphasis in the commandment is not so much on the sequence of the days, as if the moral content included the last day of the week, but on the meaning of the Sabbath itself. Nowhere does the Old Testament tell us to keep the Sabbath of the seventh day *of the week*, but it tells us to keep the seventh day. Whether the Sabbath follows or precedes the other six days of the week, it is still a seventh day in relation to the other six days. Indeed, Adam's first day was the day following his creation; thus, he did not first work six days and then rest, but on his first day rested with God, and rejoiced in God's work before he began his own. Further, the reasons adduced in Exodus 20 and Deuteronomy 5 to enforce Sabbath observance help us understand the significance of the Sabbath, but in the nature of the case cannot be part of that content that can never be changed or omitted. Rather, they are extra words suited to the situation of the recipients.

The unchangeable or strictly abiding content of the fourth commandment must be found in the principle of one day in seven as a Sabbath, with the actual day to be decided by other factors, such as creation or redemption, that are consistent with its fundamental nature. It is a likely assumption that the particular day on which proper Sabbath observance was restored to Israel, as recorded in Exodus 16, was reckoned from the day of deliverance from Egypt, since the commencement of the year for Israel was dated from that event (Ex. 12:2).

Observance

On the subject of Sabbath observance there are surprisingly few details in the Old Testament. The essential emphasis is the cessation of ordinary employment and the use of the day for spiritual celebration. Psalm 92—a psalm for the Sabbath, according to its title—indicates that praising the Lord, making music to him, singing for joy at the work of God's hands, trusting in his righteousness, and praising his constant love and power are Sabbath activities. The Sabbath was not to be a day of doing nothing, nor a day of mere external religious duties, but a day of special spiritual activity.

As for specific prohibitions, work during the plowing and harvest times was prohibited on the Sabbath (Ex. 34:21), presumably because people claimed that the limited period available to complete these tasks justified ignoring the Sabbath. Nehemiah (13:15–22) and Jeremiah (17:21–27) prohibited the bearing of burdens on the Sabbath, but the context indicates that commercial activity was involved. There are two other prohibitions. Fire in dwellings is banned in Exodus 35:3, but occurs in the context of instructions about the building of the tabernacle, no doubt to offset any tendency to justify working on the materials for the tabernacle on the Sabbath. In other words, building a place of worship was not a proper activity for God's day. The other reference (Num. 15:32–36) sets the death penalty for gathering wood, but the context is that of defiant transgressors. The case in question is surely that of a fuel merchant who plies his trade on God's day. One other text (Ex. 16:23) has been taken as excluding any preparation of food gathered the previous day, but this is to draw too much from the passage. This approach to the cited passages is essentially that found in writers such as Thomas Shepard (1604–49) in his work on the Sabbath published in the year of his death, and reminds us that Puritans were not necessarily the rigorists often alleged.

These few general statements stand in marked contrast to the more than one thousand rules built up by the Pharisees in the time of Jesus, and even their rules were not always as rigid and detailed as those of other Jewish sects.

Canaan Not the True Rest

When the people of God settled in the Promised Land following the exodus from Egypt and the wilderness wanderings, they entered into the place God had prepared for their rest, but they had not thereby reached their ultimate rest (see Heb. 4:8–9). To those of Abraham-like faith there lay ahead "a heavenly country," "a city which is to come," of which blessing the Sabbath was both an emblem and a pledge. A greater than Joshua would bring them into this true rest. Canaan was only a type or picture of the heavenly country.

The Ministry of Jesus

During Jesus' ministry we find that Jesus is regular in his attendance at the synagogue on the Sabbath day (Luke 4:16), and that he also healed many people on this day. Two important sayings bearing on the Sabbath, and a significant passage in the epistle to the Hebrews, will now be considered.

John 5:18

The healing of a man at the pool of Bethesda called forth the criticism of the Pharisees, whereupon Jesus responded: "My Father is always at his work to this very day, and I, too, am working" (John 5:17). The Jewish leaders then sought the more to kill him, since, in their eyes, he was not only breaking the Sabbath but committing blasphemy, "calling God his own Father, making himself equal with God" (John 5:18). But Jesus answered that whatever the Father does, the Son also does. In other words, Jesus justified his healing of a man on the (earthly) Sabbath by the parallel case of his Father in continuing to sustain the creation each moment during his (heavenly) Sabbath.

For our present purpose, two points may be noted:

1. God's rest following creation (Gen. 2) does not close with the usual formula, "And there was evening, and there was morning," since it embraces all future history, yet during it the Father is not idle but continues to uphold his creation and act for its benefit.
2. Jesus' healing of the man is entirely in character with the observance of the earthly Sabbath, just as are the Father's activities during his heavenly Sabbath. Thus, not to do good on the Sabbath is to profane it (cf. Matt. 12:12).

Mark 2:27–28

One of the most remarkable sayings of Jesus is found in Mark 2:27–28: "The Sabbath was made for man, not man for the Sabbath. So the Son of Man is Lord even of the Sabbath." The context is the criticism of the disciples by the Pharisees for picking some grains of corn as they walked through a field on the Sabbath. Judged by the law of the Sabbath as given in the Old Testament, such criticism was without foundation. But crushing the grains was "work," according to the detailed regulations developed later by the rabbis. Jesus gives an illustration from the Old Testament to show that the rigidity with which the Pharisees interpreted the law was not countenanced by the Old Testament. He then makes the statement already quoted.

The saying does not mean merely that Jesus has the right to free the Sabbath from Pharisaic abuses. Who doubts that he has such a right? But it means that his relationship to the Sabbath is such that he has full authority to determine all things related to it. After all, the Sabbath was made for man to ensure his well-being, not to make him a slave to legalistic regulations. The term "Son of Man" has its background in Daniel 7. It indicates universal authority as Messiah, while the emphasis "*even* of the Sabbath" stresses the greatness of that authority. It is a messianic claim.

As the Sabbath points to the eternal fellowship with God that comes only through him who is the Way (John 14:6), the saying includes the thought that Jesus is Lord of the Sabbath to bring to realization what the day represents. In Matthew's account (12:1–8), Jesus points out that the work of the priests in the temple on the Sabbath defiled it, yet they were innocent. He adds that "one greater than the temple is here." The priests were carrying out God's work in offering the sacrifices, but Jesus, the true Servant of the Lord, had now come, and inaugurated the time of the new wine that old wineskins could not hold without splitting (Mark 2:21–22). As Christ inaugurates a new creation, the renewal of the pre-Mosaic, pre-fall Edenic Sabbath is completely in order. Resting in Christ, who has fulfilled all righteousness for us, we go about our work, and we look forward to the consummation when we enter into the heavenly country he has gained for us.

Christ's Fulfillment of the Law

Christ did not come to abolish the law but to fulfill it (Matt. 5:17). The Mosaic covenant *is* superseded. The shadows of the Mosaic administration give way to the reality of Christ's saving work, for the law was given through Moses, but grace and truth were realized through Jesus Christ (John 1:17). Still, the Ten Commandments were always special among the laws God gave, being written by God's finger on the back and front of stone tablets. Christians do not receive them as rules for life from the hands of Moses, the mediator of a superseded covenant. But they do embody the principles in the moral law of love for God and man from creation, and so Christians receive the law from the hands of Jesus, the Mediator of the new and better covenant. Their appreciation of them is deepened through the positive exposition of them by Christ's obedience and in his own teaching and example (Matt. 5:17ff.). Thus, the righteousness of the law is fulfilled in believers who do not walk after the flesh but according to the Spirit (Rom. 8:4–5).

The unique position of the moral law is seen in the following facts:

1. Only the Ten Commandments were spoken by God's voice.
2. They alone were accompanied by the shaking of Mount Sinai.
3. They alone were written by his finger.
4. They alone were written on enduring stone tablets rather than merely being written in a book (Ex. 24:4; Deut. 4:10–14).
5. They alone of the various laws were placed in the ark of the covenant (Deut. 10:5).
6. They formed the introduction to the Mosaic covenant, which, in fact, expounds them in a manner appropriate for the people at that time (Deut. 6–26).
7. They were fully complete, the tablets being written on the front and the back, so that there was no room for other commandments of the same unique kind, for there were none (Ex. 32:15).
8. They were regarded as superior to the ceremonial law (e.g., Ps. 51:16–19; Jer. 7; Amos 5).
9. The greatest commandment, on which everything else depends, is total love for the Lord (Matt. 22:37, quoting the exposition of the first commandment in Deut. 6) and also love for one's neighbor—a command that, while explicit in a context of laws of different character, is a necessary corollary to the other, given that humans bear the divine likeness (Lev. 19:18; cf. Matt. 7:12).
10. Hence, these considerations lead to the common view that the Decalogue is a reflection, in a form suited to the historical situation of Israel, of the moral law, the law of love, written on Adam's heart at his creation.

We have already noted that the wording of the Ten Commandments is adapted to the condition of those who received them. In applying them in the New Testament dispensation, we also see modification in form while preserving the unchangeable essence. Thus, Paul quotes the fifth commandment in Ephesians 6:3 but substitutes "earth" for "land" without at all touching the fundamental principle of the command. Similarly, some believers had died prematurely because they did not have proper regard for their fellow believers (1 Cor. 11:30). Again, God's example in the Old Testament identified the particular day to be observed as the Sabbath, and Christ's example does the same in the New Testament.

Jesus Christ and the Attainment of Rest

Jesus (in Hebrew, "Joshua") is the true deliverer from bondage to sin. Through him man's destiny can be realized, and the eternal Sabbath entered. Jesus himself said, "Come unto me, all you who are weary and burdened, and I will give you rest" (Matt. 11:28).

A very important statement on the significance of the present time in the light of the salvation achieved in Christ is provided in Hebrews 3:7–4:11. The writer presupposes that Israel in the wilderness and the church on earth today are in parallel situations, for there has always been only one redemptive covenant (3:5–6). Both receive a promise of rest (3:11; 4:1), and both are subject to dangers and temptations that can lead to failure to enter the rest (3:12, 19), and so both receive exhortation to obedience in faith. The rest is defined as the rest of God's seventh day (4:4), and is represented as future and as a place of rest to be entered by believers, as was Canaan, although Canaan was not the true rest (4:8).

This language does not fit a subjective experience of rest that the believer gains now. The true rest into which believers will enter is a heavenly country (11:16), the city with foundations (11:10), the city that is to come (13:14). God's purpose in the creation is thus realized through the consummation of redemption: the redeemed enter into God's creation rest, the eschatological country, the promised inheritance.

This being the perspective of Scripture, the gift of the earthly Sabbath has as much relevance today as in the beginning before sin. As Hebrews 4:9 states: "There remains, then, a Sabbath-rest [Greek: *sabbatismos*] for the people of God." The weekly sign of this eternal hope continues. Believers rest in the Lord, rejoice in his works, and go forth to labor for his glory, having the assurance that, through the last Adam, they have a blessed destiny.

It is often argued against this position that the believer in Christ enters into the rest of God when he abandons trust in his own works and rests in Christ, a position common among the early Reformers. But this argument does *not* fit the context of Hebrews 4. Verse 10 says that when one enters God's rest, he rests from "his own work," *as God did from his*. The parallel with God's rest from his (good) work requires the believer's "own work" to be the works of faith done on our pilgrimage and not the evil works of unbelief from which we turn when we believe. We rest from our labors and our works follow us when we reach the *end* of our pilgrimage (Rev. 14:13), even though it is granted that we find that rest in principle upon believing in Christ.

We conclude that this passage in Hebrews confirms that the rest of God's seventh day speaks of the goal to which creation is called, and teaches that it is still future. It provides no basis for the cessation of the weekly sign of that rest that was given even before sin entered the human family. Nothing in the passage suggests that it ceases now through the coming of Christ, and everything suggests that it continues with enriched meaning until what it represents is realized in the world to come.

The Change to the First Day of the Week—the Lord's Day

There is no unambiguous text in the New Testament stating in as many words that the principle involved in the fourth of the Ten Commandments has been abolished, or that the day of its observance has been changed to mark the inauguration of the new era. Naturally, what is unchangeable in God's law cannot be abolished, since it expresses God's character. But as to the change of day, there are relevant Scriptures. We should also keep in mind that the good and necessary consequences of scriptural statements are as binding as a precept explicitly stated (e.g., Luke 20:37–38; cf. Westminster Confession of Faith 1.6). Let us now proceed further, bearing in mind what we have already learned of the origin and nature of the Sabbath.

The New Testament shows that the resurrection of Christ, which secures the eternal destiny of Christ's people, occurred on the first day of the week, very early, and not on the Sabbath day as then observed. Christ is "the firstfruits" of those who have fallen asleep (1 Cor. 15:20), and this reminds us of the first sheaf of the harvest that was to be presented the day after the (Saturday) Sabbath at the close of Passover (Lev. 23:9–14). On the day of his resurrection Christ appeared to his disciples, and likewise a week later (John 20:19, 26), another first day of the week. After his final parting from them, marked by the ascension, he poured out the Spirit. This event occurred on the day of Pentecost, fifty days after Passover, and also fell on the first day of the week in the New Testament period. Pentecost is otherwise known as the feast of firstfruits (Ex. 34:22; Lev. 23:15ff.), and the outpouring of the Spirit on that day marks the beginning of the harvest of which Christ, the firstfruits, is the guarantee. This singling out of the first day of the week is significant.

Not only is Christ the one through whom all things were created, he is also "the beginning and the firstborn from among the dead" (Col. 1:18). He has inaugurated a new order of existence, a new creation, by his redemptive work. Still, the redemption he brings does not annul the first creation but restores and perfects it. In Christ, believers have all things, but they have not yet entered into the heavenly country that is their inheritance. They still have the recurring sign of the believer's hope in the gift of the Sabbath, but a Sabbath enriched by Christ's accomplishment of redemption. The change of day reflects the reality of what has come, that creation's goal is through the risen Lord, while the continuation of the day of rest points to what is yet to be in the consummation: already, but not yet.

It is in the light of such principles that the true significance of the New Testament emphasis on the first day of the week is seen. The significance of Christ's honoring of the first day of the week is as great as the divine example provided in Genesis 2.

All New Testament references to Christians worshiping on the Jewish Sabbath occur in situations in which we would expect overlapping because of missionary and evangelistic efforts. No doubt, inadequate grasp of fundamental theology on this matter as on others led the church into mistaken views quite early. The sabbatic (rest) character of the first day of the week might be denied because of a reaction from Jewish legalistic notions of what the Sabbath meant and the observance it required. But the essential idea of joyful celebration of the Lord's greatness and goodness was still retained.

No established Christian writer of the second century rejects the fourth commandment, only the rabbinical, Judaistic Sabbath. Christian literature of the second century evidences the use of the term "Lord's Day" found also in Revelation 1:10. Its most natural meaning there is to refer to the day that was peculiarly the Lord's because of his inauguration of the new era, the beginning of the new creation, on the first day of the week. That is certainly how the term was used by the second-century writers.

Acts 20:6–12: The Meeting at Troas

The meeting referred to in this passage was held on the evening of the first day of the week and not on the Sabbath, despite Paul's presence during the previous week. The first point to note is that the Jewish expression "the first day of the week" is used, as it also is in 1 Corinthians 16:2, where Paul exhorts that an offering be put aside on that day.

By the New Testament period the Romans had introduced a week of seven days, but with the days named after the seven heavenly bodies then known. The first day of this week was named after Saturn, and was often a festival day on which work was prohibited. In the early part of the second century, the increased importance of the sun cults led to the transfer of the name of the second day to the first and the adjusting of the name of each of the other days, so that Saturn's day became the last day of the week, as it still is with us. The Romans also measured the day from midnight to midnight, whereas the Jews measured from sunset to sunset. Thus, what we would call the evening of one day was to the Jews part of the next day.

With this background we come to the passage. The Greek text of Acts 20:7 reads literally, "And on one of the Sabbaths," but "weeks" and "Sabbaths" are interchangeable terms in Hebrew and Greek because of the function of the Sabbath in the weekly cycle, and the phrase means, "And on the first [day] of the week" (the cardinal numeral being used in the sense of the ordinal). Since it is a Jewish expression, we might suppose that Luke is using a Jewish system of counting from sunset to sunset. This interpretation is followed by the New English Bible and the Good News Bible, and they paraphrase accordingly: "On the Saturday night"; "On Saturday evening." The question, however, is not settled by these two versions. It should not be forgotten that John 20:19 refers to the evening of the "first day of the week" in a context where what we would call Sunday evening must be meant. So a Jewish weekly cycle with days indicated by ordinal numbers *can* be combined with a Roman reckoning of days from midnight to midnight.

Let us look now at the specifics of Acts 20:6–12. All admit that the meeting was an evening one, and the phrase "many lamps" in verse 8 suggests that those present may have had to travel in darkness to get there. If the meeting was Saturday after sunset, however, one must explain how "daylight" (v. 11) could be on "the next day" (v. 7) rather than later the same day. Only by forcing the Greek grammar can the natural meaning implying a Roman system of time (midnight to midnight) be avoided.

With the requirements of the text just referred to, supported by the similar usage in John 20:19 and the natural reading of the whole narrative, the Sunday-evening position supposes that Roman time is used, so that the day runs from midnight to midnight; that a regular meeting was held on the Sunday evening, with Paul as the visiting preacher; that a fellowship meal, possibly including the Lord's Supper, was observed; and that after the more formal part of the meeting was over, there was a time of less formal discussion, with Paul taking his leave at daybreak on Monday.

This position has some implications:

1. The use of the Jewish expressions "the first day of the week" and "to break bread" in reference to a Gentile church shows that these terms were carried over into common Christian use because of their association with the Lord Jesus. One also has the term "[come] together" (Acts 20:7; cf. 1 Cor. 11:20; 14:23).

2. Debate on whether the Christian day of rest/spiritual celebration should run from midnight to midnight or from sunset to sunset is irrelevant, for this can be adapted to the common mode of time reckoning in a particular country.

The likelihood is that Christians in Gentile areas had reasonable freedom to meet on the first day of the week. This is because it was commonly a day when work was not done by Gentiles because of the worship/cult of Saturn observed on that day. The Troas example may suggest that the normal meeting time there was what we would call Sunday evening, perhaps because some of the believers, particularly slaves, would not be free from duties owed to their masters during the day.

Does the New Testament Reject a Special Day?

We now consider three texts that are sometimes claimed to show that there is no special day of Christian worship in the New Testament.

Galatians 4:9–11

The Galatian church was plagued by Judaizers, who advocated the necessity of observing the law of Moses for salvation (4:21) and, in particular, the religious observance of the Jewish holy days, what Paul calls "special days and months and seasons and years" (4:10). The most natural meaning is that he refers to the weekly Sabbath or other similar days, New Moon and New Year observances, extended religious festivals, and sabbatical and Jubilee years (cf. Lev. 23; Num. 28:11–15; Isa. 1:13), which indeed are no longer obligatory. But it is important to note that Paul is dealing with legalism, with salvation by works, as taught by the Judaizers. Paul's words do not touch the question of the pre-Mosaic creation Sabbath, nor indeed observance for other nonlegalistic reasons of the Mosaic Sabbath. This leads us to consider Romans 14:5–6.

Romans 14:5–6

In this passage it is evident that some Christians of Jewish background had not yet fully grasped all the implications of the gospel. Thus, while not observing the special Jewish days as a means of justification, they did hold scruples that led them to regard these days highly, while others in the church had no such scruples. The gospel is not being compromised by these views, and Paul counsels the strong to exercise forbearance toward the weak on this issue as well as on the associated dietary scruples.

If we regarded Paul's indifference to religious days and food in Romans as absolute, we would have a contradiction with Galatians. But two points are obvious:

1. Paul looks at the motive in the particular case, just as he did with the question of circumcision—in which in one situation he circumcised Timothy (Acts 16:3) but in another rejected it outright (Gal. 5:2–3). Lord's Day observance is not to be regarded as a means of justification any more than is obedience to the other nine commandments that sum up the law of love.

2. The issue relates to the Mosaic administration of God's covenant, which Christ had fulfilled. The point at issue does not bear upon the creation rest that now, from the fact of Christ's resurrection and inauguration of a new creation, finds fitting expression on the first day of the week. God's day is a gift to be received and celebrated. It is certainly not to be neglected (cf. Heb. 10:25).

Colossians 2:16–17

In this letter Paul classes the Sabbath with the ceremonial law of the Jews as a shadow of things to come, which has been fulfilled in Christ. This reminds us that the Sabbath, which had its origin in the nature of the relationship between God and man established at creation, nevertheless had a very close connection with the old-covenant administration in Israel, and was unique to that nation. Indeed, the

Sabbath is virtually equated with the covenant made with Moses (Ex. 31:12–17), and its principle is elaborated beyond the weekly cycle to other times, such as the sabbatical year every seventh year.

Now the old-covenant administration *is* fulfilled in Christ, but it does not follow that the principle of the creation Sabbath is abandoned. That idea the writer to the Hebrews expressly rejects, while he also makes clear that the "rest" of the creation Sabbath is yet future. Although in principle achieved in Christ, it is yet to be realized. Indeed, if Paul's rejection of holy time and holy food in Colossians is absolute, then he contradicts his own express teaching that the feast of the Lord's Supper should be kept by God's people (1 Cor. 11:23), and his own practice in observing the first day of the week rather than the Jewish Sabbath (Acts 20:7).

Thus, it would be perilous to conclude that the weekly rest day is in every sense fulfilled in Christ so that it is no longer to be observed. We might well argue, however, that the New Testament does not use the name "Sabbath" for the Christian day of celebration just because the newness of the time inaugurated by Christ deepens our understanding of the Sabbath and far transcends the limited and provisional vision of the Old Testament promise. (Note, too, the absence of the noun "Sabbath" in Gen. 2.) Further, the bad connotation of the word because of rabbinic distortions of Sabbath observance is relevant.

It is not that we cannot call the Lord's Day the Christian Sabbath, but we must ensure that the gospel of grace shines through in our attitude to and observance of the day. Christ has indeed brought a deeper significance to the day of rest, illuminating its true nature as a day of joy and gladness in the God of salvation (cf. Ps. 92). It is indeed the Lord's Day: the creation Sabbath restored and perfected, and the blessed destiny of which it speaks secured to all believers.

Conclusion

Seeing that the fourth commandment sets out the principle established at creation for man's well-being, and seeing that through Christ the destiny of which it speaks is ours, the Lord's Day is for our Lord. Let us beware the encroachments that can so easily be made on it by less important things. Let us grasp its great principle and apply it gladly and wholeheartedly for our spiritual profit.

The Lord's Day! We can use it for worship, fellowship, spiritual enrichment—and how we need these! Also, as we put aside the ordinary activities of the week, we may enjoy spiritual, physical, and emotional refreshment in activities that further the aim of the day. Avoiding business, shopping, and the like, we are to be active in doing good. In some occupations there will be everyday work on this day, and rightly so (the cows must be milked, the hospitals must be open, police will be needed), for the Sabbath is made for man and not the reverse. There will be particular difficulties in some occupations in our industrialized society, and obviously a Christian will not be eager to cut into the opportunities for Christian worship by working overtime on Sunday.

A strong church, a prosperous nation, must cultivate Christian values. The present impoverishment of the church and our national direction owes much to neglect of God's provision for us. We are great on physical muscle-building and find great amounts of time and money for it. But what about our spiritual muscles? Consider the human restlessness characterizing our time because God's rest is ignored. How important it is to raise our eyes heavenward! And will not the church find sufficient funds for the spread of the gospel if on the first day of the week—the day that reminds us of the destiny we have in Christ because of his love for us—we set aside as the Lord has prospered us (1 Cor. 16:2)!

Appendix: A Little History

One does not put new wine into old wineskins. The early church with no argument accepted the first day of the week for Christian worship. In Jewish areas, however, there would not have been immediate abandonment of the Jewish Sabbath. In Jerusalem about A.D. 60, the mainly Jewish converts were zealous for the law and the customs (Acts 21:20–21). About A.D. 85, the Jewish synagogues introduced a curse on Christians, with a view to excluding their presence and participation in synagogue services.

Nevertheless, this does not mean that there were not distinctive meetings for Christian believers. Such gatherings were a necessity from the beginning, and the evidence is quite overwhelming that the first day of the week was the day observed. On the other hand, Christians and Jews were sharply distinguished when Paul reached Rome about A.D. 61 (Acts 28:17, 28–29). Nero, who had married a Jewish proselyte in A.D. 62, blamed the Christians and not the Jews for the fire in the city in A.D. 64. A different or additional day of worship may have had something to do with this more ready identification. With the destruction of Jerusalem in A.D. 70, Jews and Christians were more sharply distinguished in Palestine, and greater realization of the distinctive identity of the Christians as the people of God came about.

The early postapostolic church did not always grasp the principles involved in much church practice. Some Christians still kept a Saturday rest day and a Sunday resurrection festival. But with the passing of anti-Judaism decrees by Emperor Hadrian in A.D. 135, the church at Rome seems to have been active in promoting Sunday observance. The sun cult was transferred to the first day by the pagans, and it was easy for Christians to exhort that Jesus, the Sun of Righteousness, be worshiped on that day. Anti-Jewish prejudice played a large part in the eventual rejection of Saturday observance in favor of Sunday as both the rest and worship day. There was a tendency to base the change on the authority of the church rather than careful explanation of the biblical text, while the hesitation of the postapostolic church to affirm the sabbatic character of the Lord's Day is understandable because it was rightly wary of Jewish legalism and inactivity infecting the meaning of the day. Nevertheless, during the medieval period, the practice of the church was such that Sunday was treated as a nonbusiness day and as a day for worship.

In later medieval theology, particularly as systematized by Thomas Aquinas (ca. 1225–74), a close connection between the Lord's Day and the fourth commandment is upheld by making a distinction between ceremonial aspects (such as stringent work restrictions, a particular time) and the moral content (some time, not necessarily one-seventh) for God's worship.

The Protestant Reformers

Martin Luther (1483–1545) teaches that the Ten Commandments should be observed only because they clearly expressed the law of nature written on our hearts, and not because of their presence in the law of Moses. So far, so good. He specifically rejects the religious necessity for any particular day of worship now, regarding this as a ceremonial aspect that has ceased. He regards the external observance of Old Testament times as fulfilled in an inward Sabbath as the believer rests from sin each and every day. Yet he does see the need for a particular day for practical reasons, and in fact Sunday was observed in a religious manner in Lutheran circles.

Similarly, John Calvin (1509–64) sees the moral obligation of the fourth commandment, typified by the Sabbath, as resting from sin every day of our lives. That spiritual rest is now enjoyed by believers through the death and resurrection of Christ, and so the necessity of observing the day ceases, he claims. But an analogy exists between the position of the Jews of old and Christians today. Because the practical need of a day of worship for all and of rest for working people still remains, it is right that the church, for the sake of good order, choose a particular day for such religious worship and rest. Calvin preferred the Lord's Day to be that day but would not condemn other churches who chose some other day.

These views, which appear consistently in Calvin's writings, occur in the context of belief in the Sabbath as a creation ordinance predating the fall into sin (most clearly expressed in Calvin's *Commentary on Genesis* 2:3). And it is here that their inconsistency lies: that which dates from the beginning of God's very good creation cannot be meaningful only in the light of the existence of sin. It is one thing to prohibit sin; it is another to presuppose that it exists in man from the beginning and to require the mortifying of it (and who can rest from sin perfectly each day, anyway?).

It is not surprising that Luther's and Calvin's views are not upheld by all the other Reformers. While William Tyndale (1494–1536) follows Luther, the English bishop John Hooper (ca. 1495–1555) and Theodore Beza (1519–1605), Calvin's successor, are among those who adopt a view more closely tying together the Lord's Day and the fourth commandment. Beza is explicit that one day in seven is required by the commandment.

One might well conclude that the interpretation given by some of the early Reformers was affected by a concern to avoid legalism, and assumed too readily that some provisions of the Old Testament were extremely rigorous. At the same time, it must be recognized that religious observance of the Lord's Day was not in doubt among mainstream Reformers. Diverse arguments may have been employed, but the actual observance of the Lord's Day was very similar. Given this unity, there was the less incentive to examine the question in great detail.

Later, with the coming of a spiritually weaker age, the sometimes inadequate grounding of the commandment contributed to what has been called "the Continental Sunday," wherein the day was available for recreation and amusement after a brief service, since, it was held, the fourth commandment and the Lord's Day have no connection.

The Lord's Day in Britain

In Britain the relationship of the Sabbath to the Lord's Day became a subject of thorough examination from the 1590s with such volumes as Nicholas Bownde's *Doctrine of the Sabbath* (1595; enlarged 1606). Yet it would be a mistake to say that a morally binding Sabbath was a Puritan creation. There are ample testimonies to the contrary both before the English Reformation and in its early decades. The Puritan view of the Sabbath certainly became dominant and was enshrined in the Westminster Confession of Faith (1647) and catechisms, the Savoy Declaration (1658) of the Congregationalists, and the Baptist Confession of 1677/1689. The latter two confessions expressly add that the observance of the last day of the week is abolished.

In these creeds the light of nature is said to teach that a proper proportion of time is to be set aside for the worship of God, and that in his Word God asserts "a positive, moral and perpetual commandment, binding all men in all ages" to observe one day in seven holy to God; and that from the resurrection of Christ the first day of the week is the Christian Sabbath. The unattainable standard for observance set out in these confessions should not be misunderstood.

214

Every part of God's law is beyond our attainment in our present state (cf. the Sermon on the Mount), but God's law is not to be adjusted to suit our capacity.

This Sabbath position has strongly influenced English-speaking Christianity. It has not itself always been free from petty or gross legalism, but it has also been observed in a biblical manner, which has been to the untold good of multitudes. It remains true that a lively Christian faith goes hand in hand with a day for rest, spiritual reflection, worship, evangelism, and acts of mercy. If we do not use it for such ends, we not only dishonor God, but impoverish ourselves. It is given for our benefit. Let us receive it and use it as such.

Note Regarding Seventh-day Sabbath-Keepers

There were a few seventh-day Sabbath-keepers in England in the seventeenth century. The first *Seventh Day Baptist Church* was formed in London in 1617, and the first in North America in 1671. This group was never very large, but it contributed its Sabbath view to a small number of disappointed Adventists who had set a date for Christ's return (1843–44). Subsequently, some of them held that the "spirit of prophecy" had been restored to the remnant church in the person of Mrs. Ellen White. From a very small beginning, what became known in 1860 as the *Seventh-day Adventist Church* took its rise and has a following of several millions today. It considers that in a soon-to-come testing time, Sunday observance will be enforced by law. Those who then comply will have the mark of the beast (Rev. 14:6–12), since, in the Adventist view, such observance rests on mere human authority. This is not a credible claim, and fails to grasp the full significance of the creation Sabbath and the realization of creation's goal of which it speaks through the One who is the Lord of the Sabbath.

Select Bibliography

Acts of the Reformed Ecumenical Synod, Sydney, 1972. Grand Rapids: Reformed Ecumenical Synod, 1972, 146–66 (majority and minority reports on the Sabbath issue).

215

Bacchiocchi, Samuele. *Divine Rest for Human Restlessness*. Berrien Springs, MI: Biblical Perspectives, 1988 (Seventh-day Adventist).

Carson, D. A., ed. *From Sabbath to Lord's Day*. Grand Rapids: Zondervan, 1972 (nonsabbatic evangelical).

Dennison, C. G., and R. C. Gamble, eds. *Pressing toward the Mark: Essays Commemorating Fifty Years of the Orthodox Presbyterian Church*. Philadelphia: Committee for the Historian of the Orthodox Presbyterian Church, 1986 (includes R. B. Gaffin Jr. responding to Carson et al. regarding Heb. 3:7–4:13, pp. 33–51).

Gaffin, R. B., Jr. *Calvin and the Sabbath*. Tain, Ross-shire: Christian Focus, 1998.

Macdonald, Fergus A. J. "The Lord's Day." In *Hold Fast Your Confession*, edited by Donald Macleod, 129–55. Edinburgh: Knox Press, 1978.

Parker, Kenneth L. *The English Sabbath: A Study of Doctrine and Discipline from the Reformation to the Civil War*. Cambridge: Cambridge University Press, 1988.

Pipa, Joseph A. *The Lord's Day*. Tain, Ross-shire: Christian Focus, 1997.

Strand, K. A., ed. *The Sabbath in Scripture and History*. Washington, DC: Review and Herald, 1982 (Seventh-day Adventist).

Wilson, Daniel. *The Lord's Day*. Reprint, London, 1956 (Lord's Day Observance Society).

8

Unity or Disunity? Covenant Theology from Calvin to Westminster

Anthony T. Selvaggio

The Reformation, almost from its very inception, had a confessional impulse. Martin Luther nailed his Ninety-five Theses to the door at Wittenberg in 1517, John Calvin penned his first edition of the *Institutes of the Christian Religion* in 1536, and Calvin and William Farel produced a catechism for the church in Geneva in 1537. The Continental Reformers followed in the path of Calvin and Luther by producing what is known today as the "Three Forms of Unity," which consists of the Belgic Confession of Faith (1561), the Heidelberg Catechism (1564), and the Canons of Dort (1619). The English Reformation produced its own series of confessions, including the Scots Confession (1560), the Thirty-nine Articles (1563), and the Irish Articles (1615). While all of these statements of faith resound to the glory of God and articulate the essence of the Reformed faith, the crescendo of this symphony of confessions was not reached until July 1, 1643, when a group of ministers, Scottish commissioners, and members of Parliament gathered in Westminster Abbey in London to reform the government, doctrine, and worship of the Church of England. This grand assembly produced a variety of documents to guide the church, the best known of which are the Westminster Confession of Faith and the Larger and Shorter Catechisms.

What sets the Westminster documents apart from other Reformed confessions? It is the fact that the Westminster documents were the first to be overtly and explicitly organized around God's covenant relationship with man. The great Princeton theologian B. B. Warfield recognized the centrality of covenant theology (also referred to as federal theology) to Westminster's work: "The architectonic principle of the Westminster Confession is supplied by the schematization of the Federal theology, which had obtained by this time in Britain, as on the Continent, a dominant position as the most commodious mode of presenting the corpus of Reformed doctrine."[1] The father of Reformed biblical theology, Geerhardus Vos, came to a similar conclusion, noting, "The Westminster Confession is the first Reformed confession in which the doctrine of the covenant is not merely brought in from the side, but is placed in the foreground and has been able to permeate at almost every point."[2] What distinguishes the Westminster Confession from all the other Reformed confessions preceding it is its mature and detailed articulation of covenant theology.

Because the Westminster documents were the first to explicitly organize Reformed theology around the covenant concept, many scholars suggest that Westminster represents a new theology that is inconsistent with the theology of Calvin and the early Reformers. These scholars contend that a great gulf is fixed between Calvin and Westminster. The following quotations from one of these scholars, R. T. Kendall, will suffice to encapsulate the sentiment of this school: "Westminster theology, then, represents a substantial departure from the thought of John Calvin," and "Westminster theology hardly deserves to be called Calvinistic—especially if that term is to imply the thought of Calvin himself."[3]

More recently, in the present justification controversy and debate over the New Perspective on Paul, an entirely new group suggests a theological divergence between Calvin and Westminster. Some advo-

1. B. B. Warfield, *The Works of Benjamin B. Warfield*, 10 vols. (Grand Rapids: Baker, 2000), 6:56.
2. Geerhardus Vos, "Doctrine of the Covenant in Reformed Theology," in Richard B. Gaffin Jr., ed., *Redemptive History and Biblical Interpretation: The Shorter Writings of Geerhardus Vos* (Phillipsburg, NJ: Presbyterian and Reformed, 1980), 239.
3. R. T. Kendall, *Calvin and English Calvinism to 1649* (New York: Oxford University Press, 1979), 212.

cates of the so-called Federal Vision (Auburn Avenue Theology) suggest that Westminster's emphasis on covenant theology, particularly its articulation of the covenant of works, is inconsistent with the theology of Calvin and the Reformed confessions preceding it. For example, Rich Lusk writes that "careful inquiry into the precise origins of federalism shows it grew out of a rather narrow strand of British Puritanism that deviated considerably from Calvin's more pastoral, organic approach to biblical theology."[4]

The primary aim of this essay is to provide a brief survey of the historical development of covenant theology from Calvin to Westminster in order to demonstrate the progressive and organic theological unity between them.

Methodology

As we begin to examine the theology of Calvin to see whether it embodies the essence of the covenant theology present in the Westminster documents, we must first define the nature of covenant theology. At its core, covenant theology represents a systematic expression of the biblical revelation regarding God's covenant relationship with man. Over the centuries, Reformed covenant theologians have developed a sophisticated collection of theological terminology to articulate and describe that covenant relationship. The development of this sophisticated vocabulary has led many scholars to erroneously conclude that this terminology, rather than the concepts giving rise to it, must be present in Calvin's theology in order to characterize him as a covenant theologian.[5] As we begin this study, it is vital to comprehend

4. Rich Lusk, "A Response to 'The Biblical Plan of Salvation,' " in E. Calvin Beisner, ed., *The Auburn Avenue Theology: Pros and Cons* (Fort Lauderdale: Knox Theological Seminary, 2004), 119.

5. Paul Helm makes this very point in his article "Calvin and the Covenant: Unity and Continuity," *Evangelical Quarterly* 55, no. 2 (1983): 67. While it is indeed true that Calvin does not use the terminology of Westminster regarding covenant theology, he does employ the term "covenant" extensively in the *Institutes*. For example, Peter Lillback, in his article "Ursinus' Development of the Covenant of Creation: A Debt to Melancthon or Calvin?" *Westminster Theological Journal* 43 (1981): 270, stated that Calvin used the words *"foedus"* and *"pactum"* (both covenant terms) a combined total of more than 150 times in the *Corpus Reformatorum* edition of the *Institutes*. Lillback supplies a helpful chart on page 270 of his article that outlines the number of times these covenant terms appear in each book of the *Institutes*. It must be

that the terms developed by covenant theologians are subservient to the revelation that spawned them. In other words, the essence of covenant theology is not its terminology, but its doctrinal conceptions that flow from God's Word. Accordingly, the pertinent question is not whether Calvin used the terminology of Westminster, but rather whether he espoused the theological doctrines and concepts that are the substance of the covenant theology expressed by the Westminster Assembly.

Therefore, in order to proceed with this inquiry, it is appropriate to first briefly define the requisite theological components of covenant theology. Paul Helm provides a helpful summary of the core ideas. He suggests that the essential concepts of covenant theology are threefold: (1) covenant of redemption; (2) federalism; and (3) covenant of grace.[6] Brief definitions of these three components will facilitate our inquiry.

The "covenant of redemption" (also referred to as "*pactum salutis*," or "counsel of peace") refers to the covenant forged in eternity wherein God the Father decreed the plan of salvation and God the Son consented to its execution. "Federalism" primarily refers to the representative roles of Adam and Christ. Adam served in a representative, or federal, capacity for the human race in the "covenant of works" (also referred to as "covenant of creation," "covenant of nature," and "covenant of life").[7] In this covenant, Adam failed to maintain the terms of his probation, and his failure resulted in the imputation of original sin to all his natural-born posterity. Christ, as the second Adam, fulfilled the requirements of the covenant of works, and his righteousness is imputed to those he federally represents—the elect. This brings us to the third essential component of covenant theology: the "covenant of grace." The covenant of grace is the implementation

---

acknowledged that although Calvin used the term "covenant" extensively, he did not use it in the same structure as Westminster (i.e., "covenant of works"/"covenant of grace"), and therefore, as Helm has rightly cautioned, one must not overstate the case by claiming that Calvin's *Institutes* represents a sophisticated and mature treatise on covenant theology similar to the works of William Perkins, Herman Witsius, or Francis Turretin.

6. Helm, "Calvin and the Covenant," 67–80. Helm's work is very insightful, and I would like to acknowledge both my reliance on his work and my indebtedness to it.

7. This covenant is succinctly described in Westminster Confession of Faith 7.2: "The first covenant made with man was a covenant of works, wherein life was promised to Adam; and in him to his posterity, upon condition of perfect and personal obedience."

of the eternal covenant of redemption in history. The covenant of grace is first revealed after the fall in Genesis 3:15, where we learn that the seed of the woman (Christ) will conquer Satan. The covenant of grace is a shorthand way of referring to the unified plan of salvation that flows through both testaments of the Bible.

Having defined these essential components of covenant theology, we can now turn to examination of Calvin's thought to determine whether these theological concepts are present.

John Calvin (1509–64)

One of the errors that scholars frequently make when they study Calvin's theology is to restrict their examination solely to the *Institutes*. While the *Institutes* certainly represents a significant summary of Calvin's theological thinking, it by no means exhausts his thinking. Calvin, after all, was a preacher at heart, and his commentaries provide helpful insights into his theology. It is in Calvin's commentaries that one finds the most evidence for the existence of the essential components of covenant theology.

Evidence that Calvin taught the substance of the covenant of redemption can be gleaned from his commentary on the gospel of John. Covenant theologians have long recognized that John 17 reveals the substance of the eternal agreement between the Father and Son that covenant theologians refer to as the covenant of redemption. Calvin reflects a similar understanding of this text, particularly in his comments on John 17:4:

> When he adds, *I have finished the work which thou gavest me to do,* he means that he has completed the whole course of his calling; for the full time was come when he ought to be received into the heavenly *glory.* Nor does he speak only of the office of teaching, but includes also the other parts of his ministry; for, though the chief part of it still remained to be accomplished, namely, the sacrifice of death, by which he was to take away the iniquities of us all, yet, as the hour of his death was already at hand, he speaks as if he had already endured it. The amount of his request, therefore, *is* that the Father would put him in possession of the kingdom; since, having

completed his course, nothing more remained for him to do, than to display, by the power of the Spirit, the fruit and efficacy of all that he had done on earth by the command of his Father, according to the saying of Paul, *He humbled and annihilated himself, by taking the form of a servant. Therefore God hath highly exalted him, and given him a name which is above every name, (Philippians 2:7)*.[8]

Calvin's comments on this verse reveal an understanding of two prominent principles of the covenant of redemption. First, Calvin describes the work and ministry of Christ as occurring within the framework of a completed plan. Calvin writes that Jesus "completed the whole course of his calling" and that he did so "by the command of his Father." Further evidence that Calvin conceived of Christ's work as including his submission to an eternal covenant is his linking John 17:4 together with Philippians 2:7. Second, by stating that "the Father would put him in possession of the kingdom," Calvin infers that Christ's fulfillment of the eternal decree of the Father resulted in his receiving of the reward of the elect.

The argument that Calvin taught the substance of the covenant of redemption is bolstered by his comments on John 17:6:

Thine they were, and thou hast given them to me. By adding these words, he points out, first, the eternity of election; and, secondly, the manner in which we ought to consider it. Christ declares that the elect always belonged to God. God therefore distinguishes them from the reprobate, not by faith, or by any merit, but by pure grace; for, while they are alienated from him to the utmost, still he reckons them as his own in his secret purpose. The certainty of that election by free grace lies in this, that he commits to the guardianship of his son all whom he has elected, that they may not perish; and this is the point to which we should turn our eyes, that we may be fully certain that we belong to the rank of the children of God; for the predestination of God is in itself hidden, but it is manifested to us in Christ alone.[9]

---

8. John Calvin, *Calvin's Bible Commentaries*, trans. William Pringle, 22 vols. (Edinburgh: Calvin Translation Society, 1843; repr., Grand Rapids: Baker, 1979), commentary on John 17:4.

9. Ibid., John 17:6.

In his comments on John 17:6, Calvin alludes to the eternal nature of the covenant of redemption by speaking of "the eternity of election" and specifically connecting this phrase to the giving of the elect to Christ as a reward for his faithful work of redemption ("thou hast given them to me"). Calvin brings further attention to the fact that Christ received the elect as a reward from the Father as a direct result of his fulfillment of the covenant of redemption by first noting that the elect were originally in the Father's possession ("the elect always belonged to God") and then noting that they were transferred to Christ's care by the Father ("commits to the guardianship of his son all whom he has elected"). From Calvin's commentary on John, we can ascertain that Calvin articulated the theological substance of the covenant of redemption.

Not only did Calvin teach the substance of the covenant of redemption, he also taught the essence of the second component of covenant theology: federalism. Calvin unequivocally sets forth the doctrine of federalism in the *Institutes*:

> We hear that the uncleanness of the parents is so transmitted to the children that all without any exception are defiled at their begetting. But we will not find the beginning of this pollution unless we go back to the first parent of all as its source. We must surely hold that Adam was not only the progenitor but, as it were, the root of human nature; and that therefore in his corruption mankind deserved to be vitiated. . . . There is consequently but one way for us to interpret the statement, "We have died in Adam": Adam, by sinning, not only took upon himself misfortune and ruin but also plunged our nature into like destruction. This was not due to the guilt of himself alone, which would not pertain to us at all, but because he infected all his posterity with that corruption into which he had fallen.[10]

In this quotation from the *Institutes*, Calvin articulates the federal role of Adam by referring to him as the "first parent of all." He also sets forth the doctrine of imputation by stating that Adam "infected all his posterity with that corruption into which he had fallen."

10. John Calvin, *Institutes of the Christian Religion*, ed. John T. McNeill, trans. Ford Lewis Battles, Library of Christian Classics (Philadelphia: Westminster, 1960), 2.1.6.

In addition to recognizing the federal role of Adam, Calvin also fully acknowledged the theological implications of the federal parallel between Adam and Christ. Calvin's grasp of this parallel may be witnessed in the following quotation from the *Institutes*:

> This the apostle makes clear from a comparison of Adam with Christ. "As through one man sin came into the world and through sin death, which spread among all men when all sinned" [Rom. 5:12], thus through Christ's grace, righteousness and life are restored to us [Rom. 5:17]. . . . But if it is beyond controversy that Christ's righteousness, and thereby life, are ours by communication, it immediately follows that both were lost in Adam, only to be recovered in Christ; and that sin and death crept in through Adam, only to be abolished through Christ.[11]

From these samples from the *Institutes*, it is clear that Calvin embraced and expressed the fundamental essence of the federalism that would be more fully developed by the covenant theologians who followed in his footsteps.

Calvin's grasp of federalism is also visible in his articulation of the theology of the covenant of works. Many scholars deny that Calvin taught this covenant, but once again we must not look solely for terminology, but rather for the theology behind that terminology. As previously mentioned, the covenant of works is a legal or works-based covenant in which fulfillment is found only in perfect obedience. Therefore, the question is not whether Calvin used the phrase "covenant of works," but whether he conceived of Adam's relationship to God in the pre-fall state as a legal one.

That Calvin conceived of Adam's relationship to God as being legal, rather than gracious, may be demonstrated by means of the following quotation from the *Institutes*, in which he discusses the nature and implications of Adam's transgression:

> Because what God so severely punished must have been no light sin but a detestable crime, we must consider what kind of sin there was in Adam's desertion that enkindled God's fearful vengeance

11. Ibid.

224

against the whole of mankind. . . . Adam was denied the tree of the knowledge of good and evil to test his obedience and prove that he was willingly under God's command. . . . But the promise by which he was bidden to hope for eternal life so long as he ate from the tree of life, and conversely, the terrible threat of death once he tasted of the tree of the knowledge of good and evil, served to prove and exercise his faith. Hence it is not hard to deduce what means Adam provoked God's wrath upon himself. . . . For Adam would never have dared oppose God's authority unless he had disbelieved in God's Word. Here, indeed, was the best bridle to control all passions: the thought that nothing is better than to practice righteousness by obeying God's commandments; then, that the ultimate goal of the happy life is to be loved by him.[12]

This language reveals that Calvin understood Adam's relationship to God as primarily a legal one. For example, note the predominance of legal terms: "punished," "detestable crime," "obedience," and "commandments." Furthermore, Calvin described the prelapsarian state specifically as a "test" of Adam's "obedience." Clearly, Calvin understood the prelapsarian relationship in probationary and legal terms that would result in a judicial decree by God in which God would grant Adam either life or death.[13] As Helm rightly notes, "Those who say that Calvin did not have a legal view of the relationship between the Lord and Adam are clearly mistaken."[14]

Peter Lillback also contends that Calvin taught a covenant of works. Lillback attributes the origin of Zacharias Ursinus's expression of a covenant of works to Calvin: "It is entirely possible that the appellation of 'foedus creationis' is Ursinus's, but the substance of the concept is a debt Ursinus owes to Calvin."[15] Lillback's most interesting argument in favor of a covenant of works in Calvin's thought is drawn from Calvin's understanding of the relationship

12. Ibid., 2.1.4.
13. This probationary concept also appears in Calvin's commentary of Genesis, where he describes the command regarding the tree as follows: "Therefore the prohibition of one tree was *a test of obedience.*" Calvin, *Commentaries,* on Gen. 2:16, emphasis added.
14. Helm, "Calvin and the Covenant," 74.
15. Lillback, "Ursinus' Development of the Covenant of Creation," 288. Note: "*foedus creationis*" is Latin for "covenant of creation," which is another way to refer to the covenant of works.

between sacrament and covenant. Lillback argues that in Calvin's theology, sacrament and covenant are two sides of the same coin. In other words, where one is present, the other must also necessarily be present. Lillback notes that Calvin, in his commentary on Genesis, refers to the Tree of Life as a sacrament, just as he refers to the Lord's Supper as the sacrament of the new covenant in 1 Corinthians 11 (see the appendix at the end of this chapter).[16] Lillback deduces from this usage that Calvin's theology logically leads to a prelapsarian legal covenant:

> On this basis, provided Calvin is consistent with his own view of the relationship of sacraments and covenants, there must be a pre-fall covenant. Since this covenant was built on the basis of obedience to law, it appears entirely justified to call this pre-fall covenant of Calvin's a covenant of works.[17]

Lillback builds on his conclusion that a covenant of works is present in Calvin's theology in his much more developed work on this subject, *The Binding of God*.[18] In this work, Lillback adds other evidence that substantiates this argument. First, he notes that the writings of Augustine contained the "concept of a pre-fall covenant," and Lillback surmises that this influenced Calvin's theology, given his "massive use" of Augustine.[19] Second, Lillback argues for a covenant of works in Calvin based on the structure of the *Institutes*. Lillback notes that Calvin commenced his *Institutes* by discussing the knowledge of God the Creator and "postponed" his discussion of the covenant of grace until book 2. According to Lillback, this "provides the structure for a distinction between the postlapsarian covenant and a possible prelapsarian covenant."[20] Third, Lillback notes that for Calvin, the concepts of covenant and kingdom are related, much as the concepts of covenant and sacrament are related. Lillback maintains that Calvin spoke of the pre-fall Adam as being

16. Ibid., 284–85.
17. Ibid., 285.
18. Peter A. Lillback, *The Binding of God: Calvin's Role in the Development of Covenant Theology* (Grand Rapids: Baker, 2001).
19. Ibid., 287.
20. Ibid.

in God's kingdom, thus suggesting that Adam was also in covenant with God in his pre-fall state.[21] Based on these factors and the others discussed in this section, Lillback concludes that Calvin did indeed express the theology of the covenant of works: "Thus Calvin develops the prelapsarian experience of Adam in language consonant with the covenant of works: probation, prohibition, law, obedience, divine liberality and innocence, aiming at ultimate perfection and life";[22] and, "Thus the basic foundation for the existence of a covenant of works in Reformed theology was established by the great Genevan Reformer."[23]

As we have seen, Calvin taught the substance of the covenant of redemption, federalism, and the covenant of works. In addition to these elements of covenant theology, Calvin also taught the substance of the covenant of grace. First, Calvin's writings reflect that he taught a unified plan of salvation spanning both testaments of Scripture, which is a core principle of the covenant of grace. The following quotations from the *Institutes* demonstrate Calvin's conception of this unified plan:

> The covenant made with all the patriarchs is so much like ours in substance and reality that the two are actually one and the same. Yet they differ in the mode of dispensation. . . . They [the Jews] had and knew Christ as Mediator, through whom they were joined to God and were to share in his promises.[24]

> For the same reason it follows that the Old Testament was established upon the free mercy of God, and was confirmed by Christ's intercession. For the gospel preaching, too, declares nothing else than that sinners are justified apart from their own merit by God's fatherly kindness; and the whole of it is summed up in Christ. Who, then, dares to separate the Jews from Christ, since with them, we hear, was made the covenant of the gospel, the sole foundation of which is Christ?[25]

21. Ibid., 288.
22. Ibid., 289.
23. Ibid., 304.
24. Calvin, *Institutes*, 2.10.2.
25. Ibid., 2.10.4.

Furthermore, Calvin also recognized another core concept of the covenant. Covenant theologians maintain that the first revelation of the covenant of grace occurred in Genesis 3:15, which is referred to as the *"protoevangelium."* That Calvin concurred with this view is evidenced in the following quotation from the *Institutes*:

> Accordingly, at the beginning, when the first promise of salvation was given to Adam, (Gen. 3:15), it glowed like a feeble spark. Then, as it was added to, the light grew in fullness, breaking forth increasingly and shedding its radiance more widely. At last—when all the clouds were dispersed—Christ, the Sun of Righteousness, fully illumined the whole earth [cf. Mal., ch. 4].[26]

Clearly, Calvin's theology included the concept that God established a covenant of grace with the elect that was first revealed in Genesis 3:15 and progressively unfolded in the Old Testament until it reached its consummation in Christ and the new covenant.

In summary, a careful survey of all of Calvin's writings reveals that Calvin maintained the essential elements, albeit in nascent form, of classic Reformed covenant theology. Calvin's theology contained the substance of the covenant of redemption, federalism, the covenant of works, and the covenant of grace. Therefore, it is not without sufficient warrant that one can firmly assert that Calvin was a covenant theologian.

Having established that the seminal elements of covenant theology are extant in the thought of Calvin, we now proceed to connecting this covenant theology to that of Westminster. The following sections will demonstrate the essential linkage between Calvin and Westminster by describing the historical and theological progression of covenant theology as it grew on the continent of Europe and ultimately spread to the British Isles.

The Influence of Zurich

In order to track the development of covenant theology, we must leave Geneva and move to Zurich. Most scholars agree that cov-

26. Ibid., 2.10.20.

enant theology first began to be systematized by the Reformers in Zurich. Covenant theology matured more rapidly in Zurich because the Reformers in that city found themselves in the midst of an intense theological conflict with the Anabaptists.[27] This conflict forced the Zurich Reformers to sharpen the principles of Calvin's theology regarding the sacraments (particularly infant baptism), the unity of the testaments, the unity of the people of God in both testaments, and the unity of the plan of salvation.[28] The Zurich Reformers faced realities that Calvin did not face, and this led them to articulate more clearly the fine points of covenant theology. This pattern of fine-tuning orthodoxy in the face of heterodoxy is common in church history; one need only think of the climate that resulted in the ecumenical creeds. The Zurich Reformers were engaging in a spiritual battle similar to that of the early church fathers. While there were several significant Reformers in Zurich, most notably Ulrich Zwingli (1484–1531),[29] we limit this survey by focusing on the Reformer who had the most signifi-cant impact on covenant theology, Heinrich Bullinger (1504–75).

Bullinger was the leader of the Reformed church of Zurich from 1531 to 1575 and was a prolific writer, publishing 119 works dur-ing his life.[30] He was the author of the Second Helvetic Confession (1566), which became the most significant Reformed confession of the sixteenth century.[31] Among Bullinger's many works is his treatise *The One and Eternal Testament or Covenant of God* (1534), which Charles S. McCoy and J. Wayne Baker describe as the "fountainhead of federal-ism."[32] Bullinger's treatise was so significant because it was the first treatise written by a Reformer specifically on the topic of covenant

27. Vos, "Doctrine of the Covenant," 236.

28. Ibid.

29. It is important to note, as Lillback has, that Bullinger owed a great debt to the work of Zwingli. Lillback writes: "Zwingli's first published expression of this covenantal idea was on November 5, 1525. . . . Thus Zwingli's work with the covenant idea antedates Bullinger's *De Testamento seu Foedere Dei Unico et Eterno* by nine years, since it was published first in 1534. In point of fact, Bullinger himself freely acknowledged his dependence on Zwingli at this very point." Lillback, "Ursinus' Development of the Covenant of Creation," 247.

30. Charles S. McCoy and J. Wayne Baker, *Fountainhead of Federalism: Henrich Bullinger and the Covenantal Tradition* (Louisville: Westminster/John Knox Press, 1991), 17.

31. Ibid.

32. Ibid., 12. Interestingly, this treatise does not represent Bullinger's first use of the cov-enant concept. In fact, as McCoy and Baker point out, Bullinger had been using the covenant concept in his debates with the Anabaptists since 1525. Ibid., 19.

theology. Therefore, it is proper to state that it was with Bullinger that covenant theology began to be systematized as a separate subject.

Bullinger prepared his great treatise while he was in the heat of battle with the Anabaptists. Bullinger himself testified of this fact in a letter he penned to his friend Joachim Vadian, in which he acknowledged that *The One and Eternal Testament or Covenant of God* had been written directly "against the many heresies rising up today."[33] Given the nature of the specific battle in which Bullinger was engaged, his treatise does not present a two-covenant structure (covenant of works/covenant of grace), but rather focuses primarily on the unity of the covenant of grace in both the Old and New Testaments. The absence of a discussion of a prelapsarian covenant is understandable because the substance of the debate with the Anabaptists focused on the unity of the Old and New Testaments. Bullinger's main concern in responding to the error of the Anabaptists was to demonstrate the unity of the covenant plan of salvation and the unity of God's people in both testaments.

Bullinger followed *The One and Eternal Testament or Covenant of God* with a series of sermons entitled *Decades*, published from 1549 to 1551. In these sermons, he expounds on God's covenant dealings with his people. Bullinger's particular historical circumstances forced the Reformer to advance the covenant theology articulated by Calvin. Bullinger is an important link in the chain that unites Calvin and Westminster. As Peter Golding notes, "In tracing back the full-blown federalism of the Westminster Confession of 1648, one would undoubtedly have to proceed from Bullinger."[34]

The next major advancement in the development of covenant theology also has a link to Bullinger. One of Bullinger's students, Ursinus (1534–83), further honed the covenant theology originally found in Calvin's thought. Although a German by birth, Ursinus was heavily influenced by the theology of Zurich, having spent part of his life studying there.[35] While he was naturally committed to Germany, his theological allegiances were with Zurich. For example, he once stated of Germany, "I am well content to quit my country when it

---

33. Ibid.
34. Peter Golding, *Covenant Theology* (Tain, Ross-shire: Christian Focus, 2004), 22–23.
35. Vos, "Doctrine of the Covenant," 236.

will not tolerate the confession of truth which I cannot with a good conscience renounce."[36] In contrast, Ursinus's affinity for Zurich is evidenced in the following comment: "My mind is made up to turn to the Zurichers . . . whose fame stands so high with other churches, that it cannot be obscured by our preachers. They are pious, learned, great men, in whose society I am disposed, henceforth, to spend my life. . . ."[37] While Ursinus may have been German by birth, he was clearly Swiss in his theology.

Ursinus is best known for being a coauthor of the Heidelberg Catechism and the author of a commentary on that work. In his commentary on the Heidelberg Catechism, he cogently defines and defends the unified covenant of grace.[38] Yet Ursinus's most significant contribution to the development of covenant theology was his clear articulation of a prelapsarian covenant.

Ursinus clearly teaches a prelapsarian covenant in his Larger Catechism, which was part of his *Summa Theologiae*, published in 1561. There he specifically refers to a prelapsarian legal covenant by positing the following question: "What does the divine law teach you?" to which he provides the following answer: "What kind of a covenant God entered into with man at the creation and how man behaved in the keeping of that covenant."[39] Lillback notes that in his *Summa Theologiae*, Ursinus specifically employed the term "covenant of creation" (or "covenant of nature") to refer to the prelapsarian state.[40] Therefore, Ursinus's significance is that he represents one of the first theologians to systematize covenant theology explicitly in the two-covenant structure that later served as the framework for the Westminster Confession. Lillback summarizes Ursinus's contribution to the maturation of covenant theology as follows: "As Ursinus stated

36. Zacharias Ursinus, *The Commentary of Dr. Zacharias Ursinus on the Heidelberg Catechism*, 2nd American ed., trans. G. W. Williard (1852; repr., Phillipsburg, NJ: Presbyterian and Reformed, 1985), xii.

37. Ibid.

38. See ibid., 97–101.

39. Vos, "Doctrine of the Covenant," 237. Vos provides some excellent information regarding Ursinus's catechisms in the footnotes on pages 236 and 237. He points out that Ursinus developed a Larger and a Shorter Catechism and that the Larger contained these strong covenant statements. In footnote 3 on page 236, however, he points out that the Shorter Catechism "had the greater influence on the composition of the Heidelberg Catechism."

40. Lillback, "Ursinus' Development of the Covenant of Creation," 247.

the covenant of nature or of creation in opposition to the covenant of grace, and defined the goal of the covenant as life by means of perfect obedience, he had laid the foundation for later covenant theologians' discussion of this idea."[41]

The theology of Zurich, as articulated by Bullinger and Ursinus, represented a significant advancement in covenant theology. It was in Zurich that the covenant theology found in Calvin became an organized theological system. This advancement was primarily attributable to the Zurich Reformers' need to provide a clear polemic against the error of the Anabaptists. It was particularly Ursinus who served as the link to the next phase of covenant theology's maturation by exporting covenant theology to the British Isles. R. Scott Clark and Joel Beeke note that Ursinus's Calvinism and his articulation of covenant theology served as a "notable part of the stream of Continental Reformed theology that flowed into England in the late sixteenth century and nourished the young English Calvinists who would take their places in the Assembly of Divines."[42] It was through Ursinus that covenant theology traversed the English Channel and influenced the thought and discourse of the theologians who directly contributed to the theology of Westminster.

Maturation in the British Isles

Covenant thought commenced quite early in Britain and developed, to a great extent, in tandem with work on the European continent. One example of an early British theologian who discussed the covenant concept is William Tyndale (1494–1536), who traveled to continental Europe and interacted with Luther.[43] Many scholars consider Tyndale as the first English theologian to express the covenant idea. In fact,

41. Ibid., 248.
42. R. Scott Clark and Joel Beeke, "Ursinus, Oxford and the Westminster Divines," in J. Ligon Duncan, ed., *The Westminster Confession into the 21st Century: Essays in Remembrance of the 350th Anniversary of the Westminster Confession of Faith*, 2 vols. (Tain, Ross-shire: Christian Focus, 2004), 2:54. Clark and Beeke note that the connection between Ursinus and the English Calvinists was particularly strong in those Calvinists trained at Oxford University.
43. David N. J. Poole, *Stages of Religious Faith in the Classical Reformed Tradition: The Covenant Approach to the* Ordo Salutis (Ceredigion, Wales: Edwin Mellen Press, 1995), 153–55. Robert Cavendish was another early British covenant theologian, who published his treatise

he wrote of the covenant as early as 1534.[44] While there were many covenant theologians in the British Isles during the period preceding the Assembly, three of the most significant were William Perkins of England, Robert Rollock of Scotland, and James Ussher of Ireland.

William Perkins (1558–1602) is a prominent figure in the coalescence of covenant theology among the English Puritans. He gave a detailed and systematic treatment of covenant theology in his writings and was both widely read and highly respected among the Puritans.[45] The fact that Perkins clearly articulated a covenant of works is evidenced by the following quotation:

> The covenant of works is God's covenant made with condition of perfect obedience and is expressed in the moral law. . . . The law hath two parts: the edict commanding the obedience and the condition binding to obedience. The condition is eternal life to such as fulfill the law, but to transgressors everlasting death. The Decalogue, or Ten Commandments, is an abridgement of the whole law and the covenant of works.[46]

It must be acknowledged, however, that while Perkins did indeed articulate a covenant of works, he did not directly apply this concept to a prelapsarian covenant with Adam.[47] In this regard, Perkins's works must be seen as primitive in comparison to what followed in Rollock, Ussher, and the Westminster Assembly.

In addition to espousing a covenant of works, Perkins taught a unified covenant of grace, which he described as being dominated

---

The Image of Nature and Grace, Containing the Whole Law and Condition of Man's Estate in 1571. Poole, *Stages*, 159.

44. Golding, *Covenant Theology*, 30. Tyndale referred to an everlasting covenant in his "Prologue upon the Gospel of St. Matthew."

45. Stephen Strehle, *Calvinism, Federalism and Scholasticism: A Study of the Reformed Doctrine of Covenant* (Bern: Peter Lang, 1988), 329.

46. William Perkins, *The Works of William Perkins*, ed. Ian Breward (Appleford, Berkshire: Sutton Courtenay Press, 1970), 211.

47. This fact has been noted by Paul Helm in his article "Was Calvin a Federalist?" *Reformed Theological Journal* 10 (November 1994): 49. Helm notes that Perkins used the phrase "covenant of works" to "describe the Mosaic economy, or to be more precise, to describe one aspect of the Mosaic economy." Essentially, Perkins believed that in the history of Israel the covenant of works and covenant of grace existed in parallel. For Perkins, the Mosaic economy was both a "covenant of works" and a "covenant of grace."

by promise and which he contrasted with the legal nature of the covenant of works.[48] Further, Perkins grasped the essentials of federal theology—he referred to both Adam and Christ in federal terms. For instance, Perkins stated of Adam that he "was not then a private man, but represented all mankind."[49] He also alluded to Christ's federal role by noting that Christ fulfilled the covenant of works on behalf of those he represented (the elect): "The end and use of the gospel is first to manifest that righteousness in Christ whereby the whole law is fully satisfied and salvation attained."[50]

Robert Rollock (1555–99) was a prominent Scottish theologian whose writings significantly impacted the theology of the Westminster Assembly. Rollock espoused a mature form of covenant theology. His covenant theology was probably influenced by his friend Robert Howie, who was a student under Caspar Olevianus (1536–87), the German Reformer.[51] In 1597, Rollock published his "Treatise of Our Effectual Calling," which contained an appendix entitled "Short Catechism concerning the Way in Which God from the Beginning Reveals Both Covenants to the Human Race."[52] The very title of this shorter catechism reveals that Rollock maintained a two-covenant structure. He expressed a very advanced understanding of the covenant of works, an understanding demonstrated by the following quotation from his "Treatise of Our Effectual Calling":

> After God had created man in His image, pure and holy, and had written His law in man's heart, He made a covenant with him in which He promised him eternal life on the condition of holy and good works which should answer to the holiness and goodness of the creation, and conform to the law of God.[53]

Rollock also articulated the fullness of the covenant of grace, particularly with regard to its relationship to the covenant of works:

48. *Works of William Perkins*, 213.
49. Ibid., 191.
50. Ibid., 213.
51. G. D. Henderson, "The Idea of the Covenant in Scotland," *The Evangelical Quarterly* 27 (1955): 8, as quoted in Golding, *Covenant Theology*, 33.
52. Vos, "Doctrine of the Covenant," 239.
53. As quoted in ibid.

This is the use then of the covenant of works, to work in us the sense of sin and misery, and to prepare men to receive grace. Therefore, the doctrine of the gospel begins with the legal doctrine of works and of the law moral; for the gospel should preach and promise in vain righteousness and life to the believers, if they were not first prepared by feeling their own corruption and miserable condition, to hear and receive grace by the gospel.[54]

Rollock's "Treatise of Our Effectual Calling" was widely read and had great influence on the theology of the British Isles.[55]

James Ussher (1581–1656) was an archbishop in Ireland and the draftsman of the famed Irish Articles (1615). Although he was unable to attend the Westminster Assembly, his writings and theology exercised considerable influence on its work. One cannot read the Irish Articles and the Westminster Confession of Faith without recognizing the similarity in organization, word usage, and doctrine between the two.[56] Like the Westminster Confession, the Irish Articles employ the two-covenant structure (covenant of works, covenant of grace). For example, the Irish Articles unequivocally set forth a prelapsarian covenant of works:

Man being at the beginning created according to the image of God (which consisted especially in the wisdom of his mind and the true holiness of his free will), had the covenant of the law ingrafted in his heart, whereby God did promise unto him everlasting life upon condition that he performed entire and perfect obedience unto his Commandments, according to that measure of strength wherewith he was endued in his creation, and threatened death unto him if he did not perform the same.[57]

54. Robert Rollock, "A Treatise of Our Effectual Calling," in W. M. Gunn, ed., *Select Works of Robert Rollock*, 2 vols. (Edinburgh: Woodrow Society, 1849), 1:43–44, as quoted in Jeong Koo Jeon, *Covenant Theology: John Murray's and Meredith G. Kline's Response to the Historical Development of Federal Theology in Reformed Thought* (Lanham, MD: University Press of America, 1999), 37.

55. J. T. McNeill, *The History and Character of Calvinism* (New York: Oxford University Press, 1967), 307, as quoted in Golding, *Covenant Theology*, 34.

56. See Vos, "Doctrine of the Covenant," 241.

57. Irish Articles, "Of the Creation and Government of All Things," sec. 21.

The Articles also reveal a mature federalism with regard to Adam: "By one man sin entered into the world, and death by sin; and so death went over all men, forasmuch as all have sinned";[58] and with regard to Christ: "He fulfilled the law for us perfectly: For our sakes he endured most grievous torments immediately in his soul, and most painful sufferings in his body."[59] The Irish Articles expressed a full-orbed and advanced covenant theology that was exceeded in confessional form only by the work of the Westminster Assembly approximately thirty years later.

The Covenant Theology of the Westminster Assembly

The Westminster Assembly represents a cresting point in the development of covenant theology. While the members of the Westminster Assembly were clearly indebted to the Continental Reformers, it is important to recognize that the covenant theology of the Assembly was of a distinctly British variety. By the time of the Assembly, the theologians of the three kingdoms had contributed much to advance the work of their Continental forefathers. Therefore, the members of the Assembly had a vast pool of British theological resources from which to draw. Warfield posited that the Assembly primarily relied on the theology of men such as Robert Rollock, Thomas Cartwright, William Perkins, William Ames, and John Ball.[60] Vos suggested that Ussher's Irish Articles and Ball's theology were the major influences.[61] Clearly, while the theology of Westminster was connected to that of its Continental predecessors, it had significantly matured in the British Isles. As Vos so aptly noted, "Apparently the Westminster theologians were, therefore, not under any foreign influence, but simply summed up what in their own country had ripened as the fruit of slow development."[62]

58. Ibid., "Of the Fall of Man, Original Sin, and the State of Man before Justification," sec. 22.
59. Ibid., "Of Christ the Mediator of the Second Covenant," sec. 30.
60. Warfield, *Works of Benjamin B. Warfield*, 6:56.
61. Vos, "Doctrine of the Covenant," 240–41.
62. Ibid., 239.

It also appears from the historical evidence that there was a general theological consensus regarding covenant theology at the Assembly. While the Assembly had many controversial issues to deal with, including the form of church government and the role of the civil government in church discipline, there is no evidence of a similar heated debate regarding covenant theology. Therefore, it is reasonable to conclude that Westminster was not formulating a new doctrine when it articulated its covenant theology, but was rather simply expressing an already received Reformed orthodoxy.

The actual written expression of covenant theology by the Assembly displays mature theological precision. The Westminster Confession clearly outlines a two-covenant structure. The first of these two covenants is referred to in the confession as the covenant of works.[63] This covenant is described in Westminster Confession of Faith 7.2:

> The first covenant made with man was a covenant of works, wherein life was promised to Adam; and in him to his posterity, upon condition of perfect and personal obedience.

After Adam's failure, God revealed a second covenant to mankind, which the Assembly referred to as the covenant of grace and which is described in Westminster Confession of Faith 7.3:

> Man, by his fall, having made himself incapable of life by that covenant, the Lord was pleased to make a second, commonly called the covenant of grace; wherein he freely offereth unto sinners life and salvation by Jesus Christ; requiring of them faith in him, that they may be saved, and promising to give unto all those that are ordained unto eternal life his Holy Spirit, to make them willing, and able to believe.[64]

---

63. The covenant of works, however, is also referred to as the "covenant of life" in the Shorter Catechism.

64. The Larger Catechism speaks of the covenant of grace as being made with Christ rather than the elect. This may be reflecting thought regarding the covenant of redemption, or *pactum salutis*. The Larger Catechism 31 deals with this matter: "With whom was the covenant of grace made?" Answer: "The covenant of grace was made with Christ as the second Adam, and in him with all the elect as his seed."

Although repeatedly under attack, even in the present-day controversies over the doctrine of justification, this expression of covenant theology has remained the benchmark of Reformed orthodoxy for over 350 years.

Conclusion and Assessment

This essay has demonstrated that there is a historical nexus between Calvin and Westminster with regard to the development of covenant theology. It would be an oversimplification and an overstatement to suggest that one can draw a straight chronological, or theological, line from Calvin to Zurich and then to the Assembly. The development of covenant theology was not that neat and tidy. It cannot be expressed purely in a linear or chronological fashion because covenant theology was developing simultaneously on the Continent and in the British Isles. During this bifurcated development, however, there was interaction among the various players and basic consensus regarding doctrine. The two traditions were like two trees growing from the same seed and benefiting from cross-pollination.

As noted in the beginning of this essay, many theologians disagree with this perspective of continuity. Scholars such as R. T. Kendall, David A. Weir, and Holmes Rolston III see a great gulf fixed between Calvin and Westminster.[65] The following quotation from Rolston exemplifies the basic thesis of this discontinuity school:

> We shall challenge afresh the assumption that the Calvinism of the Westminster Confession is true to the Reformer himself. Indeed, it has seldom been realized by persons otherwise well versed in the Reformed tradition that the twin covenant tectonics which dominates the substructure of all later Reformed dogmatics is totally absent from Calvin. Worse than that, its fundamental incompatibility with Calvin's thought has gone all but unnoticed.[66]

65. Other scholars in this school include James Torrance, Donald Bruggink, and Charles Bell.

66. Holmes Rolston III, *John Calvin versus the Westminster Confession* (Richmond: John Knox Press, 1972), 11.

Kendall comes to a similar conclusion and calls for scholarly work to be performed to explain the true separate historical development of the theology of Westminster. Kendall states, "But the time is surely overdue that historical theology present a more accurate picture of what really happened between Calvin's era and that which witnessed the emergence of Westminster theology."[67]

Weir is one theologian who takes Kendall's call seriously. Weir attempts to provide an answer to that call in his book *The Origins of the Federal Theology in Sixteenth-Century Reformation Thought.*[68] Weir's work will be examined and discussed as a representative sample of the school of discontinuity. By briefly examining Weir's work, I hope to demonstrate the essential weakness in the discontinuity school.

Weir's thesis is that federal theology is distinct from Calvinism particularly because federal theology articulates a covenant of works that, according to Weir, was simply not present in the thought of Calvin.[69] Weir grants that Calvin and the early Reformers "discussed the importance of the postlapsarian covenant of grace," but he maintains that they "never taught the federal theology with its prelapsarian covenant motif."[70] Weir makes this point even more bluntly: "Calvin makes no mention in any of his works of a prelapsarian covenant with Adam."[71]

Weir contends that covenant theology did not emerge until after Calvin's time. He suggests that the true origin of covenant theology is to be found in the "controversy over the sovereignty of God and Adam's Fall."[72] Essentially, Weir contends that covenant theology originated from the post-Calvin dogmatic debate over predestination and the "working out of the decrees of God."[73] He makes this contention explicit by stating that "federal theology's distinguishing

---

67. Kendall, *Calvin and English Calvinism*, 213.

68. David A. Weir, *The Origins of the Federal Theology in Sixteenth-Century Reformation Thought* (New York: Oxford University Press, 1990).

69. It should be noted that Weir makes a distinction between federal theology and covenant theology. But this seems to be a distinction without much of a difference, as has been noted by Mark W. Karlberg, "Covenant Theology and the Westminster Tradition," *Westminster Theological Journal* 54 (1992): 137.

70. Weir, *Origins of the Federal Theology*, vii.

71. Ibid., 9–10.

72. Ibid., viii.

73. Ibid., 157.

characteristic—the prelapsarian covenant with Adam—had its origins in the predestinarian discussions which took place during the sixteenth century."[74] This thesis leads Weir to argue that the emergence of covenant theology is founded on scholastic theology rather than exegetical theology. He contends that this scholastic covenant theology, which according to him was a departure from Calvin, was embodied in the Westminster Confession. Weir describes the covenant theology of Westminster as stemming from "systematic, dogmatic thinking, not from the exegetical study of Scripture."[75]

Weir, like many others in the discontinuity school, concludes that Calvin and the other early Reformers emphasized the Bible, grace, and dependence on God, whereas the federal theologians who followed them emphasized scholasticism, legalism, and man's duty to God. For instance, note how Weir compares the First Helvetic Confession (1536) with the Westminster Larger Catechism (1648) on the topic of the purpose of Scripture: "The first teaches that the Scriptures principally expound grace; the second teaches that the Scriptures principally expound duty. Even responding to God's grace is a duty of all men, according to the Westminster standards."[76]

If Weir is correct in his reading of the early Reformers and the motives of the Assembly, then much of what we call Reformed orthodoxy today has little to do with Calvin. But there are plenty of reasons to question Weir's analysis. Weir's thesis is built on two foundations:

1. Covenant theology was a product of the sixteenth-century debates regarding predestination.
2. Calvin's theology did not include a prelapsarian legal covenant (covenant of works).

I believe Weir is wrong on both points, as I will demonstrate in the following paragraphs.

First, Weir is incorrect regarding the origins of covenant theology. As we have seen, he suggests that the scholastic debate over predestina-

74. Ibid., 158.
75. Ibid.
76. Ibid., 153–54.

tion gave rise to covenant theology. As has been argued in this essay, however, there is strong historical evidence that covenant theology matured in the climate of the debate between the Reformers and the Anabaptists. The Zurich Reformers, particularly Zwingli and Bullinger, were forced to further articulate the covenant theology that was nascent in Calvin because of the opposition they faced from the Anabaptists. As Lillback notes: "Zwingli developed the idea of the covenant in his confrontation with the Anabaptists. By stressing the covenant unity of both Testaments, he was able to defend his appeal to circumcision as a type of baptism."[77] Helm argues in a similar manner: "Zwingli and Bullinger seem to be particularly significant, for it was at Zurich that the conflict with Anabaptism was intense and the covenantal character of divine revelation, and of the sacraments, [was] developed."[78]

Second, Weir is also mistaken in his contention that the theology of the covenant of works is foreign to Calvin's thought. In his book, Weir discusses and concurs with Rolston's analysis of the discontinuity between Calvin and Westminster. Rolston specifically argues that Calvin considered the prelapsarian state as one of "pure grace" and that Calvin's theology was therefore totally antithetical to a works principle's being operative in Eden.[79] Weir then expresses his essential agreement with Rolston's assessment of Calvin: "Rolston is very perceptive in seeing that the federal theology is concerned at its very root level with a 'concept of a responsible man,' and that the prelapsarian covenant lies at the very foundation of such a concern."[80] Weir concludes, along with Rolston, that Calvin conceived of Adam as dependent solely on God's grace in the prelapsarian state and that it was only later, with the federal theologians, that the prelapsarian state was conceived of in terms of Adam's meritorious obedience independent of God's grace.

As has been demonstrated in this essay, however, Weir's reading of Calvin's conception of the prelapsarian state is incorrect. Based on Calvin's commentaries, it has indeed been shown that Calvin taught

77. Lillback, "Ursinus' Development of the Covenant of Creation," 270.
78. Helm, "Calvin and the Covenant," 74.
79. Weir, *Origins of the Federal Theology*, 27.
80. Ibid.

that Adam's life was dependent on his obedience to God's commands. Calvin used legal and probationary language to describe Adam's condition in the prelapsarian state. Weir seems to ignore these elements of Calvin's theology. Lillback, who contends that Calvin did express the theological elements of the covenant of works, concludes the following regarding this second component of Weir's thesis: "At the end of this analysis of Calvin's prelapsarian covenant, one can feel the hollowness of the sweeping generalization of David Weir, 'Calvin makes no mention in any of his works of a prelapsarian covenant with Adam.' "[81] Both of Weir's premises are unfounded, and so is his allegation of an essential discontinuity between Calvin and Westminster.

In conclusion, the path from Calvin to Westminster represents a progressive maturing of one and the same theology. Much like the covenant of grace, this doctrinal tradition simply unfolded and became clearer as time progressed from Calvin to the Assembly. Helm captures the essence of this maturation process:

> A doctrinal tradition, is, literally, the handing down over a course of years a body of teaching. This is what happened in the Reformed Churches, and it is possible to trace this tradition from Calvin through Beza, his successor in Geneva, and men such as John Knox and Ames and Perkins, to the time when it achieved classic, precise expression in the various confessions of faith and formularies, notably (in the British Isles) the Westminster Confession of 1648 and its sister documents the Savoy Confession of 1658 and the Baptist Confession of 1689.[82]

The mere existence of diversity in terminology employed by theologians who were part of this doctrinal progression does not suggest discontinuity, but rather simply reflects the natural changes that occur as doctrinal tradition matures. As Helm rightly notes of theologians and theology of this doctrinal tradition:

> There are undoubtedly differences between them and among them, difference in styles, emphasis, theological organization, and terminol-

81. Lillback, *The Binding of God*, 304.
82. Paul Helm, *Calvin and the Calvinists* (Carlisle, PA: Banner of Truth, 1982), 3.

ogy. But it is one thing to recognize development and change within a tradition, quite another thing to imply that the federal theology was a degenerate form of Calvin's theology, one that overturned his views of God and grace.[83]

Accordingly, the Westminster Assembly was not at odds with the doctrinal tradition represented by Calvin and the early Reformers, but rather embodies this tradition in its fully matured and ripened state. In other words, Calvin planted the seed of covenant theology, the Zurich Reformers watered it, and the divines, by the grace of God, reaped the harvest.

Appendix: Sacrament and Covenant in Calvin's Thought on Genesis 2:9; 3:22; and 1 Corinthians 11:25

Calvin states the following regarding the sacramental nature of the Tree of Life in his commentary on Genesis 2:9:

> He gave the tree of life its name, not because it could confer on man that life with which he had been previously endued, *but in order that it might be a symbol and memorial of the life which he had received from God. For we know it to be by no means unusual that God should give to us the attestation of his grace by external symbols. He does not indeed transfer his power into outward signs; but by them he stretches out his hand to us, because, without assistance, we cannot ascend to him.* He intended, therefore, that man, as often as he tasted the fruit of that tree, should remember whence he received his life, in order that he might acknowledge that he lives not by his own power, but by the kindness of God alone; and that life is not (as they commonly speak) an intrinsic good, but proceeds from God. Finally, in that tree there was a visible testimony to the declaration, that "in God we are, and live, and move." But if Adam's hitherto innocent, and of an upright nature, had need of monitory signs to lead him to the knowledge of divine grace, how much more necessary are signs now in this great imbecility of our nature, since we have fallen from the true light? Yet I am not dissatisfied with what has been handed down by some

83. Paul Helm, "Was Calvin a Federalist?" 58.

of the fathers, as Augustine and Eucherius that the tree of life was a figure of Christ, inasmuch as he is the Eternal Word of God: it could not indeed be otherwise a symbol of life, than by representing him in figure. For we must maintain what is declared in the first chapter of John (John 1:1–3,) that the life of all things was included in the Word, but especially the life of men, which is conjoined with reason and intelligence. Wherefore, by this sign, Adam was admonished, that he could claim nothing for himself as if it were his own, in order that he might depend wholly upon the Son of God, and might not seek life anywhere but in him.[84]

Calvin states the following regarding the sacramental nature of the Tree of Life in Genesis 3:22:

There is a defect in the sentence which I think ought to be thus supplied: "It now remains that in future, he be debarred from the fruit of the tree of life"; for by these words Adam is admonished that the punishment to which he is consigned shall not be that of a moment, or of a few days, but that he shall always be an exile from a happy life. They are mistaken who think this also to be an irony; as if God were denying that the tree would prove advantageous to man, even though he might eat of it; *for he rather, by depriving him of the symbol, takes also away the thing signified. We know what is the efficacy of sacraments; and it was said above that the tree was given as a pledge of life.* Wherefore, that he might understand himself to be deprived of his former life, a solemn excommunication is added; not that the Lord would cut him off from all hope of salvation, but, by taking away what he had given, would cause man to seek new assistance elsewhere. Now, there remained an expiation in sacrifices, which might restore him to the life he had lost. Previously, direct communication with God was the source of life to Adam; but, from the moment in which he became alienated from God, it was necessary that he should recover life by the death of Christ, by whose life he then lived. *It is indeed certain, that man would not have been able, had he even devoured the whole tree, to enjoy life against the will of God; but God, out of respect to his own institution, connects life with the external sign, till the promise should be taken away from it; for there*

84. Calvin, *Commentaries*, on Gen. 2:9, emphasis added.

244

never was any intrinsic efficacy in the tree; but God made it life-giving, so far as he had sealed his grace to man in the use of it, as, in truths he represents nothing to us with false signs, but always speaks to us, as they say, with effect. In short, God resolved to wrest out of the hands of man that which was the occasion or ground of confidence, lest he should form for himself a vain hope of the perpetuity of the life which he had lost.[85]

Note how Calvin uses similar language of sacrament and covenant in his comments on the Lord's Supper in 1 Corinthians 11:25:

This cup is the New Testament. What is affirmed as to the *cup*, is applicable also to the *bread*, and thus, by this form of expression, he intimates what he had before stated more briefly—that *the bread is the body.* For it is so to us, that it may be a *testament in his body*, that is, a covenant, which has been once confirmed by the offering up of his body, and is now confirmed by eating, when believers feast upon that sacrifice. Accordingly, while Paul and Luke use the *words—testament in the blood*, Matthew and Mark employ the expression—*blood of the testament*, which amounts to the same thing. For the blood was poured out to reconcile us to God, and now we drink of it in a spiritual sense, that we may be partakers of reconciliation. *Hence, in the Supper, we have both a covenant, and a confirmatory pledge of the covenant. I shall speak in the Epistle to the Hebrews, if the Lord shall allow me opportunity, as to the word* testament. *It is well* known, *however, that sacraments receive that name, from being* testimonies *to us of the divine will, to confirm it in our minds. For as a covenant is entered into among men with solemn rites, so it is in the same manner that the Lord deals with us. Nor is it without strict propriety that this term is employed; for in consequence of the connection between the word and the sign, the covenant of the Lord is really included in the sacraments, and the term* covenant *has a reference or relation to us. This will be of no small importance for understanding the nature of the sacraments; for if they are* covenants, *then they contain promises, by which consciences may be roused up to an assurance of salvation. Hence it follows, that they are not merely outward signs of profession before men, but are inwardly, too, helps to faith.*[86]

85. Calvin, *Commentaries*, on Gen. 3:22, emphasis added.
86. Calvin, *Commentaries*, on 1 Cor. 11:25, emphasis added.

9

The Doctrine of the Atonement from the Westminster Assembly to the Twentieth Century

Richard C. Gamble

Within Reformed theology, it is granted that the Scriptures speak in broad or general terms on the design of Christ's death. It is also generally agreed that Christ's death secured benefits for the nonelect as well as those benefits and salvation for the elect. Third, from a strictly objective sense, on the condition of faith, Christ's atonement is "available" to all those who hear the gospel, even the nonelect. Finally, Christ's purpose in tasting death was to save those who are saved (the elect).[1]

One of the hallmarks of Reformed theology, relative to Christ's death, is that his vicarious work was both definite (a certain number) and personal. This was the teaching of the Westminster Assembly on the atonement.

The Westminster Assembly on the Nature of the Atonement

The Assembly's work on the atonement is found in chapter 8 of the Westminster Confession of Faith. The Assembly's teaching in that

---

1. A. A. Hodge, *The Atonement* (Philadelphia: Presbyterian Board of Publication, 1867), 371–72.

chapter, however, makes more sense in light of the Westminster divines' previous work. After handling the nature of Scriptures and God as Trinity, the Assembly entitled the third chapter, "Of God's Eternal Decree." The divines worked hard to hammer out this difficult chapter.[2]

The third section of that chapter contains the phrase "fore-ordained to everlasting death." Some commissioners to the Assembly did not want the doctrine stated so sharply.[3] Nevertheless, the delegates were very determined to have reprobation clearly asserted in this place of the confession.[4]

Another area of debate on the doctrine of the atonement connects to section 6. There, the *ordo salutis* was presented. Apparently, a small but capable group entertained a notion of what is called a "Calvinistic universal redemption."[5] The divines clearly rejected this teaching, and worded the confession in such a manner as to exclude it.[6]

Chapter 4 of the confession is on creation, and chapter 5 is on God's providence over his creation. Chapter 6 teaches about Adam's fall and concomitant punishment. As expected, the Assembly defined the word "sin" very carefully. Sin was understood as both guilt and depravity.[7] In chapter 7, human salvation from sin concerned election and the covenant. The Westminster Confession teaches redemption in a covenantal structure.[8]

2. See B. B. Warfield, "The Making of the Westminster Confession," in *Collected Writings*, vol. 6, *The Westminster Assembly and Its Work* (New York: Oxford University Press, 1932). Debate occurred on the chapter's title as well as the first section, on "His Own Counsel." Ibid., 122–28. The second section, on the decree, was also treated with diligence. The divines wanted especially to underline the independence of the decree. Ibid., 129–30.

3. Ibid., 132. Stated more precisely, at least one commissioner. For example, Whitakers moved for an alteration of the section even after the confession had been completed—and then had his dissent recorded when the alternative failed.

4. "We must esteem the clear and firm statement of the doctrine of foreordination to death, therefore, a matter which the Assembly deemed of the highest importance." Ibid., 133. "It is very clear that the Assembly by a very large majority—doubtless, in this case practically unanimously—deemed that important concerns were guarded by these words." Ibid.

5. Ibid., 142. This group is associated with the names Cameron and Amyraut. For more information, see Richard B. Gamble, *The Whole Counsel of God*, vol. 3, *God's People in God's World* (Phillipsburg, NJ: P&R Publishing, forthcoming).

6. Warfield, "The Making of the Westminster Confession," 143.

7. John Murray, "The Theology of the Westminster Confession of Faith," in *Collected Writings*, 4 vols. (Edinburgh: Banner of Truth, 1976–82), 4:253.

8. The Westminster Confession of Faith "guards the unity of redemptive history, relates this history to the consummating time and event, the coming of Christ, and accords to soteriology the covenantal structure that is indispensable if it is scripturally conceived." Ibid., 4:254.

Christ's atoning work is the subject of chapter 8. That central doctrine was carefully related to Christ's own election to office, and to the election of his people in him. Atonement was also connected to his person and mediatorial offices. There was an interdependence, and the doctrine was woven together in such a fashion that disjunction between Christ's person and his work was not possible.[9]

From this foundation, Reformed theology has continued to debate and refine the doctrine of the atonement.[10]

Two Broader Areas of Debate on the Atonement

Beginning beyond the Reformed community, two areas of debate relative to the atonement are also important within the Reformed community.

Penal Substitution

The first controversy concerned the nature of the atonement theories itself. In the history of doctrine, the work of the atonement has generally been described under three headings or theories.[11]

The first atonement theory has been called the "moral influence theory," and is associated with the medieval theologian Peter Abelard. This school of thought is rejected by Protestantism.[12]

9. "The atonement occupies a central place in the Christian faith. But centrality is misconceived if it is not related to the whole of which it is the centre." Ibid., 4:255. "The interdependence is set forth in such a way that disjunction is not only avoided but is perceived to be impossible." Ibid.

10. At about the same time as the work on the confession, there was also a debate called the "Marrow controversy," stemming from a book published in 1646. The controversy concerned how the atonement related to all humankind, including sinners.

11. That does not mean that there are only three theories! In the ancient church, there was also a "ransom-to-Satan theory" and a "recapitulation theory." At the Reformation, the Socinians developed an "example theory." Later, a "mystical theory" was proposed by liberals such as Friedrich Schleiermacher. For more information, see Louis Berkhof, *Systematic Theology* (Grand Rapids: Eerdmans, 1972), 384–85, 387, 389–90.

12. Hodge, *The Atonement*, 267; Berkhof, *Systematic Theology*, 386; J. Gresham Machen, *God Transcendent* (Edinburgh: Banner of Truth, 1982), 193–94. "These persons hold simply that Jesus on the cross gave us a supreme example of self-sacrifice. By that example we are inspired to do likewise" (Machen, *God Transcendent*, 194). "They make the cross of Christ merely an example of a general principle of self-sacrifice" (194).

The second school, which is sometimes known as the "governmental theory" or the "governmental influence theory," was further developed in American Presbyterianism.[13] In this view, Christ's death was seen as a deterrent from sin, as well as an aid in Christian discipline.

From this vantage point, after Christ's bloody death on the cross, salvation was then offered on different terms to his followers. At first, salvation had to be based on perfect obedience to God's law. Now, the new basis was "faith." This view should also be rejected.[14]

The third view of the atonement is called the "penal-substitution theory." This teaching was first associated with the medieval theologian Anselm. In this view, the atonement is both objective (it propitiates God and reconciles him to the sinner) and also vicarious (not paid for by the sinner).[15] This is the generally held Reformed position.

Piacular Theory

Another broad area of debate on the atonement concerns the nature of Christ's sacrificial work. The Old Testament priest's task is often seen as twofold. The priest both offered gifts and made sacrifices for sin. Of course, Christ offered the all-sufficient sacrifice for sin. There are different conceptions regarding the nature and origin of the sacrificial idea.

Relative to sacrifice is the "gift theory"—in which the offerer hoped that his gift would secure favor with the deity. Another idea is the "sacramental-communion theory," a primitive notion of an animal "containing" deity and the offerer then "partaking" of the deity's nature. Next is the "homage theory," with the sacrifice demonstrating the offerer's submission to and dependence on the god. In this theory of sacrifice, sin is a fundamental consideration. In the homage view, the worshiper's

13. In some texts, this school is referred to as the Edwardsian teaching. Yet Jonathan Edwards did not hold this position. For further information, see Hodge, *The Atonement*, 269, 296; Berkhof, *Systematic Theology*, 388ff.; R. L. Dabney, *Systematic Theology* (repr., Edinburgh: Banner of Truth, 1996), 508. This theory emphasizes God's moral law and government, and God's acceptance of Christ's satisfaction. It is also known as the "New School" theory. J. Gresham Machen says of this school: "The death of Christ was not necessary in order that any eternal justice of God, rooted in the divine nature, might be satisfied." *God Transcendent*, 195.

14. "Even the governmental theory denies that there is any real underlying necessity for the punishment of sin." Ibid., 198.

15. Berkhof, *Systematic Theology*, 373–83.

repentance and engagement to give back his life to God is essential. A fourth notion is called the "symbol theory," in which the sacrificial offerings are "signs" of a restored relationship. The last notion is the "piacular theory." In this view, the sacrifices are expiatory. The animal was killed as a vicarious atonement for the offerer's sins.[16]

Of all those ideas, the piacular theory is the one in accord with Scripture's presentation of Christ's work. Yet even among those who have held to the piacular theory, there has been some debate about the origin of this type of sacrifice.[17]

Some Areas of Atonement Debate within the Reformed Community

The first debate concerned the reasons for the necessity of the atonement. The question was whether the atonement was necessary out of the free, sovereign will and love of God, or whether it was necessary because of the demands and threats of the law, of justice, and of sin.

The second concerned the nature of the atonement. While it was agreed that the atonement is limited to the elect, must there be a "decree" of reprobation, or does God elect some and simply "pass over" others?

The third debate was on the substance of the atonement. Did God in some sense lower, or even dispense with, the exact letter of the law in the atonement, or is the substance of the atonement the precise penalty against sin?

Before continuing, it could be asked whether these atonement details are important. J. Gresham Machen rightly reminded us that any detail relative to Christ's atonement is of the highest importance.[18]

16. Ibid., 362–63.
17. B. B. Warfield, "Christ Our Sacrifice," in *The Person and Work of Christ* (Philadelphia: Presbyterian and Reformed, 1950), 396–400. Warfield said that the origin of sacrifice is a matter of debate; there was apparently no command for it from God. He conceded that sacrifice may have been invented by man, but "by this act piacular sacrifice was instituted by God." Ibid., 397. "Sacrifice may represent the reaching out of man towards God: in its piacular conception it represents the stooping down of God to man." Ibid.
18. "It is the most momentous question that can come to any human soul." Machen, *God Transcendent*, 196.

With some of the parameters of the debate before us, let us examine some of the more important Presbyterian contributors.

Nineteenth-Century Presbyterianism on the Atonement

William Symington (1795–1862)

The great Scottish pastor and theologian William Symington was also a professor at the Reformed Presbyterian Theological Hall in Glasgow. His first book was entitled *On the Atonement and Intercession of Jesus Christ.*[19] Symington, like his American colleagues, was deeply involved in debates on the nature of the atonement.[20]

Symington, after defining technical terms, entertained five general objections made against the atonement, and answered those objections.[21] He then went to an analysis of the necessity of the atonement. Of course, without Christ's death on the cross, all other attempts to procure pardon for sin would fall short.[22]

The debatable part of Symington's work primarily concerned the nature and necessity of the atonement. Symington, like most other Reformed divines, held to the penal-substitution theory. Within that category, however, he added some complications.

Symington separated not just the meaning of the words, but also the doctrine of "the atonement" from the doctrine of "redemption."[23] The center of the atonement, for Symington, involved Christ's sufferings and procuring of salvation.[24] He comprehended the doctrine of the atonement in a more restricted sense than he did the doctrine of redemption. From a foundation in "atonement," Symington then moved on to a doctrine of "redemption."

---

19. First published in 1834, with a second edition the following year. The volume was printed in the United States in 1836 and went through many editions through the next twenty-five years. It was published in Pittsburgh in 1859 by the General Assembly of the United Presbyterian Church as *Symington on Atonement.*

20. For more information on the debates, see Roy Blackwood, *William Symington: Churchman and Theologian* (n.p., 1999), 153ff.

21. William Symington, *On the Atonement and Intercession of Jesus Christ* (New York: Carter and Bros., 1854), 20–46.

22. Ibid., 57–64.

23. Ibid., 13–15. The word that we translate "atone," said Symington, means "to cover," while "redeem" means "to be released from a debt."

24. Blackwood, *William Symington*, 150.

Sometimes the word "dominion" was close in meaning to his notion of "redemption." Symington's doctrine of redemption centered in Christ's applying the procured benefits to, or bestowing them on, his people. For Symington, redemption, in the broadest sense, involved Christ's kingship over the universe.[25]

Thus, Christ's death, for Symington, gave legal satisfaction to the claims made by the divine law for the sins of men, and subsequently took away Satan's legal ground to exercise his "lawless usurpation."[26] From this general teaching, Symington had particular notions concerning other areas of the atonement.

Symington's analysis, in focusing on the nature and necessity of the atonement, concluded that the atonement was necessary out of the free, sovereign will and love of God. Symington held that God's love was a primary motive for the necessity of the atonement.

Because God's love was the primary motive, "the necessity for atonement was a relative or moral necessity and not an absolute or natural necessity," says Roy Blackwood, "and by his explanation of that position Symington identified himself with the earlier reformers."[27] Since the atonement springs from God's free purpose to save sinners, it was not a natural but rather a moral necessity. The first movement of this prior purpose (for redemption) was God's love.[28] Thus, Symington should not be counted in that class of theologians who held to an absolute necessity of the atonement.[29] Symington rejected the notion that something external to God's nature could force him to do anything.[30]

---

25. Ibid., 151.

26. Ibid.

27. Ibid., 153. The last part of Blackwood's statement connects to his thesis that Symington sided with Calvin against Turretin on certain atonement issues (see note 29).

28. Ibid.

29. "There were significant differences between this doctrine and that of Turretin and those who followed his school of Atonement theology, both before and after Symington. Turretin insisted upon 'the doctrines of absolute necessity' and he classified all other Divines as being either those who believed no atonement necessary, or those who affirmed 'a hypothetical necessity', wherein 'God has decreed that an atonement is to be made, therefore it is necessary.' " Ibid., 155.

30. Symington "has denied that any thing in God's nature could demand the sacrifice of Christ, on the basis of its being an infringement of the sovereignty of God. In so far as God's actions subsequent to his original resolve were concerned, Symington believed that the moral conditions and 'necessities' of the individual sinners *were* factors in the case." Ibid., 155–56.

A. A. Hodge on the Atonement

Moving to America, there was a distinguished succession of systematic theologians at old Princeton Seminary. The line began with the first professor, Archibald Alexander. From him, the chair of systematics proceeded to Charles Hodge, who also contributed to the doctrine of the atonement.[31] Charles's son, who succeeded him in systematics, was named Archibald Alexander Hodge (1823–86).[32]

Concerning broader atonement debates, A. A. Hodge held to the piacular theory of Christ's sacrificial work, against many other theologians of his time.[33] In addition, he defended the penal-substitution theory against those who denied that biblical teaching.[34] Hodge also fought against the governmental and moral views of the atonement.[35]

Looking at the Old Testament, Hodge held to the piacular view of those sacrifices. The sacrifices actually expiated, and they were types and symbols of Christ's expiation.[36] "The Scriptures declare that the ancient priest was in all these respects a type of Christ."[37] Specifically, Hodge taught that Christ reconciled the elect to God.[38]

Focusing on places where Reformed theologians have disagreed, Hodge saw the motive for Christ's work of redemption in God's love. "The Scriptures habitually affirm that the motive which led

31. Charles Hodge wrote *The Orthodox Doctrine Regarding the Extent of the Atonement*. This pamphlet was also published in Scotland, edited by William Symington.

32. A. A. Hodge, while teaching in Pittsburgh, originally wrote the book as a series of articles for the *Presbyterian Banner* of Pittsburgh.

33. Hodge, *The Atonement*, 125. Hodge was vigorous in his attacks against the "broad church writers," including Horace Bushnell (1802–76), *The Vicarious Sacrifice* (New York: Scribner's, 1865) and Frederick D. Maurice (1805–72), *The Doctrine of Sacrifice Deduced from the Scriptures* (Cambridge: Macmillan, 1854). See Hodge, *The Atonement*, 122–30, 218ff. With a slight note of surprise, Hodge added that the piacular theory is held "even among [some] modern German writers." Ibid., 127.

34. Ibid., 198ff.

35. Ibid., 218–21.

36. Ibid., 275.

37. Ibid., 411.

38. "In its classical sense the word *[h]ilaskesthai* means to propitiate an offended deity by means of expiatory sacrifices or penances." Ibid., 181. "Thus, Christ is made a faithful high priest, in things pertaining to God, to make reconciliation for (*[h]ilaskesthai*) the sins of his people." Ibid. "The Hebrew word is the principal one used by the Holy Spirit to express the precise effect designed and accomplished by these sacrifices, in respect to sin as a covering, and hence in respect to God as a means of reconciliation." Ibid.

the Father to give his Son, and the Son to die, was not a mere general philanthropy, but the highest, most peculiar and personal love."[39] From God's love, Christ died for his own, and for only his own.[40]

Another area of special interest for Reformed theologians is the atonement and Christ's active and passive obedience. Hodge agreed (in accord with Symington—while not mentioning it) that the word "atonement" was in many senses inadequate.[41] Furthermore, again in agreement with Symington, he limited his understanding of the word "atonement" to "only the expiation of our guilt by Christ's vicarious sufferings," holding that it expressed "nothing concerning the relation which his obedience sustains to our salvation, as that meritorious condition upon which the divine favor and the promised reward have by covenant been suspended."[42]

At this place, his analysis is quite similar to the earlier work of the Scotsman. Furthermore, Hodge proposed the word "satisfaction" (instead of Symington's "redemption") as that which "exactly and exhaustively expresses all that Christ has done as our Substitute, in our stead, for our sakes." "His whole work was of the nature of a satisfaction."[43]

Hodge said that Symington wrongly separated Christ's obedience and his sufferings.[44] Yet it appears that Hodge's criticism of Symington may not be just.[45]

---

39. Ibid., 408.

40. "It is inconceivable that this highest and most peculiar love, which moved God to give his only-begotten and well-beloved son to undergo a painful and shameful death, could have had for its objects the myriads from whom, both before and after Christ, he had withheld all knowledge of the gospel; or those to whom, while he gives them the outward call of the word, he refuses to give the inward call of his Spirit." Ibid., 409.

41. Ibid., 248.

42. Ibid., 249.

43. Ibid.

44. Ibid.

45. "It would also be a mistake to identify the theology of Symington and Hodge as being 'the same' on this subject because Hodge, after complaining that the meaning of the term 'atonement' was too 'ambiguous,' went on to equate it with 'satisfaction,' and this same Atonement-Redemption distinction also lay at the root of his criticism of Symington's whole doctrine." Blackwood, *William Symington*, 152. Blackwood further charges, "Everything that Hodge has gone on to say here about the necessity for considering both the sufferings and obedience of Christ, Symington has said with at least equal emphasis" (152 n. 57).

At the end of Hodge's life, in the latter half of the nineteenth century, there was tremendous pressure from within American Presbyterianism to revise the Westminster Confession of Faith. The pressure was, at least in part, related to the doctrine of the atonement. The faculty at old Princeton stood against this movement.[46] From within that context, debate on the atonement continued.

Early-Twentieth-Century American Presbyterian Atonement Theory

B. B. Warfield (1851–1921)[47]

Warfield also examined the origins and nature of Old Testament sacrificial worship. Like his predecessor A. A. Hodge, Warfield was not hesitant to defend the old Princetonian views of the atonement in general, and concerning the nature of Old Testament sacrifice in particular.[48]

The first assumption concerning Old Testament sacrificial worship was to recognize that there was a broken relationship between God and humanity. From that assumption, Warfield saw the origin of sacrificial worship, at Genesis 4:3–4, with the narrative concerning Cain and Abel. When it was time to make an offering to the Lord, Cain offered from the fruit of the ground while his brother offered an animal. There was, in fact, no reason why Jehovah should prefer a lamb to a sheaf of wheat, thought Warfield. The answer to God's

46. See David Calhoun, "Old Princeton Seminary and the Westminster Standards," in J. Ligon Duncan, ed., *The Westminster Confession into the 21ˢᵗ Century*, 2 vols. (Tain, Ross-shire: Christian Focus, 2004), 2:33–61.

47. B. B. Warfield wrote a number of articles on the atonement. The most important are collected in *The Person and Work of Christ* (repr., Nutley, NJ: Presbyterian and Reformed, 1970), entitled: "The Chief Theories of the Atonement"; "Modern Theories of the Atonement"; and "The New Testament Terminology of Redemption." Although he focused on the phrase "the whole world," his work entitled "Jesus Christ the Propitiation for the Whole World" in volume 1 of *Selected Shorter Writings*, 2 vols. (Nutley, NJ: Presbyterian and Reformed, 1970, 1973), is also helpful.

48. Warfield, "Christ Our Sacrifice," 401–4. Warfield recognized that there were some incorrect theories of sacrifice that did not allow a place for the hideousness of sin in all its essential implications. Those incorrect theories were termed "recognition," "gift" (the most common), and "communion."

choice was that Abel offered "by faith." God was concerned with the human heart as well as with the specific offering of the hand.[49]

This early biblical account provided the foundation for Warfield's analysis of two different conceptions of the nature of sacrifice. On the one hand, as we have seen, there was what has been termed the "homage theory" of sacrifice, and on the other the "piacular theory."[50] Warfield was convinced that Abel held to the piacular theory, and that this conception was the fundamental ground for the sacrifice's acceptance by God. Warfield was convinced that "the Levitical system is the elaborate embodiment of the piacular idea."[51] Warfield thus concurred with A. A. Hodge.

There was a further development of the "expiation" concept. According to Warfield, this important theological concept was first elaborated in the postexilic period. In expiation, the sin offering was of the highest importance.[52] Warfield, in his constant battling with theological liberals, was glad that even they would agree that "the expiation of guilt is the leading purpose of the Levitical sacrifices."[53]

Warfield also examined the New Testament position on the nature of sacrifice. One important question for him was whether the New Testament writers had been influenced by the Levitical system, or by the notions of sacrifice that were apparently current at their own time (i.e., the first century). Most scholars, said Warfield, agreed that "substitutionary expiation" was the Jewish notion at the time.[54] In the book of Hebrews particularly, "it is distinctly of expiatory sacrifices that the author is thinking when he presents Christ as dying a sacrificial

49. Warfield thought that this "seems to suggest that the supreme excellence of his sacrifice is to be sought not in the mere nature of the thing offered, but in the attitude of the offerer." Ibid., 396.

50. "Cain came to the Lord with an offering in his hand and the Homage theory of sacrifice in his mind: Abel with an offering in his hand and the Piacular theory of sacrifice in his heart." Ibid., 397.

51. Ibid., 408.

52. Ibid., 409.

53. Ibid., 412.

54. "The sense of the writers of the New Testament when they spoke of Christ as a sacrifice . . . is that of an expiatory offering propitiating God's favor and reconciling Him to guilty man." Ibid., 416–17. Later, Warfield said, "The theology of the writers of the New Testament is very distinctly a 'blood theology.' " Ibid., 423.

death." Hebrews agrees with the Levitical terminology, and it agrees with the theories of both Paul and John.[55] Warfield was able to surmise that "every important type of New Testament teaching, including the teaching of Christ Himself, concurs in representing Christ as a sacrifice, and in conceiving of the sacrifice which it represents Christ as being, as a substitutive expiation."[56]

Warfield's powerful conclusion was that Christianity came to announce the perfect sacrifice for sin. Based on that perfect sacrifice, the Christian was bold to live a life of grace and power in the face of a watching world.[57]

Geerhardus Vos (1862–1949)

Geerhardus Vos was Warfield's colleague and friend for over twenty-five years, was Machen's teacher and colleague, and was also John Murray's teacher and then colleague for the year that Murray taught at Princeton. Both Machen and Murray held Vos in the highest regard.[58]

Concerning Christ's sacrificial work, Vos in his conception of the atonement generally followed Warfield's pattern. He, too, recognized the foundational problem of a broken relationship between God and humanity. Likewise, he understood that a man could not resolve this situation even by offering his own life, and that there was thus a need for a vicarious sin offering.[59]

55. Ibid., 420.
56. Ibid., 421.
57. Ibid., 425–26. Warfield's own expression is very powerful: "To proclaim the real sacrifice for sin which God had provided in order to supersede all the poor fumbling efforts which men had made and were making to provide a sacrifice for sin for themselves; and, planting men's feet on this, to bid them go forward. It was in this sign that Christianity conquered, and it is in this sign alone that it continues to conquer. We may think what we will of such a religion. What cannot be denied is that Christianity is such a religion." Ibid., 426. This differentiated Christianity from other religions.
58. Murray said, "Dr. Vos is, in my judgment, the most penetrating exegete it has been my privilege to know, and I believe, the most incisive exegete that has appeared in the English-speaking world in this century." As cited by Sinclair B. Ferguson in the introduction to Vos's sermon *Grace and Glory* (Edinburgh: Banner of Truth, 1994), ix. Murray states that "it was the Seminary, and perhaps the instruction of Geerhardus Vos in particular, which instilled in him the conviction that doctrine must be arrived at through a painstaking examination of the Scriptures in their original languages." Murray, *Collected Writings*, 3:29.
59. "All Biblical sacrifice rests on the idea that the gift of life to God, either in consecration or in expiation, is necessary to the action or the restoration of religion." Geerhardus Vos,

For Vos, the importance of vicariousness or substitution came into particular focus in the life of the patriarch Abraham. Abraham was commanded by God to offer life, the precious life of his son Isaac, as a sacrifice. Nevertheless, God demonstrated that substitution was acceptable; God himself provided the substitute for the son. "Thus there was placed side by side with the emphasis on the divine creative omnipotence," said Vos, "the stress on the necessity of sacrifice."[60]

Moving to the New Testament, Vos also examined the book of Hebrews' doctrine of the atonement as it relates to sacrifice. He rightly asked why so much attention was paid in that book to the priesthood and sacrifice, while the atonement was hardly mentioned at all. His conclusion was that the author was more interested in the result, rather than the atonement's mode and progress. On this point, the author of Hebrews is not very different in his thinking from Paul. Thus, the "atonement" language of Hebrews is metaphorical; it is the "blood that cleanses."[61]

Specifically, Hebrews 9 provides a rationale for the sacrificial act of Christ. Regarding verse 12, Vos observed, "Christ through His blood obtained eternal redemption [*lytrōsin*]." This word, noted Vos, was a forensic Pauline term. At Hebrews 9:15, there was the same conception: "redemption from the sins of the first *Diatheke*."[62]

Of course, Paul's doctrine of the atonement as it relates to sacrifice was also very important. This was an area of controversy during both Warfield's and Vos's eras.

Scholars at that time granted that Paul's conception was based on the Old Testament. Vos was ready to acknowledge that the Old Testament did not present an unambiguous theory of sacrifice.[63] Yet it was also clear that philosophical presuppositions had unduly and

Biblical Theology (Grand Rapids: Eerdmans, 1975), 92–93. "The second principle underlying the idea is that man in the abnormal relations of sin is disqualified for offering this gift of his life in his own person" (93).

60. Ibid., 92–94.

61. Geerhardus Vos, *The Teaching of the Epistle to the Hebrews* (1956; repr., Phillipsburg, NJ: Presbyterian and Reformed, 1985), 117–18.

62. Ibid., 119–20. Also, at Hebrews 9:28, "*enengkein* is literally taken from the LXX." Ibid., 120. Finally, he sees the same at Hebrews 11:39ff. Vos noted that the perfecting accomplished by Christ is carried back to Old Testament believers. Ibid., 124.

63. "The Old Testament itself nowhere presents us with what could be fairly called a theory of sacrifice." Geerhardus Vos, "The Sacrificial Idea in Paul's Doctrine of the Atonement,"

negatively influenced some contemporary studies of Paul's conception.[64] Those philosophical presuppositions produced rotten fruit in contemporary Pauline studies, for the apostle was no longer able to present his own views.[65] Thus, Vos also followed the old Princetonian tradition of strong defense of biblical teaching.

Vos was convinced that Paul's notion of the atonement closely associated the two ideas of "redemption" and "sacrifice." For Paul, Christ was both the sacrificial victim and the sacrificer.[66]

Vos's conclusion was that the previously common view of Paul's theology, that "the essence of sacrificial propitiation consists in the exhibition of penal righteousness," was correct.[67] There was thus a unity of opinion between the two great Princetonian professors Warfield and Vos.

From the clear teaching of his predecessors, J. Gresham Machen developed his concept of the doctrine of the atonement.

J. Gresham Machen

A short analysis of Machen's atonement views should begin with Christ's priestly work. Christ's priestly work cannot stand apart from his prophetic work, he thought.[68] The only way to have access to God

---

in Richard B. Gaffin Jr., ed., *Redemptive History and Biblical Interpretation* (Phillipsburg, NJ: Presbyterian and Reformed, 1980), 374.

64. Vos, *Biblical Theology*, 159. Vos's principle of Scripture interpretation is clear here. For both Old Testament and Pauline interpretation, "no preconceived theory of atonement should be allowed to color our understanding of the law, but the reverse should happen."

65. "We find that on the one hand the fact of the prominence of the sacrificial idea in Paul's epistles is denied, and that on the other hand, where the fact is acknowledged, the significance that has been by the church attached to the fact is explained away." Vos, "The Sacrificial Idea in Paul's Doctrine of the Atonement," 373.

66. "The thought that Christ was victim and mercy seat in one has nothing strange in it; an equally bold combination occurs in the epistle to the Hebrews, and Paul by the emphatic phrase, 'in his own blood,' has himself marked its peculiarity." Ibid., 376. "The word, thus interpreted, bears witness to the fact that Paul regarded the sacrificial aspect of our Lord's death not as a secondary or figurative mode of viewing it, but as pertaining to its very essence, as most literally expressing its central significance." Ibid.

67. Ibid., 377.

68. Machen, *God Transcendent*, 168–72. This connected to the modernist movement, which Machen combated, that dethroned Christ by saying that only the gospel of Christ was important, not the gospel about Christ. For Machen, "Jesus is both the author and the substance of the gospel" (172).

is through the work of a priest.[69] It is in his priestly work that Christ offered himself as sacrifice.

Second, Machen, like Symington and A. A. Hodge, also thought that "the word 'atonement' in the first place, is ambiguous, and in the second place, is not broad enough."[70]

Third, Machen also examined the nature of Christ's active and passive obedience.[71] Christ took our place with respect to the law of God. The primary end for Christ's death on the cross was the satisfaction of God's eternal justice.[72]

John Murray on the Atonement

Murray, like Hodge and Symington before him, wrote an entire volume on the atonement entitled *Redemption Accomplished and Applied.*

The Definition and Nature of the Atonement

Debate continued in Murray's day within Reformed scholarship about the best way to define the doctrine of the atonement.[73] Murray struggled with the issues as well.

He thought that the atonement should be viewed in light of the intra-Trinitarian economy of salvation. He further asserted that the atonement was a work of the Holy Spirit, citing Hebrews 9:14.[74] Nevertheless, when he defined the atonement itself, he conceived of it as specifically the work of Christ. Furthermore, the source of the atonement was in the love of the Father.

Murray's precise definition was this: "The Atonement is a term appropriated by theology to designate the work of Christ, which in the express terms of Scripture is explicated as obedience, sacrifice, propitiation, reconciliation, and redemption."[75]

69. Ibid., 174.
70. Ibid., 177.
71. Ibid., 190.
72. Ibid., 198.
73. See Roger Nicole, "The Nature of Redemption," in Carl F. H. Henry, ed., *Christian Faith and Modern Theology* (New York: Channel Press, 1964), 205.
74. John Murray, "The Atonement," in *Collected Writings*, 2:148.
75. Ibid., 142–43.

Murray's definition means that the atonement focuses on the satisfaction of justice. Even though it is a legal term, and furthermore a legal notion, it is also, said Murray, a biblical concept. Murray found one of the most important biblical grounds for the notion in Isaiah 53:10.[76] In Isaiah, the servant was crushed and was made a trespass or guilt offering.

To connect Murray's analysis with the earlier examinations of Warfield, Vos, and Machen, for Murray, "the atonement must more broadly be subsumed under the mediatorial work of Christ, and more specifically under the priestly office."[77] Yet defining the atonement in no way begins to exhaust its meaning.

For a "dour Scot," Murray used language on the nature of the atonement that is quite beautiful:

> We are but touching the fringes of the mystery of God's will and we should be aware that thought and word fail. Here we have unreachable wisdom, facets of revelation that pertain to ways past finding out. But it is only as our feeble minds become engaged with this mystery and we seek to explore its depths that we catch glimpses of its marvel and we exclaim: "O the depth of the riches both of the wisdom and knowledge of God!" (Rom. 11:33).[78]

Thus, the nature of the atonement, for Murray, was a bloodletting. The nature was judicial, like the concepts of expiation, propitiation, and reconciliation.

But for Murray the nature of the atonement also involves believers' union with Christ, and therefore our dying with him, too. This relates the concept of atonement or redemption to sanctification.[79] To further comprehend Murray's views, we should examine Christ's work, the necessity of the atonement, and the believer's freedom wrought by Christ.

76. "Yet it was the LORD's will to crush him and cause him to suffer, and though the LORD makes his life a guilt offering, he will see his offspring and prolong his days, and the will of the LORD will prosper in his hand" (Isa. 53:10). Unless otherwise indicated, Scripture quotations in this chapter are from the New International Version.

77. Murray, "The Atonement," 148.

78. Ibid., 150.

79. John Murray, *Redemption Accomplished and Applied* (Grand Rapids: Eerdmans, 1955), 46–48.

The Work of Christ and the Atonement

For Murray, Christ's work in the atonement focused on his obedience, on his redeeming sinners, on his making a sacrifice and propitiating sin, and on reconciliation.

In Christ's great work of atonement, he was obedient. Christ's obedience was the unifying principle of his entire work. Christ's obedience was of his will and emotion. It was not just *doing* certain things, such as going to the cross. Rather, it was an obedience that was learned throughout his life.[80]

Christ's obedience on earth related back in time to an intra-Trinitarian agreement. In the covenant of grace, said Murray, the Mediator assumes on behalf of his people the conditions of the old, broken covenant. Life had been promised to Adam upon the condition of perfect continued obedience, which Adam did not fulfill. There was punishment to be taken for breaking God's law, and Adam—and his descendants—received that punishment.

Thus, the second Adam (Christ) had to both obey all the parts of the covenant, which he did, and yet still receive the penalty due for the sin of the first Adam, which he also did. This was certainly "not fair" to Christ.

Therefore, as part of his state of humiliation, Christ was made to be under the law, which was explained by Paul in Galatians 4:4ff.[81] Stating the nature of Christ's obedience another way, he actively lived a life of obedience to God. Christ fulfilled all the precepts of the covenant and perfectly obeyed the law of God; this achievement is termed Christ's "active obedience."

But Christ also suffered for our sins. This activity on our behalf, when his Father's white-hot wrath was poured out on him on the cross, is called Christ's "passive obedience."[82]

Thus, Christ's obedience as the second Adam, theologically considered, is deemed both active and passive. The law of God required penal sanctions against lawbreakers (encompassing Christ's passive

---

80. "Jesus grew in wisdom and stature" (Luke 2:52).

81. "But when the time had fully come, God sent his Son, born of a woman, born under law, to redeem those under law, that we might receive the full rights of sons" (Gal. 4:4).

82. See also A. A. Hodge, *The Confession of Faith* (Edinburgh: Banner of Truth, 1978), 145.

obedience) and presented positive demands to be completed (Christ's active obedience).[83]

And Christ did even more. Redemption was purchased by a ransom. It was a ransom from the bondage to which our sin had consigned us.[84] Murray was not proposing the "ransom theory of the atonement" here. Christ's work is the work of a ransom: his life was the ransom price paid to God (not to the devil!), and it was substitutionary.

In addition, Christ's work was related to sacrifice. Christ is the agent in the reconciling action that flows from sacrifice.[85] In agreement with his predecessors, Murray acknowledged that the Old Testament concept of sacrifice is rightfully termed "expiatory." The sacrifices were modeled on the Mosaic ritual, and commented on in the New Testament in Hebrews 9:6–15[86] and 13:10–13.[87] Murray's thesis was that "what was constitutive in the Levitical sacrifices must also have been constitutive in the sacrifice of Christ."[88]

Of course, Christ's sacrifice was unique because he offered himself both as sacrifice and as Priest. Murray stressed two important points on the nature of Christ's sacrifice: that this type of sacrifice was not possible in the Old Testament parallels, and that it connected him to the priestly function after Melchizedek.[89]

83. Murray, *Redemption Accomplished and Applied*, 20–22.
84. Ibid., 42–43. "The word ransom and its cognates were frequently used with reference to a payment which insured the liberation of prisoners and the emancipation of slaves. It secured a deliverance from the thralldom of servitude or, although more rarely, from the penal consequences of the violation of law." Nicole, "The Nature of Redemption," 202.
85. Murray, "The Atonement," 149.
86. "When everything had been arranged like this, the priests entered regularly into the outer room to carry on their ministry. But only the high priest entered the inner room, and that only once a year, and never without blood, which he offered for himself and for the sins the people had committed in ignorance. The Holy Spirit was showing by this that the way into the Most Holy Place had not yet been disclosed as long as the first tabernacle was still standing. This is an illustration for the present time, indicating that the gifts and sacrifices being offered were not able to clear the conscience of the worshiper" (Heb. 9:6–9). "How much more will the blood of Christ, who through the eternal Spirit offered Himself without blemish to God, cleanse your conscience from dead works to serve the living God?" (Heb. 9:14 NASB).
87. "We have an altar from which those who serve the tabernacle have no right to eat. For the bodies of those animals whose blood is brought into the holy place by the high priest as an offering for sin, are burned outside the camp. Therefore Jesus also, that He might sanctify the people through His own blood, suffered outside the gate. Hence, let us go out to Him outside the camp, bearing His reproach" (Heb. 13:10–13 NASB).
88. Murray, *Redemption Accomplished and Applied*, 27.
89. Ibid., 28.

Christ's work is also related to the concept of "reconciliation." For Murray, the concepts of reconciliation and its polar opposite, of alienation, are vital for a proper conception of the atonement.[90] Yet a proper concept of reconciliation must be defined in terms of Scripture. Scripture provides a number of passages that help believers to develop a proper understanding of the nature of reconciliation. Besides Isaiah 59:2,[91] which powerfully expresses the importance of reconciliation, Murray found help in Matthew 5:23ff.[92] There, the interruption of worship is the *fact* of the alienation. The important matter is not who was mad at whom and for what reasons. The issue of justice or injustice is not mentioned. Christ emphasized that the needed reconciliation was an *act*. The man must remove the ground of estrangement.[93]

Similarly, in 1 Corinthians 7:10ff., the separated woman must remain unmarried or be "reconciled" to her husband. Subjective hostility between the two partners was not the issue. For "reconciliation" to occur, they were to take action; they must cease their separation and resume the marriage.

When Murray considered the casting away or rejection of the Jews, which "is the reconciliation of the world" (Rom. 11:15), he saw once again that the problem was not subjective hostility but reestablishing a relationship with the person who was alienated.[94] Similarly, Romans 5:8–11 carries a parallel between the believer's being justified by Christ's blood and being reconciled to God.

Murray wanted to underline the legal nature of the sinner's justification and reconciliation.[95] The teaching of Romans 5 is amplified

90. See Nicole, "The Nature of Redemption," 195–96, for an excellent definition of "reconciliation."
91. "But your iniquities have made a separation between you and your God, and your sins have hidden His face from you, so that He does not hear" (Isa. 59:2 NASB).
92. "Therefore, if you are offering your gift at the altar and there remember that your brother has something against you, leave your gift there in front of the altar. First go and be reconciled to your brother; then come and offer your gift" (Matt. 5:23–24).
93. Murray, *Redemption Accomplished and Applied*, 34.
94. Ibid., 37.
95. "The tense indicates that it is an accomplished fact, wrought once for all when Christ died." Ibid., 39. Rom. 5:9–10 is in parallel. At Rom. 5:11, reconciliation is received: "We also rejoice in God through our Lord Jesus Christ, through whom we have now received reconciliation." In Rom. 5:10, if "enemies" is to be understood in a passive sense, then "the antithesis instituted between enmity and reconciliation is exactly that between alienation and reception

in 2 Corinthians 5:18–21. The reconciliation between man and an offended God is the work of God (2 Cor. 5:18), it is a finished work (5:18–19, 21), and it is a forensic work (5:19). The work's accomplishment was seen by Murray as nothing less than the message of the gospel.[96]

The work of reconciliation focuses on human alienation from God and the divine method of restoring sinners to his favor. Murray followed his predecessors Warfield, Vos, and Machen when he outlined that reconciliation presupposes a disrupted relationship. It is this alienation from God, because of our sin, that Christ's reconciliation contemplates and removes.[97] From this alienation, reconciliation establishes a relationship of favor and peace.

In summary, removing the ground for alienation constitutes the new relationship. Reconciliation is accomplished by Christ's being made sin for us; it contemplates the relationship of God to us, and legally or forensically transmits Christ's righteousness to us. Murray's notion of reconciliation rightly underlines the beauty of Christ's great work for us.

Murray also explained Christ's work as "propitiation." One of the hotter debates during his lifetime concerned whether the word "propitiation" was suitable to describe Christ's atoning work. Murray held that it was an appropriate term,[98] and he also applauded Roger Nicole's contributions to the discussion of propitiation.[99]

Although Murray freely admitted that the word "propitiation" itself appears infrequently in the New Testament, he was nevertheless convinced that it was not only suitable but also a necessary term. Its frequent reference and particular use in the Old Testament, when combined with the New Testament connection to the Old Testament

---

into divine favor." Ibid., 40. "For if, when we were God's enemies, we were reconciled . . ." (Rom. 5:10).

96. Murray, *Redemption Accomplished and Applied*, 40.

97. Ibid., 33. See also Murray's commentary on Rom. 5:10 in *The Epistle to the Romans* (Grand Rapids: Eerdmans, 1968), 169–75.

98. For more information, see Nicole, "The Nature of Redemption," 196–98.

99. Murray used these words: "See the careful and detailed study by Roger R. Nicole: 'C. H. Dodd and the Doctrine of Propitiation.' " Murray, *Redemption*, 29 n. 1. This description was Murray's highest praise for an orthodox author. Dr. Nicole's article is found in the *Westminster Theological Journal* 17 (1955): 117–57.

Levitical rituals as a pattern for Christ's sacrifice, necessitated, thought Murray, that the concept be applied to Christ.[100]

In other words, "propitiation" was a necessary term to describe Christ's work for sinners, not an optional concept. The word means "appeasement" (of the wrath of God against sinners).[101] In sum, Murray thought that "the doctrine of propitiation is not to be denied or its sharpness in any way toned down."[102] From this foundation, Murray examined the necessity of the atonement.

The Necessity of Christ's Redeeming Work

Murray asked and answered the standard questions; for example, that if reconciliation could not be done some other way (than a horrible death on the cross), then God was not powerful. On the other hand, if it were asserted that God could procure salvation via some other avenue, but would not, then it could be concluded that God was not wise.

Murray's response to the apparent dilemma, like that of his predecessors, was clear. First, the answer to redemption cannot be found in the simple repentance of Adam (or of us). Scripture does not assert that repentance is an adequate ground for God's forgiveness. Murray reminded his readers that human laws recognized this truth as well.

Since saying "sorry" will not meet the need, Murray proposed that the atonement's necessity was "absolute."[103] His reasons were based

100. Murray, *Redemption Accomplished and Applied*, 29.
101. "The doctrine of propitiation means that Christ propitiated the wrath of God and rendered God propitious to his people." Ibid., 30. Nicole says: "This word, both in Greek and in English, connotes appeasement, averting of wrath by means of an appropriate transaction of sacrifice. The presence of this terminology bears additional witness of a very clear nature to the fact that the reconciliation envisioned in Scripture is primarily that of God to man." Nicole, "The Nature of Redemption," 197.
102. Murray, "The Atonement," 145. "The essence of the judgment of God against sin is his wrath, his holy recoil against what is the contradiction of himself (cf. Rom. 1:18)." Ibid. "If Christ vicariously bore God's judgment upon sin, and to deny this is to make nonsense of his suffering unto death and particularly of the abandonment on Calvary, then to eliminate from this judgment that which belongs to its essence is to undermine the idea of vicarious sin-bearing and its consequences." Nicole, "The Nature of Redemption," 217.
103. Murray, *Redemption Accomplished and Applied*, 11. Is Christ's work a "hypothetical" necessity? No, said Murray, for the gravity of sin is such that effective expiation is indispensable. In the history of theology, Murray's position differs from that of both Augustine and Aquinas at this place.

on exegesis of Hebrews 9:23 and Galatians 3:21, where Paul wrote that if justification could have been secured by any other method, then it certainly would have been secured. But the cross was a demonstration of the love of God. It was also, according to Murray, the vindicatory justice of God.[104]

Murray was even more precise when he asserted that the necessity of the atonement is what is termed a "consequent absolute" necessity. His reasons for this position are found primarily in John 3:14–16 and in Hebrews 1:1–3 and 2:10, 17. It was "fitting" for Christ to do these things; he must be lifted up as he provided purification for sin.[105] Furthermore, there must be a real substitute for the atonement if it is to be effective. One person must stand in for another, and the actual physical and spiritual penalty must be endured by the substitute. Christ, according to Murray, not only endured the sinner's punishment, but also brought the believer a great freedom.

Freedom in Christ

Murray's analysis came under two topics, freedom from the law and freedom from sin. Certainly, freedom in Christ relates to the law.[106]

Murray clearly articulated three ways in which Christ's atoning work has set believers free from the law. The first was that there is freedom through Christ from the curse of the law. In Galatians 3:13, we read, "Christ redeemed us from the curse of the Law, having become a curse for us" (NASB). Murray localized that curse of the law specifically in its "penal sanction."[107]

Second, there is freedom from the ceremonial law. Murray, citing Galatians 3:23–26, meant that the ceremonial law functioned as a "teacher" or was temporarily "put in charge." Jesus Christ, who was born in that historical era, fulfilled all the requirements of that economy. Necessarily, no Christian must be submitted again to that law.

104. Ibid., 15–17.
105. Ibid., 12–14.
106. Ibid., 43.
107. Ibid., 44.

There is also, in Christ, a freedom from the law of works. That is, there is freedom from the law as the condition of our justification and acceptance. Indeed, the law under which we now live is a perfect law of liberty (James 1:25). It is important to notice that Murray puts this freedom last, and not first, in his list. The reason for his structuring, I think, is that earlier he had mentioned that Christians are *not* "free from the Law." Murray would insist that when believers speak of the freedoms purchased by Christ's active and passive obedience, we must carefully delineate the nature of that freedom.[108]

Besides freedom from the law, there is also, in Christ, freedom from sin. Murray reminded his readers that the freedom from sin that was purchased by Christ is freedom in all of sin's aspects and consequences. Important for Murray in this regard are two passages, Hebrews 9:12 and Revelation 5:9.[109]

On first thought, Murray's teaching on freedom from sin does not seem apparent—for the presence of sin is found everywhere. What Murray had in mind in this regard is what he termed the "eschatological consummation."[110] In the eschaton, there will be no further consequences from sin.

From this brief analysis, we see that Murray is in basic continuity with his old Princetonian predecessors, but he also made some contributions to our understanding of the atonement.

Contribution to the Doctrine of the Atonement

On one hand, it would be correct to assert that Murray had nothing new to say on the doctrine of the atonement. Certainly, by the time of the great theologians of the sixteenth through eighteenth centuries, and the confessions, the doctrine of the atonement had been well established. On the other hand, Murray did in fact contribute to our understanding of the doctrine. He was well aware of the theological

108. Ibid., 45, 43.
109. "He did not enter by means of the blood of goats and calves; but he entered the Most Holy Place once for all by his own blood, having obtained eternal redemption" (Heb. 9:12).
110. Murray, *Redemption Accomplished and Applied*, 46.

debates surrounding the atonement during his own day,[111] as well as the earlier discussions.[112]

Murray made advances in at least three places.[113] One concerned the nature of the Levitical sacrifices and Christ's sacrifice. The second was on the atonement and Christ's mediatorial reign. The third way that Murray aided biblical scholarship was by focusing attention on the source of the atonement.

An advance in the doctrine of the atonement concerned the nature of the Levitical sacrifices. Murray's thesis was that the Old Testament sacrifices had in fact been patterned after the heavenly exemplar.[114] This assumption inseparably connected the two: Christ's sacrifice was constitutive of the Levitical offerings, and the Levitical patterns were themselves patterned after Christ.[115]

There is a complementary truth that since Christ offered himself as a sacrifice, he was then also a Priest. Thus, Christ's abiding work as Redeemer and his abiding work as Priest go hand in hand.[116]

111. Two areas of debate important to Murray, but not analyzed here, concern the relationship between the atonement and the free offer of the gospel. This topic was important to Symington as well. One side of the debate relates to what is called "common grace." In this debate, Murray, the Scot, engaged in what was primarily a Dutch-American controversy. The debate on the free offer of the gospel concerned Murray's own denomination, the Orthodox Presbyterian Church. See his "The Atonement and the Free Offer of the Gospel," in *Collected Writings*, 1:59ff., and "The Free Offer of the Gospel," in *Collected Writings*, 4:113–32.

112. Almost immediately after the Reformation, great controversies surrounding the extent of the atonement sprang up. Murray placed himself squarely within the camp of those who held to what is termed "limited atonement." He did not write extensively on limited atonement, probably because so many had written on the topic immediately before him. Within the camp holding to limited atonement, there were still heated discussions. One concerned whether Christ had died for all human beings in some sense. On that topic, see Hodge, *The Atonement*, 381–85.

113. By asserting that Murray made advances, I do not mean that the following insights were absent from his predecessors. Rather, Murray underlined, expanded, and offered correction.

114. "In this connection we must also keep in view what we have reflected on already, that the Levitical sacrifices were patterned after the heavenly exemplar, after what the epistle to the Hebrews calls 'the heavenly things'." Murray, *Redemption Accomplished and Applied*, 27.

115. "This serves to confirm the thesis that what was constitutive in the Levitical sacrifices must also have been constitutive in the sacrifice of Christ." Ibid. "We must interpret the sacrifice of Christ in terms of the Levitical patterns because they were themselves patterned after Christ's offering." Ibid.

116. "It is the recognition of Christ's priestly function that ties up the sacrifice once offered with the abiding priestly function of the Redeemer. He is a priest for ever after the order of Melchizedek." Ibid., 28.

The second contribution to the doctrine of the atonement was Murray's underlining the relationship of the atonement to Christ's mediatorial kingship. Murray knew that unbelievers, as well as believers, benefited from Christ's death. Those benefits came from the fact that Christ's mediatorial dominion is universal. By that mediatorial dominion, Murray meant that "Christ is head over all things and is given all authority in heaven and in earth." The dominion was a direct result of Christ's suffering and obedience, as explained by Paul in Philippians 2:8–9.[117]

The third advance concerned the love of God the Father as the source of the atonement. For Murray, the love of God was the cause or source of the atonement.[118] The source of the atonement is the good pleasure of God. It is not what has been termed the "arbitrary will" of God. The combined source of the atonement was the love and justice of God.

It is evident that Murray's article in the *Collected Writings* represents an advance over his earlier thought on the nature of the atonement as found in *Redemption Accomplished and Applied*. Murray carefully prepared the work on the atonement for inclusion in his collected writings, which was written just before his death. In that chapter, he presented his most mature thought on the love of the Father as it relates to the atonement.

With the insights gleaned from noting the Father's love as a source or *the* source of the atonement, Murray was convinced that many objections to the doctrine could be eliminated, and a practical problem of faith and devotion could be addressed.

If the love of the Father were the source of the atonement, as Murray presented, then a false notion of God could be eliminated. The false notion was one of the Son as the sole embodiment of mercy and love—while the Father was the unrelenting, wrathful one.[119] "The Father's action in the reconciliation," said Murray, "prevents any construction of the atonement in which Christ is set forth as the

117. Ibid., 61ff.
118. Ibid., 10ff.
119. Murray, "The Atonement," 145. Murray's stress on the love of the Father suggests Symington as a possible predecessor.

representative of love, mercy and compassion, and the Father, by way of contrast, as the representative of holiness, justice, and truth."[120]

Murray was adamant that "much confusion, misunderstanding, and misrepresentation have arisen" from a failure to note the love of God the Father as the source of the atonement. He was particular in his dissatisfaction, pointing to "even Reformed believers."[121] This is why Murray was convinced that although the atonement properly addresses the work of Christ, it should be seen as originating in the Father's love.

In characteristic fashion, Murray did not identify any of the objects of his criticism. In the Reformed community, such a view could obviously not be found in Symington. Later, Hodge saw God's love as the motive for redemption. Regarding that love, Hodge said that "the same identical essence and attributes are common to the Father and the Son. The justice demanding satisfaction, and the love prompting to the self-assumption of the penalty, are co-existent states of divine feeling and purpose."[122] In general, Hodge was not guilty of this incorrect view. But Murray stated that "the source of the atonement is the love of God the Father specifically," not the combined love of the Father and Son. Under that microscope, Hodge could be found guilty—in that the Father demands satisfaction, and "love" prompted the Son to assume the penalty.

A more clearly guilty unnamed person, however, was J. Gresham Machen. "The satisfaction of the eternal justice of God," said Machen, "was the primary end for which Christ died."[123] That was the essence of the whole substitutionary view of the atonement, for Machen.

Therefore, while stressing the love of God the Father as the source of the atonement may seem like a relatively minor point (and we do

120. Ibid., 149–50.
121. Ibid., 144. Murray's criticisms were uncharacteristically very sharp. "This should not have been the case. The accent of Scripture is apparent and pervasive. The simple fact is too patent to be overlooked. But the analysis of both fact and implications has too frequently been neglected, and the faith of believers has thereby suffered, and attacks upon integral elements of the faith have frequently been advanced." Ibid. Later, he said, "There are several ways in which even Reformed believers have failed to do honor to the love and grace of God the Father, and this aspect of the Father's love is basic to the correction of this default of faith and devotion." Ibid., 144.
122. Hodge, *The Atonement*, 29.
123. Machen, *God Transcendent*, 198.

not expect major changes!), it brought a needed light to the doctrine. Murray's careful words put his thesis clearly: "The propitiation which God made his own Son is the provision of the Father's love, to the end that holiness may be vindicated and its demands satisfied."[124] A more balanced analysis of that relationship cannot be found.

In conclusion, in the old Princetonian tradition a large volume of material was printed on the nature and necessity of the atonement. May it please God that his bride come into a fuller and deeper understanding of the great work of Christ's redemption, both accomplished and applied.

124. Murray, "The Atonement," 146.

10

The Use and Abuse of
Christian Liberty

D. G. HART

At the opening of his third lecture on Calvinism, delivered in 1898 at Princeton Theological Seminary to Presbyterians engaged in debates about revising the Westminster Confession of Faith, Abraham Kuyper asserted with characteristic confidence the relationship between the Reformed faith and liberty that was typical of a time when Protestantism appeared to be responsible for all the blessings of modernity. The Dutch theologian who performed a remarkable degree of sphere sovereignty in politics, church life, economics, and higher education believed that "every competent historian" understood that "Calvinism has led public law into new paths, first in Western Europe, then in two Continents, and today more and more among all civilized nations." One of those historians was the American George Bancroft, whom Kuyper quoted glowingly on Calvinism's wonder-working political genius: "The fanatic for Calvinism was a fanatic for liberty, for in the moral warfare for freedom, his creed was a part of his army, and his most faithful ally in the battle."[1] By the end of his lecture, after developing the specific reasons for Calvinism's support for liberty and qualifying the nature of such freedom, Kuyper was no less confident

---

1. Abraham Kuyper, *Lectures on Calvinism* (1898; repr., Grand Rapids: Eerdmans, 1931), 78.

of the link between Reformed theology and liberty of conscience. He did concede that Reformed magistrates had in practice "made a desperate effort to hinder the spread of literature which they disliked, by censure and refusal of publication." But these breaches in executing statecraft could not alter the necessary affinity between Calvinism and liberty. The Netherlands was a case in point, a nation where "the free expression of thought, by the spoken and printed word . . . first achieved its victory." In fact, "the logical development of what was enshrined in the liberty of conscience, as well as that liberty itself, first blessed the world from the side of Calvinism."[2]

Kuyper's Whiggish view of Calvinism's liberal politics looked less plausible only seventy-five years later after the liberties enjoyed by Western democracies turned into the license that characterized the 1960s and that decade's social and cultural legacy. The recent case of the Emory University historian Elizabeth Fox-Genovese is instructive here. A conservative feminist, and a recent convert to Rome, Fox-Genovese in explaining her decision to join the Roman Catholic Church acknowledged that she had grown up in a mainline Protestant family where Christian morality (e.g., the Decalogue) was taken "with utmost seriousness." Still, as a child, and later as an adult, she was nothing more than a nonbelieving Christian—that is, Christian in ethos but still not believing in Christ. Fox-Genovese's outlook began to change when she tried to challenge the pro-choice orthodoxy of modern feminism. She writes, "The defense of abortion especially troubled me because of my inability to agree that any one of us should decide who has the right to live. . . . It seemed difficult to imagine a world in which each followed his or her personal moral compass, if only because the morality of some was bound, sooner or later, to clash with the morality of others. And without some semblance of a common standard, those clashes were more than likely to end in one or another form of violence."[3] In contrast to an idea of Protestantism that exalted its understanding of human freedom, Fox-Genovese recognized in Rome a source of moral authority that challenged the skepticism and relativism that inevitably seemed to

---

2. Ibid., 108–9.
3. Elizabeth Fox-Genovese, "A Conversion Story," *First Things* 102 (April 2000): 41.

afflict Protestant societies. Unlike Kuyper's day, then, when Roman Catholicism appeared to be the enemy of liberty, today Rome seems for many thoughtful people the best hope for ordering liberty and preserving it from its excesses.

Because the relationship between human freedom and Protestant Christianity is much more complicated at the beginning of the twenty-first century than it was when Kuyper gave his famous lectures, some attention to the Westminster Confession's teaching on Christian liberty may be instructive. Is it the case that Protestantism, and especially its Calvinist wing, advocated liberty of conscience in ways that set into motion liberal political theory and the exaltation of individual human rights? Or was Protestantism closer in outlook to Roman Catholicism on the question of human freedom, with the later antagonism that pitted Protestant liberty against Roman Catholic authoritarianism a distortion of Protestantism's original genius? Since the Westminster Confession is the rare Reformed creed in the sixteenth and seventeenth centuries that includes an entire chapter on Christian liberty, its discussion of liberty of conscience along with related teachings on the authority of the church and the magistrate offers valuable assistance in wrestling with these questions. But before looking specifically at the teaching of the Westminster Assembly, a brief survey of various American Protestant accounts of liberty may be useful for appreciating the subtlety of the Westminster divines' original formulation of Christian liberty.

The Abuse

American Protestants, especially those of the Reformed persuasion, have been convinced that their faith and political liberty went hand in hand since the heady debates over independence from Great Britain when Presbyterians and Congregationalists overwhelmingly supported the American Revolution. John Witherspoon's sermon "The Dominion of Providence over the Passions of Men"[4] was a notable and famous expression of this synthesis of faith and politics.

---

4. Witherspoon's sermon is reprinted in Ellis Sandoz, ed., *Political Sermons of the American Founding Era, 1730–1805*, 2 vols. (Indianapolis: Liberty Fund, 1998), 1:549.

Based on Psalm 76:10 ("Surely the wrath of man shall praise thee: the remainder of wrath shalt thou restrain," KJV), and delivered on Friday, May 17, 1776, a day designated by the Continental Congress as one set aside for prayer, the sermon proved to be useful for the purposes of American independence and was published the next month in the city where the Continental Congress met. Its popularity also accounts for Witherspoon's election in late June of 1776 to serve in Congress as a representative from New Jersey, a post that placed him in good stead to sign the Declaration of Independence. The logic of Witherspoon's devotional discourse was equally powerful in giving voice to a conception of liberty that would prove to be enduring among American Calvinists.

In the second part of the sermon, in which he applied the meaning of the text to the political situation in the Colonies, Witherspoon attempted to inspire his listeners to patriotic greatness by exhorting them to trust in God and hope "for his assistance in the present important conflict."[5] The patriots could, he believed, have confidence in divine assistance if their cause was just, their principles pure, and their conduct prudent. Although he ended the sermon with exhortations to greater moral integrity, a signal that Witherspoon was worried about spiritual degeneracy among his contemporaries, he had little doubt about the justice of their grievance with England. "The cause in which America is now in arms," he declared, "is the cause of justice, of liberty, and of human nature." Witherspoon explained that the colonists had not been motivated by "pride, resentment, or sedition." Instead, the desire for independence from England arose from "a deep and general conviction" that religious and civil liberty, as well as "the temporal and eternal happiness of us and our society," depended on political autonomy. Here Witherspoon had a precise conception of the relationship between civil and religious liberty. "The knowledge of God and his truths," he elaborated, "have from the beginning of the world been chiefly, if not entirely, confined to those parts of the earth, where some degree of liberty and political justice were to be seen."[6] In effect, Witherspoon was articulating the fundamental Protestant

5. Ibid.
6. Ibid.

logic that assumed that true religion, namely, Protestant Christianity, flourished only if civil magistrates protected civil liberties. The flip side of this assumption was the similar belief that Protestantism was the best soil from which civil liberty naturally grew. Witherspoon made this relationship crystal clear when he asserted, "There is not a single instance in history in which civil liberty was lost, and religious liberty preserved entire." For this reason, if the colonists were to "yield up [their] temporal property" to Parliament through unfair taxes, they would also be delivering their consciences "into bondage."[7]

With such a central place in the intellectual origins of the American founding, the mutual blessings of Protestantism and liberty would become a recurring theme in American Protestants' arguments about the identity and purpose of their nation. One notable example of Protestantism's political potency was Lyman Beecher's *A Plea for the West*, published in 1835.[8] The father of a remarkable set of children, including Harriet Beecher Stowe and Henry Ward Beecher, the Boston Congregationalist in the mid-1830s moved to Cincinnati to preside over Lane Seminary, a joint endeavor of Congregationalists and Presbyterians. Uprooted from the stability of New England's Puritan culture, Beecher was worried about the future of the United States. Specifically, he was alarmed by the number of European immigrants who were surging into the American heartland and who had no familiarity with the nation's political institutions and ideals. But the Roman Catholic immigrants were perceived to be a special threat to America's future.

Beecher specifically addressed the political meaning of Christianity about midway through his book in response to his imaginary interlocutor's questions about one faith being "just as good as another." His answer was to defend Calvinism, a religious system that he admitted was often denounced as "severe, unsocial, self-righteous, uncharitable, exclusive, persecuting . . . dealing damnation round the land."[9] The grounds for Beecher's defense were all anecdotal even if it was obvious to him that the Calvinistic system "has always been on the side of liberty in its struggles against arbitrary power." Here

7. Ibid.
8. Lyman Beecher, *A Plea for the West* (Cincinnati: Truman and Smith, 1835).
9. Ibid., 79.

Beecher looked for support to the twin legacy of British legal and Protestant culture:

> Through the puritans, it breathed into the British constitution its most invaluable principles, and laid the foundations of the republican institutions of our nation, and felled the forests, and fought the colonial battles with Canadian Indians and French Catholics, when often our destiny balanced on a pivot and hung upon a hair.[10]

In fact, Beecher added, political liberty "wept, and prayed, and fasted, and fought, and suffered through the revolutionary struggle, when there was almost no other creed but the Calvinistic in the land."[11] Nonetheless, he had confidence that if Roman Catholic immigrants to America would simply breathe in the fresh air of liberty without having it filtered by the papacy's tight regulations, they would choose freedom. Beecher wrote:

> If they associated with republicans, the power of caste would wear away. If they mingled in our schools, the republican atmosphere would impregnate their minds. If they scattered, unassociated, the attrition of circumstances would wear off their predilections and aversions. If they could read the Bible, and might and did, their darkened intellect would brighten, and their bowed down mind would rise. If they dared to think for themselves, the contrast of protestant independence with their thralldom, would awaken the desire of equal privileges, and put an end to an arbitrary clerical dominion over trembling superstitious minds.[12]

At the close of the nineteenth century, another prominent Protestant with Congregationalist ties sang the common refrain of praise for political liberty's Protestant roots. In his best-selling book *Our Country: Its Possible Future and Its Present Crisis,* Josiah Strong asserted the dependence of American liberty on the right kind of faith. In his chapter on "Romanism," Strong outlined the basic antagonism between "the fundamental principles of our government" and "those

10. Ibid., 80.
11. Ibid.
12. Ibid., 118.

of the Catholic church."[13] He listed quotations from the pope as well as other church officials and publications indicating Rome's opposition to freedom of conscience, free schools ("one of the corner-stones of our Government"), and the subjection to the laws of the United States as opposed to loyalty to the pope himself.[14] On the other hand, Strong continued to assert that civil liberty followed wherever Protestantism flourished. The two greatest characteristics of Anglo-Saxons were civil liberty and spiritual Christianity, thus explaining why the English, the British colonists, and the people of the United States were both the most free and the most devout. "It is not necessary to argue," Strong wrote, "to those for whom I write that the two great needs of mankind, that all men may be lifted up into the light of the highest Christian civilization, are, first, a pure, spiritual Christianity, and, second, civil liberty."[15] Such confidence made complete sense to Strong's Anglo-American Protestant readers used to a century of such apologies for the United States' system of government.

It also made sense to American Presbyterians. Although Beecher and Strong were Congregationalists, Presbyterian authors were no less reluctant to invoke the tie between liberal democracy and Protestant faith. In his short little book *Presbyterianism: Its Affinities*, the New School Presbyterian Albert Barnes observed that one of Calvinism's chief ideals was a representative system of government. Presbyterianism, in effect, represented a middle course, "distinguished, on the one hand, from the monarchical principle, and on the other from strict and radical democracy."[16] In fact, "all just notions of liberty in modern times" were connected with the fundamental principles taught by Presbyterian understandings of government.[17] Barnes's nemesis in the Old School–New School controversy, Charles Hodge, was also vulnerable to the logic that premised Protestant conviction and concluded with modern liberty. At the end of a lecture on the nature of Presbyterianism in 1855 at the Presbyterian Historical Society,

13. Josiah Strong, *Our Country: Its Possible Future and Its Present Crisis* (New York: Baker & Taylor, 1885), 47.
14. Ibid., 49.
15. Ibid., 161.
16. Albert Barnes, *Presbyterianism: Its Affinities* (New York: J. M. Sherwood, 1863), 10.
17. Ibid., 11.

Hodge perceived significant ties between Calvinism and republican forms of government. "It is the combination of the principles of liberty and order in the Presbyterian system," he declared, "the union of the rights of the people with subjection to legitimate authority, that has made it the parent and guardian of civil liberty in every part of the world."[18] Hodge conceded that this was simply "an incidental advantage" of Presbyterianism. But even for a theologian less inclined to derive social programs from theological reflection, Hodge was caught up in Calvinistic apologies for the American polity. In this regard he was not far from the sort of reasoning that informed William Henry Roberts's argument in 1895 in *The Presbyterian System*, in which he concluded, "True Calvinism has been and is the most potent source of good to both the individual and the State, in the one of right conduct, and in the other of social order." In fact, the northern Presbyterian Church's stated clerk averred, Calvinism's "choicest products are the God-fearing believer and the law-abiding citizen."[19]

Commentators, older and more recent, have suggested a number of reasons for the affinities that Calvinists have felt between their own religion and political liberalism. To the English author Robert H. Murray, whose *Political Consequences of the Reformation* is a valuable but neglected guide to the Reformers' politics, John Calvin's understanding of divine will was a basic check on political tyranny. "No one can read the last paragraph of the *Institutes*," Murray wrote, "without seeing that all the time the conscience of the subject is held, as it were, in reserve over the authority of the King."[20] A similar point came from Mark Pattison, whom Murray quotes to the following effect: "To raise the enfeebled will, to stir the individual conscience, to incite the soul not only to reclaim its rights, but to feel its obligations; to substitute free obedience for passive submission—this was the lofty aim of the simple, not to say barbarous, legislation of Calvin."[21]

18. Charles Hodge, *What Is Presbyterianism? An Address Delivered before the Presbyterian Historical Society* . . . (Philadelphia: Presbyterian Board of Publication, 1855), 79.

19. William Henry Roberts, *The Presbyterian System: Its Characteristics* (Philadelphia: Presbyterian Board of Publication and Sabbath School Work, 1895), 28.

20. Robert H. Murray, *The Political Consequences of the Reformation: Studies in Sixteenth-Century Political Thought* (London: E. Benn, 1926), 109.

21. Ibid., 126.

In his recent book *America's God,* American church historian
Mark A. Noll assigns a similar weight to the relationship between
theology and political theory, though he is less convinced than Murray
that doctrine determined politics. For this reason, Noll's account of
American Calvinists' embrace of republicanism, a theory of government advocated before 1750 only by the heterodox, features as much
what political philosophy did to Reformed theology as the religious
affinities between Calvinism and political liberty. In the case of Presbyterians and Congregationalists, allegiance to the politics of American
independence from Great Britain compromised important aspects of
Reformed orthodoxy. Even so, the effort to harmonize religion and
politics during the revolutionary era turned what had once been an
intellectual novelty into an American habit. "Americans have long
been accustomed to think of the values of religion and the values of
republicanism as supporting each other," Noll writes, but "the long
American habit of uniting these value systems has dulled awareness
of how strikingly original the new nation's 'Christian republicanism'
actually was."[22]

One last valuable account of Calvinism's endorsement of political
liberty comes from David Gress in his 1998 study of the idea of the
West, *From Plato to NATO.* The specific dynamics of theology and
politics are of less concern to Gress than the factors that shaped the
grand narrative of Western civilization. The role of Protestantism and
the Reformation in the construction of "the West" was less influential
than the use to which Enlightenment thinkers put the Protestant
break with Rome. According to Gress, progressives and radicals had
no way of accounting for "the secular, rational freedom of modernity"
in Europe's Christian past. "That Christian freedom could be in any
way responsible for the modern understanding of political and social
liberty," he argues, "was abhorrent to those Enlightenment radicals
for whom freedom was to be asserted against Christianity, against the
censorship, ignorance, superstition, and irrationalism of a hierarchical
church and its theological apparatus of justification."[23] Consequently,

22. Mark A. Noll, *America's God: From Jonathan Edwards to Abraham Lincoln* (New York:
Oxford University Press, 2002), 54.
23. David Gress, *From Plato to NATO: The Idea of the West and Its Opponents* (New York:
Free Press, 1998), 261.

the Reformation became useful to Enlightenment thinkers as a break with Christendom and the harbinger of a new era of liberty. Although Gress does not say so, the implication of this shift was equally decisive for Protestant leaders such as those studied by Noll. If Reformed theology were to have a meaningful role in modern society, it would need to show itself serviceable to the modern project of political liberty. These may be good explanations for Presbyterian and Reformed sympathies with the political ideals of liberal democracy, but they hardly address the actual teaching of historic Protestantism on the nature of Christian liberty. To understand the theological idea of freedom and its political consequences is crucial for recognizing the nature of American Calvinists' abuse of Christian liberty.

The Usefulness of Christian Liberty

If a confessional basis for the American identification of religion and political liberty existed, the Westminster Confession of Faith would be one good place to look. Of the Protestant creeds and confessions to be written between Ulrich Zwingli's Sixty-seven Articles (1523) and the Westminster Assembly, the latter's confession is the only one to devote an entire chapter to Christian liberty.[24] Other statements, of course, rely on this doctrine. But the Westminster Confession stands out for developing Christian liberty in an even more elaborate manner than the Trinity. Chapter 20 of the confession unfolds straightforwardly, with one section on Christian liberty per se, and three subsequent sections that qualify the original statement with brief discussions of the doctrine's implications.

Chapter 20 opens with the following three sentences, the entirety of section 1:

> The liberty which Christ hath purchased for believers under the gospel consists in their freedom from the guilt of sin, the condemning wrath of God, the curse of the moral law; and, in their being delivered from this present evil world, bondage to Satan, and dominion

24. See, for instance, Arthur C. Cochrane, ed., *Reformed Creeds of the Sixteenth Century* (1966; repr., Louisville: Westminster/John Knox, 2003).

of sin; from the evil of afflictions, the sting of death, the victory of the grave, and everlasting damnation; as also, in their free access to God, and their yielding obedience unto him, not out of slavish fear, but a childlike love and willing mind. All which were common also to believers under the law. But, under the new testament, the liberty of Christians is further enlarged, in their freedom from the yoke of the ceremonial law, to which the Jewish church was subjected; and in greater boldness of access to the throne of grace, and in fuller communications of the free Spirit of God, than believers under the law did ordinarily partake of.

Two aspects immediately stand out in this relatively brief definitional paragraph. The first is that the chief part of Christian liberty is the enjoyment of those benefits purchased by Christ and enumerated in the Shorter Catechism (32–38) as justification, adoption, sanctification, and the several benefits that accompany these, as well as the ones to follow believers in death and resurrection. Of course, the divines in chapter 20 do not use the same language or terms as on display in the Shorter Catechism. But the ideas are virtually the same, from "freedom from the guilt of sin" and so on (justification), "free access to God" (adoption), "delivered from this present evil world" and the like (sanctification), to being delivered from "the sting of death" (souls immediately passing into glory) and "the victory of the grave" (resurrection). In effect, Christian liberty is synonymous with salvation in Christ, not a subsidiary blessing, because freedom from the law, sin, and death is at the heart of what Christ accomplished in his obedience, death, and resurrection.

The second aspect that stands out in chapter 20 is the relation between Christian liberty and the law. This chapter follows directly after the divines' teaching on the law, and since freedom and law generally dovetail in understanding the privileges and duties of citizenship, so chapters 19 and 20 are the proverbial two sides of the same coin. Here in chapter 20 the divines work out further implications of the difference, described in 19.3 and 19.4 between Israel and the church. Just as the law meant different things to the Israelites and Christians, so Christian freedom takes a different shape in the lives of Old and New Testament saints. The divines affirm, on the one hand, that both the Israelites and Christians enjoy the same benefits that pertain to their similar spiritual status. But in the unfolding of the history of redemption and the complications that confront believers, whether before the first or second advent of Christ, the form of Christian liberty will inevitably evolve depending on the degree to which Christ's work is complete. In fact, the liberty that Christians enjoy has direct bearing on their worship and forms of devotion. Less obvious, then, are its implications for political or judicial arrangements in the era of the church.

In the second section of chapter 20, the divines begin the process of qualifying their initial statement. It reads:

> God alone is Lord of the conscience, and hath left it free from the doctrines and commandments of men, which are, in anything, contrary to his Word; or beside it, if matters of faith, or worship. So that, to believe such doctrines, or to obey such commands, out of conscience, is to betray true liberty of conscience: and the requiring of an implicit faith, and an absolute and blind obedience, is to destroy liberty of conscience, and reason also.

On one level this statement is another definitional one with a brief delineation of liberty of conscience. But 20.2 also begins to put barriers around what might look like a recipe for license in 20.1. The first hedge on Christian liberty, then, is the Word of God. Those who enjoy the benefits of Christ's redemption do not have the liberty to disobey God's Word. In this respect, Christian liberty is a variation on what political philosophers call "positive liberty," that is, freedom to do the good, rather than "negative liberty," which is freedom from restraint. Just as the divines affirm in 19.6 that the law is of "great use" to believers, so in 20.1 they define Christian liberty in part as "yielding obedience" to God, not out of fear but out of love.

In this context, liberty of conscience can be construed as a significant implication of the doctrine of *sola scriptura*, which the divines affirm both here and in 1.6 and 1.10. In the same way that the divines affirm the sole authority of Scripture (1.6) in contrast to the traditions of men and new revelations of the Spirit, so in 20.2 they reiterate the point; Christians have freedom, and this liberty involves following

God's law, especially if being compelled to disobey on the basis of either human authority or good intentions. This affirmation of *sola scriptura* and its corollary teaching, liberty of conscience, explains why 20.2 echoes 21.1 on the regulative principle of worship, which teaches that in worship whatever is done (i.e., the elements) must have warrant from the Bible. Otherwise, it is forbidden. In 20.2 the divines do not have merely worship in view, but corporate worship is clearly a chief part of the religious duties they are considering—obedience to God's Word, faith (or devotion), and worship. In other words, Christian liberty does not free the believer from religious responsibilities, only from ones that do not derive their substance from Scripture.

The duties of believers are further underscored in the third section of chapter 20:

> They who, upon pretense of Christian liberty, do practice any sin, or cherish any lust, do thereby destroy the end of Christian liberty, which is, that being delivered out of the hands of our enemies, we might serve the Lord without fear, in holiness and righteousness before him, all the days of our life.

This section yields another qualification of Christian liberty, and is a good brief statement against any antinomian reading of the gospel. Although, as 20.1 puts it, Christians are free from the "guilt of sin," the "wrath of God," and the "curse" of the law, this liberty is not license. So the law, as 19.6 teaches, is still the norm for believers. In fact, the aim of Christian liberty, as 20.3 explicitly says, is to serve the Lord in "holiness and righteousness." This is not merely an assertion, as already indicated, of positive liberty—namely, freedom to do the good. It is also a condensed explanation of the relationship between justification and sanctification that the Reformation recovered. Since believers have been made right with God, that is, "delivered out of the hands of our enemies," they can now endeavor to lead holy lives "without fear." This is another way of affirming that Christian liberty reorients the believer's relationship to the law, which is the norm for holiness. Having been freed from its curse through Christ, the believer is now free to serve God, free from the sense of guilt or fear of punishment. To revise Martin Luther's commendation to believers to "sin boldly" because of the liberty they enjoyed in Christ, the logic of the divines here in 20.3 is to "be holy boldly" because of the freedom Christians enjoy from all penalties and claims of the law, thanks to Christ's life of holiness.

After qualifying the nature of Christian liberty with regard to worship and the Christian walk, the divines finally consider in section 4 the subject of politics, but they do so in the larger context of legitimate authority (that is, the powers that God has ordained to govern human life between the fall and the consummation):

> And because the powers which God hath ordained, and the liberty which Christ hath purchased, are not intended by God to destroy, but mutually to uphold and preserve one another, they who, upon pretense of Christian liberty, shall oppose any lawful power, or the lawful exercise of it, whether it be civil or ecclesiastical, resist the ordinance of God. And, for their publishing of such opinions, or maintaining of such practices, as are contrary to the light of nature, or to the known principles of Christianity (whether concerning faith, worship, or conversation), or to the power of godliness; or, such erroneous opinions or practices, as either in their own nature, or in the manner of publishing or maintaining them, are destructive to the external peace and order which Christ hath established in the church, they may lawfully be called to account, and proceeded against, by the censures of the church.

Two aspects of this statement deserve comment, especially with regard to the assumed links between Protestantism and the rise of political liberty in the modern West.

First, advocates of political liberty will be hard-pressed to find justification for their convictions in the Westminster Confession. In fact, 20.4 is explicit in rejecting any construction of freedom from the yoke of the law through faith in Christ as the basis for limiting the power of the magistrate. This part of the chapter is clearly upholding the teaching of Romans 13, which recognizes the legitimacy of governors such as those in first-century Rome as authorities ordained of God. Thus, Christian liberty may not be used to resist the magistrate's authority that comes from God. Although the divines do not explicitly say so, the impression they give is that if Christian liberty takes shape in a way that is at odds with the rule of the magistrate, the believer's duty is to suffer the consequences either of submitting to the state or, if the Christian's conscience may be violated by such a submission, of suffering the penalty for refusing to obey the magistrate. But rebellion is not an option because the rule of government is an "ordinance of God" and so a form of disobeying God himself.

Second, 20.4 is striking in its affirmation of the power of the church. Typically, the institutional authority of the church was not even a factor in those arguments that attempted to derive political liberty from Protestantism. For most advocates of the link between the Reformation and democratic liberalism, the authority of the church was a given, in the sense that it was so marginal that it did not need to be explicitly opposed. The modern Protestant idea that political liberty sprang from right religion generally held that Roman Catholics believed in church power, but Protestants did not, or at least the authority of Protestant churches was essentially negligible.

But the divines would hardly permit such an interpretation of Christian liberty, or of church authority. Like the state, the church's power is as an ordinance of God, something also affirmed explicitly in 31.2, in which the Westminster Confession teaches that the rulings of councils and synods "are to be received with reverence and submission," not merely as in accordance with God's Word but also as "being an ordinance of God appointed thereunto in his word." Even when American Presbyterians would revise chapter 23 on the magistrate and affirm the autonomy of the church, setting it free from the Erastian pattern that had prevailed in the relationship between England's Parliament and the Westminster Assembly, the intention was not to champion political liberty. Instead, the goal was to assert the independence of the church from state oversight, to eliminate a sphere of human life from state control and regulation—something that had bedeviled Scottish and Northern Irish Presbyterians from the very beginnings in 1560 of Presbyterianism in the English-speaking world, and that would continue to influence communions such as the Covenanters, the Associate Reformed, and the Free Church Presbyterians to leave the Presbyterian establishment in the United Kingdom. Consequently, Christian liberty as formulated in the Westminster Confession could not be construed to justify political liberalism, the freedom of the Christian from church power, or even the right of private judgment.

What emerges from a closer reading of chapter 20 is a conception of personal liberty and legitimate authority that is at odds almost as much with the Whig cultural ideal that dominated nineteenth-century American culture as with Roman Catholicism. This ideal was the strange mix of religion, politics, and historical outlook that undergirded anti-Catholicism throughout American society. It pitted the tyranny of Rome against the liberty of Protestantism, the superstition of Catholic teaching and practice against the reasonableness that Protestantism nurtured, the bigotry of Rome's hostility to modern society against Protestantism's openness to novelty in cultural and political endeavors. In sum, the Whig cultural ideal was responsible for statements about America's Christian character by the likes of Beecher, Strong, and the Presbyterians who followed their lead. These Calvinists (both vestigial and vigorous) considered the advance of liberty, markets, and human knowledge to be the outgrowth of Protestant faith. But in fact the Whig cultural ideal had no mooring in the theology of the Westminster Standards. Indeed, the place where that ideal might receive its most explicit support was actually hostile to any such construction of the Reformed faith. How Protestants in that tradition came to embrace Whiggism is a large and complicated subject.[25] But on paper, the convictions of those nineteenth-century American Protestants were very distant from the teachings of the Westminster Confession of Faith.

The Paradox of Christian Liberty

Of the several implications to emerge from a closer reading of Christian liberty in the Westminster Confession, the most obvious for the purposes of this essay bears on politics. A difference of some substance to emerge within Reformed circles during the last quarter of the twentieth century, thanks to the influence both of Kuyperianism (that is, the importance and necessity of a Reformed world- and

25. See Noll, *America's God.*

life-view) and of theonomy (the attempt to make biblical teaching generally and the Old Testament specifically normative for the modern state), is the nature of the lordship of Christ within the sphere of politics. American Calvinists have come to believe that the Reformed approach to politics is different from the Lutheran one because of a vigorous reassertion of divine sovereignty in all walks of life, an additional insistence on the relevance of the Bible to all human affairs, thanks to the sufficiency of Scripture, and a demand that genuine Christian faith not be confined to religious life but spread to influence so-called secular endeavors also. Unlike the Lutheran outlook, which has relied on the doctrine of the two kingdoms to recognize and delineate the separate spheres in which the state and the church operate, Reformed believers have argued that Calvinism sees the relationship between politics and religion differently, and that the state is bound to adhere to the norms of special revelation in ways comparable to those of the church. In other words, to suggest that the state has a different standard for its policies other than God's revealed will, as the Lutheran position implies, is to cede to politics a secular realm while reserving the religious sphere for the church.

The Westminster Confession's teaching on Christian liberty is a reminder that Calvinists may in fact share more of the two-kingdom outlook than contemporary Reformed Christians are willing to admit (though, it should be added, this similarity stems less from Calvinists' mimicking Lutherans and more from each tradition's Augustinian roots). The relationship between church and state, or the norms for these ordained authorities, does not explicitly emerge in chapter 20 of the confession. But by insisting that Christian liberty is distinct from political considerations, the Westminster divines did support the fundamental Augustinian insight that the aims of the church are distinct from those of the state, and that the church's means of liberating men and women from the tyranny of sin and the devil have nothing directly to do with the means that the state uses to execute justice and ensure the well-being of its citizens. In this way, the Westminster Confession echoes Calvin, who warned about the danger of confusing the spiritual realities undergirding the church with the temporal affairs of the state. In book 4 of the *Institutes*, he wrote that "whoever knows how to distinguish between body and soul, between this present fleeting life and that future eternal life, will without difficulty know that Christ's spiritual kingdom and the civil jurisdiction are things completely distinct. Since, then, it is a Jewish vanity to seek and enclose Christ's Kingdom within the elements of this world, let us rather ponder that which Scripture clearly teaches is a spiritual fruit, which we gather from Christ's grace."[26] Calvin added that government is not inherently polluted, as if distinguishing between the spiritual and the temporal makes this world evil.[27] The rule of magistrates is a help for the Christian pilgrimage and ought not to be disregarded by believers. But the sphere of politics is distinct from Christ's kingdom, and the spiritual government of the church, not the civil laws of the state, is the one that prepares believers for "an immortal and incorruptible blessedness."[28]

Although Calvin lived in an era prior to the writing of the Westminster Standards, one American Presbyterian who clearly saw the two-kingdom character of Reformed theology was J. Gresham Machen, the principal founder of Westminster Seminary and the Orthodox Presbyterian Church. Under the influence of the Westminster Confession's teaching and in defense of Calvinism, Machen wrote with great effect about the danger of mixing the standards of religion and politics:

> You cannot expect from a true Christian church any official pronouncements upon the political or social questions of the day, and you cannot expect cooperation with the state in anything involving the use of force. Important are the functions of the police, and members of the church, either individually or in such special associations as they may choose to form, should aid the police in every lawful way in the exercise of those functions. But the function of the church in its corporate capacity is of an entirely different kind. Its weapons against evil are spiritual, not carnal; and by becoming a political

26. John Calvin, *Institutes of the Christian Religion*, ed. John T. McNeill, trans. Ford Lewis Battles, Library of Christian Classics (Philadelphia: Westminster, 1960), 4.20.1.

27. On the Kuyperian opposition to dualism, see Albert M. Wolters, *Creation Regained: Biblical Basics for a Reformational Worldview* (Grand Rapids: Eerdmans, 1985); Cornelius Plantinga Jr., "The Concern of the Church in the Socio-Political World: A Calvinist and Reformed Perspective," *Calvin Theological Journal* 18 (1983): 190–205; and Henry R. Van Til, *The Calvinistic Concept of Culture* (Philadelphia: Presbyterian and Reformed, 1959).

28. Calvin, *Institutes*, 4.20.2.

lobby, through the advocacy of political measures whether good or bad, the church is turning aside from its proper mission.[29]

The point here is not about politics per se. Instead, the issue that Machen and Calvin along with the Westminster divines, who all experienced very different forms of state power, were driving at was that Christian liberty is far removed from political considerations. The blessings of freedom in Christ, in other words, are far more sublime and make the liberties of modern statecraft seem trivial by comparison. To confuse these liberties is, to use another translation of Calvin, "folly."

The other implication of the Westminster Confession's teaching on Christian liberty is one that concerns more generally the paradoxical nature of the gospel. In the classic treatment of the relationship between Christ and culture, H. Richard Niebuhr categorized Calvinism as transformational. By this he meant that Calvin's views of vocation, church and state, humanism, and the resurrection lead "to the thought that what the gospel promises and makes possible, as divine (not human) possibility, is the transformation of mankind in all its nature and culture into a kingdom of God."[30] In conceiving of Calvinism this way, Niebuhr set it apart from Lutheranism, which makes "sharp distinctions between the temporal and spiritual life, or between what is external and internal, between body and soul, between the reign of Christ and the world of human works and culture," and which insisted that these distinctions not be confused.[31]

Again, Niebuhr's reading of Calvinism, in contrast to Lutheranism, has gained considerable influence, thanks to Kuyperianism and theonomy. But the Westminster Confession is a reminder of why this particular Dutch reading of the Reformed faith was originally called neo-Calvinism, as in a novel or new rendering of the historic Calvinist position. In its original outlook, as the Westminster Confession shows, the realities and truths of the gospel were one thing, and they were

29. J. Gresham Machen, "The Responsibility of Our Church in the New Age," in D. G. Hart, ed., *J. Gresham Machen: Selected Shorter Writings* (Phillipsburg, NJ: P&R Publishing, 2004), 376.

30. H. Richard Niebuhr, *Christ and Culture* (New York: Harper and Bros., 1951), 217–18.

31. Ibid., 171.

no less true even if the circumstances (political, cultural, economic) under which Christians lived were seemingly at odds with these spiritual truths. Where neo-Calvinism disdains dualism, Calvin and the Westminster divines had no hesitation in distinguishing all sorts of dualities, with Christian liberty being a chief example. It very well could be that they made such distinctions because the apostle Paul himself, in reflecting on the meaning of Christ's accomplishment, recognized them as crucial to life in the new order of the church, between the first and last advents of Christ.

The Westminster Confession's teaching on Christian liberty, then, provides a further challenge to the transformationist view that now dominates Reformed Christianity in North America. By distinguishing the liberties enjoyed by believers because of Christ's saving work from political considerations (seemingly) of all kinds, the divines were demonstrating precisely the sort of dualism that has become a sign of weakening Calvinist resolve by those who insist on the Reformed world- and life-view as essential to Calvinism. Even more, their implicit distinction between the liberties of the Christian and political liberty captured the paradoxical character of the gospel that is so often missing among transformational Calvinists. For the divines, the attempt to calculate the progress of the gospel by its temporal or earthly successes was to confuse two realms fundamentally distinct. Just as the cross is the great paradox of the Christian religion, since by death came life, so evaluations of Christian influence that correlate the gospel's relevance with the advance of the true, the good, and the beautiful miss the fundamental tension in Christian existence in the age of the church.

The Calvinism of the Westminster divines may seem like a pie-in-the-sky faith. But that could be because the divines believed that the truths of Christian liberty were eternal, and that those of political liberty were temporal and ephemeral. At a time when Reformed Christians again seem to be caught up in the "sacred cause of liberty," reacquaintance with the true meaning of the liberties found in Christ as the Westminster divines explained it may be as surprising as it is comforting.

Contributors

Joel R. Beeke is president of and professor of systematic theology and homiletics at Puritan Reformed Theological Seminary, pastor of the Heritage Netherlands Reformed Congregation in Grand Rapids, Michigan, editor of *Banner of Sovereign Grace Truth*, editorial director of Reformation Heritage Books, president of Inheritance Publishers, and vice president of the Dutch Reformed Translation Society.

R. Scott Clark is associate professor of historical and systematic theology at Westminster Seminary California.

Richard B. Gaffin Jr. is an ordained minister in the Orthodox Presbyterian Church (Presbytery of Philadelphia) and Charles Krahe professor of biblical and systematic theology at Westminster Theological Seminary, Philadelphia, where he has been a member of the faculty since 1965.

Richard C. Gamble is former professor of systematic theology at Reformed Theological Seminary, Orlando, and is currently professor of systematic theology at the Reformed Presbyterian Theological Seminary in Pittsburgh.

D. G. Hart is director of fellowship programs and scholar-in-residence at the Intercollegiate Studies Institute, Wilmington, Delaware.

David McKay is professor of systematic theology, ethics, and apologetics at the Reformed Theological College, Belfast, and pastor of Cregagh Road Reformed Presbyterian Church, Belfast.

Jerry O'Neill is president of and professor of pastoral theology at the Reformed Presbyterian Theological Seminary in Pittsburgh.

Anthony T. Selvaggio is pastor of the College Hill Reformed Presbyterian Church in Beaver Falls, Pennsylvania, and adjunct professor of New Testament studies at the Reformed Presbyterian Theological Seminary in Pittsburgh.

Carl R. Trueman is professor of historical theology and church history at Westminster Theological Seminary, Philadelphia. He previously served on the faculties of the Universities of Nottingham and Aberdeen.

Rowland S. Ward is the minister of Knox Presbyterian Church of Eastern Australia in Melbourne.

C. J. Williams is professor of Old Testament studies at the Reformed Presbyterian Theological Seminary in Pittsburgh.

Index of Scripture

297

298

Index of Subjects and Names

305